DEAD TO THE CORE

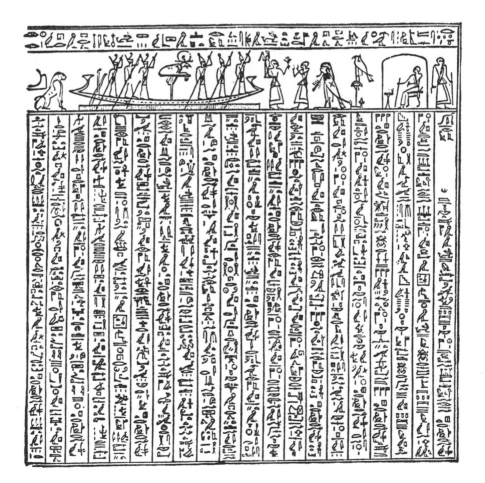

DEAD TO THE CORE

BY ERIC F. WYBENGA

Delta
Trade Paperbacks

A Delta Book
Published by
Dell Publishing
a division of
Bantam Doubleday Dell Publishing Group, Inc.
1540 Broadway
New York, New York 10036

Library of Congress Cataloging in Publication Data

Wybenga, Eric.
Dead to the core : an almanack of the Grateful Dead / by Eric Wybenga.
p.   cm.
ISBN 0-385-31683-6
1. Grateful Dead (Musical group)—Miscellanea.   2. Grateful Dead
(Musical group)—Anecdotes   I. Title.
ML421.G72W9   1997
782.42166′092′2—dc21
[B]   96-39726
                                                                 CIP
                                                                  MN

Design by Bonni Leon-Berman

Manufactured in the United States of America
Published simultaneously in Canada

August 1997

10 9 8 7 6 5 4 3 2 1

BVG

For my
mother and father
and Jennifer

and for
Jerry Garcia
1942–1995

"I don't know how many of you know that today is Ho Chi Minh's birthday. . . . It's true, I read it in my almanac."
—Bob Weir, Fox Theater, May 19, 1977

DEAD TO THE CORE

INTRODUCTION

We begin with the inescapable It. Jerry is gone, and there will be no more Grateful Dead shows. There will come a time when these sad facts no longer bear mentioning, and already their effect upon those of us who call ourselves Deadheads has changed. The character of Deadheads' mourning has subtly shifted from head-shaking wordlessness to a grim acceptance of simple truth. Even an accepted truth can surprise people, though, such as when the hankering for a show bubbles up from the unconscious or when they are confronted with images captured on video.

Jerry Garcia was not a saint, a fact that we have been acquainted with amply in the stories and books that have followed in the wake of his passing. But he was a pretty damn fine example of a human being. One gets the feeling that he was a man possessed of such boundless creative and interpretive power that he would have left his mark on any field of artistic endeavor he chose. As such, music was lucky to have had him, especially given the young Garcia's struggles with whether to follow the muse of visual art or music. I suspect that in an odd little corner of the Eep dimension, there once lived a painter by the name of Jerome J. Garcia, an artist whose canvases bore the mark of brushstrokes both obsessively fine and audaciously broad, whose palette played host to colors of his own invention, whose work encompassed the fiercest strains of abstract expressionism and the humblest folk art, an artist who sent people home from galleries weeping and laughing over small works of portraiture that perfectly captured their subjects' essence yet reserved for them the personal mystery at the heart of verisimilitude. This Señor Garcia, beloved of many, would for his personal amusement pick up a guitar from time to time. Those who were lucky enough to behold the fruits of his avocation commented on how closely his music matched the restless wit evinced in his better-known paintings.

Of course, *our* Jerry Garcia chose guitar over paintbrush, and his life's work would fill a very large canvas indeed. Because he chose the supremely expressive medium of music, he has touched us all. One can argue endlessly and pointlessly about the technical merits of Jerry's guitar playing, but one thing on which all seem able to agree is that his playing possessed an almost matchless ability to convey emotion and mood. The same is true of his voice, though this quality in his performances often goes unheralded. In Jerry's homespun blend of vocal styles—a bit of Bill Monroe, a little Bob Dylan, a pinch of Lennon *and* McCartney—he created for himself a voice of unforced affect. His interpretive talent—which sprang from the same nook of his creative mind whence came all those eloquent guitar phrasings—was such that he seemed to live so many of his songs rather than simply emote them. In later years, his voice raspy and weathered, singing as he always has at the upper limits of his range (and always, no matter how shot the voice, on key), he became in performance the very personification of the wisdom of years. The plainspoken honesty of his playing and singing, coupled with the wit and intellectual playfulness we saw in interviews, made us feel not only as if we knew him but that he was someone very special to know.

Jerry and the Dead are sorely missed and will continue to be, with all those shows unplayed and songs left unwritten (or at least uncovered!). And we also feel the loss of the total experience of touring and the shows themselves. But we also miss the personality of the Dead, for they were a band that possessed this in abundance. This character wasn't always good or kind or happy, and that's just the point. Here was a band that was remarkably honest in how they allowed us to see them. Because of this unwillingness to construct elaborate facades in performance and life, they became a part of our lives, our friends, the Boys, who really knew how to play music. This gave the music and the band's history a living drama, a vibrancy, it might not otherwise have possessed ("Listen to that solo—you can tell Jerry's pissed at Weir for blowing the verse"). It is in a sense ironic that we call Dead concerts "shows" because compared with most rock bands there was very little "show" at all. There was instead music played by interesting people with a fantastic history.

What a history! There are so many facts of the Grateful Dead's life, both happy and sad, that could not have been more perfect if they had been scripted—that they were the house band at the Merry Pranksters' Acid Tests; that both Robert Hunter and Ken Kesey were turned on to acid while acting as guinea pigs for government-sponsored LSD studies, then went on to play a large role in inventing the cultural component of what we now think of as the sixties; that the Dead's earliest patron and benefactor was Augustus Owsley Stanley III, aka Bear, the sixties' most legendary tabber of acid; that this band of misfits and their benefactor would essentially invent the modern rock sound system; that the Holy Grail of Dead tunes, Dark Star, would be the first tune that the Dead and Hunter wrote as a group; that they would one day play at the foot of the Pyramids and that a lunar eclipse would coincide with one of their shows there; that a large shooting star would streak across the sky as they were about to revive Dark Star at the Greek Theater; that Brent Mydland's last show would fall on the ten-year anniversary of Keith Godchaux's death; that the Dead's last year would "fulfill" two tongue-in-cheek Deadhead prophecies—"Trouble Ahead, Jerry in Red" (he wore a red T-shirt onstage at the start of the last tour) and the belief, spurred by an offhand remark made by Phil Lesh, that if Unbroken Chain were ever played live, it would spell the end of the Dead; and finally that Days Between, a haunting meditation on the past and on unfulfilled dreams, would be the last song Hunter and Garcia would write together.

These are only the sensational elements of the story. When one considers the eclecticism of the band members' interests, backgrounds—Phil's devotion to avant-garde classical music, Mickey's percussion-based ethnomusicology, Jerry's vast knowledge of traditional music—and accomplishments, one begins to get to the root of why the gestalt of the Dead's music, history, and personality hold such fascination for us Deadheads. Throw in the fact that the Dead are, personally, a bunch of genuinely funny guys and the given at the root of all this—that the music is fantastic—and you've got yourself a fascinating and lively subject for conversation. So let's talk about the Grateful Dead.

This little book about the Dead first took seed in the many pleasant hours I've spent over the years "talking shop" with friends. Conversation about the Dead's music inevitably tangles with talk of their history, both as written in fanzines and books endlessly pored over and, more importantly, in the oral realm of rumors and ephemera. And of course there are the tapes, those endlessly circulating pieces of plastic that bear performances both sensational and horrible (though always interesting), amusing bits of stage chatter, "overheard" technical talk among the band and its crew, and now, sadly, the sum of the Grateful Dead's music. When I get a tape of a "new" show, the first thing I want to do is listen to it, the second, share it. This is the currency of interest in the Dead—the sharing of the music and the stories, opinions, and ideas that go with it.

Dead to the Core is meant to be my end of an extended conversation about the Dead with you, the reader. My hope is that reading this book will be an interactive process. I hope that you'll find yourself checking out tapes you haven't listened to in years or become inspired to search out shows of which you weren't aware. Given the subjective nature of much that I've written here, maybe you'll find yourself arguing with the book—hopefully that, too, will send you to your tape collection, to relisten to a performance I've panned and you like, or vice versa. My intent is to engage you in a good old conversation about the Dead. Let's chill and pull out some tapes.

My inspiration for the form of this book is old-fashioned almanacs, books that not only supplied farmers with necessary information on the seasons, planting, and growing but were filled with stories, folk wisdom, recipes, and humor. Here our main discussion is of the Dead and their performances, but sidebars on the interpretation of songs, the observations of fellow Heads, and pieces of trivia and lore can be the asides and tangents that sprout from any good conversation.

There's a certain organic symmetry between the way an actual almanac is laid out, with emphasis on the seasons, and a discussion of the Dead's career. Seasons have always had significance for the Dead and Deadheads within the touring year, and one can find parallels to the seasons in the story of the Dead's career as a whole. It's almost completely natural to take such a view, given the cyclical and seasonal motifs present in so many of the Dead's songs. Hunter and John Barlow have incorporated the birth and nourishing decay of the natural world, as well as evocations of specific seasons, into much of their best work for the Dead, and the tunes that the Dead chose to cover often shared these elemental themes. This book, which focuses on what are arguably the richest years to mine for exceptional performances, is organized according to seasons, with the conceit that the Dead's spring represents their earliest years, and so on.

With so much music out there, I've tried to focus the bulk of my attention on the "monster" years and eras. These are of course also a subjective matter, but I've chosen 1966–67, 1968 (in the form of the Mickey and the Hartbeats shows), 1969, 1970–71, 1972, 1973–74, 1977, 1978, 1979–81, 1985, 1987 (Dylan and the Dead), 1989–90, and 1990–91. Even with so many years covered, there were some agonizing decisions: I dropped 1976 and added 1978; I thought long and hard over whether to include 1982 and 1988 but ultimately decided they weren't as consistently fine as the other years represented. This subjective approach has also left the Dead's last few years out of the closer picture at least, to which you may take issue. My feeling is that the Dead reached a peak in 1990 that carried over into 1991, took a precipitous dip in 1992, experienced a renaissance of sorts in 1993 with new material and some generally mind-blowing performances, and declined gradually but definitely from that point on. To help remedy the "gaps" in my coverage, I've included an appendix of additional show reviews from throughout the Dead's career. Perhaps some champion of the years I've passed over will come forth with a book focusing on those—I'd enjoy the "conversation" and insights such a book would offer. As it is, we have many years of killer shows to go through, so make yourself comfortable and let's talk about the Dead.

SPRING

M A R C H

Ah, spring. The season of sowing is also the one in which the seed of the Grateful Dead was first planted, Phil Lesh replacing Dana Morgan, Jr., on bass on the cusp of summer in 1965. Spring is the season closest to the heart of the East Coast Deadhead, the Dead, warmth, light, and life returning as separate manifestations of the most wondrous spoke in the wheel of eternity. Spring of '96 was unseasonably cold in the East, bearing a chill that blew from without and numbed and saddened from within. Who knows if generous doses of sunshine would have made it all the worse for evoking that which is now forever beyond our

27 *3/27/85 Nassau* ✿ *Half-Step revival, first Tom Thumb's*

28 *3/28/81 Grugahalle, Essen, Germany* ✿ *With Pete Townshend*

29 *3/29/90 Nassau* ✿ *With Branford Marsalis*

30

31 *3/31/85 Portland, Maine* ✿ *Spring Fever in a nutshell!*

reach? Each gray rainy day bore reminders of songs no longer sung.

We'll see sunny spring come again to fire the ochers of budding branches, but we won't hear the likes of *this* band again, won't renew our acquaintances on a trek to tired arenas into which life is breathed for a few nights. How much more wonderful now is the gift of so many hours of live recordings? Spring seems a good time to write the band a thank-you letter for their generosity in letting us gather over the years all the notes they've spilled. Hope springs eternal, and though the song is over, it should be remembered that the heart has songs of its own—here's a chance to sing to the Dead.

So much solace to be found in so many amazing spring tours and shows—'69, Europe '72, '74, '77,

1 *April Fool's Day* ❋ *The Dead have never played on April 1st*

2 *4/2/82 Duke* ❋ *The Switch*

3 *Jesse James, d. 1882* ❋ *Richard Manuel, b. 1945*

4 *4/4/85 Providence*

5 *Allen Ginsberg, d. 1997*

6 *Bob Marley, b. 1945* ❋ *4/6/71 Manhattan Center*

7 *4/7/87 Meadowlands*

8 *Hank Aaron bests Babe Ruth's home-run record, 1974* ❋ *4/8/85 Philly*

9 *4/9/88 Worcester*

10

11 *Civil Rights Act signed by LBJ, 1968*

12 *FDR, d. 1945*

13 *Jack Casady, b. 1944* ❋ *4/13/83 UVM* ❋ *Scarlet* ➤ *Fire!*

14 *4/14/82 Glens Falls*

15 *Tax day* ❋ *4/15/82 Providence*

16 *4/16/83 Meadowlands* ❋ *With Stephen Stills*

17 *Benjamin Franklin, d. 1790* ❋ *4/17/71 Princeton* ❋ *Pigpen fest*

18 *San Francisco Earthquake, 1906* ❋ *4/18/82 Hartford* ❋ *Phil's "Earthquake" Space*

19 *4/19/82 Baltimore* ❋ *Phil's "Raven" Space*

20 *4/20/83 Providence*

21 *4/21/84 Philly*

22 *Richard Nixon, d. 1994* ❋ *4/22/69 The Ark*

23

24 *4/24/78 Normal*

25

26 *4/26/72 Jahrhundert Hall, Frankfurt, Germany*

'82, '83, '85, '90. A canopy of anticipation for East Coast versions of new tunes no longer spreads above our heads, but the seed that was planted more than three decades ago fell on good soil, was nurtured, and grew tall and mighty. The roots are firm. The decay of days past can nourish as well. With that in mind and so many shows to fill our ears it seems as natural as can be to keep on growing. It's the spring of the year, and the time is here. . . .

27 *U. S. Grant, b. 1822* ✸ *4/27/71 Fillmore East*
✸ *4/27/91 Las Vegas*

28 *4/28/71 Fillmore East*

29 *4/29/71 Fillmore East* ✸ *Closing of Fillmore East*

30

spring spring spring spring spring spring spring spring spring spring spring spring spring spring spring spring spring spring spring

M A Y

1 *5/1/81 Hampton*

2 *5/2/70 Harpur College*

3 *5/3/72 Paris*

4 *Four students killed by National Guardsmen at Kent State* ❈ *5/4/81 Philly*

5 *Cy Young pitches first-ever perfect game, 1904* ❈ *5/5/67 Fillmore*

6 *5/6/70 MIT* ❈ *Dead play during student strike over Kent State* ❈ *5/6/81 Nassau* ❈ *He's Gone for Bobby Sands, Caution breakout*

7 *Bill Kreutzmann, b. 1946* ❈ *5/7/77 Boston Garden* ❈ *Half-Step!*

8 *5/8/77 Cornell* ❈ *Scarlet* ➤ *Fire!*

9 *5/9/77 Buffalo* ❈ *Comes a Time!*

10 *5/10/87 Laguna Seca* ❈ *Desolation Row!*

11 *Bob Marley, d. 1981* ❈ *5/11/72 Rotterdam* ❈ *Longest Dark Star on record... or tape, that is*

12 *Yogi Berra, b. 1925* ❈ *5/12/91 Shoreline* ❈ *C. C. Rider, Train to Cry bustouts*

13 *5/13/77 Chicago Auditorium Theater* ❈ *"Calling Dr. Beechwood..."*

14

15 *Dan Healy's birthday* ❈ *Wavy Gravy (né Hugh Romney), b. 1936* ❈ *5/15/70 Fillmore East*

16 *5/16/81 Cornell*

17

18 *Mount St. Helens erupts, 1980*

19 *Pete Townshend, b. 1945* ❈ *5/19/74 Portland, Oregon* ❈ *Truckin' (etc.)!* ❈ *5/19/77 Fox Theater* ❈ *Terrapin* ➤ *Playin'* ➤ *D/S* ➤ *Wheel* ➤ *China Doll* ➤ *Playin'*

20

21

22 *The Great Train Robbery, 1868* ✳ *5/22/77 Pembroke Pines* ✳ Dick's Picks Volume Three

23

24 *Bob Dylan (né Zimmerman), b. 1941*

25 *Miles Davis, b. 1926* ✳ *Babe Ruth hits number 714, 1935* ✳ *5/25/95 Seattle*

26 *5/26/72 London* ✳ *Foundation of Europe '72 jam* ✳ *5/26/73 Kezar*

27 *5/27/93 Cal Expo* ✳ *Shakedown!*

28 *5/28/82 Moscone Center* ✳ *With John Cipollina, Flora Purim, and Boz Scaggs*

29 *John Cipollina, d. 1989*

30 *5/30/92 Las Vegas* ✳ *Spanish Jam revival*

31

spring spring spring spring spring spring spring spring spring spring spring spring spring

Dawn of the Dead
1966–1967

Let us remember that for one brief, shining moment there was…Tripalot. Ken Kesey's acid-munching and freely freaking Merry Pranksters, who created the scene where the Dead became the Dead and whence the first Deadheads arose, were no lotus-eaters dreaming of Xanadu upon cushions of Chinese silk. Theirs was a real-time trip of freak energy unleashed in the construction of the moment. One didn't write poetry on acid, one lived it.

Their trip was no less ambitious a project than a chemically induced evolution of human consciousness. Antiwar rallies? Those were for the gray world of *Homo sapiens*. The Pranksters were molecular *Übermenschen*, privy to Technicolor visions of the world as it *really* was, pushing the envelope of reaction time in pursuit of the ineffable *moment* in which to live, with the psyche a greased pathway between ego and id, superego and all its hangups out to lunch.

One of the most striking things one comes away with after reading accounts from this era is the hard work that the northern California Heads put into having fun. Serious fun. Up at Kesey's spread in La Honda, a Prankster initiate is snubbed for not contributing: He sits and smokes—cigarettes, no less—while learning Sanskrit instead of designing and constructing mad machines to graft onto the Pranksters' Rube Goldberg gestalt of film, tape loops, audio delay, strobe lights, and thunder machines. Rock-and-roll bands—for the most part kids in their late teens and early twenties—band together to form cooperative ownerships of ancient San Francisco ballrooms, not with dreams of preserving riches from the grasping hands of promoters but with the driving ambition of preserving the vibe, of giving themselves and their audiences the ideal place to revel, freak freely, and *have fun*. Here was a generation who, at least for a time, pursued good times with the single-minded zeal with which their forebears had pursued the comforts of a middle-class life.

The Dead came away from their casual stint as house band to the Pranksters' Acid Tests aware of the transportative effects of their music and with minimal or no adherence to conventional divisions between performer and audience, the entertainer and the entertained. The Acid Tests knew no such distinctions, and if the Dead at times had to compete at the tests with babbling tape loops or the avant-garde whimsy of the Pranksters' own "band," they were also thankful that they could stop playing and walk away from the stage if the visuals got too intense.

With the Acid Tests as the template for the Dead's own trip, as Garcia acknowledged, the Dead's earliest performances were very intimate affairs. Their electronic chamber music, to borrow one of Phil's characterizations, was played in small, funky old ballrooms left over from dance-hall days, mostly the Fillmore, the Avalon, and the Matrix (and, perhaps funkiest of all, the Old Cheese Factory in November 1966). Group bills accounted for larger halls, such as early shows at Winterland. By late '67 they were playing a wider assortment of venues and made brief forays into New York, Toronto, and Denver, where they played at a Family Dog outpost. The Dead tour was born.

In tapes from shows at venues both small and relatively large, there is in this period an easy rapport between the band and the audience, with the ambience suggestive of a gathering of friends that, at these early San Francisco shows at least, is pretty close to the reality. The stage chatter from this era is hilarious and often crazed—witness, for example, the rantings of the 5/5/67 Fillmore show. An energetic sense of playfulness and openness reigned.

Tapes from this period don't seem to get much play time on the Nak, but these early shows are definitely worth listening to, and oh-so-fun to pop nonchalantly onto the deck to blow the minds of those who maybe expected you to throw in Cornell '77— again. What these protobootlegs reveal is a blues band that at first flush seems wholly dominated by Pigpen's swirling organ sound. But then you hear Jerry, playing endless loops of crazy, lightning leads on his Gibson ES or Les Paul. Phil, mere months into his relationship with the bass, is already playing lead lines and rapid counterpoint to Jerry. Bobby, too, has already started down his idiosyncratic road, playing little filigrees and very little true rhythm, which doesn't provide much mooring for the band when Garcia takes off on his solo flights. Jerry hasn't really begun yet to throw in little rhythmic comps here and there in his solos to orient Weir, so there are times when the groove begins to drift out from under him, a disorienting sensation to encounter in music that is already so strange. This is, amazingly, the sound of a band learning to play their instruments. Odd, my guitar lessons never sounded quite like this! The original Boys, the "quintessential quintet" of Grateful Dead Hour host David Gans's apt alliteration, dropped broad hints of Deadness and their respective musical personalities from the beginning, though one of the most interesting aspects of listening to a number of tapes from this period is how rapidly their evolution was taking place. This blues-and-dance band is, while learning their instruments, inventing psychedelic music (as it invents them), quickly shedding the cocoon of their fairly straightforward readings of tunes such as Hey Little One and It's All Over Now, Baby Blue, drying off their wings, and fluttering hither and yon through rhapsodic meanderings on the primary riffs of blues and jug-band standards such as Viola Lee Blues, I Know You Rider, and Next Time You See Me.

New tunes—Golden Road, Cream Puff War—started to emerge in early 1967, supplanting the Dead's earliest, now obscure originals such as Cardboard Cowboy and Alice D. Millionaire. Robert Hunter's first compositions for the band came later in the year. Meanwhile the jams kept getting longer and the playing better, with Pigpen's self-assured vocals beginning to share significant time with Jerry's manic leads, as Pig bades him "Play your guitar," like the bandleader he was at that point. It may take some digging to get tapes from this period because, although the relatively few shows in existence or circulation are fairly common, many Heads just don't listen to stuff that far back. If you take the time to do so, you'll find that the best of the shows are worth having for more than purely archival or historical reasons.

3/25/66
TROUPER'S CLUB

This is the earliest non–Acid Test tape in many Heads' collections, or at least those who have any interest in pre-1969 Dead (and you should, you should). As with the 7/3/66 Fillmore show (with which it's often found coupled), the sound is not great, but the tape is definitely listenable—my copy evidently started its life as a bootleg album, indicated by the telltale pops and hisses (a nostalgia-inducing sound in its own right!) between songs. Like other tapes from early to mid 1966, it's packed full of songs in their putative debut versions. And while it may not become a tape that enters your heavy rotation, it's somewhat more than merely an archival curio. The band at this point was obviously starting to truly jell as a unit, and Garcia's playing is even at this early date plenty out there and perhaps a bit flashier (in some senses at least) than we've grown accustomed to. He's fast as hell and more metallic—brassy—sounding, cutting like a trumpet through the organ-dominated sound of the rest of the band.

The "opening" (since the tape is evidently incomplete, there's a high probability that it's not the actual opener) Stealin' rocks, with some genuinely successful harmonies (and this before Crosby, Stills, and Nash showed them how it was *really* done). The real treat, though comes next, with a *big* blues jam, informed in part by the Stealin' just played but definitely its own creature. Pigpen goes all-out, if simply, and Jerry is simply everywhere on guitar—effervescing upward, brassily asserting himself, and growling restlessly. I haven't been able to find an earlier jam by the Boys (at least not as the Grateful Dead), and *DeadBase* also lists this one as the first occurrence of that beloved Dead phenomenon, though doubtless there are scads of earlier exemplars that are lost to us forever (sob). It is, at least given the surviving record, a truly historic moment, the "birth" of one of the happiest and most venerable Dead traditions. This is probably a rehearsed instrumental, but the veils of time keep us from being sure.

The sole surviving Hey Little One that follows comprises one of my favorite proto-Dead ballad moments. The band creates an ideal moody setting for the song (owing in no small part to Pig's haunting organ), and Jerry's impassioned singing is great, even if his voice at this point was still a bit immature to be entirely convincing for this sort of throaty, all-broken-up, delivery—it's a bit reminiscent of how Dylan sang in conscious imitation of Leadbelly and Cisco on his first album.

The humorous Hog for You comes next, and my tape closes with the first-known You Don't Have to Ask, a Dead rarity that, while interesting, was not destined to become a classic. Some versions of this tape also have Cold Rain and Snow and Next Time You See Me as the last two songs, though these are most likely filler from a much later show.

Even if you're not historically inclined, get this tape, if only for the unique Hey Little One, a real treat, and the *ur*-Dead blues Jam.

7/3/66
FILLMORE AUDITORIUM

You may have thought that the band's speediness on their first album was an anomaly—after all, the Dead themselves had expressed dismay over how incredibly fast the whole thing was. Well, turns out that playing amped-up blues and jug-band chestnuts at blazing tempos was known territory for the band. June 3, 1966, at the Fillmore Auditorium (*not* the Fillmore West, but the "original" Fillmore) 🎵 is a show I'd rate as a must for the collection, with a number of tunes that exist here in their earliest known incarnations and a style of playing that was evolving almost month by month. The

🎵 Q: WHICH SAN FRANCISCO BALLROOM, ORIGINALLY OWNED BY THE FAMILY DOG AND SITE OF MANY LEGENDARY SHOWS BY THE AIRPLANE, BIG BROTHER, AND THE DEAD, BECAME THE FILLMORE WEST WHEN BOUGHT BY BILL GRAHAM?

A: THE AVALON, A FORMER IRISH DANCE HALL.

sound is pretty good for the early date, with clear stereo channel separation and not much hiss, though there is some general fuzziness to the recording as a whole.

The show opens with the Viola Lee Blues, a version that is every bit as fast as the one that appears on *Grateful Dead.* The Big Boss Man that follows, a "first" (that is, first "known" version) serves as a nice, laid-back tonic to the speedy Viola Lee, and it features Pigpen in his element, singing in a relaxed blues style and blowing a very proficient harp.

Sittin' on Top of the World comes next, one of those early Dead tunes that really serves to define the proto-Dead song, wacky harmonies, *ur*-Jerry solos—even at this point, he has that "bubbling up" effect going—and exuberant lead vocals by same.

Dancin' in the Streets (yet another "first") is of course a very different arrangement from the post-"retirement" "disco" version; it is in fact very close to the Martha and the Vandellas original, down to the opening organ riff and the placement of the backing vocals. What distinguishes the Dead version even at this early point is the middle jam that features Jerry soloing over a rhythm section that starts at allegro and ends up somewhere between molto and molto *molto* allegro, Billy *pounding* on the drums as if his life depended on it.

Owing to the fact that it's a song that starts with a run through the chorus, stand-alone Riders sound a bit naked and abrupt, especially to ears well acclimated to China → Rider. That this Rider is cut, however, is one of the great losses of this tape. The Dead play it remarkably similar to the way they have throughout its almost thirty-year run. The main differences here are the inclusion of the "I'd rather drink muddy water . . ." verse (during which, unfortunately, the song cuts), the close harmonies, and the little sixteenth- and thirty-second-note licks Jerry crams into every available space—proof that Jerry could play as fast as he damn pleased and that slowing down was for him a stylistic decision. Play this for all those worshipers of other guitar gods to shut them up at long last. ❧ The "Jerry is slow" rap always rankles, as does a frequently heard Deadhead defense that goes something like "What Jerry lacked in virtuosity he made up for in style and tasteful playing," often heard or seen—on computer newsgroups—in endless and inane Trey Anastasio (of Phish) versus Jerry

❧ I REMEMBER TELLING MY COLLEGE ROOMMATE, A BIT OF A FAIR-WEATHER DEADHEAD, THAT I'D HEARD THAT MARK KNOPFLER WAS JERRY'S FAVORITE CONTEMPORARY ROCK GUITARIST, TO WHICH HE REPLIED, "SURE! HE'S THE ONLY GUY SLOWER THAN JERRY!"

Garcia arguments. Well intentioned as this sentiment is, it obscures the fact that Jerry was a virtuoso's virtuoso. Rock Scully, among many others, has noted that Jerry's primary compulsion in his spare time was endless diddling with scales, and you can bet they weren't C and G Major. I mean, the guy played improvisational material his whole career! I'm likely preaching to the choir here, but it's in hopes of supplying fellow Heads with some argumental ammunition against the followers of the Fender-toting British Invasion hordes.

Finally, how about that strange vocal tremolo Jerry adopts for He Was a Friend of Mine—was he going for emotional effect or sheer trippiness? Most likely the sheer trippiness was going for *him*. It's that *extremely* "high lonesome sound," Bill Monroe in the mushroom fields.

7/16–17/66
FILLMORE AUDITORIUM

This tape, backed with the following night at the Fillmore strikes like a revelation. The recording quality is as good as that of the better known 11/19/66 Fillmore tape with the additional virtue of being from an earlier show. The Dead's playing at this point is assured and inventive, and just plain joyful. I'd rate this show and the next night as the class of the field from 1966. If any shows from this proto-Dead era are likely to get heavy play in your collection, it's these.

The show kicks off with what is, as far as I know, the first Bill Graham introduction for the band captured on tape, and it's a typically sardonic one: "The oldest juveniles in the state of California, the Grateful Dead!" His voice sounds exactly as it did in later years, making this moment a poignant bridge across all the days between. The Dead respond with a unique (from the available evidence) minor-key vamp led, as the Dead was at this time, by Pig. The chord progression segues into Viola Lee Blues in a manner that bears more than a passing similarity to the opening of the 6/15/85 Greek China → Rider—not that I think that the 1985 instance was a conscious allusion, mind you. The Viola Lee Blues itself just about wins my vote for best ever. It's not nearly as awkwardly speedy as the fortnight-older July 3rd version and is generally played with greater sophistication. The vocal mix on the chorus is splendid, and the band plays a sick all-out jam before going back for the last chorus. The song's speedy part is played especially so here, and the return to the original tempo concurrent with the chorus is executed flawlessly.

Phil back-announces Viola Lee, as they say in radio, with "That was a song about jail," and then turns his attention to the Don't Ease to follow with "This next song is about, well . . . no, it's a funny song." The comment from the band or audience that provoked his "no" and assertion of Don't Ease's humorous merits is lost to history, and Phil's euphemistic reply owes, no doubt, to the song's risqué subject matter, "Miss Brown" being slang for the female sex organ. The Don't Ease that follows is fortunately not lost. This is the song that would become the Dead's first single, ⌇ released right around the time of this show, possibly a bit after.

Q: WHAT WAS THE B-SIDE TO DON'T EASE?

A: STEALIN', A TRADITIONAL SONG THEY PLAYED LIVE IN 1966.

Q: UNDER WHAT LABEL WAS THE RECORD RELEASED?

A: SCORPION RECORDS.

This early Don't Ease cooks along admirably. Talk about a song with a long shelf life! ⌇ Generally not a huge favorite (though it's one of the best recognized tunes among casual Heads) it's maybe a bit of a mystery that Don't Ease stayed so long in the Dead's repertoire—nostalgia for that first single perhaps. Perhaps, but not bloody likely. This version is a gem, though, with an open, different feel from what the song has become. It's homier: Miss Brown was Ma Brown back then.

Q: WHEN DID THE DEAD LAST PLAY DON'T EASE?

A: A LITTLE MORE THAN A WEEK SHY OF TWENTY-NINE YEARS (!) LATER ON 7/8/95 AT SOLDIER'S FIELD—THEIR NEXT-TO-LAST SHOW.

We are lucky to have two surviving versions of Pigpen's obscure Pain in My Heart. They're both strong and available in (for 1966) high quality—this is the earlier of the two. Here is a kinder, gentler Pig, singing in a soulful mode he executes so well—it's too bad there aren't more surviving Pig ballad turns like this.

Bobby, however, shows us a side we've seen quite a bit of since, wailing away on New Minglewood Blues (same arrangement as on *Grateful Dead*) and proving that Bobby in 1966 was already . . . well, Bobby. Jerry counters with an upbeat Sittin' on Top of the World and then Bobby again for the obscure (and dated as few Dead tunes are) ditty You Don't Have to Ask. The ending of this one is significant for what may be the earliest instance of Weir doing his Estimatedesque "No, no, nah" thing. Yes, Bobby was already Bobby.

Then, ah then . . . the blissful trifecta of Cold Rain and Snow, a "first" Good

Morning Little Schoolgirl (and a great one at that), and a bittersweet It's All Over Now, Baby Blue.

The Cold Rain is very well played, with some tricky stop-start rhythmic stuff in the beginning. At this stage, though, Jerry has yet to give it the anthemic feel it will assume in later years.

An especially raunchy Schoolgirl highlights the better known facet of Pigpen's stage persona, with leering grunts after each "you're so sweet and pretty." When his harmonica blasts out of the right speaker, it's as if he's standing there, stage right, splay-legged and defiant, blowing hard and soulful.

Jerry's last tune is a very well done Baby Blue. You can really hear that Jerry is still searching for his own vocal style in this version. Nonethless he succeeds in delivering a tune by the master of song interpretation in a way that is wholly his own.

The next night is every bit as hot in the first and exists in even better sound quality. Pig's organ is maybe a little loud in the mix (indeed, firsthand reports from this era cite the organ as the Dead's dominant sound), given his fairly repetitive playing (it gets a little much in Standing on the Corner, especially), but, hey, that was the Dead back then. I sure wouldn't be bitching about it if I could be at the show.

Pigpen atones for his organ playing, too, with some inspired blues harp in Big Boss Man. The boys follow with one of only two known Standing on the Corners, which moves into a Beat It On Down (seven beats to open, for those keeping score at home) that is positively joyous. It in turn moves into the Dead's one and only In the Pines, known in some quarters as Where Did You Sleep Last Night. The arrangement is an interesting one, and though the execution isn't all it could be, with some flubbed vocals and entrances on the last go-through, Jerry's singing is heartfelt throughout. And talk about your rare nuggets! As with its fellow "one-timer" Hey Little One, one can only hope that additional versions eventually see the light of day, and think wistfully of what might have been had they worked them up more. Then we get the sole surviving Cardboard Cowboy, a weird little Bobby tune. The song does have its moments, though, especially when the band brings it way down near the end. Perhaps this tune's biggest drawback is the lightning speed with which it is played—it's seriously amusing to hear various band members realize this and try to rein it in, all to no avail.

The tape ends in style with the "first" Nobody's Fault (with significantly different words from later versions) and a vintage Next Time. Both are gorgeous versions, made all the more enjoyable for their availability in such high quality. Nobody's Fault especially is a gem, with Garcia nailing his vocals and inspired playing all 'round behind him. And oooh, Pig's harp solo in Next Time! Good Ole Grateful Dead indeed!

They're out there, and you owe it to yourself and your friends to get 'em.

A Vintage History of the Historic Dead

Vintage Dead. Historic Dead. The History of the Grateful Dead. They've puzzled casual Heads for years, first in the record racks with the Dead's official releases in stores that sold no bootleg albums, and for years now in record collectors' stores. Many passed them over in the first instance because they looked pretty shady—and besides, why buy what you can get for the price of a blank tape? Now they're rare vinyl and as such often prohibitively expensive—*Vintage Dead,* for example, can go for about fifty bucks.

Just what are these live albums doing on MGM, a legitimate label that is decidedly not the Dead's (and never *has* been)? The recordings, which are mostly from the Avalon Ballroom, with a few from the Carousel thrown in, are all from 1966. As such they predate the Dead's deal with Warner Bros., a loophole that MGM managed to take advantage of by means that are not entirely clear. These "official" bootlegs didn't sit particularly well with the band, though, who found it at the very least ironic that the MGM executive who had put out *Vintage* and *Historic Dead,* Mike Curb, was the same man who had led a purge at the label of all "drug" bands.

The performances captured on these albums are, to be sure, historic ones, though that's pretty much a truism for 1966

3/18/67
WINTERLAND

It didn't take long for this soundboard, rumored to have originated from Bill Graham, to acquire broad fame in Deaddom. With its remarkable sound quality, given its vintage, and generous first- and second-set helpings of many of the Dead's earliest tunes—including the rare originals Golden Road and Cream Puff War—it's not hard to see why.

The tape opens with a very energetic Me & My Uncle, sung with wild lunges out of key by Weir. Jerry plays a mysterious, Spanish-sounding flourish between the lines of the verses here. A quick Next Time You See Me may owe its brevity to Pigpen's lack of a D harmonica—he was apparently unable to cop one from the audience either. He Was a Friend of Mine is sung with less intensity here than in some '66 versions; on the other hand it definitely achieves more of a laid-back groove. This performance typifies the almost mannered attention the band pays to dynamics in this show, jibing with accounts from this era that this was a part of their playing upon which they were trying to improve.

As for Smokestack Lightning, is it just too hideously heretical to venture

Avalon and Carousel shows. *Vintage Dead* and *Historic Dead* were combined into the last of the trio, *The History of the Grateful Dead*, which was released in 1972 under MGM's Pride label. As *History* is considerably less rare than its two predecessors, it can be found at relatively bargain prices. Unless you're a record collector, this is the one to go for (if any), since it contains almost all the material from the first two: Side one—Dancing in the Street (6:37), Lindy (2:49), Stealin' (3:00), It's All Over Now, Baby Blue (4:52), I Know You Rider (4:18); side two—In the Midnight Hour (18:23), It Hurts Me Too (4:17).

The recordings, except for Stealin', seem to share an ambience suggestive of a common show. Stealin' and Lindy are seemingly singled out as not having been recorded at the Avalon, though the liner notes are vague on this point, as well as the question of whether the bulk of the material, which is said to be from the Avalon, is from the same night at that venue. If one assumes that it is, the closest match from *DeadBase* would be September 16, 1966: Rider, Hurts Me Too, Baby Blue, Schoolgirl, Lindy, Dancin', with Midnight Hour as the encore. This list is itself of questionable provenance in terms of the date, and for this list to be a match (which it most likely is), shuffling of the songs on the album must be presumed.

The recording quality is fair (save for the Stealin', which is horrid), which means pretty damn good for this period. As for the tunes themselves, the first side kicks off with a hot Dancin', replete with those giddy "whoa-oh, whoa-ohhh" backing vocals. It's a nice long, leisurely version, well worth hav-

a preference for Weir's treatment? Bobby's fierce attack seems to suit this song better than Pigpen's roly-poly delivery. That said, Pigpen's harmonica solo and Jerry's guitar make this version one to behold, especially when they start to duet, with Bobby laying down feedback-enriched power chords in the background. Jerry adds some cool punctuation to Pig's vocals too—check out the slide down and up the neck (*Baaaawhuuummp!*) after the line "Whoa-oh, who got your baby sister?" for example. This song also evinces an almost self-conscious attention to dynamics. A short Morning Dew is most noteworthy for the testament it bears to Bobby's growing maturity as a rhythm player.

There's some interesting instruction from Jerry to the band regarding the Beat It On Down intro beats: "Two, and leave out the one." The version that follows is breathlessly fast, at the end of which one of the band exclaims, "Olé!" There's some additional fun with the audience as Phil cries out, "Aw, look out, look out!" amid mounting guitar weirdness. What does it all mean? Phil admits that "we're only doing this to kill time, you understand." The set (at least as captured on tape) closes with an excellent, lively Dancin', with an early example of the clever seasonal variations the Dead would give this song over the years: "It's the spring of the year, the time is here for Dancin'. . . ."

The second set opens with a raucous Golden Road, from which the beginning is unfortunately cut. Jerry offers ing. Lindy, an old dusted-off dance-hall 78, is a great little rare nugget. Here's Jerry and Bobby doing vaudeville, and they are surprisingly quite good at it—picture Jimmy Durante on acid. One could say that it's reminiscent of some of Paul McCartney's Beatles stuff, such as the White Album's "Honey Pie" and *Magical Mystery Tour's* "Your Mother Should Know," except that it predates both those albums. So there, lovable moptops.

They beat McCartney to the punch on that one, but Baby Blue shows Jerry doing his best Dylan imitation (and it's not a bad one at that), with Pigpen laying down his best Al Kooper organ riffs. The first side closes with an amphetamenic Rider that features a must-have proto-Garcia solo. Hearing this leaves no question as to why the Dead earned loyal fans from the very start.

The album's real showstopper, though, is the Midnight Hour that kicks off side two. This is true to the form of this era, as Midnight Hour was a tune in which Pigpen would really take charge (Rio Nido '67 jumps to mind) and stretch out on the ribald lyrical improvisations ("So if you want to take care of business, now you got to find yourself a fox now and pretend that you're a hound"). When the frontman turns to sideman Garcia and bids him "play your guitar," sideman Garcia surely obliges, even finding a way to fit a couple of his patented Andalusian riffs into this R&B standard. This tune alone makes the album worthwhile, especially for Pig-o-philes—eighteen minutes plus of self-assured swagger, howlin' and screamin'.

And if that wasn't enough, we also get many thanks to the crowd after it's done and takes the opportunity to welcome all to "set number two, or the post–Chuck Berry set [he shared the bill]." Turning his attention to what's to come, he shares his desire "to continue the proceedings with a song we affectionately call Cream Puff War." The version that follows is full of life, the band seeming genuinely fired up to be performing one of their own compositions. It's a monster performance, too, with some long (and loud), frenzied jamming at the end. By way of contrast the band moves next into the hypnotic terrain of Willie Dixon's "The Same Thing," the closing jam of which contains some of their finest playing from this period.

Cold Rain and Snow soars. It's beginning to take on the *big* feel it would assume in later years—it's earliest days as a swinging little Jerry ditty are clearly over, a point driven home by Jerry's throat-rending passion. He and Phil make this one the hot little number it is. The clear highlight of the set, though, is a performance of Viola Lee Blues that may, from the evidence at hand, have to take best-ever honors. This one is an epic, rocking hard from the first resounding atonal chord. The Dead's musical chops are shown off to extremely good effect here as they go completely sick and all-out but manage to retain absolute control over the form of the song at all times. This, Cold Rain, and The Same Thing elucidate nicely what was meant by contemporary comparisons of the band's the flip side of the "Midnight-Hour Pigpen," a soulful, achingly empathetic It Hurts Me Too. This is Pig's whiskey heart open and bleeding all over the stage, a song I always like to picture as being sung to sometimes lover and always soul sister Janis. Vintage Dead. Historic, even.

sound to "rolling thunder." And to think that they hadn't yet added Mickey!

Unfortunately the tape ends with a very unkind cut of what was shaping up to be a powerful Death Don't Have No Mercy.

5/5/67

FILLMORE AUDITORIUM

This tape contains what is probably the best version extant of the rare Golden Road to Unlimited Devotion. The tape itself is of questionable provenance, yanked from *DeadBase* because their crack scholarship has Alligator, the third tune on the tape, not debuting until June of that year. Memories of that time being hazy, though, and with verifiable Alligators appearing so soon afterward, I'm inclined to give it the benefit of the doubt. To further confuse matters, *DeadBase VII,* which does list the show, has the show erroneously opening with He Was a Friend of Mine. It's clear, though, that He Was a Friend of Mine should come after the Alligator (Golden Road → New Potato Caboose, Alligator, He Was a Friend of Mine)—there's a continuity on the tape between the Alligator and He Was a Friend, during which Phil asks, "Are you all turned down for this one?" a question that, because the band isn't, Phil has to repeat. Phil then exclaims, "Hey, I just saw a narc in the audience! He was right around in there. If you see one, step on him." He Was a Friend of Mine is gorgeous, with Phil laying down a fat bass foundation and Jerry playing shimmery, feedback-laden lines that are oh-so-pretty—what a shame that it's cut.

I don't think it's unfair to venture that this was one of those early shows where the band (save Pigpen of course) was, um, *enhanced.* As evidence I offer the following, which opens the tape:

> (coughing, heavy breathing, ululations, animal sounds over Pig's organ noodling—then silence)
>
> JERRY: "We're stalling. We're stalling while our, uh, drum—I'll tell you, we'll tell you exactly what's going on up here so nobody has to wonder anymore—"
>
> BOB: (without missing a beat, in a drawl) "Lay it awwn me."

JERRY: "What's going on is our drummer is putting a corn plaster on his bass drum."

PHIL: "He's licking his left thumb."

JERRY: "That's what's happening."

(thunderous bass drum beats, over cheers: "Hurray, hurray, yeah, way to go!")

BOB: "Okay, now, this is a dropout song. It inspires you all to drop out and dance, dance, dance."

JERRY (?): (screaming) "Waaaaaaaahhh!!!"

PHIL (?): (ditto) "Waaaaah!"

JERRY (?): "Wait, wait, did somebody say, 'Waaaaahhh!'?"

BOB: "Everybody say, 'Waaaaaahhhh!'"

BAND: "Waaaahhh! Waaaaahh! Wheeeew!"

AUDIENCE: "Waaaaaahh!"

BOB: (deadpan) "Thank you."

JERRY: "Gosh."

PIGPEN: "Lemme hear everybody say, 'FUCK!!!'"

AUDIENCE: (disjointedly) "Fuck!"

JERRY: (slyly) "Loowwwderrrr . . ."

BOB: "Everybody say, 'Dope!'"

AUDIENCE: "Dope!!"

JERRY: "Ha. Ah . . ."

SOMEONE ONSTAGE: "Everybody say, 'Dope!'"

BOB: "Everybody say, 'Primate!'"

AUDIENCE: [silence]

JERRY: "What, say what?"

BOB: (coyly) "Heh, heh. Oh yeah?! Everybody say, 'WHAT!!!'"

AUDIENCE: "What!!!"

ONSTAGE: "What!"

JERRY: "Hey, that was good, that was good."

PHIL: "Everybody say, 'OH NOOO!!!'"

AUDIENCE: "Oh no!"

PIGPEN: (singing) "Sh'ain't nothin' ta me . . ." [Billy and Phil join in instrumentally for a moment]

JERRY: (to band) "We all here together?"

BOB: (to the band) "Begin, begin, begin . . ."

JERRY: "Two, three, four . . ."

The Dead play the Golden Road that follows with all the exuberance that the preceding madness would suggest; it definitely inspires one to drop out and dance, dance, dance. That it segues into an excellent New Potato Caboose, followed by a typically frenzied Alligator makes one all the more hungry for the rest of this show. As it is, it's about the best side-of-a-tape filler one could hope for. Back it with Rio Nido 9/3/67 for an intense rarities mix.

9/3/67 (*or* 9/4)
RIO NIDO

All that remains of this show is a tour-de-force Pigpen performance of Midnight Hour. At over a half an hour in length it serves as a synopsis of sorts of the Dead's playing at that time: Pigpen in putative charge, and the band— Jerry and Phil especially—firmly entrenched in their love of jamming.

When Pigpen tells Jerry to "play your guitar now," he obliges with a trippy, soaring solo that bears a passing resemblance to the special passage before Rider in '73–'74 China → Rider—it's got that same bright, rolling feel. Then comes a long stretch with Phil, Jerry, and Bobby collaborating for some sinuous psychedelic passages, laden with feedback, that are very reminiscent of the best of the Allman Brothers.

After this marathon stint of jamming has temporarily abated, it's Pigpen's turn again, ragging the audience into dancing—"C'mon, get up and dance with that girl . . . I know what you're here for, brother, and you ain't here to sit around . . . with your hands in your pockets and your face lookin' like a fool"—exhorting everyone in his view to lose their inhibitions and hook it up. "Y'know, Bobby wants you to dance, he'll dance with you [Jerry (?): That's right!] . . . you can even come up here and dance with him if you want to—he won't mind. . . . Hey, Bobby, why don't you go down there and dance with her if she won't get up and dance with you. C'mon, you can stop playin' your guitar. . . ." Pure hilarity. The wonder is that anyone could resist this onslaught, as this girl apparently did. Pigpen, unable to give up, adds a plaintive little "C'mon, baby, c'mon up" as the tune ends.

This epic slice of Dead history actually exists in pretty good sound quality, with lots of bass and excellent channel separation. It's good for what ails ya.

11/11/67
SHRINE

This is a classic show that shows the Dead at that point where they really started to become the act we've known for all these years. The closing New Potato Caboose → Alligator → Caution alone take up a whole side, and whoa, Nellie! Caboose shows the true size of this acid beast in the media's "Summer of Love." "All graceful instruments are known" *is* the vocal sound of the early Dead—goofy, crazed, joyous, and complex. The "truly monstrous groove" that the band envisioned when Mickey first joined Billy behind the skins has begun to take fearsome shape here.

At one point at the jam that ends Caboose, Phil, Jerry, and the drummers get crunching, and it could be the Dead at their best, any place, any era, the timeless music of the spheres.

The Alligator jam and the closing Caution theme are huge, exploring all sorts of places, with Jerry somehow getting his guitar to make strange, flute-like noises a good twenty years before the advent of MIDI technology. There's also plenty of good feedback weirdness to be found in this duo that wraps it all up in a bundle of freakiness.

"Fate Music"
Mickey and the Hartbeats

he details remain sketchy to this day, but the story as it's come down is this: Sometime around or during the recording sessions for *Aoxomoxoa*, that is, fall of 1968, Jerry and Phil asked Bobby and Pigpen to leave the band. Pigpen, so it's related, was not able to keep up with the band's increasingly seat-of-the-pants psychedelic excursions, and Bobby's rhythm playing was not of the caliber and solidity to hold down the fort while Jerry and Phil went flying off into the contrapuntal noonosphere. With Bob and Pigpen gone, Jerry, Phil, Billy, and Mickey became Mickey and the Hartbeats for a passel of shows in October 1968 (but not exclusively—there are Hartbeats shows as late as early 1969), in which they were frequently joined onstage by the likes of Jack Casady, Paul Butterfield, and Elvin Bishop.

It can't be quite as cut-and-dried as all that, though. For one, Jerry and Phil have at various times downplayed the notion that Pigpen and Bobby were "kicked out of the band." Bobby has maintained that he was and that it was a painful, soul-searching time for him. But there are full Grateful Dead shows amid even that October '68 concentration of Hartbeats shows.

Aoxomoxoa, however, is notable for its lack of contributions by Weir and McKernan, even though they are credited on the album. And perhaps the promoter(s) for the Dead gigs sprinkled among the Hartbeats shows gave a "Grateful Dead or nothing" ultimatum. Or maybe these shows were "second chances" for the booted.

Whatever the particulars, the Hartbeats shows evince a raw power and improvisational genius that must have made the move seem like a good idea at the time, at least musically. Despite the fact that the Hartbeats shows were roughly contemporaneous with the recording of *Aoxomoxoa*, the performances are like night and day to one another. As one might surmise from the guest artists mentioned above, the live shows were not excursions into carefully crafted rococo psychedelia but raw, hard-core psychedelic blues jam sessions.

These Hartbeats shows seem as if they gave the Dead's two main melodic voices—Jerry and Phil—the opportunity to fully explore the fairly new original material—Dark Star, The Other One, The Eleven—as only they among the band's members at that time (excluding the drummers) had the talent and chops to do. In the extended, freeform jams they had a chance to stretch out improvisationally in a much more open space than that afforded by the instrumentation, repertoire, and group dynamics in the

Dead—and step *out* they did. By so doing they forged musical understandings both explicit and implicit that stood them in good stead for the remainder of the Dead's performing life. One can draw a fairly direct line, for example, from the musical terrain staked out in this Other One to such outstanding versions as that of, say, 11/5/77. The Dead were, to be sure, able to carve out new musical territory both before and after Mickey and the Hartbeats, but these shows and the freedom they gave the participants to push the envelope as far as only they could, provided the bedrock on which their future, seemingly unconscious, contrapuntal improvisations were built.

10/8/68
THE MATRIX

This first Mickey and the Hartbeats show cast the die for those that were to follow, with breathtaking jamming and a song list that seems to belong to some other universe. What these shows must have been like!

The tape I have is of the first set only, and if you're not familiar with Hartbeats tapes, you might be surprised that a first set—positively earthbound compared with the other two sets—can consist of Jam → The Eleven (jam) → Death Don't, The Seven, Dark Star (jam) → Cosmic Charlie. The second set? Jam, Space → Jam, Jam, The Other One → Jam → Caution → Jam.

You get the idea. At least the first set has the advantage (for reviewing purposes anyway) of carrying some recognizable points of reference.

The opening jam starts with the band clearly stating the Next Time You See Me theme and then turning that into a blues-jazz fusion jam that is simply all Jerry with a rhythm section. (Those who would say to this, "In other words, Mickey and the Hartbeats," do a disservice to the lead contributions Phil made to this ensemble.) The bass line at the end restates the Next Time theme, as Phil begins to really assert himself, moving the jam into The Eleven. He carries the main melodic line, freeing Jerry to add a reggae-flavored counterpoint that works quite nicely until some frenzied drumming pushes the jam along at a fevered pace. The Eleven is, as is typical of Mickey and the Hartbeats, sans lyrics. It melts slowly, though, into a full-fledged song, a slow, mournful Death Don't Have No Mercy. Garcia delivers some blistering licks on the Gibson between verses sung with self-assuredness.

The Seven, a rare rhythmic jam in 7/4 time, is sweetly hypnotic, with Phil playing a whimsical bass line through the many repetitions of the theme. The drummers conspire to mix it up a bit rhythmically after a while, inspiring Jerry to undertake some tasty soloing before returning to the original vamp. Only a few bars are played before Phil takes over, laying down some hot bass leads and then making several rushes and feints at an ending before the band actually brings the jam to its climax.

My tape of this set seems to be from a bootleg album; interestingly, when I first got it, it was mislabeled "4/25/69 Electric Theater." There's a harsh cut and fade in the beginning of Dark Star, but luckily it resumes in time to catch Jerry and Phil jamming hard, playing counterpoint to each other with joyous abandon. Phil's lead bass style is shown here in its full glory, both in the way he carries the main melodic line and in his improvised counterpoint. This Dark Star is technically a jam, but Jerry's lead lines throughout the instrumental verses are as nuanced and expressive as any vocals. Some very bluesy playing follows the verse, with Garcia stating cannily familiar lines and formulations within the idiom over Mickey's guiro playing, so essential to the Dark Star sound in that era.

The main Dark Star theme returns and quietly mesmerizes for a time before Jerry turns up the volume for some piercing licks on his way into the second "verse," which is in turn followed by shimmering cascades of notes, built to a crescendo and brought back down. Garcia wrings a few more lead lines out of Dark Star, then jangles into Cosmic Charlie, the sole vocal performance of the set. Jerry obviously experiences discomfort with the range required for this song, but then again its charms are based more than slightly on its idiosyncrasies, of which the vocals are a part.

It's a ringing, upbeat close to an archetypal Mickey and the Hartbeats show—long on virtuosity, creativity, and intense jamming.

10/30/68
THE MATRIX

This tape, better known than 10/8, is of the next Hartbeats show in circulation. Like its predecessor and other available Hartbeats shows it crackles with vitality from the opening—in this case it's Dark Star, played with some interesting variations on the intro. Jerry and Phil execute a scintillating pas de deux around the main theme, never wholly acceding to the dictates of its primary melodic line. This is just—excuse me, but—the shit. After about fifteen minutes of this virtuoso improvisation, the band slides into a hot little blues jam, Billy whipping the drums along with heavy cymbals and Mickey riding a cowbell into what becomes the Death Letter Blues, a tune both sad and smoking.

In the pause that follows, Jerry says, "Uh, I might explain that we're really here just playin'—just goofin'—I mean we don't have really anything in mind or anything. Yeah. We're just thrown together by fate. So we're playing fate music, call it luck music." This trademark piece of Garcia humility (an echo of comments he also made at the 10/10/68 Hartbeats show) is of course followed by a show-stopping, jaw-dropping Other One jam. It deviates several times from the main theme, Jerry and Phil erecting spontaneous and discrete musical structures that buttress and accentuate the whole—this in the finest tradition of Dark Star. All kinds of ground, most of it new, is covered. It even includes some early Phil bombs. Further words cannot do it justice. You must check it out.

A brief Lovelight jam serves as the bridge to the slow-burning fuse of an Eleven jam that, when it catches, explodes into an electric frenzy. A slow, searing Death Don't brings things down again, and then a pair of jubilant jams with Elvin Bishop bring the craziness to the fore again. The show (such as we have it) ends as it came in as the top layer of a delicious Dark Star sandwich is applied.

Baroque Dead
1969

he significant eras of the Dead's history are often demarcated by keyboard personnel. Repertoire is another good guide. On both these scores, 1969 is unique, a year at the crossroads of the Dead's development. The beginning of the year, which began musically on November 23, 1968, with Tom Constanten's first show, was spent recording and performing the psychedelic chamber *cum* dance-hall music that would appear on *Aoxomoxoa*. The second half of the year saw the band begin to veer toward the folksier *Workingman's Dead* material, a fairly substantial change of gears and one that would be at least partly responsible for T.C. leaving the group early in 1970.

Nineteen sixty-nine was the year in which the Dead's pure psychedelic vision peaked. The ascent to this acme had begun in late 1966 and throughout 1967 with the band's first original compositions, and had picked up considerable speed in 1968 with the full integration of Mickey and the maturation of the synaptic cross-wiring between Phil and Jerry that is especially evident in the Mickey and the Hartbeats shows. It was in '68 that Phil brought his friend T.C. into the studio to record "prepared piano" tracks for the That's It for the Other One suite. By 1969 the Dead were feeling their avant-garde and improvisational oats, moving farther away from the electric-blues roots that, even in the trippiest of 1968 performances, were always evident. This direction was both father and heir to T.C.'s joining the group.

If the Beatles had ever found a way to perform their *Sgt. Pepper* material live and had excelled in playing long, improvisational passages and bridges between songs, they might have sounded like the Dead in 1969. Indeed T.C. might have brought the Beatles a long way toward realizing live renditions of their studio experimentations, for his 1969 performances with the Dead show him adept not only in providing the organ and calliope colors of Beatlesque whimsy but the simulation of studio psychedelia such as backward masking of tape. The Dead's prime '69 material could also be termed Beatlesque without engaging in too much of an associative stretch. The hauntingly beautiful Mountains of the Moon bears a passing modal resemblance to "Blackbird," and one can hear cosmetic similarities at least in Doin' That Rag and Beatles dance-hall psychedelia such as "Being for the Benefit of Mr. Kite."

The Beatles of course never did bring their lysergically inspired compositions to the stage; the Dead did so with their own night after night in 1969 (as they did before and after). The thing was, playing the involved set pieces that are so heavily identified with this period—Mountains, Doin' That Rag, the old arrangement of Dupree's Diamond Blues, and even St. Stephen (which Garcia famously termed at one point a "musical policeman . . . a cop")—proved to be something of a cul-de-sac for the Dead. Dark Star was ever open and easy to play through, and so it remained. The Other One, as well, though the Cryptical parenthesis had waning appeal for the band after '69. The Eleven could be played through, but its locked-in rhythm and chord changes straitjacketed the jamming to an extent. Once the band had mastered and turned in many extraordinary performances of the *Aoxomoxoa* material, it fell by the wayside, since it was cumbersome and no longer a challenge or a novelty.

It's interesting how quickly this cutting-edge psychedelicism, held up by many Heads as the Dead's finest hour—and in some ways it was—as an end in itself peaked and dissipated in its hold upon the band's attention. January through March 1969 yielded a legendary group of performances, including those that were to appear on the benchmark *Live Dead* album and the revered March 1st show at the Fillmore West— the *Aoxomoxoa* material as well as the quintessential Dead linkage of Dark Star → St. Stephen → The Eleven → Lovelight were all heavily featured in this time frame. A cross-country tour in April and the band's return to California in May saw much of the same. But in June, right around the time that *Aoxomoxoa* was released, the *Aoxomoxoa* material exclusive to 1969 (i.e., Mountains of the Moon, Doin' That Rag, and Dupree's—prior to its late seventies' revival, that is) began to gradually slip out of the Dead's rotation, leaving Cosmic Charlie alone among the performed album tracks that had not been in the Dead's lineup for some time (i.e., aside from St. Stephen and China Cat). And even St. Stephen's performances began to winnow as the year progressed. Simply put, by the time *Aoxomoxoa* had come out, the Dead had tired of playing much of the material on the album! (For a study in contrasts, compare the lead-up time and postrelease playing for the *In the Dark* material.) One can imagine much gnashing of teeth and tearing of hair among Warner Bros. execs.

The Dead were shedding their skin: Tunes similar to those on *Aoxmoxoa*, such as New Potato Caboose, were also being phased out at this time. While these unwieldy, arrangement-heavy songs (Jerry once said apropos of this era's compositions that even China Cat was "marginal") were exiting the rotation, the *Workingman's* material was creeping in, as were other tunes of the folk-country variety. Me & My Uncle, a tune from the earliest days, had been revived and played heavily since April. Dire Wolf made its first known appearance on June 7th. An appearance as Bobby Ace and His Cards From the Bottom of the Deck (minus Billy and Pigpen)—Weir's cowboy fantasy—at

SOME CHINA ➤ RIDERS OF NOTE

✵ 4/18/71 SUNY Courtland
Nothing too crazy here, just a really homey and well-played early China ➤ Rider. Note the appearance of Bobby's China Cat guitar line in Rider during "I wish I was a headlight."

✵ 4/27/71 Fillmore East
Nails *the "I wish I was a headlight" line plus a unique take on the transition jam.*

✵ 8/27/72 Veneta
Like the rest of this show, the China ➤ Rider is smoking.

✵ 2/24/74 Winterland
An especially groovy transition.

✵ 5/19/74 Portland, Oregon
Some very hot licks in the China Cat and a gorgeous example of the "Feelin' Groovy"-ish '73–'74 transition jam.

✵ 6/26/74 Providence
Just get the show. Really. Go on now, what are you waiting for? Go!

✵ 12/29/77 Winterland
This breakout version, though not among the finest technically, merits inclusion for the synergy between crowd and band. Garcia's opening notes unleash a two-way torrent of joy that washes through each part of the songs and the transition between them. Note the thrice-played coda to Rider.

✵ 12/1/79 Stanley Theater
Fantastically well jammed, with a big feel.

San Francisco's California Hall on June 11th seems to signal a turning point of sorts. Clearly under the influence of guests John Dawson, David Nelson, and Peter Grant, the Boys turn out a song list that includes Silver Threads and Golden Needles, Mama Tried, The Green, Green Grass of Home, and The Race Is On. The closest they come to rock-and-roll, much less psychedelia, is the Beatles' I've Just Seen a Face.

The June 11th show was so unusual that one might dismiss it as an anomaly. But then, on June 20th, the very day that *Aoxomoxoa* was released, we have the surviving set list of King Bee, Cold Jordan, Dire Wolf, Casey Jones (first known appearance), Mama Tried, Lovelight, Alligator. So much for marketing synergy. . . . Granted the Dead played two shows that night and may have stocked the other show with album tunes, *and* this setlist is no doubt incomplete . . . but talk about a sudden change in musical direction!

By December the Dead had begun to play acoustic sets. By January 1970, T.C. was gone. Woodstock had come and gone, as had Altamont. As had *Aoxomoxoa* and Dead baroque. The Dead, without shedding their psychedelic jamming (Dark Star remained a staple, for God's sake) were about to embark on their folk, country, and western phase. The sixties were . . . (pregnant pause) . . . over (groan).

China Cat Sunflower ⬛ I Know You Rider

One of the odd little axioms of Deadhead life holds that there are China → Rider people and there are Scarlet → Fire people. You're either one or the other. What identification with either camp says about someone is open to question. Is a devotee of China → Rider, with its more driving feel from the transition through Rider (than the Scarlet → Fire transition through Fire) more a "type-A" Deadhead? Or does his affection for China Cat's acid-drenched lyrics and that dodgy little Bobby intro that scratches your brain just behind the ears brand the China → Rider head more of a psychedelic ranger than his Scarlet → Fire brethren?

Right. Well…China Cat Sunflower → I Know You Rider, a pairing with a pretty long history, served as a foundation for second sets from the early eighties on. (As did Scarlet → Fire.) In the early seventies it was one (or two, rather) of several predominantly first-set tunes that gave the band a forum for some real jamming in the opening frame. After the Winterland "retirement" run, the duo was absent for a couple of years (save one appearance) until 1979, when it returned to circulation, moving back and forth between the first and second sets until settling in as a predominantly second-set tune in 1983.

If Scarlet → Fire tends toward the color red, China → Rider is yellow. That's how Candace Brightman generally played it, and that's the emo-

✸ **8/10/82 U. Iowa**
Moves through each song and the transitions at breakneck speed, but it obviously has Jerry's full attention, filled as it is with his hot little countrified blues licks.

✸ **7/15/84 Greek**
Super bouncy. A veddy, veddy good 'un.

✸ **6/15/85 Greek**
Just about perfect. An archetype, at least for the eighties. The kickoff to an amazing second set.

✸ **3/27/86 Portland, Maine**
Jerry finds this one note in the transition and keeps working it until the intensity has gone up many notches. It stays there.

✸ **6/30/88 Rochester**
Huge.

✸ **9/16/88 MSG**
A hard-to-find monster that's worth the hunt.

✸ **12/10/89 L.A.**
An awesome version illustrative of the Dead's 1989 resurgence.

✸ **3/26/90 Albany**
A wonderful transition out of Victim.

✸ **9/20/90 MSG**
Best of the nineties? The rest of the set ain't bad either.

Bruce Hornsby really kicks it into high gear.

tional color it conjures—bright, forward-leaning, playfully psychedelic. In terms of lyrical content and genealogy they're an odd couple—a lysergic libretto juxtaposed against a bit of jug-band pining. But hey, that's a phrase and sentiment that could describe the eclecticism of the Dead themselves.

China Cat Sunflower's lyric—composed, Robert Hunter has said, in a state where contemplation of a cat served as touchstone for an interplanetary journey—is a real masterwork. It's one of the very few rock-and-roll lyrics (including Dylan's) that has as much impact on the page as it does sung, if not more. Buy Hunter's book, read it, and see for yourself—his background as a poet first, lyricist second, shows in this quality of his writing. That said, Hunter has noted that no one has ever asked him the meaning of this song (a pinch of grace from us Deadheads to him, no doubt), so I sure won't belabor it here, except to say that "It's about acid" does it less justice than the observation that it's about seeing, sensing, and making connections in a sensous world. Anyone out there remember what it was like to be three years old?

Similarly limiting in regard to this song (and much Deadsong) is the label rock and roll, though I, too, am guilty of using that appellation above. This is Dead music from their electric baroque (or *baroque electrique*) period. Play for me any other rock and roll that sounds like this and I'll cede the point; I don't expect that I will have to.

The transition to I Know You Rider and Rider itself are of course more aptly labeled rock and roll. I Know You Rider is an old black traditional, true, but as electrified-roots music it wears the rock label well. Before the song's several-year retirement that began with the Dead's own sabbatical at the end of 1974, the transitory jam contained for a time an extra element reminiscent of the so-called "Feelin' Groovy" jam present in some Dark Stars. One can hear this theme stated clearly on the excellent 5/19/74 version, for one. It's the opening Rider descant, with a twist of playful weirdness that edges onto the same sublimely affective territory as the so-called "Mind Left Body Jam." It's a sound that epitomizes the Dead at their '73–'74 best, and the editing out of this jam upon the songs' return to the lineup at Winterland on 12/29/77 was a real loss.

It's a loss that was compensated for, in a sense befitting the changes through which the Dead were going, by a change in the singing of Rider in the postretirement version: to wit, Bobby takes the line "Well, the sun's gonna shine in my back door someday" for his own, without backing vocals from the rest of the band (this change was also inaugurated on 12/29/77). The repetition of this line and the dynamics the band play behind it build to a peak that foreshadows Jerry's "I wish I was a headlight" line; the "March wind gonna blow..." line acts as a bridge between the two—a valley between a K2 and Everest among Dead peak moments.

DREAM BOWL

It's understandable that this show gets overlooked, falling as it does just before the famed late-February–early-March Fillmore West run that yielded not only much of the *Live/Dead* material but two of the best-loved '69 shows as well. It's an oversight well worth remedying, though, as this one matches the splendor of its better known '69 brethren.

The show starts with Dupree's, but my tape comes in at the beginning of Mountains of the Moon, in a version that is one of Garcia's better vocal performances of this tune. Jerry switches to his electric at the end for a playful transition to Dark Star and long, languorous riffing on the theme before the first verse. He comes on even stronger after the verse, taking an angular, jabbing, and jangling solo to a climax punctuated by several soundings of the gong by Mickey. Phil takes the reins from here, into a jam with shades of the "Feelin' Groovy" theme, until Jerry determinedly states the Dark Star theme again. From there it's into the second verse.

With the last notes of Dark Star still reverberating, Garcia counts off "One, two, three, four . . ." into Cryptical. The Other One that follows is exciting even by the standard measure of this tune, a very fast-paced version with Jerry laying down some raunchy, fuzzy riffs. The adrenaline charge is reflected in Weir's breathless, staccato vocal, which is a bit sharp. Jerry and Phil's backing parts are also slightly off-key. All this is mitigated, however, by the growling intensity Weir musters for the "Cowboy Neal . . ." line and the whole rest of that verse. It's about here that one begins to realize that, hey, this is one of the better versions of this tune, an observation that the Cryptical reprise does not alter in the least—it's well sung and nicely jammed.

SOME INTERESTING CATLESS RIDERS

❋ 5/2/70 Harpur College
The shuffling feel of this one coupled with the vocal delivery conspires to produce a feeling of preternatural sadness.

❋ 11/10/85 Meadowlands
Half-Step ➤ *Rider*

❋ 8/5/89 Cal Expo
Playin' ➤ *Rider* ➤ *Terrapin (!)*
A very intense Rider, indeed.

The second set kicks off with more vintage '69 material, Doin' That Rag. Jerry sings this one with evident relish, if slightly off-key again (except for the a cappella part, which is very off-key). St. Stephen is a fairly standard '69 rendition, which is to say very good to excellent, and the Eleven that follows revisits some of the driving kineticism of The Other One from the first set. Jerry seems to be everywhere. In later years Jerry

AND AN EARLY RIDER-LESS CAT

☀ 6/5/69 Fillmore West: China Cat
➡ Sittin' on Top of the World

From back in the days when China Cat could go into any number of tunes, this is one of the more unusual and intriguing combinations, with a well-played and energetic China Cat crossing a prosaic bridge into a similarly excellent Dark Star. The transition to Sittin' is not seamless—kind of a splice with sustain—but there is excitement there (it's also interesting to hear China Cat end!)

would say that The Eleven was hard to play through except in the most obvious ways. With this evidence in hand, I would like to respectfully disagree. Aided in no small part by Mr. Lesh, he finds a number of novel approaches to the chord cycle, all executed at blinding speed. This swollen river of jamming sweeps into a Lovelight that puts just the right joyous lid on the show, or rather blows the lid right off.

3/1/69

FILLMORE WEST

Whether or not this show actually is the best of 1969, it stands as a prime example of those extraordinary convergences of peak playing within the parameters of a given era and a setlist that is perfectly emblematic of the same.

The Dead more than live up to the billing of Graham's "Magnificent Seven" introduction in a first set marked by playing that flirts with perfection. This is astounding, really, when one considers the improvisational nature and high complexity of the tunes therein.

That's It for the Other One opens the show (not bad for an *opener*, eh?) in epic fashion, the Dead nailing down one of their finest performances of the full suite, with the jam at the end of Cryptical especially hot. New Potato Caboose is bouncy and clear as a bell, riding out on rolling waves of bass. Doin' That Rag is also very well done, and check out how Jerry pronounces the hard part of the *g* at the end of Rag, an early example of his arresting vocal quirk of overenunciating words at times. Here the effect is pretty trippy, in keeping with the feel of the song, set, and show. A faster than usual Cosmic Charlie follows with an intro that sounds more like the Beatles' "Revolution" in this version than just about any other. What a first set!

The second set opens with another Bill Graham intro, "The great high hope," to which Phil, I think, responds, "Why, you . . ." Can round two possibly top the first? A common (for '69, that is) *Aoxomoxoa* pairing of Dupree's, methodical and carnivalesque, into a gorgeous Mountains puts it in contention. Then Phil sounds the opening notes to Dark Star and the answer is yes, the second set *can* top the first. Dark Star is fluid and slippery, covering much of the same ground as the *Live/Dead* version from two shows previous, but making its own distinctive additions to the Dark Star canon as well. It serves as the sublime base for the vintage '69 string of St. Stephen → The Eleven → Lovelight, Dark Star as cerebral foreplay for a run of tunes that climaxes with Lovelight. After such intensity, the comic "make it up as we go along" Hey Jude, which Pigpen sings quite well (after the rest of the band badgers him into it), complete with an "A-walkin' on the water . . ." improvisation, is a mellow relief. Sort of like the Werewolves encore for 10/31/91, a chance to exhale and smoke 'em if you got 'em.

4/22/69
THE ARK

Here is yet another legendary show to come out of the amazing '69 spring tour, featuring one of the most engrossing and intoxicating Dark Stars there is.

The second set begins in a fashion typical of the era, with the band grousing about the PA, heaping abuse upon Bear. Phil is very funny during this bout of chatter, testing the monitors by letting loose a series of vocal ejaculations straight from the pen of *Mad* magazine cartoonist Don Martin: "Kebonk! Schploort! Th-ghazaakh! Thhsssspphh!!!"

When the problem finally gets sorted out, the Dead perform a pleasantly relaxed Dupree's, less highly mannered than the 3/1/69 version, followed by a highly expressive Mountains of the Moon. The moody noodling at the end of Mountains becomes Dark Star soon after Jerry switches from acoustic to electric guitar. Jerry leads the band off the beaten path of the main Dark Star riff early on in this one, clearing the way with a very trumpetlike tone. After the verse the drums play heavy chimes in concert with Weir, tolling sonorously through the Dark Star as if a call to worship. It's an effect that lends this Dark Star an almost gothic feel, accentuated by Jerry's often haunting variations on the main riff. Garcia closes this "paragraph" and begins a new one by emphatically stating the main theme, only to deviate from it again immediately, this time in a sunnier mode. In the unpausing passages that follow, the band tosses out endless variations on the theme in a steady stream of group invention, building to a number of peaks before letting each crumble in its own landslide of feedback.

The jam turns mysterious again after a time, Jerry playing some crypto-Spanish guitar lines with heavy distortion amid waves of feedback. In truth this Dark Star is so constantly mutable in mood and musical structure that mapping it is akin to describing each subtle variation of light on a windy, partly cloudy day with a bright sun in the sky. It finally ends its wondrous mutations with the predictable transition into St. Stephen, which is unfortunately very ragged, especially in the harmonies (which are just awful). Balance is retained, however, with an Eleven that is even more frenetic than usual, leading into a Lovelight → Caution jam → Lovelight that is, if anything, even sicker. The band is so obviously cruising at the end of the show that it would be a wonder if they stopped here. No doubt at least an encore is missing from the circulating version of this show. What there is, though, is amazing, a must for any collector.

6/14/69
MONTEREY

This is one of those shows that Deadheads love (those who've heard it) and the band would probably hate if they listened to it. There's a lot to love, especially a show-spanning Lovelight that serves as the prime vessel for the show's jam; what the band would no doubt hate is how out of tune their instruments are throughout practically all of the show.

The set that has survived for circulation opens with the aforementioned Lovelight, a marvelously long version that contains some pretty far-out playing. The end is especially strange, with Jerry playing a revolving pattern of staccato guitar weirdness. The transition into the relative simplicity of Me & My Uncle retrospectively evokes the disorientation caused by '71 and '72 Dark Star transitions into more prosaic tunes such as 12/5/71's Dark Star → Uncle → Dark Star. Indeed this could more accurately be seen as a forebear of such transitions, as mid-June of 1969 was a time of almost abrupt change for the Dead, the dawning of an era when deep psychedelic poetry would find a way to coexist comfortably with country and folk prosody.

It's Jerry front and center for a good long while, starting with him singing Doin' That Rag with as much passion as he's given that song. He Was a Friend of Mine, a real gem from the earlier years, is gorgeous instrumentally, its spareness leaving ample room for Jerry's sensitive guitar lines. It is marred somewhat, though, by badly out-of-tune harmonies. A very early Dire Wolf is next, worth mentioning for the jaunty, staccato treatment here that differentiates it from later renditions.

If Lovelight bookends this set, Dark Star is the magical tome within. This must be one of the fastest versions played, very speedy from the start. The first verse arrives pretty quickly, after which Jerry, Bobby, and Phil create a prickly jam, Garcia exiting at opportune moments for some blazing runs. The main theme returns to get an exhilarating workout, burning out finally into the familiar pile of '69 feedback ashes from which loose embers stoke the fires of St. Stephen. It doesn't take long for Stephen to rage into a three-alarm blaze—this is one of the most exciting in a year full of great versions, though it does lose considerable steam in a very ragged William Tell bridge (referred to by some Heads as the "William Tell Overture").

No matter, though, The Eleven more than atones for that momentary lapse, ripping through the changes and shining very brightly in the vocal section. It goes tearing right back into Lovelight, which consists mostly of Pigpen and the Boys riffing on the "All I need" rap, which Pig punctuates at the end with an emphatic "Feels sooooo fuckin' good!" And it does. A brief foray into Drums shows that Billy and Mickey are of the same opinion, chanting rhythmic nonsense syllables and then echoing these chants with their playing, which leads back into Lovelight *again. Who* is it, by the way, who enters Lovelight vocally before Pigpen? Doesn't sound like Bobby, Jerry, or Phil, but all onstage that night put together a show with real fire.

Q: How many Deadheads does it take to screw in a light bulb?

A: Four—one to screw it in, two to watch it burn out, and one to tape it.

or

A: None—they just follow it around for thirty years and wait for it to burn out.

11/8/69
FILLMORE AUDITORIUM

The Dark Star in the middle of this show initiates a mind-boggling nine-tune jam (with two reappearances of Dark Star) that is, if not their finest ever, certainly among the contenders. Dark Star starts off unassumingly enough, with a well-played if straightforward entry into the first verse. From here on in please make note of the fasten-your-seatbelts sign.

T.C., Mickey, and Billy take over the reins immediately after the verse to lead the band into a space with "backwards through time" effects. That is, sounds with a gradual attack and a truncated decay—the reverse of how musical notes generally sound. Mickey's slow crescendos on the gong, to which he puts a sudden stop with his hand, are particularly effective in creating this feel. Space gets spacier before a thick bass jam becomes a bat-out-of-hell Other One. Phil, as you might have guessed, is in charge here. After the first verse they really work the effect of sustaining the last beat of each measure before Phil comes pounding down on the "one," and the result is thrilling. Even more sublime pleasures are in store, though, as The Other One jam is transformed gradually and virtually indetectably (with seeming effortlessness) into a snippet of a swirling feel-good jam vaguely reminiscent of the Feelin' Groovy jam.

The Dark Star theme is stated again, with a brief return to the aforementioned jam. Then—and this will take your breath away—we are taken back to a time when Uncle John's Band was a wordless (but fully formed) calypso-flavored jam. Although the lyrics added later were ideally wed to the tune, this jammed version is uniquely affecting.

Dark Star returns after Uncle John's Jam for the second verse and, in classic form, pours its life into St. Stephen. Jerry sings the "Sunlight splatters . . ." bridge here as fine as he ever has. The transition to and construction of The Eleven are, like the rest of this show, phenomenal. The vocal harmonies are also tremendously well done. This traveling electric circus rolls next into a little town called Caution—mayor, name of Pigpen. Phil's bass turns in the internal Caution jam are preternatural, the band exploding all around him in cymbal-accented bursts of ball lightning. Pig's rap has the audience eating out of the palm of his hand and clapping rhythmically through his whole "Got my mojo working" thang. Criminally, the tape is cut here, picking up much later in the rap.

As Caution gives way to the first performance of the Playing in the Band prototype, the Main Ten, it's very amusing to hear Pigpen off in the background singing along: "Dit de dah, dit de dah, dit de dah-de-dah" in an almost ironic manner (although I'm not so sure how well the words "in an almost ironic manner" jibe with any action of Pigpen's!). Although The Main Ten is not main-tained for long, the band does manage some interesting variations on its theme in a short time. The Dead *really* step it up, though, when they return to Caution, Phil and Jerry playing their thunder-and-lightning roles with stunning speed and aplomb in and out of another long Pigpen stint. Heading into the home stretch, the band plays an especially whimsical and avant-garde Feedback—long, haunting, and exploratory.

Finally there is—what else?—We Bid You Goodnight. Some early harmony troubles result in Phil and Jerry having to carry the rest of the band on their backs (for not the first or the last time), but much is rectified for the chorus after Jerry's lead parts. Though this is one of the sloppier versions, the fact that one can hear the audience's call-and-response singing on this soundboard makes it extra special, as does the way the band takes the song down to a whisper at the end. This show and a few that followed seem to signify sort of a last hurrah for the baroque approach of '69. Bravo!

1970—1971

he dawning of a new decade saw the Dead going through some fairly dramatic changes. Their first two albums of the seventies, *Workingman's Dead* and *American Beauty,* were released in this period and the back-to-basics approach they heralded—in song form and content, instrumentation, and recording technique—had repercussions for the band's live performances that were to be felt throughout the remainder of its history.

The country, folk, and blues flavor of these albums was not, to be sure, terra incognita for sixties "rock" performers or the Dead, for that matter. Bob Dylan, to cite an obvious and influential example, had either turned his back upon or ignored or moved beyond psychedelia in the very "Summer of Love" itself with his album *John Wesley Harding,* a collection of simply constructed and played three-verse songs very much in the folk and country vein. He followed this effort with an album, *Nashville Skyline,* that was positively drenched with country. The Band had begun in the late sixties to craft songs steeped in Americana and had discovered for themselves a very effective musical and lyrical vernacular for infusing these themes with an anachronistic authenticity. And the Byrds, and then Crosby, Stills, and Nash, had created a mellow California hybrid of folk and rock that emphasized vocal performances and, as a result, the words and melody of a song. "Folk rock" seems to me, as it did to these performers, a label that trivializes more than it elucidates, but it can perhaps be elaborated upon to describe more fully what these performers, and the Dead, were doing: adding to the traditional canon of folk and traditional song, using (in some cases) the instrumentation and some of the sensibility of the prevailing idiom of the day, which was rock and roll (a phrase that, from its very first associations with music, has been the sort of umbrella label that ends up saying very little about the artists it denotes).

All of the artists mentioned above did in fact influence the new direction taken by the Dead beginning in the latter half of 1969. Robert Hunter has acknowledged the inspiration he derived from Dylan's songwriting (for Dylan, I think it's safe to assume that this applies to both his pre- and his post-electric "folk" songs) and the Band's in particular. And, on the musical side, the Dead's close relationship with David Crosby is certainly reflected at least in the vocal approach to the *Workingman's* and *American Beauty* material, and doubtless had something to do with their mining the folk-country vein in the first place. The story goes that Crosby agreed to help the band with their harmony arrangements in an informal exchange for session work on CS&N albums, including Jerry's pedal-steel work on "Teach Your Children," on *Déjà Vu.*

What should not be forgotten among all this talk of influences, though, is that, for Jerry, Bobby, and Pigpen at least, the *Workingman's* material represented a homecoming of sorts. The Warlocks, after all, had been sired by Mother McRee's Uptown Jug Champions, Jerry and Bobby's collection of "second-rate talent." Garcia's roots were bluegrass and folk, having played banjo with the Wildwood Boys and Sleepy Hollow Log Stompers, and performed folk songs with his then-wife, Sara. The father of bluegrass, Bill Monroe, was an idol of Garcia's and of fellow Wildwood Boy Robert Hunter's. And, as for Pigpen, well, he was the blues personified, an identity that came from a life hard lived and an immense blues vocabulary learned from his father, who was a DJ at a blues radio station. Indeed up until 1970 the Dead never wholly turned their back on these roots. Pigpen, to be sure, sang the blues throughout his tenure with the band. And the electrification of jug-band standards like I Know You Rider, Stealin', and Sittin' on Top of the World hardly obscured their muddy origins.

One might not search for external influences at all had the Dead's material and performances prior to them "going country" not been psychedelia of the most rococo sort, thereby making the perceived difference all the more acute and, yes, somewhat puzzling. The Dead, though, saw that they had painted themselves into a corner with material (i.e., *Aoxomoxoa*) that was, regardless of its considerable charms, unwieldy, difficult to perform, and, if not *soulless* exactly, at least very left-brained. The *Aoxomoxoa* songs (and era, as typified by T.C.) possessed a sort of dark, Brecht/Weillian whimsy, to be sure, that was in keeping with currents that ran through the band from beginning to end; there was continuity of material as well—witness Dupree's Diamond *Blues* (my emphasis). But there was very little *swing* there, an observation that is amply illustrated, I think, by a comparison of Dupree's circa 1969 and the new arrangement debuted in 1977. Don't get me wrong—I truly enjoy the swirling calliope sound of the '69 edition, but the simpler setting of '77 onward is more organic to the song's content, lending an honesty and veracity to the lyrics and authority to Jerry's delivery. Writ large, this could be considered the Dead's program for 1970–71: the stripping away of artifice.

That the prevailing musical winds were also blowing in that direction (not only CS&N, Dylan, and the Band but the Eagles and the whole trend toward singer-songwriters—James Taylor, Joni Mitchell, et al.) probably had very little to do, directly at least, with their musical program. Incidentally it may have caused the albums of this period to have been somewhat better received than they might have, but it should be remembered that if this was a trend, the Dead were in the vanguard. Better "folk rock" than the bombastic road taken by other bands emerging from the late sixties into the seventies.

At any rate the years '70 and '71 were very good ones for the Dead, musically at least (personally and fiscally, well . . .). As always the calendar is an imprecise measuring device. This era started musically in mid June of 1969, when the first of the *Workingman's* material began to trickle in to the Dead's sets, and picked up momentum in December of that year with their first acoustic-electric show and T.C.'s departure in early 1970. It could be said to have begun to end with Keith's introduction to the band in late 1971. Keith's piano playing, it is true, contained a strong ragtime element that fit nicely with the band's frontier motif, but the more modern jazz elements of his playing style would eventually pull the band in another direction.

On tape this is an era with more than a little bit for everyone. For starters there's a whole lot of it. The Dead in these years were a touring machine, more so than ever before or even since. Gratefuldeadmania did not take the country by storm, no, but their audience was certainly growing, aided by the favorable reception of *Workingman's* and *American Beauty* (I resist making qualitative comparisons with the previous albums—apples and oranges), a large number of FM broadcasts of shows, and many radio interviews granted, especially by Hunter. Fall '71 would see the release of the live album, *Skull Fuck/Skull and Roses/Grateful Dead Live*—a rose by any other name, et cetera . . . —that would get them their first gold record (which they promptly set out to burn and six-gun to smithereens). The volume of shows and the march of time ever closer to the present has given us quite a number more shows than were preserved (or at least are in circulation) from any of the previous years. Concomitant with this quantity is a generally very high quality of performance—spring and fall tours in both years were outstanding; the summer months from both years are, for whatever reasons (one being Bear's stay in the slammer) and with some notable exceptions, somewhat lesser known, but a quick perusal yields some fantastic shows— the Fillmore East and Euphoria Ballroom runs in July '70, the Yale Bowl, for one, in summer '71.

And the music itself: folk, gospel, blues, country, rockabilly, rock and roll—and that's just the acoustic sets! This is a year in which Silver Threads and Golden Needles, Casey Jones, The Other One, How Long Blues, China → Rider, Uncle John's Band, Good Lovin', and Dark Star all coexisted. That's just a small sampling. The addition of the acoustic sets in 1970 swelled the Dead's repertoire to a size that was not seen again until the late seventies. It's a testament to the Dead's musical skills and their genuine commitment to the new songs of this era that they made an effort and were able to integrate this material into their more extended jamming tunes. In other words the fact that they didn't just go whole hog and play discrete songs during this period both showed it and enabled it to be more than just a passing phase in the band's history.

It's a fact that points up the uniqueness of the Grateful Dead. Not only were they able to write—words and music alike—great, authentic songs in the folk idiom, but they were able to incorporate them into a greater whole composed in no small part of very trippy extended jamming. Not many bands would be able to do that (there might not be many that would *want* to, but I believe this lack of eclecticism is ultimately to their, and rock's, detriment). Granted the integration was not perfect. Aside from the acoustic-electric dichotomy, this is the period when the first real first-set–second-set divisions begin to creep in. But the acoustic-electric, first-set–second-set line was often crossed and as a result remained somewhat blurred. The effects of the paring down characterized by the acoustic sets were also discernible in the electric set, as both playing and arrangements became somewhat more straightforward—the revered 2/13/70 Dark Star, though complex in its own right, epitomizes this trend toward what could be loosely termed a musical directness. And any band that can go from the far reaches of an amazing Dark Star straight into the debut of a tune like Wharf Rat, then *back in* again (as they did in the epic 2/18/71 Port Chester show), deserves some recognition on this point.

On top of all of this, the treat of Pigpen accompanying himself, as he did at times, on acoustic guitar and delivering some of his most potent raps seems almost to constitute an embarrassment of riches. It's a surfeit in which we all can revel.

2/11/70
FILLMORE EAST

The highlight of this show may also stand as the highlight of the collective opus of guest artists sitting in with the Dead. The already intense psychedelic jamming out of an excellent Dark Star is brought to a whole 'nother level as Duane Allman, Gregg Allman, and Peter Green (from Fleetwood Mac, back when they were a psychedelic blues band) join the Boys onstage. A sizzling free-form jam ensues with Jerry and Duane not dueling—no, nothing so crass as that—but intertwining their signature guitar sounds to produce an effect that somehow manages to exceed the sum of its parts. What emerges is one of the most involving Spanish Jams on tape. The jam builds and builds and spawns . . . an epic Lovelight. Yow!

The first time I heard this vital piece of live Dead was at two in the morning in a friend's dorm room. Owing to the hour (I think his crazy roommate was asleep across the room) we had to keep it down. I remember that

I couldn't wait to play it LOUD, and if you haven't yet heard this mother of all guest spots (with all due respect to Branford Marsalis), you should wait no longer.

5/2/70
HARPUR COLLEGE

Though many acoustic-electric tapes from this era have joined my collection since I first got my hands on all three sets of this treasure, it has held up to high initial impressions. It's not just a fluke of clean sound and the availability of all sets. Though we're missing many of the shows from this spring tour that might give us further perspective on just how special an evening it was in that context, it is clear that this was a superlative show by any standard.

The acoustic portion of the evening opened with Don't Ease, interesting in this setting and nicely augmented by Pigpen's harp playing. The version of I Know You Rider that follows is preternaturally haunting, slower and with an entirely different rhythmic feel than the electric version to which we're so accustomed. Particularly fine is that the "muddy water" line is not only brought back but given emphasis. Friend of the Devil is also lovely. With such a fine start it's understandable that the band would give the audience a little shot between Friend Of and Dire Wolf for calling out songs frantically. It's interesting to note Garcia's dismissal of Weir's admonition that "You gotta start acting like a mature, responsible audience"—"Don't listen to him." This sort of bemusement at Weir's often gruff attitude toward the crowd is a defining feature of Jerry and Bobby's onstage relationship in this era, though it should be noted that Bobby's tongue is no doubt planted firmly in cheek here, and they all liked to razz the New York crowds a bit.

A seven-beat Beat It On Down the Line is noteworthy not only for Bobby's impassioned singing but for his hilarious Pigpen attempt before the middle solo: "Rock on out." The Black Peter that comes out of Beat It On Down is amazing, with Jerry singing this song as well as he ever has. It just goes to show that, unlike the 5/15 version just a couple of weeks later, these very slow tunes can work without the sustain of electricity if the band is on. Candyman, however, doesn't start out as well and is abandoned after only one verse, whether by premeditation or spur-of-the-moment disaffection is unclear. Whatever the motive, the effect is quite remarkable as Jerry and Bob make a drastic change in tempo without warning, ending up in Cumberland.

Jerry moves to his electric here, to play some licks over the still-acoustic playing of the rest of the band (or maybe he just broke a string). It's a delightful version of one of the best of the *Workingman's* songs, improved by David Grisman's (or is it Marmaduke's?) mandolin work (one of them is there—listen!).

The end of a real fine Deep Elem—a cautionary tale of sin in a red-light district—brings about "Gospel Time," as Jerry terms it. Weir helpfully asks, "Everybody take off your hats . . . or the men take off their hats and the ladies leave them on." A Bible-thumping, swaying Cold Jordan ensues, the first in almost a year. In the upper register, Grisman plays some fine mandolin; in the lower, Phil (or another basso profundo onstage) sings a damn impressive bass part. Grisman's playing also adds some welcome ornament to a solid Uncle John's Band.

Set two is by far the most jam laden. A fun-spirited St. Stephen leads into a flawless Cryptical, which in turn yields Drums into The Other One, highlighted by a wild middle jam, back into Cryptical. This challenging linkage is topped off by an explosive intro to the wonderfully weird, strangely shuffling Cosmic Charlie. That the Dead are able to play such a demanding and quintessentially electric group of tunes such as these right after the acoustic set—and play them with élan—is damn impressive, a real commentary on the versatility of their chops at this point in their playing.

Casey Jones is very tasty. There are crazier versions, to be sure, but this one distinguishes itself through its attention to detail. Good Lovin' starts out very rough, but the band comes *burning* out of the Drums in the middle. Garcia plays some stuff here that has no business in so innocuous a tune—his trespass is most welcome. The playing in question is an ominous, speedy jam that sounds like nothing so much as an aural representation of accounts of Neal Cassady's driving technique and the effect it had on the more sensitive of his passengers. There are no brakes here, only downhill momentum fueling exhilarating fear. When the jam becomes sunlit again (that is, recognizably a part of an upbeat song), there's a palpable sense of relief to be had—the feeling of making it down the mountain unscathed. The jam puts this version among the very best.

Jerry's tuning *during* Cold Rain and Snow doesn't much help this version, although the sound of his guitar going "wowowowow" at the end is at least entertaining. As for It's a Man's, Man's, Man's World, what can I say? This tune is flat-out amazing. Jerry, Phil, and Bobby do a creditable job of backing up Pigpen on the "de-dah-doos," and as for Pigpen himself, well, he's not James Brown, but you wouldn't say he's *no* James Brown.

The closing Dancin', Mickey banging at the cowbell throughout, manages to top even its two predecessors in the set. This one's the prize tomato of an early-1970 Dancin' bumper crop. The jaw-dropping jamming sounds as if it's almost on another theme at the end, with Jerry pouring out fast loops of lightning and Phil thundering at his heels for a good long while. Phil also makes a real Pigpenesque comment to the audience at the end of the set: "You folks should all follow the fine example of the fellow over here who got it on with his girlfriend. And we're gonna take a short break, and I want you all to feel each other for about ten minutes while we do."

But wait, there's more! The third set opens with a bass rumble—Dew! And this one really do Dew that voodoo that Dew do so well. Jerry plays with fury in the buildup to the song's climax. Check out his vocal for the delivery of the final line, though: "I guess it doesn't mattah. . . ." One of the last Viola Lee Blues comes up next (it wouldn't survive the year) with some added complexities. Jerry spaces the words a bit here, but the closing jam can make one forget the song even *has* words. Out of Viola Lee a short burst of Feedback gives way to a splendid, up-tempo We Bid You Goodnight, with Phil in especially fine form (must have been that Cold Jordan warm-up—if indeed it was him) and Jerry just going off on his part.

There's not much slack or fat here, just three tapes' worth of just about the best the band had to offer in that era. For killer filler there's a New Riders version of The Weight (with Jerry on pedal steel) that sometimes circulates with various of these sets, purporting to be from that night. While reveling in it and the three Dead sets, one can only hope that more performances from this spring tour will find their way into the light.

5/6/70
MIT

This was a free concert on a day of student strikes to protest the Kent State killings; it was also a preview for the Dead's concert at MIT the following night. What this tape lacks in quality it more than makes up for in sensational playing and atmosphere. Though it isn't quite Veneta '72 in length, song selection, playing, or tape quality, it shares that tape's sense of place. You can put yourself right there in Kresge Plaza on a cold, blustery spring day, dancing like mad just to stay warm.

The tape starts a little ways into an amazing Dancin', Weir shouting "C'mon, everybody dance around now!" Given how hot this version is, it's a wonder that the exhortation was even necessary (yes, even for MIT students).

The jams are long, thoroughly exploring every little nook and cranny that the song's structure offers. Garcia and Lesh build up a number of exhilarating runs, and some passages in here actually call to mind Dark Star. There's also some Eyes-like strumming by Jerry at one point, while Phil plays an ascending bass line similar to his part in that yet-to-be-written song. An excellent China → Rider keeps the energy level high, Jerry's guitar taking on a quarrelsome cast, as if it, too, is trying to fight off the cold. A good Next Time is followed by a huge opening for Dew, which stays big all the way through. There aren't many very quiet spaces in this one, as it builds steadily to an explosive finish. Good Lovin' gets off to a roaring start but grinds to a halt when Pigpen's mike issues only distortion, which occasions his uttering of the classically direct line "This microphone over here don't work too fuckin' good, you guys." The "guys" get it to work at least a little better, and the Dead deliver another long, psychedelic treatment of what was originally a three-minute pop song, with some blazing Jerry solo runs. At its end Phil remarks upon the playing conditions: "Well, this is getting kind of ridiculous 'cause it's so cold we can't play for shit, you see. I mean, you know, we're enjoying it, it's a lot of fun and all that, but . . . we're gonna do some more and then split."

The band continues to give the lie to Phil's claim that they can't play for shit, with one of the most rambunctious versions of Casey Jones ever and a sick St. Stephen → Not Fade. The opening to Stephen is very powerful, and the intensity reaches several feverish climaxes on its way to an equally great Not Fade, then back into a Stephen jam before returning to Not Fade for a final vocal turn. The Dead finally call it quits there, Bobby departing with, "Hey, we're gonna split. And we'll be playing for you tomorrow night. But it's too fucking cold, you know how it is," to end this classic outdoor show.

5/15/70 (late show)
FILLMORE EAST

Though far (far) from the best show of this era, the acoustic set of this show is worth having for a few standout songs and some relaxed and hilarious interplay between the band (Jerry, especially) and the crowd.

The set opens with a gorgeous debut of The Ballad of Casey Jones, to which Bobby does great credit. Next, while Bob suggests to Jerry "at the risk of being repetitive, how about another song in D," a skirmish breaks out in the audience. Jerry, laughing, admonishes, "Now, now, kids, don't fight."

The picture of Jerry and Bobby up on the stage of the Fillmore East, very laid-back, is very well conveyed by this tape, on which their onstage asides are clearly audible.

Silver Threads is also very nice, though the Black Peter that follows drags a lot, an effect that is particularly palpable when this tune is played acoustically. Things pick up, though, with the intro to Friend of the Devil, over which Jerry informs us that "We had a request to do this—we did it in the first show, we're gonna do it again now," to which Bobby adds, "That's breaking a long-standing tradition—we love to break tradition." It's unclear whether he meant repeating a song or taking a request, though the former seems most likely.

Friend Of is unfortunately where this set starts to go seriously awry, with some major feedback problems toward the end. It's also where the humor really starts to pick up. While Jerry and the crew are coping with and trying to find the source of the problem, a guy in the audience yells out, belligerently, "HEY, GARCIA!" This is what follows:

Bob: (*very* mockingly, slurring and thickening his voice) "HEY, DUHRTHEEUH."

Jerry: (also mockingly, like "I'm just *so* interested in what *you* have to say) "What?"

Audience guy: (garbled)

Jerry: "I can't hear you, man."

Audience guy: "Why did the chicken cross the road?"

Pigpen(?) Crew(?): " 'Cause he was tryin' to get away from you!"

Audience: (laughter)

Bob: (in that awful British accent he affects for this bit) "I say, my dog has no nose."

Jerry: (in a better U.K. accent than you might guess) "No nose? How does he smell?"

Bob: "Bloomin' awful!"

Jerry: "Hey man, next year we bring out the girls."

Bob: (deadpan) "Lavish revue."

Audience guy: (starts to shout again, something unintelligible)

Jerry: "I'm sorry, I'm—man, I lost interest. It went right past." (Guy shouts again.) "Yeah, yeah, have it tattooed on your arm and come show me later."

Uncle John's, in which Jerry sings, "Beg *ye* call the tune," is rough, harmony wise, a fact Jerry seems to acknowledge with "Aw, you're too kind, too kind" in response to the audience's applause. A leaden Candyman seems to seal the set's fate:

JERRY: "What we're gonna do is we're gonna finish up this wooden section of the program with a gospel tune."
BOB: "A right proper one."
JERRY: "We're gonna have, uh, David Nelson of the New Riders come up and help us a little bit, as they say."
AUDIENCE: (light, slightly delayed applause)
JERRY: (dourly) "Yeah, yeah."
BOBBY: "Skip it."
JERRY: (laughs)
PIGPEN: (from the wings) "Wait a minute, don't I get to play one before you go off and sing that fuckin' Jesus song (garble)?"
BILLY (?): "Yeah, Pigpen, play the blues!"
JERRY: (no doubt realizing Nelson's on his way up and not wanting to appear rude) "Oh, wait a minute, wait a minute, before we—"
BOB: (loudly, cutting off Jerry) "Hey, you wanna hear Pigpen?" (crowd cheers) "I don't think he heard you, I wanna hear it a little louder. . . ." (crowd cheers louder) "I *still* don't think he heard you, maybe you oughta do it a little . . . (laughs) All right, ladies and gentlemen, the dog-suckingest man in showbiz, Pigpen!"
PIGPEN: "That guy got a dirty mouth."

After Bobby's James Brown intro parody, Pigpen proceeds to absolutely steal the show with the second ever She's Mine. Now *this* is a nice, rare treat—Pigpen accompanying himself on guitar, all alone. Katie Mae, too, is superb, every bit as good as the 2/13 version preserved on *Bear's Choice*. Then, one last time before the promised "Jesus song," we get to see Jerry's quick wit in action again:

BOB: (shouting) "Phil? Paging Mr. Philip Lesh."
JERRY: (resignedly) "Or we could just do it rather than wait."
ANOTHER AUDIENCE GUY: "When are you gonna do a free concert here?!"
JERRY: (voice dripping with sarcasm) "As soon as everything is perrrfectly cool in New York City. . . . And if you're smart, you'll get out too."

Phil eventually does make it onstage to close the set with the first I Hear a Voice Callin', with heavenly harmonies to close a rowdy set.

EUPHORIA BALLROOM

This is it, the night El Paso entered the Dead's repertoire! There's even more to celebrate, though, in an outstanding acoustic set with plenty of hilarious chatter.

The tape of this show begins with a curiosity, a very noisy audience recording of the Don't Ease opener that has been grafted onto the soundboard recording of the remainder of the set. It's good to have for the sake of completion, but it reveals more about the restiveness of the audience—no quiet reverence here, it sounds like a cocktail party—than the musical quality of what seems to be a fine performance of the song. You also get to hear how low the guitars actually were in the mix (see below).

The soundboard kicks in with the next tune, a Friend of the Devil that is close to perfection. What faults there are in the performance have more to do with the way Bobby's guitar drops in and out than the playing itself, which the band addresses in the first of several amusing chatter breaks, this one primarily a ragfest on Owsley, who's manning the sound controls. Due to its consistently funny nature, I present it here in its entirety:

BOB: "Hey, can you hear the guitars out there?"

AUDIENCE: "No!"

JERRY: "There it is, man, how's about turning up the guitars *real loud* in the PA? You'd think that after five years of that you'd have an *ear*. Maybe that's the trouble. . . ."

BOB: "The trouble is that you'd think that—"

OWSLEY: "Want 'em louder than the vocals?" (Jerry snorts)

BOB: "Hey, man, they cannot *hear* the guitars out there. . . . Can you hear the guitars out there?"

AUDIENCE: "No!"

JERRY: "Make it *loud* . . . there it is, man. What exactly can you hear?"

BOB: (to Owsley) "Yes, make the guitars louder than the vocals out there."

JERRY: "No, no, don't do *that,* but make them *almost* louder than the voices— as loud *as* the voices, how's that?"

PHIL (?): "Sure, sure—do it up here, too."

JERRY: "Right, *man*."

BOB: "I mean, we can't hear what we're doing and they can't hear what we're doing."

BILLY (?): (in New Yawker voice) "So what good is it?"

JERRY: "Yeah!"

BILLY (?): "I ask ya."

JERRY: "I know, it gives one pause."

AUDIENCE: "Plaaaay!"

JERRY: "Relax, that's what we're here for, man."

Dire Wolf has a nice, homey feel, Jerry struggling not to laugh after a lyrical miscue. Then comes Humorous Chatter, Part II, which starts with a number of people at the rail shouting "MOVE BACK" in unison.

PHIL: "Like that's kind of reasonable, I think, y'know—I mean all these people are crammed up here, are crammed against the stage, so they're only standing up for air, *right?*"

JERRY: "Don't listen to him—it's not *that* reasonable . . . breathe deep, folks—"

WEIR: (interrupting) "I don't know if these people—" (he's cut off by high-pitched feedback)

PHIL: "Hey, can't you get rid of that damn ring, Bear?" (more feedback)

BOB: "I don't know if these people that are standing up (Phil hoots, imitating the feedback) are gonna be inclined to sit down, but right now they can't, 'cause they're pressed together."

JERRY: "So where's it all at, man, where's it all at?"

BOB: "Now I ask you."

OFFSTAGE VOICE: "Right here!"

PHIL: "Hey, it's ringing at two hundred fifty cycles, Bear, and it's also ringing at about two thousand cycles. You got that? That's out in the house also, man. . . . Well, just pull 'em out."

JERRY: (to Owsley) "Don't mutter, man, don't mutter."

PHIL: (exaggeratedly) "I can't hear you. What are you saying?"

OWSLEY: ". . . Oh, well, I got a vague whatever(?) . . ."

JERRY: "That's it, a vague whatever—did you hear that?"

BOB: "How can you hate a guy like that?" (Jerry laughs)

Out of muffled discussion of what to play next, Bobby can be heard saying, "I'd like to do El Paso, but if you don't want to . . ."

PHIL: "Oh, I like it."

JERRY: (his voice dripping with sarcasm) "El Paso? It's kind of early for that, *ain't it?*" (more inaudible discussion follows)

JERRY: "Bobby's looking for a capo."

BOBBY: "Commonly known in, uh, referred to in folk circles as a 'cheater,' you can put it on and . . ." (Woman offstage: "Cheat.") "Cheat. Reminds me of a good card game I know. I'll tell you how to play it sometime, next time he breaks a string. . . . Hey, it's really pathetic, man, I can't hear what I'm doing up here, and—"

JERRY: "Yeah, I can't hear Weir's guitar no-how, man."

BOB: "Turn it up yet louder . . ." (Owsley turns it up real loud) "Okay, Okay . . ."

PHIL: "Jesus."

JERRY: "Hit it—"

And so the band finally goes into Dark Hollow, which is as masterfully rendered as the *Bear's Choice* version. Bobby's voice is full and mellifluous, and Jerry just *nails* his Bill Monroe-esque harmony part, which is one of the finest the Dead have ever worked out. Candyman also features attentively nuanced Garcia vocals, especially the way he phrases the "Candyman's in town" line. The rare How Long Blues (not the same as the song with this name played by Hot Tuna) and Deep Elem are both outstanding, continuing the fine flow of the set. It ends on the strongest possible note with David Crosby adding his harmonies to knockout versions of Cumberland and New Speedway Boogie.

"*It* was just such a great feeling to be going to a show. I remember one road trip in college going from Boston to Hartford. Myself and four buddies. We had hotel reservations, plenty of money, and all the supplies we needed. I remember meeting at the Store 24 at about ten A.M. so we could finish our provisioning and hit the road. We were all positively giddy with anticipation. We got the party started immediately and relished the drive down there, waving at our fellow Deadheads all the way down. It felt like you were really a part of something so special and so fun. A place where you were totally accepted, and no matter how weird your behavior, there was no chance you were going to be the weirdest person there.

"That theme of acceptance was always such a plus for me. How many others out there have had an experience like this one?

"When I first went to Boston University as a freshman, I was unable to hook up with any of the people I knew up there that first night. I wandered around in my dorm self-consciously looking for friends to make. What I really wanted to do was find someone with some weed to smoke. Ambling around on the third floor, I came to an open door with Grateful Dead music playing out into the hall. I stuck my head in and said, 'Hey now!'

"In there I made my first friend at college, a person who is a fairly legendary taper from Rye, New York, whom I'll simply refer to as Crispy. Crispy had a bong full of fine sens for me. All his bootlegs were on reel-to-reel tapes. He had vials of liquid LSD that, after trying, I named 'Blue Star Express.' In short he was about the coolest thing I'd ever come across. That began a core group of B.U. Deadheads that remain some of my closest friends to this day.

"The point I make is that it's always such a common ground. You generally know what to expect from the Deadheads. And to this day, even with no more Dead, it's still a common ground. For instance my boss, who is a senior VP, at the company I work for, is an ex-hippie. He's about forty-five years old. It's great to listen to him reminisce about the Fillmore shows in '70 and '71. He's one of the picky Deadheads that go way beyond bitching about Vince. As far as he's concerned, the Dead died with Pigpen. Not that I agree with that, but it's good to know that even with the thirty years of Dead history, the arguments are still the same and the common ground is still the same. And picky Deadheads have been around forever. **"**

—STEVE KARR

9/19/70
FILLMORE EAST

The penultimate show of yet another impressive run at the Fillmore East, we have only the electric set (or a portion of it) from what surely was an acoustic-electric evening. Although there is history in the fact that the electric set contains Pigpen's last Good Morning Little Schoolgirl, tapes from this show are generally of the Dark Star jam. It is more than enough to satisfy. Deeply.

The Dark Star in question opens with some inventive guiro work from Mickey. After the first verse there are several seconds of complete silence followed by some very bizarre percussion (gongs, birdcalls, and other noises defying easy description), accompanied by terrifying feedback sufficient to make the hair on the back of your neck stand on end. The effect of the guitars emerging with clarity from this zone of feedback is unsurpassedly trippy—it sounds for all the world like a soundtrack for a passage through the looking glass.

Out of this yellow, shimmering place of birdcalls and strange guitars, Jerry's guitar suddenly leaps forth to frolic via a joyously irrepressible jam I've never encountered in other Dark Stars, an all-too-short bridge to what is quite possibly (along with 2/13/70) the finest Feelin' Groovy jam ever. You may differ—it doesn't really matter. What *does* matter is that this one will definitely leave you feeling groovy. If we're thinking in terms of sound tracks, this is one for running amok in a bucolic field or, at the very least, for dancing like a happy fool around your living room. The jam passes back into the main Dark Star theme with great musical deftness, then into the second verse.

From there it's a short passage to a St. Stephen that also merits inclusion among the very best—bouncy, with a lot of punch. And if you've been lucky enough to have heard this one, you'll appreciate the assertion that the drumming is fantastic. St. Stephen becomes a phenomenally hot Not Fade, augmented considerably by the elusive Darkness Jam, which goes right into a blazingly fast little China Cat jam, then back into Not Fade again. Unbelievable.

As if all this were not enough, there are some serious (or rather, not so serious) Pigpen antics to follow in the Lovelight that closes out the set. To set the stage, this version starts out as one in which Pigpen's vocals convey a real sense of heartbreak. The band plays real well, Bobby and Jerry particularly. Bobby has the quick wit to add the lick from James Brown's "Sex Machine" to a passage in the early part of Pigpen's rap where he's talking about his desires "early in the mornin' " ("Get on up!"). But none of these fine moments, nor the crunching guitar embellishments added by guitar near the end of the song, are what you will remember from this version, which features Pigpen at his randiest. I'll let Pig take it from here:

PIGPEN: "... There's a young man right there—ha! Now—ha! Would you like to go home alone or would you like to take a young lady home with you? Well, what do you say?" (varied shouts from the crowd) "He can't talk, he's got his hands in his pockets." (laughter, cheers) "Here's somebody else—you wanna take a young lady home? What you say? Awwwright! That's more like it! Hey! Okay, what else? Now, here's a young lady—would you care to take a young man home? Speak into the microphone."

YOUNG LADY: "Nooooo."

PIGPEN: "Excuse me. Ain't nobody else want to say something? You guys look like you want to say something."

GUY IN CROWD: "Leave it on, Pigpen!" (an allusion to the *Live/Dead* Lovelight)

PIGPEN: "Okay, but I want to tell you something—hold it! I wanna tell all you folks now, I'll give you a little bit of advice. Now if you're standing next to some young lady that happens to be attractive to yourself, and you're just standing with your hands in your pockets doing something kinda funny, then you got to straighten yourself out! But if you sat an' stand an' sitting by some young lady who looks kind of foxy to you, all you got to do, ain't no use in playing no games, come over and say, 'Say, er, uh, ma'am . . . let's fuck.' "

BOBBY: "Pigpen, did you say 'fuck'?"

PIGPEN: (with much passion and relish) "I said FUCK! And with that . . ." (laughter from Jerry, followed by Bobby and Jerry, away from the microphones, jokingly saying, "All you need") "Y'all wanna hear a dirty story?"

CROWD: "Yeah!"

PIGPEN: "Buy a record!" (music resumes)

He isn't quite done yet, though, and he continues to rap/sing on and off for many minutes more—including entreaties for his woman to "roll on over," rhapsodies over "sweet jellyroll," and a request that his woman "please don't mess with my dreams unless you want my meat." Then, to top it all off, he punctuates the final note of Lovelight with his plea/order/cry for the evening: "FUCK!"

When the house system begins to play "Let's Get Together" by the Youngbloods (interestingly enough they're also the performers of "Darkness, Darkness," upon which the Darkness Jam is based), signaling that the show is indeed over, the already-clapping crowd doubles its efforts. Finally Phil comes onstage to deliver the bad news, which he has to rush to get out over the crowd's expressions of disappointment: "Hey, uh, what we wanna say is, thanks very much, but it's been a really long night and Garcia's got a cramp in his hand and we're all tired and Bobby's lost his voice, so, good night."

Of course Pigpen can't help but add, "Wait a minute, wait a minute, why don't you guys go home and fuck somebody." The song comes back over the house system in almost synchronistic commentary, ". . . If you know the song I sing, you will understand—listen—you hold the key to love. . . ."

Just another night with the Good Ole Grateful Dead at the Fillmore East, as captured on a recently unearthed tape that should get wide circulation.

9/20/70
FILLMORE EAST

The superb acoustic set from this night deserves to be ranked among the Dead's best. The opening Uncle John's is lovely, as is Friend of the Devil, which David Grisman embellishes with lively mandolin riffs. Big Railroad

Blues is hair-raising due to Jerry's exceptional singing and a loose and goosey performance by the band. Dark Hollow only features what may be Weir's best, most nuanced country singing ever, framed beautifully by Jerry's harmony part—he just nails "Blow your whistle, freight train" every time, and obviously takes great pleasure in doing so.

An excellent Ripple is followed by a gorgeous To Lay Me Down, with the nice added touch of a mystery pianist and a rare (and the last we've got on tape) acoustic performance of Truckin'. Up until this point they'd all been acoustic, so it's actually the electric version that was a change, but to ears long acclimated to the full-throttle electric take on this song, the acoustic treatment is really so nice a change, a glass of cool water. Rosalie McFall is chill-inducing; David Nelson and Grisman really step out on this one. Two of the best songs from *Workingman's Dead,* Cumberland Blues and New Speedway Boogie, round out the set, both terrific performances. The Brokedown closer seems the perfect choice and it is, on the whole, well done, but one would expect a sublime rendition in light of what's followed. Unfortunately this one drags and the boys have some trouble with the harmonies, flaws that, given the esteemed musical company here, are readily noticeable.

10/31/70 (early show)
STONY BROOK

Halloween. Per usual, the Dead open with Till the Morning Comes (disclaimer: this is irony). It's not a *great* song, and the band has a pretty tough time with the harmonies throughout (not to mention the hideous blown chord near the beginning), but it is rare (especially as an opener) and the live touch of repeating the chorus definitely gives it some added excitement.

This unusual opener is not the only thing to recommend this show, though the late show probably has the edge (it's at least better known). China → Rider is very well done, and Cold Rain and Snow is *exceptional,* very anthemic in feel by this point and one of the best versions there is. The show ends even more strongly than it began with a Viola Lee Blues → Cumby → Uncle John's. Viola Lee starts out humorously with a guy in the audience yelling out the first line while the Dead tread water as if they had forgotten the words. Jerry asks, "What did the judge do?" before all dive into the vocals with confidence. It really kicks into high gear with the fast jam at the end, the vitality carrying through a very fine Cumberland into an Uncle John's of like quality. There's an unusual moment at the end of Uncle John's, right after the "Whoa

Dark Star

It is but one of many striking points of coincidence, if not outright synchronicity or magic, that the Holy Grail of Dead tunes, the song that most fully captures the band's inimitable essence, is the first song that Hunter and the band wrote together. Alligator, St. Stephen, and China Cat came first, true, but these were lyrics Hunter mailed to the band, who then wrote the music or fit them to music already written. Dark Star was the first true collaborative composition between Hunter and the Dead. Strange, isn't it, that this first "group" song would strike a chord that would reverberate throughout the Dead's history with a greater force than any subsequent effort. Chalk it up as yet another episode in Dead history that couldn't be written better as fiction.

Dark Star wins its place in Deadhead hearts because it is a tune that is by design a platform for the Dead's great strength—jamming in all its manifestations. The great Dark Stars feature jazzlike improvisations over the main thematic chord changes of the song, one or more of the jams unique to Dark Star, some moments of deep space, and maybe a thematic jam or quote from another song, and serve as a vital link in the jamming together of several other tunes that are invariably improved by being tied to it.

Dark Star's lyrics are generally given the least notice, but they're every bit as involved and complex as the music and have as much resonance, and on as many levels, with the spirit of the Grateful Dead. On one level it's an imagistic piece of poetry in the same vein as China Cat Sunflower. It's a dark, psychedelic collage, an inward-looking head trip to China Cat's outward-oriented sensory overload. China Cat takes us through daytime realms while Dark Star pulls us through an etherized night, our only guide a disembodied voice who asks, à la T. S. Eliot, "Shall we go . . . ?"

There's much more here than imagistic evocations of loss, estrangement, and tripped-out nighttime confusion. Specific visual references—a "dark star," "clouds," "nightfall," a "lady in velvet"—conjure a sense of obscurity, darkness, negativity. At the same time, Hunter provides indications of light cutting through or shining in the darkness: "searchlight casting," "nightfall of diamonds." The "lady in velvet recedes." Through these contrasts runs a current of mutability and impermanence. Traces can be found in every line (or as Hunter lays the song out on the printed page, every stanza): "crashes," "ashes," "tatters," "tear loose," "faults in the clouds," "transitive," "dissolving," and "recedes." There's an overall sense to the song of absolutes breaking down or at least of a yin and yang to experience, with a melting line between the two.

Amid this breaking down of absolutes is the piercing light of insight: the "searchlight" seeking "faults in the clouds of delusion," the breaking down of the ego as self-perceived ("mirror shatters"), and the almost centrifugal shredding of objective reality ("reason tatters"). There's also a hallucinatory quality linked with a loss of distinction between the self and external objects in the line "glass hand dissolving to ice petal flowers...." Hmmm...sounds a little bit like the effects of LSD.

But if the song is a multilayered depiction of a real head trip, it is also more than that; it is the first in a long line of self-referential Dead tunes. Much of the lyric could describe the musical process undergone by Dark Star as the Dead performed it live. The crashing of Dark Star—its musical deconstruction on stage—indeed gives rise to numerous creations that rise from its ashes, and the nature of these spontaneous musical pieces is as transitive as the nighttime fabric of the music in which one finds these gem-like jams ("diamonds"), as likely to dissolve as a glass hand.

Dark Star is a musical journey through the realm of the Dead and its many treasures.

Little Nemo in Dark Starland

In the early 1900s, when comic strips were epics (read: before TV), there was a strip called *Little Nemo in Slumberland,* written and drawn by Winsor McCay. Its perpetual plot involved the efforts of Nemo, a little boy, to reach Slumberland, where King Morpheus's daughter wanted him to be her playmate. Typically a messenger of the king would appear before him in the first panel with some manner of conveyance—stilts, a giant, a rocket ship, a passageway—for reaching Slumberland. Invariably he would encounter an obstacle or interloper that would bring about an accident, causing him to wake up. In the final panel Nemo would be back in his own room, twisted in his bedclothes, being told by his papa to "keep it down in there" while his mother berated her husband for letting him eat some or another treat before he went to bed (never eat rarebit after eight o'-clock!). As if that isn't vid enough, the drawings more than matched the trippiness of the concept. Needless to say, Garcia was a fan. And Hunter even titled one of the segments on *Infrared Roses* Little Nemo in Nightland.

It's a ride taken on horseback with bright, upbeat music in the air. But an unearthly voice is carried to you on the wind, enticing you onward with tales of strange nighttimes. Just as the music turns suddenly somber (the chorus of Dark Star resolves with the E-minor chord), your horse bolts, and you find yourself being pulled at full gallop through exhilaratingly strange, moonlit terrain. From there you might wander to a babbling brook on the other side of nightfall, be inundated by a swarm of fireflies, or you might just have your horse melt right out from under you.

In more prosaic terms, Dark Star is a place of many sick jams. Debuted in late 1967, its early performances in 1968 linked it to its Deadsong yang, China Cat. These two tunes and the That's It for the Other One suite, to which it also had early linkage, pointed the way to the future of the Dead. Its slightly later lead-in to St. Stephen, once established, laid the groundwork for many a primal Dead jam along the Dark Star → St. Stephen → The Eleven → Lovelight orangeprint. It was one of the tunes upon which the

All this by way of saying that there is a Little Nemo strip that illustrates well a Dark Star journey on horseback akin to the one I describe here. Little Nemo is given the black-and-white night horse Somnus to take him to Slumberland. The king's servant, Oomp, warns that although Slumberland "is a long way off through many miles of weird scenes" (How hip this dialogue is for 1905), his steed will take him there safely, but he must not speed him. Nemo obeys, and all goes well until he is challenged to a race "to Moontown" by a green kangaroo being ridden by a monkey and just can't resist. It turns out to be a free-for-all (rabbits on pigs, frogs on dogs, etc.) through space and over stars and planets. Nemo tries to rein Somnus in to no avail, and he eventually trips over a star, sending Nemo hurtling through space.

And then he wakes up.

The cartoons are amazing, as are the stories. Several editions of McCay's work have been put out by the Nostalgia Press, Box 293, Franklin Square, New York, NY 11010.

Dead really cut their improvisational teeth—one of their first nonblues launching pads for jamming—in 1968, getting some furious workouts in the Mickey and the Hartbeats shows especially. The early elements were in place: bending and playing around the main riff, Phil's carriage of the main thematic line, with Jerry flitting in and out liked a crazed bumblebee, the lilting organ riff, the percussion work, and the nutty, New Potato Caboosesque harmonies "in the round" on the "transitive nightfall" line. It wasn't until 1969, though, that Dark Star really started to come into its own.

T.C.'s joining the ensemble had a great deal to do with the way Dark Star began to break away from jamming on the central theme to explore new musical structures and even cast off structure entirely. Both he and Phil were enamored of modernists such as Igor Stravinsky and Charles Ives and avant-gardists, especially John Cage. So they were not only receptive to but advocates of atonality, chromaticism, and musique concrète (music as objet trouvé—found art, essentially—as discovered in non-traditional "instrumentation" such as broken glass, radio static, the squeak of a door, or, in the Dead's case, feedback; these musique conrète jams were, to quote a phrase, "formless reflections of matter"). Garcia, it seems, was not only a budding master of conventional jazz, blues, and bluegrass (via banjo) improvisation, but a musician who was game for just about anything, including this. The two-drummer setup further aided these forays into deep space, with either Mickey handling percussion—guiro, sandpaper, gong—and Billy on the set, or both exploring the sound potential of the percussive universe while Phil, Jerry, Bobby, and T.C. produced ethereal feedback and "backward masking"-type effects amid cascading and disjointed notes, sonic explorations that most other groups were hard pressed to produce in the studio, let alone live and onstage.

Cutting-edge sound collage wasn't the only innovation brought to Dark Star in 1969, however. Riffing off of the main theme, thoroughly explored in '68, became even more fluid and increasingly likely to lead off into off-the-cuff improvisations with clear musical structure that was both rhythmic and melodic. These jams existed in a wide variety of forms as well, from Phil-led atonal, angular creations—rush hour in New York with a drum pulse—to exuberant, tuneful, liquid expressions of pure Jerrified joy. The middle ground where these extremes met was a bass and fuzz guitar-driven jam, internal to Dark Star played in '69 and '70, now known by many Heads (after the *DeadBase* appellation) as either the Feelin' Groovy or 59th St. Bridge jam because of its (very) superficial resemblance to the Simon and Garfunkel tune. I prefer Feelin' Groovy because it has the advantage of also describing the emotional effects of the jam.

All these forms could, and more often than not would, exist in a single Dark Star. The tune's further evolution in 1971 brought some new thematic jams into the gray fold, including the racy, ecstatic Tighten Up jam, a quote of the only hit of Archie Bell and the Drells from the summer of '68. An outstanding version of this jam can be found on *Dick's Picks Volume Three* (10/31/71), labeled simply "Jam." Certain of the spacey sections also began to take on a character recognizable from one Dark Star to the next, to be dubbed by Heads as "Insect Fear" and "Galactic Overdrive" and other evocative titles. Much of this was, in essence, psychedelic program music.

One of the most interesting characteristics of many 1971 Dark Stars was the attempted integration of discrete songs into the fabric of Dark Star, an apt microcosmic (emphasis on the "cosmic") expression of what the Dead were trying to do in their shows as they brought the *Workingman's* and *American Beauty* type material into shows where trippier and more jamming *Anthem* and *Aoxomoxoa* tunes remained. Two of the best examples of this approach, which would continue through '72, are the 2/18/71 debut of Wharf Rat as the "meat" in a Dark Star sandwich, and the unusual 12/5/71 Dark Star → Me & My Uncle → Dark Star. Though neither of these tunes is from the albums mentioned above, their contrast with Dark Star is about the same: towering, dense, sonic insanity yielding to humble plains dwellings.

The 1972 versions are some of the most wide-open, prettiest Dark Stars the Dead ever played. Not only are there long stretches of interconnected, tuneful jamming between verses, but frequently a good deal of weirdness occurs even before the first verse. It's in '72 that we also start to get some hints of the Mind Left Body Jam in the sound of Jerry's guitar in certain spacey passages, though it doesn't make its full-fledged arrival until '73, as a Dark Star appendage. From '72 to '74 Dark Star becomes less of a set staple but if anything more of a treat—this is an era of long, langorous stretches of jam-bedecked song. And then there were none.

It's hard to go from the '72–'74 versions to the few revival editions that followed and think of the breakouts as truly being Dark Star, as they are none of them all that exploratory or even lengthy. 1/10/79 is probably the best of the bunch, 7/13/84 the least. If this was to be the Dead's approach to the song, one can understand their giving it a pass for so long. Even as Deadheads continued to crave it—more and more so—it was being supplanted in a big way by Space, the vacuum that sucked up so much second-set jamming after 1977. The 1989 breakout at Hampton, however, showed a clear commitment to doing the tune justice, with some outstanding MIDI soloing and an almost nostalgic feedback fest.

MIDI seemed to bring the Dead back to a love of long bouts of jam adventure, and it definitely added a spark to the post '89 versions. Even if it wasn't the MIDI per se that encouraged the Dead to play more freely and creatively on the Dark Stars of this period, the MIDI instrumentation was a marvelous end in itself. Just as '69 Dark Stars distinguished themselves for electronic invention, the later era of Dark Star's flowering would become marked by its orchestral feel. The Dead didn't play Dark Star at all in 1995— it was last played in March 1994—but one has to be as glad for the band as for Heads that they had some good years with it again before all was said and done. Not only does it represent an apt closing of the parenthesis of nearly thirty years, but one would hate to think that the Dead would regret not having done it and that Jerry would die without having played again in that musical space in which he felt so comfortable early on.

oh, what I want to know . . ." reprise where the drums, playing their part into the a cappella chorus, sound exactly like a person falling down a flight of stairs.

DARK STAR

✿ 10/8/68 (Mickey and the Hart-beats)
Without words, the music tells an epic tale.

✿ 2/27/69 Fillmore West
The Live/Dead *Dark Star; the Dead picked a fine representative—it's held up as a paragon of the T.C.-enhanced '69 Dark Star.*

✿ 3/1/69 Fillmore West
A fluid, shape-shifting beauty.

✿ 11/8/69 Fillmore Auditorium
One of the strongest examples (and there are many) of how Dark Star, which makes three appearances here, can be the vessel into which (and whence) a show is poured.

2/18/71
PORT CHESTER

This has got to be the mother of all breakout shows, with first-ever versions of Bertha, Greatest Story, Johnny B. Goode, Loser, Playin', and Wharf Rat. The first set also ranks as one of the best the band has ever played, not to mention the fact that it was Mickey's last night playing with the band for almost four years *and* it was one of the famed ESP shows.

What was it about this venue, anyway? Little more than four months before, the Dead had de-

�֎ 2/13/70 Fillmore East

A much-beloved version that's possessed of the great openness and clarity the Dead brought to the tune in the brief era when Dark Star was unfettered by keyboards.

✷ 9/19/70 Fillmore East

If trippy you seek, trippy you'll find here.

✷ 2/18/71 Port Chester

A very pretty, sensitive Dark Star ➡ *Wharf Rat* ➡ *Dark Star, with a killer version of the Tighten Up jam on the second go-round of Dark Star.*

✷ 11/7/71 Harding Theater

Not all that long but synesthetically stunning. Explores a number of stunning musical landscapes in a brief period of time. Such a long, long time to be gone. . . .

✷ 12/5/71 Felt Forum

A bizarre, percussion-dominated rendition.

✷ 5/11/72 Rotterdam

The longest version on record, yet with nary a note of fat.

✷ 7/18/72 Roosevelt Stadium

A jungle of Space from which a sleeping Tiger is roused.

✷ 8/27/72 Veneta

Features some of Jerry's most luminous playing in this song, or anywhere, for that matter.

✷ 11/19/72 Hofheinz Pavilion

A vast world unto itself, from which emerges, among other landscapes, the first Weather Report Suite prelude.

buted a whole passel of other tunes at the Capitol Theater as well. Maybe they liked the energy of the Connecticut kids who made runs into Port Chester to get sloppy drunk. Whatever—the Dead did the new songs credit, and the results have been preserved for posterity.

How did the debuts fare? Right off the bat, Bertha (already in its soon-to-be-customary set-opening position) is very hot, despite the fact that Jerry still has some phrasing to work out. He also sings, "I had a sinking feeling I was falling." Phil introduces an early-vintage Truckin' with a humorous allusion to Casey Jones: "Well, this isn't drivin' a train but it's almost as good." It's a strong version of the young song. But back to the debuts.

Loser is forestalled briefly by a typical bout of Grateful Dead tuning, about which Bobby wryly observes, "You're witnessing possibly the only ritual older than music, that being tuning up," a witticism to which Phil or Jerry replies, "That's a fact." Loser, when they get around to it, is good, even if the harmonies, though sung on-key, point up the fact that the Dead's vocal mix can at this point sound kind of weak live.

It's not tuning that comes next but a lively discussion among the band as to how Greatest will end.

❋ 2/15/73 Madison
Anchors a superlative string of songs and contains a delicious bassy jam.

❋ 6/10/73 RFK
A spacey and relaxed Phil-led masterpiece.

❋ 10/18/74 Winterland
Out of a jam from Phil and Ned Lagin's electronic weirdness comes an archetypal '74 edition, with much slow, meandering exploration of the main theme. This was also the last regular-rotation Dark Star until 1979 or 1989, depending on how you look at it.

❋ 10/9/89 Hampton
The mother of all revivals, at least to those who were there or on the bus at the time. And it's a damn fine version in its own right.

❋ 9/20/90 MSG
One of the most out there of the postrevival versions, with Phil giving it the MIDI juice.

❋ 12/31/90 Oakland
The Dead loved to play Dark Star with Branford; this may be the finest rendition to come from the collaboration.

❋ 4/1/91 Greensboro
Perhaps the most sublimely psychedelic version of the nineties.

❋ 10/31/91 Oakland
Kesey's rap on Bill Graham's death and the way the Dead play behind him may make this the most significant nineties entry into the canon.

You can hear Bobby laying out the structure of the song to the band. He announces it with, "We're gonna beg your indulgence and try another new song out on ya," amid Mickey trying to get him to say the name of the song and lingering confusion over how it is to be played. Bob even asks Jerry, right before the song starts, "You're gonna play it in A, aren't you?" to which Jerry replies, "No, I already tried it in A; it sounded flat." Finally all gets worked out, and Weir steps to the mike to say, "Okay, Mickey wants to call this one 'The Pump Man,' for reasons of his own," a reference to the song's origin in the rhythm of an electric pump. Jerry tells him to "Count it off," and they're in business. This is the one and only version where Weir sings Hunter's "riding up on guitar," which he manages by putting the accent on *on* instead of *up.*

After all the confusion the first Greatest comes off really well, revealing it to be a potent rocker. Right on its heels comes another first, a breathless reading of Johnny B. Goode. The playing's pretty good on this one, but Bobby's vocals need a lot of work. The song debuts over for the time being, the band turns in a good Mama Tried and a top-notch Hard to Handle—this one's got that extra something that renders it one of the better versions. The best, though, is about to come.

KILLER FILLER

The February '71 Port Chester run was originally scheduled for December '70. Would Port Chester have been the breakout run it became if it hadn't fallen in the new year? Such answers are lost in the mists of time. But Jerry and Mickey did a radio spot announcing the postponement, aided by some poor suffering soul (he chimes in with "in December" when Jerry, hopelessly goofy throughout the spot, can come up with nothing more specific than "We're not playing in Port Chester on those . . . days"). The whole announcement is a real hoot, Jerry playing banjo and Mickey Jew's harp and goofin' all the way through. A portion:

JERRY: "I'm Mickey Hart."

MICKEY: "No, no *I'm* Mickey Hart."

JERRY: "Hey, what happened to my police whistle, goddammit? . . . Hiya folks, this is Jerry Garcia. . . ."

MICKEY: "And this is Mickey Hart of the Grateful Dead, here to say to you today that we're sorry. . . ."

JERRY: "Yes, we're sorry, sorry, sorry. . . ."

MICKEY: "But we're not the only ones who are sorry. . . ."

JERRY: "You're gonna be sorry, too, as soon as we tell ya . . ."

MICKEY: "There are lots of sorry people in this world and . . ."

JERRY: "That we're not playing in Port Chester—"

MICKEY: "Jerry, tell 'em, tell 'em, Jer!"

JERRY: "On those . . . *days*. . . ."

This show's Dark Star is one of the prettiest versions of an era rife with many variations. It starts off with slippery, fluid playing on the theme, which is not stated as insistently as in earlier versions. The first verse arrives rather quickly and recedes back into a short stretch of jamming on the theme before plunging briefly into a shimmery space. It's out of this space that the first Wharf Rat emerges, as auspicious a debut position as a song can have. It lives up to its lineage as the band and Jerry do it credit. Note that the rhythm of Jerry's vocal delivery is slightly different here than in future versions; his singing is no less sensitive, as is particularly evident in the way he handles the "but I'll get back . . ." line. Also interesting is his singing "docks of the river" instead of "city."

Dark Star returns with some excellent jamming on the main theme, with hints of China Cat and Goin' Down the Road added into the mix. The combination eventually emerges into a real feel-good jam that bears strong resemblance to the Tighten Up jam in the 10/31/71 Dark Star. It rips. There's a little feedback shiver in the midst of the jam, repeated a number of times by either Bobby or Jerry, that's positively chilling, a patch of darkness in the midst of this beautiful creation. The second verse is sung

Bird Song

Sad, sweet, elegiac Bird Song could only be a Dead song. What other band could play a tune that reaches such extremes of lilting beauty and experimental jamming? The lyrics, too, a masterful blend of sorrow and grin-and-bear it pluck, bear the unmistakable imprimatur of Robert Hunter. Hunter again uses the forces of the natural world to tie the song's elements together, snow, rain, sunshine, and wind as metaphors for experience, for life as it is lived, rather than contemplated. What more is there to say when one looks into the heart of a storm? How can one cry when the wind is there to dry one's

AND YOUR BIRD CAN SING— BIRD SONGS OF NOTE

* 4/28/71 Fillmore East
* 7/18/72 Roosevelt Stadium
* 8/12/72 Sacramento
* 8/27/72 Veneta
* 11/19/72 Hofheinz Pavilion
* 6/22/73 Vancouver
* 10/31/80 Radio City
* 3/7/81 Cole Field House
* 4/16/83 Byrne
* 6/21/85 Alpine
* 11/5/85 Worcester
* 3/2/87 Kaiser
* 3/26/87 Hartford
* 12/31/87 Oakland
* 7/16/88 Greek
* 9/16/88 MSG
* 6/19/89 Shoreline
* 3/16/90 Cap. Center (appears on *Without a Net*)
* 3/29/90 Nassau (with Branford Marsalis)
* 9/20/91 Boston Music Hall
* 5/21/92 Cal Expo
* 3/20/93 Atlanta
* 9/22/93 MSG (with David Murray)
* 6/13/94 Seattle
* 8/3/94 Giants
* 6/2/95 Shoreline

tears? The song also possesses echoes of Ecclesiastes, with its times to sleep, sing, and fly—the Hunter leitmotifs of cyclical renewal and decay once again arising in the text. Bird Song shares these themes with its closest kin in the Dead's songbook, Cassidy, a cyclical elegy as well with similar jams and placement in shows.

Bird Song is for Janis, great friend of the band, sometimes lover and always pal of the Pig, fellow disciple of the cosmic blues. Like a bird, "she sang a little while and then flew on." Ask a Prankster, nothing lasts.

Played live, this was one of those songs that the Dead could take anywhere—and often did. Especially in years where there were no Dark Stars—that is, most of the eighties—Bird Song became one of the prime live forums for musical exploration, floating lazily into a thousand twilights before returning to its soothing refrain of "Don't cry now…" Usually played in the first set, it was, after the first-set–second-set division became more pronounced in the early seventies, one of the few forums for wide-open jamming in the opening frame.

beautifully and then it's the main theme again, transfiguring itself to go into Me & My Uncle, which ends the set.

There's a priceless moment illustrative of the Jerry-Bobby dichotomy as the band leaves the stage:

PHIL: "Folks, we're gonna take a short break."
JERRY: "We're gonna take a break awhile."
BOBBY: "That's right, we're gonna take a break and you can watch our dust."
JERRY: (disapprovingly) "*Nice,* Weir. You can take a break too. Everybody gets to take a break."

If you get only one set of this show, get this first one, which has room enough on it for some hilarious back-and-forth with the light man over "the big fucking chandelier in the middle of the ceiling" to start the second set, a sweet Casey Jones, and the last of the night's debuts, Playing in the Band (which you don't want to miss).

4/6/71
MANHATTAN CENTER

This show features an interesting first set that makes it stand out among so many excellent tapes from this period. The opening Bertha is still very immature, with Jerry giving even emphasis to every line, not having yet learned which to lean on for effect. A fourteen-beat Beat It On Down is fairly ordinary but well played, as is Hurts Me Too. Me and Bobby McGee features a weary-sounding Weir. After Bobby McGee Jerry has to tell people to move back before launching into an excellent Dire Wolf.

The highlight of the set, though, and the main reason for possessing this tape is the debut of Oh Boy, which, once they get it going, shows itself to be well suited to the Dead treatment. They wouldn't play it again for another ten years, breaking it out in an acoustic set at the Dance for Disarmament in December '81. Interestingly it also surfaces in the '87 Dylan rehearsal sessions, wherein Jerry takes the vocal lead (in the '71 version it's Bobby) for a rousing rendition with Dylan singing backup. To continue the rarities, the Dead back up the first Oh Boy with the last Hog for You, the first since the very early days (1966, to be precise). Jerry just lays down this *hard,* lean blues solo in the middle—kind of "I *own* this song. Damn."

The rest of the set, though not nearly as unusual, has its moments. A good early vintage Playin' comes next, followed by confusion, shouts from the stage of "Hey, Weir, hey, Weir, hey, Weir," and "Hey, Pigpen." All is understood, though, as it turns out that Pigpen just needs dome monitors. Pig's monitor volume turns out to be for a good Midnight Hour. Not a great one, a good one. This song is no longer the twenty-minute-plus beast it used to be. It's good to hear a Midnight Hour from Pigpen in 1971, but there's something melancholy about the whole enterprise. Here is a song that used to be one of the band's major vehicles for long, exploratory blues jamming, with some serious Pigpen rapping thrown in for good measure. Time was when Pig, frontman, would command Jerry to "play yo' guitar," and the whole nine yards in those halcyon days at the Avalon, the Carousel, the Fillmore. Now, three thousand miles and four years or so away from that place and space in time, Midnight Hour is a bit of nostalgia that the Dead allow into a set dominated by their own compositions, which have become the new vessels for the band's jamming energy. On the other hand, this night, with its Pigpen revivals, could be looked upon as the beginning of a resurgence on his part that would see him deliver some of his greatest raps in the weeks to come.

Good versions of Cumberland and Casey Jones are followed by one other moment worth noting, a proto "Take a Step Back." Jerry stops to plead, "You've got to move back, folks, these are human beings here. You've got to move back, back!" Phil adds, in a dreamlike voice, "Baack, baaaack!" and Billy starts to play the drums a bit in the background . . . so close!

The second set, while not as unusual, is also incredible. For one, it's got what may be the best Sugar Magnolia *ever*, Jerry playing a live-wire wah-wah lead throughout. Good Lovin' includes some prime Pigpen raunch ("Take off your clooothes and have a good time!"), and the NFA → GDTRFB → NFA → Truckin' rocks, *especially* the Truckin'. Incidentally it was the previous night's NFA → GDTRFB → NFA that, with some studio polishing, was used on *Skull Fuck*.

4/17/71

PRINCETON

This is it, the show with two of Pigpen's most epic raps. Pigpen kicks the second set right off with the "Sold—the Brooklyn Bridge!" *Good Lovin'* rap for which he's perhaps best known today (see *Playing in the Band* or *Dead-Base* for full text; better yet, get the tape). There's no question that this one's a serious piece of work, but I do hope that there's no one out there with the mistaken impression that this is the only brilliant and humorous extemporaneous rap that Pigpen ever pulled off, because at this he was truly a master.

There's another vintage Pigpen rap in this show, in Lovelight, which tends to get overlooked. This is a shame, because, as good as the Good Lovin' rap is, this is the one that shows a very sweet side of Pigpen. His Lovelight matchmaking here seems very innocent and well intentioned (as opposed, for example, to the "Let's fuck" rap from 9/19/70). He introduces Bob to Barbara, and gets them to hug. Then he manages the same for a guy named Frank and another girl named Barbara. He somehow makes human connection seem so simple here, summing it up with, "Well, that's two for two. That ain't bad. Now why don't everyone try it on their own? I can't lead you on all night, you know."

These two big Pigpen turns are quite obviously the show's highlights, but it should also be noted that Pig sings an impassioned King Bee in this set too. Sing Me Back Home is also excellent, probably the best version of this somewhat mawkish Merle Haggard tune, to which Jerry brings some real emotion here. Finally it should be noted how Lovelight came about—the band flubs the beginning of the We Bid You Goodnight coda to a very good Goin' Down the Road and responds by going back into a brief Goin' Down jam before exploding into Lovelight—interesting.

4/29/71
FILLMORE EAST

A perception that was held among Dead freaks in the early seventies and echoed by some band members and others close to the band held that the Dead played their best shows at the Fillmore East. Relative qualitative judgments are difficult to make about individual shows in an era that seems, in retrospect at least, almost uniformly hot. There can be no doubt, however, that the band's performances at this hallowed East Village venue rank among their finest of the years 1968–70. The esteem in which they are held by Deadheads has, if anything, grown in time.

The Dead bid their farewell to this bishopric of East Coast venues with one of their best shows there. The first set is distinguished by an excellent Hard to Handle, one of a number from this month, and the beautifully restrained emotional texture of Me and Bobby McGee. The sensitivity of Weir's vocals on this last finds empathetic resonance in the band's playing. Take Jerry's first solo, for instance, with its haunting echoes of missed trains. His excellent backing vocals speak eloquently of loss. The Dead end the set with Bobby's clue to the audience that if "you look real quick, you're gonna notice that we're gonna take a short break."

Part Two begins with the calling card of a Dew opener—a prodigious Phil bomb. There's even more of a quiet sense of lament than usual in this run-through, augmented by some breathtaking Phil riffs during the softer parts of the song. A solid Minglewood is followed by a Sugar Magnolia with some of the best harmonies the song has been given in live performance. After Black Peter there's a pause and then Bobby delivers the news that "Little beknownst to us, or to you guys, Phil's bass has been broken this whole time that we've been scratchin' our asses wondering what to do next. So he's gonna fix it and we're gonna stand around and scratch our asses and wonder what to do next," to which Jerry adds the reassurance "But we're not in any big hurry or anything." There's long moments of tinkering and muffled voices onstage, out of which Phil's bass finally sounds a few clear beats, to cheers from the audience. Bobby confirms, "That's Phil's bass." In true "you couldn't have wrote it any better" fashion, Jerry asks Phil, somewhat cryptically, "Twenty-five?" to which he replies "Twenty-five. Ready?" and lays down twenty-five beats to open Beat It On Down the Line. *That* gets things rolling nicely.

Indeed we soon get an Alligator → Goin' Down the Road combo that features not only a crackling, full-bore drums segment but some of the hairi-est jamming the Dead have ever laid down. The transition to Goin' Down the Road happens deceptively early; the theme is stated but only as a launching pad for more sick jamming, culminating in an explicit jam on the St. Stephen theme, right before going all out into Goin' Down the Road, for real this time. Goin' Down the Road takes a thrilling turn into a classic Cold Rain. Among the remaining tunes, China Cat and Greatest Story are especially tasty. When it's all over, Uncle John's encore and all, Phil simply bids the crowd "Good night, New York," which pretty much says it all, but the audience won't have it, immediately stomping their feet and clapping and raising a great ruckus in calling for more. This in turn draws a stern lecture from Uncle Bill. Though it seems to start as a benign valedictory, audience interruptions raise his ire:

> *"There's a question that I can't answer—is there anyone really like the Grateful Dead? It's an amazing, an amazing group.... Someone was talking about music before, and this usher said the Grateful Dead aren't just music, they're an environment, which is the most beautiful thing I ever heard." (obnoxious interruptions ensue)*

"For one time, if you want to applaud, fine, but instead of yelling more and more and more why don't you try sometime [to] think that the musicians are here, they're hanging out, and leave it up to them and don't be assholes all the time, just leave it hang and leave it up to them. 'More, more, more, more'—just hang out and leave it up to them, okay?"

The Dead eventually do take the stage for a second (and third) encore (there is no discernible abatement in the volume of the clamoring for "more" after Graham leaves the stage), Phil quipping that "They'll suck the last ounce right out of ya," and Bob, thinking historically, pointing out that "Hey, well, this is our last gig at the Fillmore East apparently and I'd just like to hear a little appreciation for Bill Graham—he runs a hell of a place." Appreciation is duly offered, and then cut short by the sonic *blast* that begins Midnight Hour. Even more of a treat, though, is the complex and quirky We Bid You Goodnight with which the Dead bid a final farewell to a hall in which they played some of their very finest shows.

10/30/71
CINCINNATI

Though the list from this night's second set isn't quite as impressive as the next night's *Dick's Picks Volume Two* selection, the performances and stage chatter are no less memorable. It gets off to a roaring start with an exuberant Casey Jones and really hits its stride on the third tune, an early Comes a Time, replete with the soon-to-be dropped third verse. Jerry is clearly still giving his utmost concentration to finding his delivery, and the result is fascinating and beautiful. His singing is earnest and almost acrobatic in its range—just an outstanding performance. It's worth noting that the expressive quality of the song comes more from the vocals at this point than the guitar, as his wrenching solo hasn't quite been worked up yet.

After Weir let's all know that "We're all carefully tuned up again," he introduces El Paso with "For all you boogie freaks out there, this next number is a waltz and it's a ladies' choice." This rendition serves as a reminder that there was a time when this tune was more vital than the repetitive bore it became. Bob keeps up the repartee afterward by "Begging your indulgence we're gonna do another song in the key of D," to which Jerry enjoins, "Well, well, what? This is one we laughingly call 'Rambling Rose.'" Bobby fakes

Brown-Eyed Women

Perhaps the most perfectly realized of the Garcia-Hunter "westerns," Brown-Eyed Women is a shining example of a tune that takes maximum advantage of Jerry's vocal talents and enthusiasms. He always managed to inhabit this melancholy tale of bootlegging and frontier disaster to the extent that he seemed an intimate party to all that happened to Delilah Jones and co. The first-person narrative abets this effect to a degree, but it's Jerry's interpretive talent that gives the song that flavor of a yarn told on the back porch by a grizzled old pipe-smoking uncle, the last survivor of the eight Jones boys—the way he'd let his voice catch on the "...looks like the old man ..." line and, more organically, the gruff character of his voice (particularly from about 1979 on) that melds perfectly with the mental images painted by the song's words.

Hunter's way with history is also at its finest in the song's lyrics, with its allusions to the stock-market crash ("1930 when the Wall caved in") and Prohibition. It's a lyric with great touches of verisimilitude, a finely crafted folk song that achieves that true folk quality of timeless (despite the historical references) familiarity from the first listen. These historical touches aren't mere embellishments, though. Not only do they ground the Jones's bootlegging in a rich context, they advance the character study of "the old man" Jones, as well.

There are three depictions of things falling or caving in. The first of these is of "the ox" falling down to receive a yoke, used to evoke a time when, perhaps, the Jones family farm was profitable (in the twenties, when "he" [again, the old man presumably] "drank to the dregs of the whiskey jar"—his cup was full, he drank in life heartily, at the end of this period, though, his glass was empty), also the time of Jack Jones's (the narrator's) happiest youth. We can be reasonably sure that "Jack Jones" refers to the narrator and not "the old man" because of his pleasure in the attentions of "ladies," while the old man seems very attached to his wife, Delilah. The second time we hear of a collapse is of "the Wall"—Wall Street. The old man manages to carry on despite this disaster, though, by bootlegging—perhaps the farm has failed. It is the second cave-in (and the third image of falling), that of the roof in the song's bridge, that does the old man in—he "never was the same again" after that incident. A resourceful man who could take his hits and find a way to fend off total indigence, even if by illegal means, the senior Jones was unable to withstand the loss of the woman who had given him eight sons.

As to the song's score, it doesn't have a second-set song's openness and easy opportunity for wildly inventive jamming, but it is invested with considerable musical charms. For one, the bluegrassy musical setting for the lyric is right on target, with a trademark Garcia bridge that matches the way the lyrics bring the story to its emotional denouement. For another, it's got that very catchy opening lick that becomes the song's thematic hook, musically. It sounds for all the world like a banjo part transcribed for guitar (a trait it shares with Cumberland, among other Dead tunes), a composition for which Garcia was uniquely qualified and which meshes nicely with the western folk flavor of the song's lyrics. It's on this ascending hook that Garcia built some of the soaring yet gritty solos he turned in for this tune. Maybe the best version of this song was turned in on 5/8/77, a rendition that benefits greatly from the more direct, postretirement arrangement of the intro; it gets extra points for being followed by an outstanding version of Mama Tried, which I've always thought of as Bobby's (and Merle Haggard's) yang to Brown-Eyed Women, telling the story as it does of the "only rebel child from a family meek and mild," which has echoes in Jack Jones's account of being the only Jones boy who turned bad.

laughter over the opening strains of Keith's elaborate introduction for the song. Keith remains a force throughout—you can even hear Jerry exclaim, "Whew!" after Keith ends a nimble solo with a rolling flourish. Here's where Jerry gets a chance to display his inimitable way with hecklers. A guy in the audience who had been shouting for Truckin' between tunes hits the height of his obnoxiousness after Ramble On, shrieking "Play Truckin', Truckin', why won't you play Truckin'?" Here is the exchange as it unfolds, with some trippy rambling afterward:

JERRY: "We don't know it."
BOB(?): (over additional screams of "Truckin', Truckin'!") "Eat it, man, eat it, eat it."
JERRY: "C'mon, man, you gonna be a cop? Is that it? 'Play Truckin', play Truckin'.' We'll play whatever we like." (audience cheers) "Of course that's not saying—"
BOB: (interrupting) "Yeah, it's a free country, y'know."
JERRY: "—that you won't like, you might like it, too, it might be all right, it might be something perfectly okay.... What about all those people who may not *like* Truckin'?"
VOICE FROM OFFSTAGE: "How many are there?"
JERRY: "Well, how about it, man?" (stoned-sounding laughter from the side of the stage, as well as: "Why don't *you* play Truckin'?")
PHIL: "We realize we're wasting valuable time, folks, but it's really okay in the long run."
BOB: "You folks up there, are you folks up there sitting right under the ba— the lip of the balcony—"
PHIL: "B-b-b-b-balcony ..."

JERRY: "B-b-b-b-eh, buh . . ."

BOB: "—you wanna watch out 'cause any minute they're gonna be droppin' a whole load of live chickens on ya. Heh."

Sugar Magnolia exists here in all its early glory, Jerry simulating the exhilaration of summer love with fast, fluttery runs. And then, as Phil announces it, "Okay, man, this is for you, this is the one you've been waiting to hear." (more screams from screaming guy) "Yeah, we know, man, we know. We hear you." Apparently there's still some ambivalence about seeming to give in to the guy. Bobby says, "We're gonna pause for about three or four seconds, scratch our asses, and think it over," to which Jerry adds the sound effect of his pick scratching one of his strings. They get over whatever reservations they had, though, as Bobby starts the tune off with "Ah-one, two, three, four!" Phil and Jerry provide the one-two sonic punch for a very well-jammed-out Truckin' that's every bit as psychedelic as some of the better '72 editions.

The set ends in true '71 style with a Not Fade → Goin' Down → Not Fade sandwich. Billy's drumming is very impressive, as is the sinuous interaction between the axmen, in the slithery transition jam that has by this date grown much more complex than a pairing of these two fairly straightforward tunes would seem to indicate. The greatest passage here, though, is the Philled transition back into Not Fade from the We Bid You Goodnight coda of Goin' Down the Road.

12/15/71
ANN ARBOR

The second set of this show is a recently unearthed treasure, a discovery in which we can rejoice—a splendidly clear soundboard, one more Dark Star to add to the canon, and one of the great Lovelights, home to a medley of King Bee and Mannish Boy (aka I'm a Man).

The tape starts with Dark Star, an auspicious beginning. This one begins in a swinging, up-tempo mode and strays from the main theme fairly quickly for some free-form playing that culminates in a very speedy, almost melodic meltdown. The scattered molecules of the song coalesce again just as swiftly into a hot little improvisational jam that soon takes on hints of The Other One and then the Tighten Up jam. It's played at great speed and oh-so-fleetingly before going into the first verse.

After the verse, the Dead plunge us into a bassy, spacey realm lit only by the stray twinklings of a guitar here and there. Soon we depart once again for a planet in the Jam system, at warp five, emphasis on the warp. The musical inhabitants of the planet upon which we alight seem to be descendants of the Feelin' Groovy and Spanish Jam peoples. Our contact with this transcendently enlightened race is alas short, as we blast off again into a buzzing, ringing jam that eventually leads us to the terra firma of Deal (surface temperature: hot!) (end of conceit, folks, I promise).

After Deal there's a Stars and Stripes Forever tuning and, after several takeoffs aborted for additional tuning, a joyous Sugar Magnolia takes wing. It is but a warm-up, though, for the Lovelight to follow. Pigpen performs the beginning of his rap very tunefully, singing it more than usual. This one *is* typically ribald, though, featuring a run-in with a certain lady of the evening, no Brooklyn Bridge–selling pimp in sight (if this allusion is lost on you, go directly to 4/17/71; do not pass Go, etc.). When she asks, "What else you got in your pocket?" His answer of course is, "Why don't you come along with me and find out?" The segue into King Bee is achieves a mighty groove, Keith laying down some blues piano that perfectly complements some of Jerry's hottest blues licks. The transition into Mannish Boy is similarly without flaws or seams. After some more serious electric blues jamming, the revisitation of Lovelight comes as an occasion for unbridled joy, accompanied by much clapping of hands and cheering from the audience. Pigpen's joyous yells on the last, fast go-around and his speed rapping over the hot climax show he's more into it than anyone. Sadly the very end is cut.

The next thing we hear is Bobby saying, cryptically, "Dark Starr . . ." (perhaps making fun of clueless or hopelessly dosed audience members clamoring for this already-played song) before he launches into a raucous Saturday night, thus bringing to a close a new window into a raucous Wednesday night some twenty-five years ago.

The sound of '72 vintage Dead is the sound of a band pulling itself in myriad directions, almost all of which are promising. The most prominent artifact of this year—the official release *Europe '72*—though a fine "live" (heavily overdubbed) album, only hints at what was going on.

What were some of the currents running through the band's performances? The integration of Keith Godchaux and the introduction of Donna Godchaux, the full flowering of Weir's talent and repertoire, Pigpen's last hurrah, and a growing and increasingly bifurcated repertoire—these are starting points, many of which point to further elements of the Dead's transition from '71 to '73.

Keith's first full year in the band not only saw him add lovely ivory touches to the band's discrete songs, such as Jack Straw, Brown-Eyed Women, and Tennessee Jed, but pull the band in a jazzier direction as well. There's a wonderful tension, or complementary interaction, between the residual folk-country flavor of the Dead's immediate past and the exploratory jazz mode of their near future that runs through the first-set tunes, often finding a middle ground akin to ragtime. His playing in the band's long stretches of jamming added light to passages that only a year before had seemed much darker. By the end of Keith's tenure with the Dead, the group would be hungry for sustain and color, but the absence of keyboard sustain in much of the outer improvisations of this period created an openness that was novel and perhaps responsible for the lyrical quality that distinguishes this year's spaciest passages. To listen to tapes of '72 shows is to realize the extent to which the band was being remade around Godchaux.

Donna's presence was obviously not felt as strongly in this year as it would be later in her tenure with the band, but she offered a fair sampling of the best and worst she had to offer. It's apparent that she's still trying to find her place in the mix and arrangements, and having even more trouble than she would later hearing herself onstage. It's either to her credit or to her detriment that she dove in feetfirst with raucous singing on Playing in the Band, for example. Once her parts became better established and more forums for her talents were explored, she would assume her more recognizable place in the mix as one of the stamps of seventies Dead.

Nineteen seventy-two was a big, big year for Weir. (It is said that his then-girlfriend, Frankie Hart, played a big role in encouraging him to step into the spotlight, and to work at being worthy of it.) The release of *Ace,* his first "solo" album, merely added punctuation to the evident way he was coming into his own as a singer, composer, and instrumentalist. The slew of tunes he had debuted in 1971 were by this year reaching maturity and receiving performances that would stand as some of their best renditions. Playin' was played at almost every show in '72, and with a crisp, evening-star quality (particularly in the sparkling stabs of guitar that peek out of the intro's initial bass darkness) that would set this year's performances of the tune apart. The newly introduced Black-Throated Wind received similarly exquisite treatment. Greatest Story really began to *move,* a forum for some fervid Garcia soloing.

And Sugar Magnolia found new life in Keith's piano (although it could be argued that this was a double-edged sword, diminishing as it did Garcia's involvement in the tune). Bobby's vocals from this period are among his finest, his baritone rich and unforced and his falsetto carrying the emotional weight it would possess less frequently in some later years—think of the higher passages in Black-Throated Wind. His rhythm playing was in the throes of a similar maturation, assuming an indigo patina in the sustained passages and spinning gossamer threads in his trademark filigrees.

Bobby's ascendancy coincided with Pigpen's swan song. Pig was, even in these last performances, moving in a new direction himself. Like the rest of the band in the early seventies, he was honing a song-oriented style. For him this meant that pieces such as It Hurts Me Too, Big Boss Man, Mr. Charlie, the very odd Chinatown Shuffle, and his astounding Two Souls in Communion took prominence over the long, bouncy jams and raps that had reached their latter-day height in the previous year. Pigpen delivered these songs with a conciseness and gut-kicking sorrow matched only by his solo performances of She's Mine and Katie Mae in 1970. His sensitivity was at its height in 1972, a poignant reflection of the physical pain he was experiencing at this time and a testament to his native genius for the blues.

The Dead drew the line of first-set–second-set demarcation with greater firmness in 1972, ratifying and advancing the trend of '70 and '71. There were, for example, six first-set Dark Stars in 1971, none in '72. Playin' became the prime first-set forum for jamming, abetted to a degree by China → Rider. Bird Song's revival in midsummer added a welcome third tune to help shoulder this happy duty. All this isn't to say that the discrete first-set songs weren't impressive—they were in fact outstanding, brimming with a vitality that flowed from Jerry and Keith's fingers, as is amply displayed on *Europe '72.*

The second sets feature some of the Dead's best open-ended playing, markedly different from what had come before, in part because of Keith's injection of swing. Truckin'

→ The Other One provides a good deal of the territory for this era's jams, as do some of the loveliest, most organic Dark Stars played. There's an evenhandedness to the ensemble work on these jams, clear evidence of musicians truly listening to one another in the fashion that would bring them to the pinnacle of the coming years. Keith, Jerry, and Bobby find an airy instrumental mix in these spaces, and Phil asserts himself fearlessly—also a portent of things to come.

The transitional and complex nature of Dead '72 makes it hard to pin down, but the excitement in the playing is as plain as a hot summer's day in Veneta. It's no accident that '72 shows are among the most beloved of serious tape collectors.

5/11/72
ROTTERDAM

A Dew opener augurs well for a long, superbly played second set, one of the best of the legendary Europe '72 tour. A superfine Two Souls in Communion—you've just gotta love the ending "whoa-oh" backing vocals—also points to it being a show with some of our last, best Pigpen moments.

The nine-hundred-pound gorilla that dominates this set, though, is Dark Star. Clocking in at just under forty minutes, it's the longest known version. Here's how it goes down: The beginning is fairly spacey, not at all the clear opening of, say, the 1970 edition. It just gets quieter and spacier, a Dark Star for a cool, breezy spring day—very fitting for Holland. After a few minutes in this mode, though, Phil rolls in some bass thunderheads, over which Jerry plays an ominous lead with anachronistic snatches of what sounds like his Let It Grow solo. Once this segment has been fully explored, Billy takes over for a short Drums. Phil takes the lead out of Billy's solo for a short bit of vague, very spacey playing that eventually resolves into the main theme and then the first verse. Appropriate to this version, Jerry sings it in a very eloooonnnggaated way. After the verse Phil, Jerry, and Keith make some truly bizarre music together, very avant-garde symphonic. When Bobby and Billy join in, this jam begins to take on monstrous proportion—dark and moody, with both Jerry and Phil playing fast atonal runs. Somehow this jam evolves into some countrified playing reminiscent of Cumberland before flying off in yet another direction: a very basic jam that builds in rhythmic cohesion and intensity before once again dissolving into spaciness. Phil drops a clear Bird Song hint here and, soon after, the space dissolves and we're at the doorstep of Sugar Magnolia—a typically fat, jamming '72 version.

With the final chord of Sunshine Daydream still reverberating, Phil and Jerry guide the band into what was to be the last full-fledged Pigpen Caution. As ever, it's a furious bout of jamming, this retrospectively historic version rendered even more special by the quick, almost subliminally stoney Who Do You Love rap that Pigpen throws in for good measure. The closing Truckin' builds to a peak worthy of what has preceded it, but the closing Uncle John's drags in places (as the Dead, even in '72, were not bionic). As they say in the Netherlands, *goede nacht* and *wel te rusten—goede ouwe* Grateful Dead!

7/18/72
ROOSEVELT STADIUM

The second set of this three-set wonder contains a primo '72 Playin' as well as a top-notch Truckin' → Dark Star → Comes a Time. And so that's where we join our program, already in progress. Bobby was just about to introduce Ms. Godchaux:

BOBBY: "I'd like to take this opportunity to introduce Donna Jean here."
DONNA: "Thank you."
BOBBY: "She's gonna help us out with this next one, and it goes something like this. . . ."

Playin' is amazing. Jerry, Bobby, and Keith are the culprits. Their improvisation here not only climbs the heights but is seemingly unique to this version. A few tunes later Truckin' is also distinguished by long, inventive jamming that never lets up in intensity. It's lengthy, but never lazy. And it goes burning into a tremendous Dark Star.

Dark Star begins with some furious jamming on the main theme, which is discernible for a long while, changing tempo only gradually until Jerry gets a bee in his bonnet and leads the band into a very fast variation on the theme. He plays some lightning-syncopated figures high up on the neck here, letting the final notes of each flurry ring out until, without warning, we're dropped back into the original tempo and the verse. After the vocals there is feedback and a brief meltdown, and then just Billy. What follows is space—the final frontier, a dissonant, driving Phil-and-Jerry-led jam that culminates in a mini-Tiger (think of it as a bobcat). After the cat there's a musical passage that sounds like a thousand molecules dispersing and recohering. When they come together again, it's in the shape of Comes a Time. As so often happens in these '72 Dark Stars, the transition from deep space to structured tune is accomplished both very smoothly and with fairly disorienting results, making even a familiar tune take a second or two to make itself known to the ear. This Comes a Time just happens to be an absolute gem, too, with Jerry's vocal acrobatics matching the guitar virtuosity he brings to the song.

The first and third sets, it should be added, are almost as tasty as the filling.

8/27/72
VENETA

This justly famous benefit show for Chuck Kesey's (Ken's brother) Creamery is, despite frequent allusions to crushing August heat, a knockout from start to finish. Jerry's playing is especially fine here, but all the band plays extremely well.

If one had to pick the real standouts from this show, they would have to be the epic versions of Bird Song and Greatest Story in the second set and Dark Star in the third set. This is pretty much the definitive Bird Song, even though Garcia has yet to develop the elaborations on the main hook he would play in later years. It floats and soars on the silvery wings of Jerry's guitar, propelled forward by Phil, Billy, and Bobby particularly. The stop and restart executed by Billy in the middle is breathtaking. It's a gorgeous rendition all the way through—just about perfect and featuring some of Jerry's sweetest, easiest playing. Greatest rocks with all-out, nail-you-to-the-wall, guy-sitting-in-the-chair-in-the-Maxell-ads abandon. This one's even better than the 9/28/72 version or, for that matter, any version, anytime.

Jerry's playing is just as fluid in the Dark Star that opens the last set. It opens with long, luminous stretches of mysterious riffing on the main theme before the first verse arrives. After the verse, Keith, Phil, and Jerry carve out a jam vaguely reminiscent (in retrospect, that is) of later Playin' jams. Jerry plays some superlatively trippy runs here, with all other players rising to the occasion. Billy seems directly wired into where Jerry's going, arriving there simultaneously with subtle punctuation for Garcia's Coltranesque sentences and paragraphs. Jerry and Phil's conversational syntax becomes progressively more insane until they reach a climax in a Tiger-propelled meltdown. From there a deep space is flavored with some very tasty licks from Jerry, hinting at Dew. Ace pulls one out of his sleeve instead, though, and the band agrees on El Paso.

These are just the maximum peaks, though, from a mountain range of a show, one of the best the Dead have ever played.

9/28/72
STANLEY THEATER

The second set of this show is one of the finest of the year and exemplifies the versatility of the Dead's 1972 incarnation—country, ragtime, rock and roll, and space music thriving side by side. Also to be found in this set is just about the hottest and most unpredictable Other One ever.

The set kicks off with a so-so Bertha, but really gets under way with an outstanding Greatest Story. The brief lead-in—a burbling bass and a few whistles (à la '81 Truckin's)—is not only very cool but signifies that this will be no ordinary version. Jerry belches wah-wah fire throughout the tune and treats us to a full-fledged St. Stephen jam that positively leaps from his guitar. Greatests like this one make you believe that his "guitar" really *did* turn into a "quasar." One only wishes that the tune would go on longer and perhaps that Donna might have restrained herself from uttering the bizarre vocal ejaculations with which she embellishes the Stephen jam.

A nice Brokedown cools things down a bit, and then a short Mexican Hat Dance tuning and a whistle from Billy signal the arrival of the western portion of our program—a strong Me & My Uncle and Ramble On, with an El Paso on which Phil is particularly assertive.

In the He's Gone that follows, Jerry's long, plaintive lead lines hold sway until Phil takes the reins and beats this Dead horse right into The Other One, duetting with Billy until Jerry and Bobby follow with relish. A long, frenetic jam ensues, accentuated with generous splashings of cymbal from the Rockin' K. Next comes another jam, this one of a totally different character from its predecessor: open, leisurely, tunefully inventive, and luxuriously long. At the end of this stretch the band steps back completely, leaving Jerry to compose a short, tight solo high up on the neck, full of piercing harmonic darts. After this it's back into the main theme and verse, which is followed by some really badass blues licks from Jerry on the way to a Tiger that screams and roars as the focal point of a giant meltdown. The "Tiger recoil" here— that spinning, winding-down noise from Jerry's effects in the wake of the "roar," like a hubcap rolling away from a wreck—is the most deliciously weird I've heard. After such a total brain fry, what else is there to do but slide into a sensitive and flawless Me and Bobby McGee?!

With the last note of Bobby McGee still reverberating, the band, perfectly in sync and without missing a beat, jumps right back into The Other One, with Phil and Jerry trading power runs until the second verse. When this brief foray back cedes to Wharf Rat, my guess is that you'll have a smile on your face.

If You Get Confused ...

ROBERT HUNTER was loath for a time to print his lyrics because he wanted to "let the songs live out their lives in the listener's ear." His versions of those Dead songs he'd written were "no more 'the real ones' than those that may have spoken to some of you through the music darkly twenty years ago"— this was how he put it in *Box of Rain,* his book of collected lyrics. With that in mind, here, then, are the "real ones."

Truckin'

"... flashing marquis out on Main Street"
"... flashing my keys out on Main Street"
You know, like twirling your keys around, looking for action.

Black Peter

"Annie Bonneau from St. Angel"
"Anyone knows from sin and gin"
As in, that's why he was lying in his bed and dying.

Don't Ease

"Don't ease, don't ease"
"Jolene, Jolene"
One of those inevitable moments that occur when you bring a friend to his first Dead show. Seems "Jolene" was his favorite song among those he knew, and when they played it, he was fired up to sing the lyrics, as he knew them, at the top of his lungs, to puzzled Heads turning all around him.

Masterpiece

"When I paint my masterpiece"
"Well, it ain't my masterpiece"
Overheard on the '89 summer tour.

Lost Sailor

"Where is the Dog Star?"
"Where is the Dark Star?"
I love how this would get cheers from Dark Star–starved Heads.

Terrapin

". . . I can't figure out"
". . . I came for you now"
By a friend who is just the king of misheard lyrics. I remember him correcting me with this one when I sang the correct line in his presence.

"Light the song with sense and color, roll away despair"
"Like the song that sends cicadas all the way to Spain"
Y'know, the same cicadas that sing later in the song.

Ship of Fools

". . . I still might warn a few . . ."
". . . it's still my point of view"
This kind of makes sense if you put a colon after it.

Brown-Eyed Women

"Delilah Jones went to meet her god"
"Delilah Jones went to meet her dog"
Just a case of cross-eyed hearing. Even more absurd would be "Delilah Jones went to eat her dog."

Half-Step

". . . this cue ain't straight in line"
". . . just queuing straight in line"
Well, it makes sense. Just not in the song.

"Cue ball's made of Styrofoam . . ."
"Two balls made of Styrofoam . . ."
Not necessarily gonads, maybe . . . other balls beside the cue ball. Whatever.

Franklin's Tower

"Roll away the dew"
"Roll away with you"
What the line would be if the Dead were a Top-40 band.

Hell in a Bucket

"At least I'm enjoying the ride"
"Peace, Love, and Joy and the Rock"
Uh, yeah. Huh-huh. The Rock and uh, huh-huh, stuff. Huh-
huh, huh-huh.

Uncle John's Band

"Have you seen the like?"
"Have you seen the light?"
Beginner's mistake.

Wharf Rat

"I love my Pearly Baker best . . ."
"I love my Pearly nakedness . . ."
Well . . .

". . . for some other fucker's crime"
". . . for some motherfucker's crime"
At times this was a misheard lyric. Frequently, though, it's what
Jerry was singing.

Viola Lee Blues

"I wrote a letter, I mailed it in the, mailed it in the air indeedy."
"I wrote a letter, I mailed it empty, I mailed it empty, yeah,
indeedy."

Sugar Magnolia

"Jumps like a Willys in four-wheel drive"
"Jumps like the wheelies hitting four-wheel drive."
Not too many people in America know just what the hell a
Willys is.

"A catch colt draws a coffin cart"
"A catch colt draws a coffee cart"

"I know the rent is in arrears"
"And no more rabbits in our ears"

"Cow is giving kerosene"
"Cow is drinking kerosene"
I could swear that Jerry actually sang this last one on occasion.

11/19/72
HOFHEINZ PAVILION

This show, a staple of many collections, features a quintessentially '72 second set, with a very spacey Dark Star surrounded by a number of much earthier, more prosaic tunes.

The set-opening Promised is played with blinding speed, just over two minutes long, which doesn't exactly accrue to its favor. The band manages to slow down long enough, though, to play a hot Ramble On Rose and a pretty, early-in-the-set Stella Blue. After Stella, Bobby informs us that "Pigpen's not with us tonight. He's still at home recovering from multiple and serious illnesses. And we're hoping that he'll be with us next time we're in this area," a poignant piece of history and a bit of news that even the ever-ebullient Mr. Weir delivers with evident sorrow. A more typically Bobby comment follows in the form of "We're gonna tune up on account of you can't be too careful." Jack Straw is also a very strong version.

You guessed it, though, it's the Dark Star that makes this show special. This one is a gem that contains some very long and *very* exploratory jamming, with Keith favoring us with some trippy organ work and Phil positively dominating during a period of deep space in the middle. While Phil's doing his best *Götterdämmerung* imitation, Jerry makes his guitar scream out with a sound eerily like that of a little girl. For a long stretch that follows it's Phil Phreak heaven, with Phil soloing over Bobby's barking. When the full band rejoins them, it's for a triumphant, feel-good jam (which has cosmetic similarities to the Feelin' Groovy jam), Jerry tugging further on your heartstrings with each upward climb.

What happens next is just as strange and wonderful as the preceding jam was exuberant and wonderful: The Weather Report Suite Prelude, as of yet unknown and unattached to that piece of music, floats across the stage borne by ether and, perhaps, a curious space-time anomaly that has sucked it back from 1973. You can hear the disturbance in the space-time continuum reverse itself as Jerry, who had until this point been playing quietly along, goes *completely* BERSERK in perfect tandem with Bobby (wonder how they worked that out beforehand. My theory is that they didn't—they were just being subjected to the inevitable aftereffects of a tear in the fabric of space and time). When the band joins in, it sounds, appropriately enough, as if they're playing backward at high speed.

Out of nowhere the cosmic radio dial is tuned through the static of weirdness, and suddenly we're listening to a station that's playing Half-Step, the weirdness of Dark Star behind us, little eddies of energy and ozone still swirling about and gradually dissipating. The Half-Step itself is verrry slow, a Half-Step at half speed.

1973–1974

daptability, as evolution has taught us, is a boon to survival. The Dead's longevity speaks of not only the strength of the "genetic diversity" of their musical influences (i.e., their eclecticism) but their ability to adapt to playing in the changing situations of numerous musical styles, three decades, countless venues, and six different keyboardists (or eight, if one counts Ned Lagin and Merl Saunders, who appeared with the band in 1975). The Dead were not only able to change and adapt when circumstances and their desire to do so dictated, but were able to do so quickly. Witness how they went from a dance–electric-blues band to psychedelic monster in the span 1965–67, and how they went from being a supremely hot jamming band in 1968 to an ensemble that pushed some of the outer boundaries of modern music within months of T.C. coming on board. How they just as quickly moved into the country-folk realm, each change taking their music into new territory while retaining much that was significant from what came before.

The Dead seldom had long to work in a given mode or configuration without being pulled in another direction by forces from without or within. Nineteen seventy-two was the only year they needed, then, to fully integrate Keith into the band. Pigpen's departure and Donna's addition were two big developments that also left their mark on that year, but they were not ones that would substantially affect the development of the band's ensemble playing. The band had for some time treated the Pigpen tunes as a separate piece, so as devastating as his absence may have been on a personal and artistic level, it wasn't as if they had to effect drastic alterations on their group playing once he ceased touring. And though Donna's presence was certainly felt in the final presentation of a song on the stage, the fact that she was not an instrumentalist meant that her parts did not really affect the way the band interacted.

As for repertoire, the Dead had new tunes to explore in '72, sure, but they represented no dramatic shift of direction on the order of that between the first album's material and *Anthem/Aoxomoxoa* or of these two albums and *Workingman's/Ameri-*

can Beauty; nor did the band inundate themselves with new compositions as they had the previous two years.

This isn't to say that there wasn't growth and change in Keith's first full year in the band. There were both, in abundance. It's just that the Dead were, contrary to their previous style, changing incrementally, organically. They were seeing where having Keith on keys would take them musically, but not moving as dramatically in one direction or another as they had upon both T.C.'s arrival and his departure. The Dead's power to adapt was such that they could have come to what became their '73–'74 sound and repertoire sooner than they did. That they took a year or so to get comfortable in their new configuration before saddling themselves with new tunes and the new musical approach they required no doubt contributed to the extraordinary ensemble playing of the '73–'74 era.

If Pigpen's organ playing tended toward the blues and T.C.'s an avant-garde whimsy, Keith's approach spoke readily of his fairly deep jazz background. And this is precisely the direction the band began to take, with broad hints in 1972, especially in the ragtime and swing mode. With the Dead's first show in 1973, though, their new direction was announced in unmistakable terms with the debut of the eminently jazzy Eyes of the World (Oh, that major seventh chord!). And what a welcome debut it was, a song as open and ready to be played through as The Other One, Playin', and even Dark Star. The Dead, at the top of their playing form and clearly thrilled to have a keyboard player who could stay with them through every musical landscape, used all these jam builders to put together some astounding musical constructions, with groundbreaking intertune jamming a feature of almost every show. By late '73 it became evident that the individual band members were tapping in to musical skills that had steadily improved from the early years and were now improving almost exponentially. To this they no doubt owed the steadiness of the band's course, which meant that a year older truly equaled a year better (and more). The experience of sharing a stage with others able to reach deep into their bag of tricks night after night was proving inspirational, challenging, and ultimately beneficial to their overall sound. If the vocals (particularly the harmonies) were kind of rough at times, the playing had never been more fluid or quicker to turn corners. It is Billy, especially, who must be lauded for this last trait, his easy, cymbal-liquid drumming a perfect match for the band's newfound jazz milieu. The fact that he was now the lone drummer, a role to which he had more than readjusted since 1971, also lent itself to split-second turns down new avenues in midjam.

Billy and Keith were *there,* Jerry was game to follow—his playing already bore the mark of one who had done his share of listening to jazz guitar greats like Kenny Burrell and Wes Montgomery—and more than able, as was Phil (Phil was *everywhere*), and Bobby, well, what choice did he have? This last is not meant as a poke at Bobby but rather a commentary on how he was the band member at the time with the least jazz background—his musical roots were firmly in folk and the blues. He had, however, arrived naturally at a rhythm-guitar style that bore a rather remarkable similarity to bebop keyboard style. His restless compositional imagination also served him well in this area, and he acquitted himself as well as his coconspirators.

The Dead brought this developing approach to bear in playing some fantastic versions of their best tunes. The Eyes from this era are, as noted above, superb—'73 is *the* year for beautiful Eyes. As were Playin', China → Rider, Truckin', The Other One, He's Gone. Dark Star was played far fewer times than in previous years, but those that they did play are classics, long, lazy versions that make one wish there were more. China Doll and Stella Blue were given gorgeous treatments, as two sides of the same coin— Stella Blue rain and China Doll ice. And then there were Here Comes Sunshine and the Weather Report Suite, compositions heavily identified with this era (Sunshine more with '73, the full Weather Report Suite with '74) because the Dead played them no longer after their retirement, save a revival of Here Comes Sunshine in late 1992. Their characters seem to speak to their respective years as well. Here Comes Sunshine, a series of brash yellow stabs of Jerry's light, reflects the brightness and experimentation of '73, musical optimism with guitar jangles and lyrics alike speaking of clearing skies. On the other hand, The Weather Report Suite, with its transcendental moodiness and the almost mannered instrumentation of part one, epitomized the musical complexity and sensitivity of the Dead in 1974. The transition to the abandon of Let It Grow provided as good a showcase as any for the Dead's versatility.

The most sublime musical moments of this era did not occur in songs, however, but between them. The Dead's improvisational playing during these years stands as among the most interesting and exciting ever laid down by a group with electric instruments. This was a period of truly epic jamming, when one bout of improvisation could move the band from deep space to ethereal jazz to hard blues, all without missing a beat. The thematic jams were also in full flower. The Spanish Jam had been revived and the Dead brought full body to Dark Star explorations in producing the so-called Mind Left Body Jam. Both added considerably to the wordless transportation of shows in '73 and '74, with racing, emotional highs and poignant, stabbing notes that mark shows that contain them, such as 6/28/74, as the favorites of many Heads.

It seems fitting that this time of long shows, elaborate jamming, and all-around fantastic playing should also see the Dead's sound at its apex of sophistication to that point. The mental and sonic pictures invoked by mention of the '73-'74 era are one and the same: that of the mighty Wall of Sound, the three-story, six-hundred-plus speaker behemoth of a PA that was the apotheosis of Owsley and Dan Healy's continual pushing of the rock-and-roll sound system's technological envelope, a glorious child with a genealogy that dated back to the band's early days. Audience tapes from Wall of Sound shows and earwitness accounts tell a story of an ultracrisp, clean sound, which was indeed the system designers' aim. Healy would later point out that the Dead's later system achieved much of the same results with far greater efficiency, and

Owsley, while conceding the Wall's unwieldiness and relative inefficiency, seemed reluctant to have thrown the baby of the concept out with the bathwater of its money-gobbling enormity. Even if later Dead systems did match the Wall of Sound's clarity of output, one thing's for damn sure—no PA in rock history ever looked so fuckin' bitchin'.

And it's in front of that Wall of Sound—Jerry pinging the moons of Jupiter and wringing the space between them from the Wolf, Phil using his elaborate Alembic bass as the hammer of the gods, all engaged in the creation of lightning greased to slide through the skull—that tapes from this period allow us to view the band in the mind's hall. The only pity is that the Wall contributed to the physical and fiscal burnout that caused them to stop capitalizing on the momentum that built and built from the first kinetic cannon shot out of 1972.

2/9/73
STANFORD

This is one of those rare shows in the canon, like 2/18/71, that would no doubt have attained "epic" status almost regardless of the playing, owing to the large number of song debuts. Happily it shares the '71 Port Chester breakout fest's distinction of also being remarkably well played considering the unknown territory being explored. Another thing this show holds in common with Port Chester is the generous amount of chatter it contains. Here the focus of the band members' conversation is generally the initial protoversion of the Wall of Sound, which also made its debut this night, in somewhat more rocky fashion than the songs.

The opening Promised Land was not more than a few seconds old in fact when half the speakers in the new single-source PA fried before the breakers in the system could save them. The remainder of the show was performed by jury-rigging what remained. You can hear adjustments being made at about the midpoint of Promised as Jerry's guitar disappears from the right channel to reemerge faintly, then gradually stronger from the left. There's also a dropout of a few seconds, but it's not clear if the problem originates with the taping or the PA.

The technical difficulties do not, however, keep Jerry and Phil from romping all over on Promised. Jerry in particular is a lick-creation machine here. Next up is the first-ever Row Jimmy, which is not without its birthing pains: Jerry's singing is fairly off-key throughout and he flubs a number of the lyrics (it also sounds as if he says "glass shack" here). The arrangement, though, is as it would stay for the remainder of the song's run, except for the reggae-tinged feel that the song's ending acquired in the eighties.

The set continues with a Black-Throated Wind that is perhaps less sensitively sung than some but more energetic than most. Deal is forgettable, but Jerry adds some frenetic playing to the first of what would be many standout versions of Me & My Uncle in 1973—clearly a peak year for this song. After Uncle the Dead address the PA situation, Bobby saying that "this is sort of the 'get the bugs out' night" and Phil interjecting that "if you have been following us for any number of years at all, you will realize that this happens everyplace we go, every time we play." The rest of the exchange, before it's cut on the tape, goes as follows:

BOBBY: "Well, if it irritates you, tonight is going to get you crazy." (crowd roars) "On the other hand toward the end of the evening we hope that this PA, this *all new* PA of ours, is going to really stand up and grow some hair."

PHIL: "Is there anybody back there who can't hear?" (assorted cries of affirmation from the audience) "Well, uh . . ."

BOBBY: "You can't hear? What can't you hear?"

PHIL: "Everything."

BOBBY: "Enunciate, please. Listen, if, uh . . ."

PHIL: "What they mean is that it doesn't sound like their home stereo."

A solid Sugaree follows (Jerry sings only "sewn up," skipping the "tight"), and then a standard Looks Like Rain, most notable for its paucity of Donna vocals. Loose Lucy is the next debut, with a number of verses different from subsequent versions, and Jerry scrambling those that would remain. This must have been quite the humorous tune to have heard them break out for the first time. A nice, fully developed "Roll Out the Barrel" tuning signals, as Bobby lets us know, that "That's right, it's polka time." Mexicali and the Brown-Eyed Women played next are solid, and Jerry is all over El Paso with some lovely runs.

Nineteen seventy-three finds one of its first marks of quintessence with the first-ever Here Comes Sunshine. The harmonies don't quite work (which was to become a familiar scenario for this tune), but it's a game try nevertheless and an exciting debut. Wish they'd stuck with it over the years, though the revival in '92 was definitely a happy surprise. Despite all the historic markers, though, the high point of the set is the closing Playin'. It shows none of the kinks that mark much of the rest of the set, as if the band poured their pent-up energy and frustration over the sound problems and the fact of having to play all these songs that they didn't know that well yet into a song that they sure as hell *did* know how to play. I'm not sure what a "perfect" Playin' would sound like, but this seems as good a candidate as any.

The second set begins with Wavy Gravy and an associate, "Asa," announcing that baskets will be making their way through the audience in solicitation of funds to buy the North Vietnamese a new hospital to replace the one the United States had bombed in Bak Mai. Wavy starts his spiel with an acknowledgment of the Dead's long-standing policy of wanting to use the mikes only for music, complete with an interesting rationale for violating it: "I am told to make this announcement—short—and not political. I'll make it short, but political is weird. Like, taking a shit is a political act. Smoking it is a more political act, but world politics and a rainbow on a pole is what we're all about." The band's discomfort is practically palpable as Wavy and Asa deliver a hurried but long enough message, with a fairly substantial political subtext at least.

China → Rider, though, is certainly *not* political, a nice musical tonic. The jam upon the Rider descant is not yet fully developed here, but it definitely represents an elaboration over how they had played it in '72. At any rate the transition is raging, with Jerry playing some lightning scale runs. A solid Jack Straw is followed by more commentary from Bobby on the PA: "We just located a bug in our new system and it sounds like about a forty-foot cockroach . . . and we're gonna iron him out right now." (cheers) "We've located the source of the problem—it's a dead battery somewhere. It's true, that's the God's truth."

They Love Each Other gets a fast first go-round, this inaugural version drenched with the joy evident in the cutting licks Jerry trots out throughout the tune. The song ends to an infernal buzzing coming from the PA—more trouble, more Bobby: "It all started with that stack over there, then that one started to buzz, now this one's starting, pretty soon that one's going to buzz." (buzzing stops) "And now we want to know if they're working and they *are*." (someone in audience: "It's about time!") "You said a mouthful."

It's funny to hear the cheer Jerry elicits with his first words of the evening, checking a microphone with "Hello, hello, hello . . . are they on or are they not on?" He'd already begun to talk less onstage at this point in the Dead's history, and after Bobby lets the audience know that "We're as happy about that [the sound returning] as you are," Truckin' starts, to numerous frenzied cries of "Jerry!" Truckin' is outstanding, an ideal stage setter for one of the best debuts ever, the first version of Eyes of the World. No first-time jitters here, just an excellent '73 Eyes with Phil asserting himself and Jerry playing with all the confidence in the world. The two really spend some time exploring at the end, too, playing the *ur*-version of what would become the standard '73–'74 tag to the tune, that Stronger Than Dirt-ish series of rhythmic riffs. That the Dead go from there into the first ever China Doll is just an incredible bonus. It's a short one, true, and the harmonies aren't quite there, but what an historic night!

The rest of the night escapes anticlimax with continued superlative playing. Big River rips, owing to Jerry's total involvement, and Ramble On Rose is here in an all-time version. Box is subpar, with Phil, he of the perfect pitch, singing off-key here and there and flubbing a line or two. Perhaps the former is as good an indication as any that the band were also having trouble hearing themselves onstage with the new sound system and its attendant problems.

There's something that's just so likable about Wave That Flag, with its spontaneous rhyming rap that's equal parts Groucho Marxesque and childlike. Bobby next introduces Sugar Magnolia with the tongue-in-cheek statement, reminiscent of his Truckin' intro on *Europe '72*, that "This is our new single. . . . It broke big as hell in Pittsburgh . . . that's a fact too." This is one of the best-ever renditions, a judgment sealed early in the song by the piercing harmonics Jerry plays in his first short solo break. It's a barnburner throughout, with an extra-fun Sunshine Daydream, Jerry's loopy closing line and all. The show ends strong with a pretty Uncle John's, and a suitably boogying Around and Casey Jones encore. For 1973 this was only the beginning, in more ways than one.

2/15/73
MADISON

Believe it or not, the highlight of this show is not the debut of You Ain't Woman Enough (irony alert). Nor is it an El Paso bursting at the seams with Jerry licks. It's not even one of the best, most jammed-out Here Comes Sunshines ever, or a Sugar Magnolia with a positively delirious and seemingly endless Sunshine Daydream. During a tour when the Dead were test-driving some of their best new tunes and emerging from 1972 with a more distinctly jazzy sound, their playing was suffused with an energy and skill that renders this, the second show of the year (and second with the first incarnation of the Wall of Sound), flush with noteworthy versions. The whole tour was like that.

So what is the highlight of this show? It's the Dark Star → Eyes → China Doll in the middle of the second set. Phil leads the band into two incredible jams in Dark Star, the second of which is so well defined as to be a completely different tune in and of itself. Jerry's entrance into Phil's solo must rank among the Dead's most beautiful live passages. It's pretty much just Phil and Jerry here, going about their business with breathtaking improvisational skill, building to a crescendo that drops right into Eyes. Though only the second-ever version of this song, they play it as if they've been doing it all their lives. Phil and Jerry once again rule the roost here, especially in the long jam at the end, where Jerry plays some remarkable variations at the end of each phrase that are, as far as I know, unique to this version. Finally, China Doll, also in its second-ever performance, suffers only a minimal sophomore slump. It's marred somewhat by Jerry's out-of-tune guitar, but the overall effect is very good, helped along by Bob's delightful, phaser-affected contrapuntal arpeggios.

5/26/73
KEZAR STADIUM

This famous show offers three knockout sets. It's in the third, though, with its jam of He's Gone → Truckin' → The Other One → Eyes → China Doll that the vintage 1973 action takes place.

It can be hard to single out individual versions of He's Gone because it's a song that the Dead played so consistently well over the years. This one stands out even from such a distinguished field. The Godchauxs, Donna especially, are a big part of what makes this one special. Donna adds some emotional vocal embellishments, the best of which is the "whoooa" after the first "Nothing's gonna bring him back." Keith delivers with some lovely upper-register flourishes in the coda. Jerry also distinguishes himself with some nice mellow riffing to keep the twilighty end jam moving until the big push into Truckin'.

The body of Truckin' is very good if not spectacular, but as is so often the case, the end jam gets seriously ambitious. Jerry lays down a series of *nasty*, harmonics-bedecked blues licks before a brief return to the main theme, from which Phil takes the lead with soloing that touches on some Groovyish places with a hint of The Other One. Lesh briefly jams on another theme, then the whole band pounds into The Other One.

Phil and Jerry take an interesting approach in the first-verse lead-in jam. It's shorter than many '73 versions and not exactly quiet, but subdued and unhurried. The jamming out of the first verse leads to a Jerry, Bobby, and Phil interaction that oozes into a meltdown featuring a roaring Tiger in all its crazed electronic glory. A descending, Jerry-led jam takes the band into a twinkling, gravity-free space out of which Eyes suddenly appears. It's a real up-tempo version, with plenty of the Phil-Jerry contrapuntal runs that make this year's versions pretty much the best. It burns off considerable energy before being plunged into the icy waters of China Doll.

The Sugar Magnolia that wraps things up is exuberant even by that tune's standards, Bobby giving vent to his zeal with a joyous vocal improvisation. It's a frenzy that the Casey Jones that follows reclaims in a slow, locomotive build to the end of the song's raucous vocal repetitions.

6/10/73
R F K

This three-set wonder is regarded as a classic among tape collectors and rightfully so. The first set possesses one of the finest song lists of the year, and the Dead are joined by the Allman Brothers and Merl Saunders in the unusual third set. It is the second set, though, that strikes closest to the heart of those who love 1973.

Round two starts off with what may be the finest Eyes ever played. Garcia and Lesh's effortless counterpoint soars from the first note, set off by Garcia's jubilant strumming at key points. Jerry's guitar bubbles up in the first solo and, once in open, air dries its wings and flits around like a bee. Phil and Jerry maintain a lively conversation throughout, moving with uncanny speed and sensitivity through extremes of light and dark, hope and peril during the generous jam at the end. Keith, Billy, and Bobby make their presence felt in the greatest way during the vintage '73 rhythmic jam at the end, one of the most extended and best-played examples of this delectable part of this era's Eyes. The spaciness at the end, driven by Phil and Billy, eventually gives way to a hot, sinfully short series of harmonics-rich blues licks from Garcia, which in turn drops into a lovely Stella Blue. This version is lent considerable shine by Keith especially. Big River nears country nirvana, and a long, dreamy Here Comes Sunshine also showcases his keys work as well as great playing by Phil.

Dark Star starts very low-key, with the lead every bit as much Phil's as Jerry's. Indeed it is Phil who takes the jam into the penumbra of night, with only light twinklings here and there from Jerry's guitar. From there Phil charges into a bass-heavy, grinding jam. This one takes shape ever so slowly, Jerry joining in well after Phil has staked out the territory, and then only very gradually. The jam's slow cohesion renders all the more satisfying the moment when it finally does kick in full force. When it ends, Jerry makes his most direct statement of the main Dark Star theme, signaling the approach of the verse, which soon follows. Out of the vocals Phil again lays down a thick carpet of bass while Bobby plays some chiming harmonics. It's over this background that Garcia plays progressively more spacey passages laden with reverb and feedback. It's not long before Jerry and Phil are playing the Martian blues and heading for the farther reaches of the solar system. Jerry starts playing Tiger runs and then lets it roar and growl fiercely afterward, while Phil's bass bellows danger on the way to total feedback meltdown.

It's out of the gooey residue of this brain fry that He's Gone emerges, nimbly wending its way past steaming puddles of dissolved bass notes. Jerry's keening blues licks and Keith's rolling piano make this one a fine addition to the many excellent '73 versions. One almost expects the song to turn into a celebratory New Orleans funeral march at the end. Jerry's rays of guitar sunshine stabbing through the clouds of the blues licks he also plays suffice nicely, though. Keith and Phil join in as Billy and Jerry speed the jam to heights of expression and an electrifying transition to Wharf Rat. This rendition is not without some technical flaws, but it is mesmerizing nonetheless, due in no small part to the way Jerry holds on to the last note of each vocal phrase. An extremely hot, extravagantly explored Truckin' rounds out the jam. The joyful strains of Sugar Magnolia cap the set, Bobby adding some hyped-up vocal improvisations at the end. And to think that the Dead came out with the Allmans after all this!

TRUCKIN' WITH GAS

*" 'Truck*ing*'? No, no, no—that's not how you say it. Anyway we're not gonna play that now anyways. ". . . Some tunes later: "The correct pronunciation of this tune is 'Truckin'!"*

—PHIL, 9/28/75

* 5/11/72 Rotterdam
* 5/26/72 London
* 7/18/72 Roosevelt Stadium
* 8/27/72 Veneta
* 5/26/73 Kezar
* 11/20/73 Denver
* 5/19/74 Portland
* 9/3/77 Englishtown
* 11/6/77 Binghamton
* 2/5/78 Cedar Falls
* 6/30/84 Indianapolis
* 7/15/89 Deer Creek
* 9/14/90 MSG
* 9/20/90 MSG

Eyes of the World

Eyes is a tune where the Dead try to have their cake and eat it too—and succeed. It is constructed with enough openness to allow a good measure of rhythmic variation and melodic exploration, making it an ideal forum for jamming. Its ringing, affirming chorus also makes it a very catchy tune.

Lyrically Hunter begins by asserting that "outside" of a "lazy summer home"—in the "real" world, with its quotidian struggles—"you don't have time to call your soul a critic." What does it mean to call one's soul a critic? Since your soul is your essential being, anything you do that your soul would criticize would be an action that goes against your very fiber. If you're calling your soul a critic, you are recognizing a disparity between your actions and your beliefs. When one is engaged with everyday life and hassles, one often doesn't have the opportunity for the sort of reflection that makes such a disparity evident—one might say, without introspection, that one is acting according to one's beliefs on any given day. It is only when rest—laziness—buys one time for contemplation that one's internal contradictions become evident. And one might realize that self-criticism of this or that action is coming from deep inside—one's soul. As for the nuthatch line that ends the verse, it seems as if the wonder at the nuthatch's migration is metaphoric amazement at the bird's easy transition from "summer" to "winter" home.

But what is the nuthatch? It is a creature, a part of nature. Its prescribed nature is not contemplative but instinctive. It could serve as a metaphor for one who "goes with the flow." Migratory, it never really leaves summer, but moves from warm region to warm according to the seasons, to its "winter's summer home." If a "summer home" is a place where contemplation is possible, it is always in this space. "Wings a mile long" seem to allude to a guiding and abetting mechanism, an extension of the bird's self into the whole of its environment.

Observation of the nuthatch brings about the epiphany of the title: "Wake up to find out..." *But*—this is one of the most important words in this song—"but the heart has its beaches...of its own." How are we to reconcile a view of man as part of nature's gestalt with a self-awareness that gives us an interior landscape as well? Jerry did not generally sing the "but"; it does, however, appear in Hunter's lyrics. Though Garcia often omitted parts of Hunter's lyrics to maintain ambiguity or otherwise affect meaning, I think it's safe to conclude that this change was made solely to make the song sing more gracefully.

The next verse is especially tricky, and I caution that the analysis that follows is, like all of this, mere speculation. "There comes a redeemer..."—a savior: Jesus? Jesus, the "son of Man" and the son of God, according to the New Testament, gave of himself so that man's sins (initiated by Adam and Eve and repeated by their progeny) could be expiated and mankind would henceforth gain entrance into heaven. Man would follow him into his father's kingdom—again, heaven. Sure enough, behind this redeemer "follows a wagon … that's loaded with clay." The name of the first man—Adam—means "clay," the material from which, according to Genesis, he was fashioned. The "seeds that were silent" line might be an echo of Jesus' parable, told in Matthew, of the sower who sows some of his seeds upon stone and some upon fertile ground. The yield of the good ground became the belief and the disciples of Christ's teachings. Bloom Christianity—the "redemption" of mankind—did, and "decay" it has as well. Spiritual decay set in almost immediately, as the very formation of a separate religion was hardly in accordance with the teachings of Jesus, a strict and observant Jew, and the revisionist contortions through which his life story were put to justify Christianity made it stray it farther and farther from Jesus' message. And decay in Christianity's influence over the Western world was certainly in full swing by 1973, when the song was unveiled. The sixties saw, famously, a popular questioning and realignment in regard to traditional beliefs; organized religion was certainly one of them. When old beliefs (in any "redeemer" followed by clay/man) lose their hold, a spiritual vacuum ensues—"he slowly too fades away" and "night comes so quiet."

Now, Robert Hunter is never so literal-minded as to write a song with an exegesis of the rise and fall of Christianity "encoded" in its lyrics. The above only seeks to point to threads of meaning that may inform this song with spiritual seeking.

Getting back to the spiritual vacuum, what is to fill it? The answer comes immediately with the chorus—you. Mustn't the soul find sustenance, though, in a belief in something greater than oneself? You are, because you are a part of the entire world, and you are that part that is aware and observant. Moreover "you" have inside you—"the heart has its …"—an infinity and eternity of landscapes and days. This last points not only to imagination and emotion but to Jungian strains of collective memory.

The spiritual argument is settled, to a degree, in the last verse. If the middle verse spoke of following a redeemer, the last one speaks of following one's own path, marching to the beat of one's own "drummer"—"Sometimes the songs that we hear …" There's a moderation to be found: One must ultimately follow one's own heart and visit that "homeland" within, but there are times when one can (or must) visit the spiritual "country" of others. The chorus, as it comes around for the last time, reminds us that though we each have an internal spiritual terrain, each of these "homes" (note how prevalent the word and concept of "home" is in this song) is ultimately a part of the same gestalt, as each person who listens to the song must be reminded that he is a part of the greater whole—"eyes of the world."

That said, isn't it a lot nicer the way Hunter writes it? This is the genius of Hunter's writing—to contain so much meaning in such an economical and moving collection of lines. And that offered above, which may or may not be close to the mark, only captures one of the many points of view that are radiated, prismlike, from a song that is even more lyrically and significantly open than it is musically.

Just as the song has one set of lyrics from which multiple variations of meaning can be extracted, the tune has a structure that is rhythmically sound and simple enough to allow for an almost endless variety of melodic variations in the jams. Jerry and Phil, especially, used this song to do just that. It's rare and rough for a song to debut as strongly as this one did. Some of the very early 1973 versions are so well developed and explored that it's hard to make a convincing argument for the song's improvement after that year. Whether it got any "better" after 1973 is open to argument, but the Dead did put it through a number of distinct phases, more so than many other tunes, distinguished by alterations in details such as tempo, Weir's harmony part, and so forth. As a result, versions from 1973–74, 1977, 1982–83, the late eighties, and 1990 (beginning with 3/25/90) are all very different in feel. The biggest change in the song came after the Dead's "retirement," when the Stronger Than Dirt-ish rhythmic jam at the end was dropped. Of these postretirement editions, those from the late eighties are probably the weakest in arrangement. They are very hurried, without the leisurely, lingering quality the song demands. The early eighties versions are also fast, but with more attention paid to detail, especially by Bobby, whose embellishments or lack thereof can make or break Eyes.

11/17/73
PAULEY PAVILION

This show marked the second time in a week that the Dead played the tasty sandwich Playin' → Uncle John's → Dew → Uncle John's → Playin'. There's something so pleasing about the symmetry of this combination and the way it moves in tempo from faster to slower and then back out again. It's also a journey back in time in terms of repertoire (and of course forward again).

Best of all, though, it's three great tunes in outstanding versions (this was, mind you, 1973) with the Dead's transitional playing at its peak. Playin' starts off a bit shaky vocally, but quickly rights itself with a long, full-bodied jam (lots of bass). This is one Playin' jam where the emotive power of the playing matches the band's creativity and speed. The transition into Uncle John's is subtle and seamless, a simple piece of fabric in which first one thread then another change melodic and tonal color until, before one can truly say when the change took place, it's a fait accompli. The same can be said for the passage from Uncle John's into Dew—though more readily perceived, it's executed with considerable panache and freighted with the emotional content that the Dead are magically able to convey without resorting to words. If anything, the transition back into Uncle John's Band is even more stirring. The second run-through of Uncle John's features some very intense jamming in which everyone gets involved. Once the jam begins to melt down, Bobby plays some piercing harmonics that soar through Jerry's descending lead like darts aimed at your solar plexus. That an excellent '73 Eyes → Sugar Magnolia (emphasis on the Eyes, which is truly fantastic) takes place in the same show is really more than one can ask.

As for the putative debut of this Playin' sandwich a week earlier (11/10/73), it is of course somewhat different: Uncle John's has more of a laid-back, reggae feel, and Dew is *very* fully jammed—more so than the 11/17. So take your pick—11/17 has the edge on the jams, but 11/10 has some better interior playing. Actually don't pick, get both and decide not to decide.

12/2/73
BOSTON MUSIC HALL

December 1973 was an exceptional month for the Dead, marked in large part by some of Keith's best and most assertive playing for the band. The second set of 12/2/73 illustrates all of this nicely.

An opening Wharf Rat, given strong backbone by Phil, cedes to one of the hottest, most finely played Half-Steps of a year that, along with '77, is home to some of the very best. This one possesses some real fire, often lacking in pre-'77 versions. The highlight of the tune comes in the "Across..." bridge, where Keith begins playing the arpeggios that generally belong to Jerry. This crossing of established ensemble roles is exciting in and of itself, but it becomes all the more so when Jerry begins to play the same part, but staggered so that his notes fall in between Keith's. The effect is gorgeous—guitar and piano rain falling down to fatten the lazy river.

The set intensifies with a swing into Playin', yet another tune that saw some of its most amazing performances in '73. At the end of the year the band was in the zone when it came to this piece. The body of the song is very well played here, well on its way to being an excellent version. What happens next, though, sets it apart: Total Meltdown. It begins instrumentally, as the playing becomes increasingly abstract, then equipmentally, with the axmen unleashing merciless torrents of feedback. Phil taxes the PA (you can hear it "clipping") and just about any pair of home speakers with wave after wave of bass, white and pink noise, the aural equivalent of dread. Simultaneously the guitarists initiate an assault of earsplitting screeches—sonic icepicks. Whatever its transformative effects on my consciousness, it didn't seem to do my cat any good. She started to twitch a bit when the bass rumbles hit her, and when the high-pitched needles began to come through the speakers, she slooowly inclined her head kind of sideways and gave me the strangest look.

So my cat's fucked up pretty good now and I think I might just get me a lawyer. I'll take the contents of the Vault as compensation for breaking my cat.

When the smoke clears to reveal the smoldering ruins of time machines, a graf zeppelin, and the Wall of Sound (not to mention the catatonic form of my supine feline), Jerry's guitar can be heard strolling through the wreckage playing what sounds like the intro to Dear Prudence. But of course—it's time for your mind to leave your body. This is one of the fullest, most affirming versions of the Mind Left Body Jam ever played. Phil and Jerry seem to take one side of the musical discussion while Keith offers his commentary from another tonal point of view, not as mere keyboard ornament. Dead literature is rife with talk of jams rising "phoenixlike" from the ashes of a meltdown. If ever this metaphor was apt, though, it's in description of what occurs on this tape. It's not for the faint of heart (or fragile of pet), but it pays off mightily.

Mind Left Body deposits us at

WILD EYES

✳ 2/9/73 Maples Pavilion
As fine a debut as a Dead song has ever had—this one leaped from the womb almost fully formed.

✳ 2/15/73 Madison
If the debut version was "almost fully formed," this second version saw it reach maturity.

✳ 6/10/73 RFK
Just plain organic and beautiful.

✳ 6/18/74 Louisville
A very jazzy, elegant version.

✳ 10/19/74 Winterland
This Grateful Dead Movie *version is possibly the best in the early arrangement.*

✳ 8/13/75 Great American Music Hall
The first Eyes with two drummers must be deemed a success. Phil takes some great solo turns.

✳ 5/7/77 Boston
Fast, with unconscious interplay between Phil and Jerry.

✳ 9/3/77 Englishtown
Better than the famed (overrated?) Half-Step from this show.

✳ 4/20/83 Providence
An especially rock-and-roll version.

✳ 4/6/84 Las Vegas
A rare Eyes out of Space.

✳ 6/23/84 Harrisburg
One to play for any annoying friends who try to tell you Jerry is slow.

✹4/8/85 Philly
Fast and furious.

✹ 6/27/85 SPAC
Ditto.

✹ 3/29/90 Nassau
Branford adds another dimension to this song; the result is even greater than the sum of its parts.

✹ 3/31/91 Greensboro
A long, *wonderful version.*

✹ 6/26/94 Las Vegas
A great Eyes in a monster show.

✹ 10/17/94 MSG
A long, lazy summer home of an Eyes.

the threshold of an excellent He's Gone in which Jerry, Keith, and Phil all assert themselves at different times for bouts of inspirationally weird soloing. An already good Truckin' improves considerably with the Nobody's Fault jamlet that Jerry initiates at the end. Phil steadfastly refuses to let this blues tune become in any way standard, with some tricky packing of the blues meter with bass lines. Jerry's solo lines soar with a clear, ringing tone. They jam this one out as much as one could hope, allowing for a good deal of invention within fairly well-established parameters. Jerry's playing at the end is particularly inspired, as is the transition into a gorgeous Stella Blue. Garcia makes excellent use of feedback to lend an edge to this version. Sugar Magnolia closes the set in fairly straightforward fashion until Keith and Phil come to dominate a top-notch Sunshine Daydream, transforming it from a good to a terrific closer.

TOASTING THE JAMS

Q: Why was Jerry Garcia so phat?
A: Because he liked the jam so much.

It's no secret that the Grateful Dead liked to jam. To the uninitiated, it seems that's all they did—bad. It often seems that way to the initiated as well—good: The more the better. Of course in the music of "the world's greatest garage band," as Stephen Stills once dubbed the Boys, jamming existed on many levels.

There is the solo jamming, of which Jerry was obviously the prime exponent—that is, taking a lead line that any "normal" band would devote a few bars to and turning it inside out nine ways to Sunday. And on the best nights, just when you thought the band was about to dive back into the verse, they'd go back for one more pass. There was a time when they weren't alone in this practice, but the seventies became the eighties and the nineties, and such meandering pursuits of the muse passed out of vogue. Time was, when Grateful

Dead shows made up pretty near the whole of my rock concert experience, I wouldn't even have considered this "jamming" as such—hell, just a good ol' rock-'n'-roll guitar solo, right? It's something that a Deadhead can still get myopic about, a point driven home to me when I shamelessly tried to convert a certain editor who shall remain nameless. I popped in my favorite piece of Dead-conversion propaganda, the Boston Garden '77 Half-Step. Not too shreepy, a good tune (if not one that would immediately pop to most Heads' minds as an exemplar), and a kick-ass driving solo with just plain unconscious lead guitar-bass interplay. "Hey, this is a pretty good tune," he said, meaning the lyrics and the chord construction. So far, so good. Midway through the main solo break I turned to him, air-guitaring Jerry's part like mad, with an "Isn't this sick?" He replied a tad disdainfully, "It's good, but it's *so long*" [emphasis added by author to denote author's disgust]. When the band went back for yet another instrumental round of verse, verse, chorus structure, I could tell that it was all he could do not to roll his eyes. Well, there's just no larnin' some folks.

There's also the "jamming out" of a tune, the workout the Dead give certain of their songs (which, by no accident, are among the best loved) after the singing's done but before they're done with them—as at the end of Terrapin, for example. For certain tunes, such as Bird Song, this jamming is followed up by a last run-through of the chorus; ideally the playing has by this point become so frenzied that the fact that the song in question has words at all comes as something of a revelation. It's in this jamming out—the process of discovering new angles from which to approach and subsequently alter the main melodic line, playing permutations on the rhythmic mathematics of a song, and, at its best, creating wholly new improvisational music—that the transition to the next tune (if there is to be one) is worked out. It is in these periods of transformation, when the band is not necessarily playing one song or another but a hybrid of the before-and-after (or even something wholly apart), that some of the Dead's most sublime music can be found. The Dead write great songs; there are some better ones by other artists, some not as good by the same. The Dead sing very well and play fantastically; there are other performers who (arguably) can match them—"Oh yeah, listen to *this* guy's voice, listen to *this* guy's solo." In their transitional jamming, though, the Dead are matchless.

Anyone who has read or heard quality interviews with the band members cannot help but come away with the insight that this was a band with a very sophisticated grasp of music theory. Such an understanding of the mechanical underpinnings of song is a sine qua non of playing by the seat of one's pants, of knowing how to make a subtle modulation that takes you from one related scale to the next and to recognize and attune oneself to those actions when they are taken by another member of the ensemble. But this sort of technical savvy will take a band or an individual player only so far. When the Dead were on, they went light-years beyond "so far."

There's an innate artistry to the way the Dead build and execute a jam. A good portion of this artistry is, to be sure, born of virtuosity—you can't run before you can crawl. Nevertheless there's an element to the best art (or sport, for that matter), usually labeled "talent," that springs from the personality of the artist. Who can say what exactly gave Mahler his complex and innovative sense of tonal relationships, Vermeer his rich palette, Michael Jordan his sense of the exact moment to break left when his defender(s) is convinced he's about to break right? Skill is what gives an artist the ability to execute, but genius lies in having the idea in the first place. The Dead's genius, in jamming out a tune and creating transitional pathways from one song to the next, is often to be found in their sense of timing: knowing the exact moment to pull off of a repetition of a note or phrase, to build the dynamic intensity or drop things down to a whisper of guitar over the rustlings of a cymbal. That the Dead, as individuals, were able to do this is impressive; ensemble playing of this sort speaks of long hours of group woodshedding followed by long years of playing together onstage. Some would say that acid helped too.

To be a bit more concrete, consider the crescendo the band builds in the 7/1/85 Merriwether Scarlet → Fire jam; in the space after, while it is still resounding in the listener's skull and only Phil and the drums continue, Jerry plays a single, plaintive "wah"—a simple, eloquent answer to a fierce argument. Or listen to the 11/17/73 UCLA Playin' → Uncle John's and the way the notes of Uncle John's gently insinuate themselves into the fabric of Playin'. One moment you're listening to a fine Playin' jam; if you so much as aurally blink, you'll realize you're in Uncle John's without the slightest notion of how you got there or when you arrived. Granted the move from Playin', in D, to Uncle John's, in G, requires only the alteration of one note, but there are real differences in the forms of the two tunes, and the Dead never fully show their hand until the game is won (i.e., until the transition is a fait accompli). In the 6/15/85 Greek China → Rider listen to the way the band uncannily determines the absolute crest of the jam and then surfs it nice and easy into Rider.

Timing is but one element, though, in the inspirational mix that makes the Dead's transitional jamming such a special part of modern popular music. The other is the Dead's passion for experimentation. To be game for any onstage experimentation at all rendered the Dead somewhat of an anomaly throughout their history, more so as time and musical fashion moved on (regressed?). But not only were the Dead willing and able to mix things up, caution be damned, they *lived* for it—wouldn't have had it any other way. The happy fruits of this aesthetic are many, many hours of improvisational wonder captured on tape: nameless jams that materialize from the deconstructed detritus of songs; long passages of impromptu playing that manage to be at once cerebral and passionate; jazzy stretches of instrumentation that follow no discernible (or familiar) dictates of tonal relation or melody or, when things are at their oddest, rhythm, yet reward the listener's patience with a palpable sense of ordered disorder. There is definitely a method to the maddest of the Dead's madness, even if the "plan" can be perceived only in retrospect. Such is the nature of the Dead, a musical beast that lived its best moments, Neal Cassady—like, on the very cusp of the "now." It's an interesting paradox that the most taped musical group in history played with so little regard for anything but the present, and it is this of course that makes their music so worth preserving and made seeing them again and again (and again) a pursuit of bliss rather than folly.

But the multiple strains of the Dead's jamming do not end here, not hardly. For the Dead were not only imaginative and accomplished musicians but remarkably eclectic, both individually and collectively, in their musical influences as well. A deep and varied frame of musical reference serves as fodder for some of the Dead's most affecting playing, as a riff or even a single note would remind Jerry, Phil, or whomever of an apt musical "quote" to be thrown into the conversation. Out of the deepest Space and recognizable tunes and even from a standing start arise bouts of thematic jamming, like radio stations playing long-forgotten tunes stabbing suddenly out of a sea of static. The musical ghosts of the Youngbloods' "Darkness, Darkness," Hendrix's "Foxy Lady," Hughes's "It's a Sin," Marley's "Stir It Up" can drift across the stage at any moment. Or the most sublime Dead moments of all, the thematic jams of their own invention, most notably the so-called Spanish Jam (aka Spinach Jam, per *Dick's Picks Volume Six*) and Mind Left Body Jam (a name derived from its seeming resemblance to the tune "Your Mind Has Left Your Body" on the Paul Kantner/Grace Slick/David Frieberg album *Baron von Tollbooth and the Chrome Nun*, on which Garcia and Hart make an appearance). Close cousin to these last are the Dead's jams on songs of their own or in their repertoire, sans lyrics. Among the jams referred to here are those on the themes of Caution, Nobody's Fault But Mine (the Nobody's jam), The Other One, Dark Star. There were times in the Dead's history when a song that had left the Dead's rotation would only exist as a jam, as in the case of We Bid You Goodnight, which was not sung for years but could be found as a brief jam appended to the end of Goin' Down the Road Feeling Bad. At other times tunes were jammed before they had lyrics, as was the case

GREAT MOMENTS IN DEAD JAMMING

❋ 3/25/66 Trouper's Club
Here's maybe the earliest instrumental captured on tape, a hot bout of psychedelic blues jamming.

❋ 2/14/68 Carousel
Not only does this historic show—Phil's favorite and the greater part of the foundation for Anthem of the Sun—*contain a very spacey Spanish Jam, but there are broad hints of the Mountain Jam (from Donovan's "First There Is a Mountain," later worked to stratospheric heights by the Allman Brothers and the Dead themselves—see 12/12/73, for example) in* Caution.

❋ 10/68 Matrix, etc.
Lovers of Dead jamming should check out any Mickey and the Hartbeats show for some of the finest exemplars of all types of jamming.

❋ 11/8/69 Fillmore
In a show that is jamming in every sense of the word, the Dead run through Uncle John's Jam and the first Main Ten—Uncle John's is especially wonderful.

❋ 2/11/70 Fillmore East
Spanish Jam with Duane and Gregg Allman and Peter Green—the whole is greater…

❋ 9/19/70 Fillmore East
The elusive Darkness Jam and a brief China Cat jam sprinkle stardust on an already magical Not Fade Away in an amazing show.

❋ 12/2/73 Boston Music Hall
An early and luxuriously long Mind Left Body Jam rises out of one of the with the Uncle John's Jam and Main Ten (a jam that contained some—not all—of the elements of Playing in the Band), and the Help on the Way and the Slipknot! from the Winterland '75 Help → Slip → Franklin's.

In all these cases it is perhaps the very fact that words *are* absent that accounts for the stirring nature of the jams. Lyrics, even those as finely crafted as Robert Hunter's and John Barlow's, are only words, and words are only symbolic representatives of emotions, things, actions, qualities. A lyrical depiction of happiness, for example, even one that is imagistic and allusively persuasive, is far less direct a conveyance than music—or even a single sustained note—that can create that emotion in the listener. This is the kind of music the Dead played in their jams—evocative and emotional music, direct connections with Heads' heads and hearts. The tone of Garcia's guitar alone, especially in some of the best Mind Left Body Jams, could be enough to bring tears to one's eyes. The way so many these jams are constructed also seems attuned with some subtle rhythm to the flow of human emotions—listen to the Stir It Up jam from 3/21/91, which exemplifies this emotive build: The band first establishes the rhythm and chord changes in the song, and the listener's body most intense meltdowns in the Dead have ever freaked out of their instruments.

�֍ 5/19/74 Portland
A somewhat racy Mind Left Body Jam, in keeping with a spacey and speedy show.

✖ 6/18/74 Louisville
A jazz jam followed by a jam on It's a Sin shows the versatility and virtuosity of that era's Dead.

✖ 6/28/74 Boston Music Hall
A slowly cohering, introspective Mind Left Body Jam—deeply affecting.

✖ 7/19/74 Fresno
A Spanish Jam steeped in spooky psychedelia.

✖ 11/20/78 Cleveland
The second set starts with a thrilling Playin' jam (listen for the passages where Jerry plays some quick lines anachronistically suggestive of the theme to the Inspector Gadget *cartoon).*

✖ 5/6/81 Nassau
The Spanish Jam and a fast, furious Caution jam provide some of Jerry's most feverishly psychedelic moments on tape.

✖ 8/28/81 Long Beach
Another hot '81 Spanish Jam.

✖ 10/6/81 London
The Blues for Allah jam out of Space creates a universe where time just stops.

✖ 11/5/85 Worcester
Not surprisingly, the Supplication jam ➡ *Playin' jam steals the show.*

✖ 3/27/86 Portland
A Spanish Jam that pulses with the

sways slowly, setting out in the stream of notes, responding to the emotional color they call forth. Then, once the wavelength has been found and assimilated by band and audience alike, Garcia elaborates with the song's melody, unleashing that which has been allowed to build inside the heart, letting the music say that the initial suspicions of joy laid out in the jam's beginning can be felt without reserve, unfettered. Can I be happy, dare I be happy? Oh . . . ecstasy!

I think that the absence of lyrics in the jams caused the Dead to imbue their playing with added emotional weight. Whether or not that was their intention, it was certainly the result, which makes these passages among the tastiest in the Dead canon. All the permutations of the Dead jam, from virtuoso soloing, to the stringing together of tunes in inspired fashion, to the improvisational creation of musical structures and rock-and-roll "tone poems," are the defining elements of the Dead's music. If the Dead had never played a Hunter-Garcia song, or any other for that matter, but had retained the jamming described above, they would still have been the Dead. That they did all this *and* played so many great songs with intelligent, philosophically resonant lyrics is what made them the greatest raw power of Jerry's guitar, brawny and loud in the mix.

❄ 3/24/90 Albany
A very fully developed Mind Left Body Jam out of Terrapin transports Dead and listener alike back to 1974.

❄ 3/21/91 Cap. Center
Jerry leads the band into a Stir It Up jam out of Fire—happy, happy music.

❄ 3/17/93 Cap. Center
The Handsome Cabin Boy with its Celtic instrumental flavor, floats across the stage out of an amazing Space to lend the perfect St. Patrick's Day touch.

❄ 9/13/93 Philly
One of the best things Vince ever did with the Dead—tubular bells.

SOME ESPECIALLY TASTY JAM SANDWICHES

❄ 11/8/69 Fillmore
Dark Star ➡ Other One ➡ Dark Star ➡ Uncle John's Jam ➡ Dark Star ➡ St. Stephen ➡ The Eleven ➡ Caution ➡ The Main Ten ➡ Caution ➡ Feedback ➡ We Bid You Goodnight

❄ 12/1/71 Boston
Other One ➡ Me & My Uncle jam ➡ Other One ➡ Uncle ➡ Other One

❄ 9/28/72 Stanley Theater
He's Gone ➡ Other One ➡ Bobby McGee ➡ Other One ➡ Wharf Rat

rock-and-roll band on the planet. Ever.

Of course not everyone would agree with that last sentiment, which points to a special trait shared by Deadheads: They like the Dead! Seriously, though, Deadheads generally share an appreciation for the nuance of feeling that music can carry, and not just melody but rhythm, harmony, and counterpoint as well. Most every Deadhead has had the experience of popping a show in the deck with a non-Head present and finding that even the most intense passages leave this other person cold. Witnessing this sort of reaction can inhibit the Head's enjoyment of and involvement with the music as well, which is part of what made shows so exciting—the mass attunement of the group heart and mind to a place of great sensitivity. This collective exercise in appreciation where a nuance of phrasing between two notes Jerry played, or an accent from Phil, or Bobby, could bring cheers and "ooohs" not only made listening a blissful group activity but, from band members' accounts, made playing one too.

✸ 11/10/73 Winterland
Playin' ➡ *Uncle John's* ➡ *Dew* ➡ *Uncle John's* ➡ *Playin'*

✸ 11/14/73
Truckin' ➡ *Other One* ➡ *Big River* ➡ *Other One* ➡ *Eyes* ➡ *Other One*

✸ 10/9/76 Oakland
St. Stephen ➡ *Not Fade* ➡ *St. Stephen* ➡ *Help* ➡ *Slipknot* ➡ *Drums* ➡ *Samson* ➡ *Slipknot* ➡ *Franklin's* ➡ *Saturday Night*

✸ 5/19/77 Fox Theater
Terrapin ➡ *Playin'* ➡ *Uncle John's* ➡ *Drums* ➡ *Wheel* ➡ *China Doll* ➡ *Playin'*

✸ 9/6/80 Lewiston
Playin' ➡ *Uncle John's* ➡ *Drums* ➡ *Not Fade* ➡ *Wheel* ➡ *Uncle John's* ➡ *Playin'* ➡ *Sugar Magnolia*

✸ 6/24/85 River Bend
Cryptical ➡ *Drums* ➡ *Space* ➡ *Comes a Time* ➡ *Other One* ➡ *Cryptical*

✸ 10/16/89 Byrne
Dark Star ➡ *Playin'* ➡ *Uncle John's* ➡ *Playin'* ➡ *Drums* ➡ *Space* ➡ *Take You Home* ➡ *Miracle* ➡ *Dark Star* ➡ *Attics* ➡ *Playin'*

✸ 11/1/90 London
Playin' ➡ *Dark Star* ➡ *Drums* ➡ *Space* ➡ *Dark Star* ➡ *Playin'*

2/24/74
WINTERLAND

One of my favorite Bill Graham intros starts this tape, another very crisp soundboard from '74: "Whatever's going on in the rest of the world, whether it's wars, kidnappings, or crimes, this is a peaceful Sunday night with the Grateful Dead." The Dead, almost by way of response, launch right into U.S. Blues. I'm Uncle Sam implies that the Dead are just as much a part of the country, and the world at large, as the things Graham has just described. The Dead and rock and roll do not exist in a vacuum, and the United States is not only red and white, but blue suede shoes as well.

The first set of this peaceful Sunday night has a number of excellent tunes. A five-beat Beat It On Down gets great harmonies courtesy of Donna Jean (this always was one of the songs she sang best), and a Candyman that recovers from early tuning problems to delight with a spacey, tremolo-laden Jerry solo. The real highlights, however, begin with a China → Rider that achieves a real deep groove—sweet, long, and totally jamming. A jubilant transition to Rider features even more jamming than usual for 1974 on the Feelin' Groovy-ish elaboration of the Rider descant, a touch that nudges this already excellent version into the all-timer column. The long, questing Playin' closer belies the fact that this is a first set. The noteworthy feature of this version is how effectively it treads the line between spaciness and drive—it's plenty freaky but never wholly loses its melodic thread or forward momentum.

The obvious high point of the second set is a Dark Star → Dew that takes up a whole tape side and then some. Dark Star loosens up right quick, dropping the main theme but maintaining rhythmic and chordal structure as the underpinnings of some nimble, interweaving jamming between Jerry, Phil, and Keith. Billy eventually adopts a jazzy feel that moves the jam along, which, when he does so, is just what the doctor ordered: a familiar and pleasing rhythmic vessel for this strange brew. After some time playing in this mode we get a rather slowly sung first verse, followed by our first taste of deep space, heralded by Weir playing a figure very reminiscent of the Weather Report Suite Prelude, which, forget ye not, was originally born of Dark Star. Jerry soon embarks on some fast, wah-laden strumming resembling the start of a Tiger, under which Bobby plays the Spanish Jam chords. A magical series of moments pass as all pick up the theme except for Jerry, who continues to fan furiously while roaming up and down the fretboard—Spanish weirdness. Some more space follows, and then an impromptu, highly melodic jam streaks across the horizon to land, smoldering, in the Morning Dew.

The first thing you're apt to notice in this version is the skill and attention that Bobby lavishes on the first couple of verses, playing beautiful harmonics and shimmering arpeggio accents. Phil, Jerry, and Keith match Bobby's care to turn in a long, impassioned performance of Dew. The rest of the set is fairly standard, if well played, notable for a hot run-through of the Not Fade → Goin' Down → Not Fade sandwich and a really nice Baby Blue encore.

5/19/74
PORTLAND

This is one of those shows that, like 5/2/70 or 5/8/77, epitomizes the form the Dead assumed—in terms of sound, playing, and repertoire—in the era of which it is a part. Like the aforementioned shows, it possesses the added virtue of being from one of the Dead's ragingly great periods. Without further ado . . .

An excellent Half-Step opens the first set. A few songs later Bobby turns in a top-notch rendition of Black-Throated Wind and from there on in the show just grows in power. It grows next into Scarlet Begonias, notable for one of Donna's most successful end-of-song wails—powerful, soaring, and on-key. She follows suit by giving powerful, if simple, backing to a Beat It On Down that's one of the great ones. The fat, joyful Loose Lucy that follows is another all-timer—as in Beat It On Down, it's simply a joy to behold the close groove that Donna establishes between herself and the lead vocal, especially toward the end of the song. Donna even turns in a creditable performance in Money, Money, a tune for which she had a fairly well-established distaste. Whatever one's regard for the (tongue-in-cheek) lyrics, this one rocks, with Keith and Jerry pulling out all the stops. The set-closing China → Rider features an outstanding, stirring example of the '73–'74 pre-Rider jam.

A Promised Land → Bertha → Greatest Story gets the second set off to a breathless start. The festivities begin in earnest, though, with an exceptional Weather Report Suite. The Wharf Rat that flows from it is also one for the ages; very powerful, with the band paying close attention to dynamics.

As for the Truckin' that comes a few tunes later—well, to borrow a phrase from the 10/31/71 Cincinnati show, this is the one you've been waiting to hear. This version becomes a launching pad for some of the best jamming ever captured on tape, as a thunderous rendition of the song's main body thrusts

CONFESSIONS OF A PHIL PHREAK

PHIL PHRIDGE

"*My* dad has a small refrigerator with Dead stickers on it. 'Lesh is More,' 'Tastes Grate, Lesh Philling,' they announce. He inherited it from me. It used to be my fridge in school, when I saw a lot of shows. But now it sits in his office, holding milk and cream for coffee instead of beer.

"This fridge doesn't have any 'The Fat Man Rocks' stickers on it, and certainly no Bobby stickers, because I don't think anyone ever made one. No, this fridge has only Phil stickers on it, because Phil was always the musical magnet that drew me to the left side of that stage. At general admission shows I would try to get in early so as to get a prime spot in the Phil Zone. Even at seated shows I would blithely try to jiggle my way down there so as to be closer to the man.

"There was no better place to listen and watch than from the Phil Zone. I was always amazed, even on off nights, at the mastery of his playing. His subtle interplay with Jerry, the way he added texture to the music but anchored it at the same time always blew my head off. Phil's deep, funky runs, in concert with Jerry's high, trippy noodling was what always made the sound for me. And of course when he sang, adding that sonorous and nasally profundo to his playing, all the better.

"I also liked watching from the Phil Zone the physical manifestations of his playing. The way he would creep when really getting into a tune, that sort of splay-footed, open-kneed sway he would get going. Phil was also seemingly the most technologically adept band member. How many shows witnessed Bobby annoyedly trying to find the right radio frequency for his guitar, Jerry stonedly fucking with his wah-wah pedal, while Phil was coolly making minute and precise adjustments to his sound on that stack that stood as tall as he did.

"The Phil Zone also provided the opportunity to study the intricate patterns on Phil's dye. Obsessively so, on a good night. Because in addition to his playing, Phil was always the most sartorially hip member of the band. Granted his competition was not very stiff; Jerry in his oversized T-shirt from Woolworth's and wearing his shapeless brown Hush Puppies, and Bobby sporting that too-tight pink Izod, or later that hideous mauve tank top, cut-offs, and Nikes. No, Phil somehow always looked cooler to me. The sweat bands on his wrist alone put him in a whole different league. Despite his superior dressing style, though, Phil never quite looked the part of the rock musician. He had to me the appearance of an accountant who had serendipitously stumbled

into a hard-driving jam that in turn barrels headlong into the Mind Left Body Jam. This version of the jam is less introspective than the next month's 6/28/74 edition, which seems fitting if one considers that this one comes out of Truckin', the other out of the Weather Report Suite. Make no mistake, though, this one is just as chillingly thrilling, Jerry's guitar carrying through it with a hoarse-throated scream.

And that's not all, as the band then tears into a serious Not Fade → Goin' Down the Road pairing. At the peak of Not Fade, just before it goes into Goin' Down the Road, Jerry does some loud, aggressive soloing under which the band's rhythmic punctuation becomes fouled, making the meter of his solo difficult to resolve. In a fine example of the Dead's alchemical way of turning base metal into gold, Jerry speeds the transition into Goin' Down the Road, relieving the tension in the most luscious fashion—another *objet trouvé* in the Dead tape museum. Jerry's solo within Goin' Down is short but very sweet. The show ends with Saturday Night and a U.S. Blues encore, blazing both. Jerry's parting sentiment, "Thanks a lot, Portland, we love ya," was no doubt returned in spades after this show.

upon a freezer full of acid and a bass guitar. And never looked back.

"My dad doesn't realize it, but Phil was the balls of that band. My dad does not miss Phil. I don't think he really even knows who he is. [If he did, he would know that he couldn't catch Phil on the Further tour, or playing with Ratdog, or any other such thing. Phil was a member of the Dead, (to me, *the* member of the Dead), and the Dead are gone.] My dad would have to be content, as the rest of us are, with turning Phil up on a good tape, opening that fridge for a beer, or some coffee, and kicking back to listen. **"**

—NUGGET

6/18/74
LOUSVILLE

The second show in an outstanding late-spring—early-summer tour, Louisville is just about perfect, offering a musical sampling of the Dead's full bag of tricks—a little bit of country, some straight-ahead rockers, very spacey (yet crisp) playing, and one jam each in a jazz and blues mode. Such a retrospective seems to make perfect sense for a time in which their playing was at its apex.

The highlight of a very strong first set is the Eyes → China Doll, a familiar formulation in this era, executed here to perfection. Eyes is jazzy and fluid, with Phil and Keith very prominent in delivering standout performances. Jerry tosses off seemingly effortless liquid runs, and Phil takes one of his most full-blown leads of 1974 (read: ever) in one of the instrumental breaks. He passes the baton briefly back to Jerry, who then passes it back to Phil for some very easy bass soloing before Eyes dips into a chilling, precise China Doll.

There aren't too many really weak versions of the Weather Report Suite, so relative qualitative judgments rely primarily upon the finer points of execution—tempo, dynamics, harmony. Well, the version in the second set of this show has all that, and an extra sense of atmosphere that marks it as well near definitive. The momentum is built through a dreamy, dewy Part One as each band member plays his part with an orchestral sense of his contribution to the whole (the astounding separation of '74 tapes augments this effect). Phil and Keith are major—yet subtle—presences here as Jerry's lines engage in a lively conversation throughout the suite with Bob's vocals. Billy's entrance at the end of Part One has that extra bit of snap and even the slight fraying of the harmonies on the "I ams" seems somehow wistful, in keeping with the mood of the song. Let It Grow hits an emotional high of joy and wonder, most keenly felt in Jerry's smooth quasi-calypso guitar lines and a fantastic closing jam.

The band brings it down real low in the spaciness that follows, Jerry extending questing guitar tentacles in search of a musical hold. It is Keith, though, who finds the handle, locking into a groove with Billy that Jerry quickly latches on to, a jazzy jam informed by the preceding Let It Grow. Keith and Phil lead the band next into The Other One, throughout which they remain the most actively inventive players. Jerry's lead lines act as a bridge between the incredible piano-bass interaction. This is an Other One that streaks across the set with the intensity and brevity of a shooting star until it burns out amid the spacey place whence it came. Jerry and Bobby play some great Venusian chamber music, with feedback, string scratching, and spacey delay effects, all above Billy's loose-limbed, "floating with the universe" drumming. When Phil joins in, he lays down a foundation of gravity and darkness on which Keith once again erects a musical structure, Billy right with him. The completely improvisational blues-jazz jam that follows is, though simple, remarkable for the attentive spontaneity with which it is played (On 6/23/74 they toy with a similar theme, but it doesn't lock together like this one does.). All are *on* here, listening to one another and contributing with élan. One almost expects Donna to start laying down some scat lines!

The Dead continue to let their music do the talking as they get down into a smoldering jam on It's a Sin. Again the playing is clearly that of a band at the top of its form. Jerry's blues licks evince a devilish mastery of the form. And it's a huge mystery to me why Keith didn't more often adopt the organ sound he employs here (very similar to that used in Crazy Fingers on *Blues for Allah*). It's all over much too soon, though the band quells one's disappointment quickly with a beautifully fragile Stella Blue.

Big River and Jed bring the proceedings perhaps too far back to earth, despite solid versions of both. After Jed Bobby and Phil react with humor to a bottle apparently thrown onstage, in a way that gets to the essence of the act's irrationality:

Bobby: "If your object is to put a bottle on the stage, please pass it forward and lay it up here; don't throw it, because someone might get hurt."
Phil: "Besides, we could use the three cents."
Bobby: "That's also something to consider."
Phil: "Yeah, maybe *you* could use the three cents."

Phil's words, besides hearkening nostalgically back to the days of three-cent bottle deposits, seem a wry commentary on the Dead's financial precariousness in the Wall of Sound era. The show closes with a hot little Sugar Magnolia that opens with Jerry's guitar sounding very trumpetlike. Jerry and Phil both kill on this one.

As if all that precedes wasn't enough, the Dead pile on the goodies with a rare Dew encore. The middle of this one is a Phil fest, augmented by Keith's accompaniment. Upper-end ivory tickling serves and Phil's melodic counterpoint define the sublimely quiet musical space from which Jerry and Bobby take off, literally fanning the flames to a flash point. It's an all-time ending to an all-time show.

6/28/74
BOSTON

Like 5/19/74 and 6/18/74, the second set of this night at the Boston Garden typifies the best of the Dead's experimentational '74 aesthetic: avantgarde, yet never coldly academic.

The set starts innocuously enough with Sugar Magnolia (though a retrospective or anachronistic view would find that unusual in and of itself). Just when it is about to go into the Sunshine Daydream coda, it is usurped by the opening Bobby riff of Scarlet Begonias. A liquid jam out of Scarlet in which all are involved overcomes some initial caterwauling by Miss D. (less egregious than at some times, but . . .) to build in volume in intensity until you'll swear Jerry's about to switch over to the envelope filter and begin the Fire descant, anachronism be damned. But no, it's just a ravishing Scarlet sans Fire that amply shows how special this tune was even before 3/18/77 rolled around and changed Dead second sets forever.

Fast-forward a bit to a harmonics-filled tuning that reveals that the Weather Report Suite, beloved staple of '74 shows, is about to surface. The prelude and Part One are as good as any from this year, maybe better, and the Let It Grow brims with exploratory jamming in the restless, jazzy '74 mode. The jamming is sucked down the cosmic drain of one of the more evocative meltdowns on tape—an aural photograph of dew sparkling on sea stones. What follows is, in this reviewer's experience at least, the ne plus ultra of Mind Left Body Jams. Though the true name or derivation of this jam is a point of contention among Deadheads, "Your Mind Has Left Your Body" seems to capture perfectly the essence (if not the true musical lineage) of the jam as played here. This one has the capacity to bring tears full of the intoxication of possibility to one's eyes, make the hair on one's arms and neck stand on end, and spread an otherwordly mixture of warmth and cold dread outward from the solar plexus. There's just something about Jerry's guitar sound on this jam—especially in this version—that cuts like a crystal shard not only through the jam but through one's psyche as well. *This* is musical therapy, a psychedelic experience without drugs. It's not *all* Jerry's doing, though—another sublime touch is added by Keith's bell-like keyboard lines, so ably imitated (consciously?) by Brent more than a decade and a half later in the 3/24/90 version (the release of this run as *Dozin' at the Knick* shows the band having a bit of fun with us by naming the jam Mud Love Buddy Jam).

From this musical and emotional summit there emerges a jam that promises to be the Wharf Rat intro but instead disintegrates back into the cosmos, passing shattered bits of Dark Star along the way until it enters the musical galaxy whence the Dark Star came for a swinging, jazzy jam that wouldn't be out of place in a Dark Star but is definitely its own wonderful entity. Jerry's guitar screams through the heavens, buffeted by winds of piano, bass, guitar. Unbelievable. The restless growlings of the Tiger at the end are but spacey icing on the cake. Particularly enjoyable here is the "Tiger recoil." The Dead alight again on planet Earth in a bouncy blues mode, out of which a top-notch U.S. Blues, of all songs, develops with an unusually long and interesting introduction.

After U.S. Blues, Phil, who is perhaps unaware that the band has left the stage itself in flames, delivers the admonition, "Careful, folks, the fire marshall is going to put you out." The Dead do nothing to quench their own fire with a rocking Goin' Down the Road that explodes into the deferred Sunshine Daydream with all the force of the energy generated since Sugar Magnolia became a Scarlet Begonia hours before. This is the first time that Sugar Mags was split from its coda—I daresay the Dead must have been pleased with the results.

7/19/74
FRESNO

A soundboard of startling sonic clarity (thanks, Gans!) brings the Wall of Sound to life once more in this very tasty piece of 1974. The highlight of this show is a Weather Report Suite—driven jam, with parallels to 6/28/74, in the second set.

The first link in the chain is He's Gone. Though somewhat flawed in the "body," of the song, it finishes triumphantly, with some good vocal interplay in the coda and a long, relaxed jam that brings it into U.S. Blues, an odd transition to these ears so accustomed to it as an encore.

But this is all warm-up, really, for what flows out of U.S. Blues. A beautiful prelude to the Weather Report Suite rings with harmonic yummies. Part One is marred a bit by some dreadful harmonies (or lack thereof), as is Let It

Vonnegut and the Dead

It's not hard to see where Kurt Vonnegut would appeal to Jerry Garcia. Vonnegut's stories and novels have, from *Slaughterhouse Five* on, always had a strong strain of science fiction running through them, a genre Jerry loved, and Vonnegut's witty digressions and idiosyncratic verbal riffing are reminiscent of both Jerry's conversation and his guitar playing. Garcia was in fact a Kurt Vonnegut nut—he even bought the movie rights to *The Sirens of Titan* and enlisted Dan Aykroyd and other *Saturday Night Live* hands to help him bring it to the screen (needless to say, it didn't happen, though storyboards and a treatment were even drawn up; others hold the rights now). And of course the Grateful Dead's publishing company is named Ice Nine, after the strain of ice that can freeze the whole world in the Vonnegut novel *Cat's Cradle*. It's possible that an allusion to Ice Nine may be detected in Robert Hunter's lyrics for Franklin's Tower: "If you plant ice, you're gonna harvest wind." Aside from being an eloquent rephrasing of the biblical "Who sows wind reaps the hurricane," it's an exact description of Ice Nine's immediate effects in the novel. After the substance is loosed upon the world—dropped into the sea—and all the earth's water turns to ice, a fierce, cold wind whips across the frozen land.

Grow, but the playing is as superb as the vintage would suggest. Jerry goes predictably off and Phil steps up in a big (and loud) way during, and especially at the end of, Let It Grow. It's here that he takes the lead part over Jerry's rhythm playing.

Jerry recaptures the lead for a short, fast jam with a certain Playin' flavor, which soon leads to a meltdown highlighted by Keith's organ/synth playing (he's playing with the sound he'd later use in the aptly titled Crazy Fingers). Postmeltdown, it's Phil at the helm again, taking the band into La Jam Española. The combination of Jerry's fuzzy guitar sound and the aforementioned organ effects get this one off to an especially freaky start. Jerry soon changes to a rounder wah-filled sound reminiscent of Mind Left Body, then to a mellower jazz-guitar tone. Props especially go to Billy for the way he insinuates himself into the jam. If you are, as am I, a collector of the Dead's thematic jams, then you simply must have this very well-developed version, which is all the better for leading into Eyes.

Although '74 Eyes don't as a rule quite match the transcendent beauty of those from the song's debut year of '73, they're not exactly weak either (actually, this is one song that was very strong throughout its run). This version comes alive as Phil and birthday-boy Keith trade some excellent runs, guiding the jam to its terminus in an above-average China Doll.

The combination of a superb soundboard in circulation and some vintage '74 jamming in all senses of the word make this a fine representative of the year to add to your collection.

DIJON, FRANCE

The Dead made a brief European jaunt before their Winterland "retirement" run, playing ten shows total in England, Germany, and France. The Dijon show is one of the better from this "last" European tour.

The first set starts off with four tunes tinged with Americana—strong versions all of Uncle John's (with that wonderful 1973–74 reggae feel), Jack Straw, a revival of Friend of the Devil (that very nice and somewhat rare fast electric version), and Black-Throated Wind. The Dead open things up a bit with a hot Scarlet before playing a haunting Row Jimmy, to which Keith adds some eerie organ textures. Other high points of the set are a very well done The Race Is On, made special by Jerry's countrified licks and a lovely, very slow To Lay Me Down. The Playing in the Band closer is the clear standout— a very fulphilling version with a long, long-running dialogue between Messrs. Lesh and Garcia. The jam they play toward the end bears a faint similarity to Shakedown Street.

The Loose Lucy that opens the set is notable only for the fact that the vocals are missing on the soundboard. The Eyes that comes next, though, is distinguished by quite a bit more. It is a Phil pheast, marked by long stretches where all else step back and cede center stage to Mr. Lesh. Most of this soloing is fantastic, but there are some places in here where it sounds as if he is pressing a bit, trying too hard to make "it" happen.

China Doll suffers from a very uneven tempo exacerbated by a missed entrance. The band treads water while Jerry tries to come up with the line and then rushes to finish up after the verse is delivered. Billy's drumming and Donna's harmonies stand out as wheat among the chaff. The quiet setting makes Billy's creative fill work all the more apparent, and as for Donna, her harmony part here is notable for being true, complex harmony as opposed to the simple singing of an octave interval above the lead that she did for much of her time with the band. Even Donna possessed greater musical complexity in 1974. Another example of Donna's fine harmony arrangements in this year can be found in Scarlet Begonias, in the part she sings during the "once in a while you can get shown the light" line and the analogous parts of that song.

He's Gone is good, if not great, highlighted by Jerry's attention to those little country licks—they almost sound like pedal steel—at the end of each line, which the song has lost at various times over its run. He plays some lovely harmonics in a number of them, making them extra tasty.

It's at the end of Truckin' that the Dead seem to find their real spark, playing the outro with style right into Drums and then an extended Caution jam, during which Phil again takes the reins. There are also strong hints here of what would eventually become Stronger Than Dirt. The energy here carries over into a finely played, sorrowful Ship of Fools before closing by rote with Saturday Night and U.S. Blues.

SUMMER

J U N E

1 *Marilyn Monroe, b. 1928*

2 *U.S. release of* Sgt. Pepper's Lonely Hearts Club
Band, *1967*

3 *6/3/76 Portland* ✳ *Comeback from
"retirement"*

4

5

6 *6/6/91 Deer Creek*

7 *6/7/91 Deer Creek*

8 *6/8/74 Oakland* ✳ *Playin'!*

9 *6/9/76 Boston Music Hall* ✳ *St. Stephen
breakout
6/9/77 Winterland* ✳ *Help* ➤ *Slip* ➤
Franklin's!

10 *6/10/73 RFK* ✳ *With the Allman Brothers
and Merl Saunders*

11 *6/11/91 Charlotte* ✳ *Victim!*

12 *Second Mount St. Helens' eruption, 1980* ✳
6/12/80 Portland ✳ *Scarlet* ➤ *Fire
transition precipitates Mount St. Helens' eruption*

13 *Thurgood Marshall becomes first black Supreme
Court Justice, 1967*

14 *Flag Day* ✳ *6/14/85 Greek* ✳ *Twentieth-
anniversary show* ✳ *6/14/91 RFK*

15 *6/15/76 Beacon* ✳ *6/15/85 Greek*

16 *6/16/85 Greek*

17 *6/17/75 Winterland* ✳ *Blues for Allah
breakout show; Help on the Way without lyrics
6/17/91 Giants* ✳ *Dark Star tease show*

18 *Paul McCartney, b. 1942* ✳ *6/18/74
Louisville*

19 *Lou Gehrig, b. 1903* ✳ *6/19/76 Oakland* ✳
Playin'!

Summer. The most
magical, unreal time of
year, when school's out
and even a nine-to-five
doesn't seem so bad.
Summer's the season that
passes the fastest—seems
no sooner is it here than
it's done come and gone,
my oh my.

Summer on tour was a
blast, hardly any other
way to put it. It was the
time when the weather
matched the musical heat
coming from the stage,
when one could dance
under the open sky and
actually contemplate the
crescent moon during
Terrapin. The sweet, ropy
smell of burning grass in
the open sunshine during a
raging Cassidy, the
smiling swirl of tie-dye . . .
what a treat. The Dead

20 *6/20/80 Anchorage*

6/20/83 Merriwether ✳ *Aborigine dreamsong rap in Sunshine Daydream*

21 *First day of summer*

22 *Kris Kristofferson, b. 1937*

23 *Robert Hunter, b. 1941*

24 *6/24/76 Tower Theater*

25 *6/25/91 Bonner Springs* ✳ *Scarlet* ➡ *Fire, Comes a Time!*

26 *Abner Doubleday, b. 1819* ✳ *6/26/74 Providence*

27 *Mel Brooks, b. 1926* ✳ *6/27/85 SPAC* ✳ *Zuckert!!!*

28 *6/28/74 Boston Garden*

6/28/85 Hershey Park

29

30

31 *6/30/84 Indianapolis* ✳ *Playin'!*

6/30/85 Merriwether ✳ *Shakedown!*

seemed such a part of our natural landscape that outdoors was where they seemed to belong. Outdoor shows also meant that Phil's bass boomed even fatter than usual, a phenomenon he once acknowledged, explaining that "standing waves in enclosed spaces tend to cancel out entire registers." Bleep.

Of course there *was* the sweltering heat to contend with at times—'82, '88 (remember Buckeye?), and '89 seem to stand out especially on that score. Total dehydration and heat prostration threatened more than once, the whole show experience seemingly reduced to an insatiable quest for water. I remember being particularly parched at the tour opener, Foxboro, in '89 and setting out across the desert of the stadium floor during the set

J U L Y

1 *Willie Dixon, b. 1915* ✽ *7/1/79 Seattle* ✽ *7/1/85 Merriwether Post Pavilion*

2 *Thurgood Marshall, b. 1908* ✽ *7/2/88 Oxford, Maine* ✽ *7/2/89 Foxboro* ✽ *Playin' opener, Friend Of to open second set*

3 *7/3/66 Fillmore Auditorium*

4 *Independence Day* ✽ *7/4/81 Manor Downs, Texas* ✽ *One More Fourth of July*

5 *Robbie Robertson, b. 1944*

6

7 *Ringo Starr (né Richard Starkey), b. 1940* ✽ *7/7/89 JFK*

8 *7/8/78 Red Rocks*

9

10

11 Skylab *plunges to Earth, 1979* ✽ *7/11/69 Flushing Meadow*

12 *7/12/90 RFK* ✽ *Dark Star!*

13 *7/13/84 Greek* ✽ *Dark Star returneth, with shooting star; Scarlet* → *Touch* → *Fire!*

14 *Woody Guthrie (né Woodrow Wilson Guthrie), b. 1912*

15 *7/15/88 Greek* ✽ *Scarlet* → *Fire!*

16 *7/16/90 Rich Stadium*

17

18 *7/18/72 Roosevelt Stadium*

19 *Keith Godchaux, b. 1948* ✽ *7/19/74 Fresno*

20 *Carlos Santana, b. 1947* ✽ *7/20/94 Deer Creek*

21 *Ernest Hemingway, b. 1899*

22

23 *Keith Godchaux, d. 1980* ✽ *7/23/90 World* ✽ *Brent's last show*

break—"water . . . water" I implored through cracked lips, unheard. Then . . . the cool sound of a drum circle from the back of the floor. I followed the beats. As they got louder and louder the crowd parted and there, like a shimmering mirage, was a celebrating group of drummers accompanying Heads dancing in ecstasy under a CASCADE OF COOL WATER from a spigot high up on the wall. Ecstasy, sweet drenching ecstasy.

There were also the twin hideousities of swollen tour ranks and stadium shows, but what of the splendor of Telluride, Red Rocks, Lewiston, the Greek? And,

24
25
26 *Brent Mydland, d. 1990* ❋ *7/26/72 Portland*
27 *7/27/73 Watkin's Glen "Soundcheck"*
28
29 *NASA established, 1958* ❋ *7/29/88 Laguna Seca* ❋ *China* ▶ *Crazy Fingers* ▶ *Rider; Complete, unsplit Playin'*
30
31

more prosaically, Laguna Seca and Oxford. Anywhere where you could see both the Dead *and* trees was a place you never wanted to leave— shades of halcyon days in Golden Gate Park.

The tours of Sugar Magnolia seasons past . . . '85, '88, Europe '90 stand out . . . the parking lot in full splendor, roaming around and taking in the Shakedown Streets, the familiar busses (and adding a few new freakmobiles to your mental collection), enjoying Frisbee and drumming and hacky-sacking and just plain cooling it in the sun, knowing that the only thing you had to do was walk through those gates in a couple of hours and then things would get even better. Time was, not so long ago, you could camp out in the parking lots—

A U G U S T

1 *Jerry Garcia, b. 1942*

2

3 *8/3/82 Starlight*

4

5

6 *8/6/74 Roosevelt Stadium*

7

8

9 *Jerry Garcia, d. 1995*

10 *8/10/82 U. Iowa*

11

12

13 *8/13/75 Great American Music Hall* ❋ Blues for Allah *release party* ❋ One From the Vault ❋ Make Believe Ballroom *bootleg*

14

15

16 *Babe Ruth, d. 1948* ❋ *Elvis Presley, d. 1977* ❋ *8/16/91 Shoreline* ❋ *First-set Dark Star*

17

18 *Nineteenth Amendment (women's suffrage), ratified, 1920*

19

20

21 *Hawaii becomes fiftieth state, 1959* ❋ *8/21/93 Autzen* ❋ *With Huey Lewis*

22 *Donna Godchaux, b. 1947* ❋ *8/22/93 Autzen*

23 *8/23/68 Shrine* ❋ *With 8/24,* Two From the Vault

24 *John Cipollina, b. 1943*

25 *National Park Service established, 1916* ❋ *Elvis Costello, b. 1954*

whole nomadic villages of Heads enjoying lazy nights as one long day melted into the next. A festival of friends, and high times indeed, the memory of which drew us to the Further Festival as much as the music. The Grateful Dead will always be the music of summer; that we can see them no longer, oh what a bummer.

26

27 *8/27/72 Veneta, Oregon* ✵ *Kesey Creamery benefit*

28

29 *8/29/83 Hult*

30 *Last Beatles concert, Candlestick, 1966*

31 *First giant squid captured alive, 1982* ✵ *"My eyestalks they are twisted, my tentacles are all in a knot"*

"The East Coast Deadhead still feels the pangs of showlessness every fall, and of course the summertime's done come and gone. . . . My antidote is a holiday week I'm trying to push: I call it Jerryweek, from August 1st to 9th every year. We celebrated in fine style this year and will do better next year; our candlelight parade from the bay to the ocean on Fire Island this year was quite appropriate, complete with music, incense, tie-dyes and posters."

—S. K.

JERRY'S PRESHOW REGIMEN

–3 hours: Meditation in crystal pyramid. Receive setlist from Jor-El.

–2½ hours: Consume large vat of steamed kale. Chase with egg cream.

–2 hours: Go to cubbyhole behind amps, pick up guitar (already tuned by Steve Parish) to bend strings; retune.

–1½ hours: Do about forty-five minutes of pure guitar finger exercises.

–45 minutes: Check effects, make sure all is in order. Check wah-wah twice.

–30 minutes: Get the feel of the place, rap a little, chill.

–15 minutes: A little Häagen-Dazs, some Reese's Pieces, maybe a root beer. Smoke a butt.

–5 minutes: Figure out with Weir whose turn it is to open.

–1 minute: "No, really, I could swear you went first last night. . . ."

0–+5 minutes: Additional tuning.

+7 minutes: "So what tune are we doing?"

+8–+10 minutes: More tuning.

You Don't Have to Ask ...

DID THE Dead take requests? Well, maybe ... In the late 5/15/70 late show they play Friend of the Devil again (they'd played it at the early show) as a request. In a week when the Dead indulged in some pretty impressive repartee with their audience, 10/30/71 has them seeming to fill a request for Truckin', 11/7/71 one for Casey Jones. And on the soundboard of 5/9/77, requests for Big River and Brown-Eyed Women are audible and requited, though coincidence is a real possibility. And there was that time when I *thought* Row Jimmy and Jerry immediately started *playing* Row Jimmy (now, if only he could have telepathically beamed what it *meant* ...).

One thing's for sure, though: the Dead *made* requests. Can you name the shows at which the following requests/questions were made/asked?

1. "Anyone want to buy a used PA?"
2. "Is there anyone here by the name of Frank Burns ... Fred Burns?"
3. "If there's a doctor in the house, would he please come backstage, 'cause there's a woman having a baby."
4. "Does anyone right nearby here have a D harmonica?"
5. "Any of you folks right in the first few rows here have a match?"
6. "If you see our bass player, won't you please return him home?"
7. "What do you wanna hear that'll take ten minutes? We've got ten minutes left."
8. "Dr. Beechwood. Calling Dr. Beechwood. Dr. Schott, calling Dr. Schott."
9. "Anybody missing a little kid named Frank?"
10. "And the riddle is, if you cross an octopus with a pig, what do you get?"
11. "Hey, can we get a little more guitars on the monitors, and a little less reverb?"

ANSWERS

1. 11/7/71 Harding Theater.
2. 4/18/71 SUNY Cortland.
3. 9/28/75 Golden Gate Park.
4. 3/18/67 Winterland.
5. 7/17/66 Fillmore.
6. 1/15/79 Springfield.
7. 4/5/69 Avalon.
8. 5/13/77 Chicago.
9. 5/6/70 MIT.
10. 2/14/70 Fillmore East.
11. 2/13/70 Fillmore East.

1977

1977

1977

1977

1977

1977

1977

1977

1977

1977

1977

1977

1977

1977

1977

1977

1977

h, 1977. Truly a great vintage for the Dead. I remember that when I first got my hands on the Bettyboards of May 5th through May 9th, I was convinced that these were the best shows the Dead had ever played. Hearing these shows led me to dub every '77 tape in sight and, on the evidence of these tapes, I became sure that this was the Dead's *year* ever, period. I know there are a lot of Heads out there who would "amen" that sentiment, and just as many who would denounce it heatedly. My feelings, for one, regarding 1977 have become decidedly more mixed. I feel that there's little doubt, though, that the aforementioned chunk of May (if nothing else in this year—and there's plenty more) ranks among the Dead's finest.

The "best year" argument is of course a pretty silly one, given the vagaries of taste and the great changes in sound (not to mention keyboard personnel) the band went through over its thirty-odd-year history. Yet there is a consensus of sorts on the hot years, and 1977 is one on many scores. There's a certain logic to this in the band's development. One starts by conceding that the years 1973–74 represented a musical peak on all scores: ensemble playing, exploratory jams, sound system, repertoire, and so on and so forth. This peak was then followed by the near total "retirement" of 1975, and their rebirth in 1976 with Mickey back. Nineteen seventy-six, as a year's work, is somewhat lacking. There doesn't seem to be much technically wrong with the Dead's playing, but the band is, for the most part (there are notable exceptions), without a real kickin' groove—to be expected, one would think, when a band like the Dead adds another part to the rhythm machine, even if that part is Mickey Hart. Hart himself has commented on this period of readjustment, noting in a 1990 interview with Blair Jackson that "the songs had slowed down [because] I was out of shape [and] Billy and I hadn't really played together for years." Late in 1976 and continuing into 1977, though, the band gets the rhythm machine to turn over with much greater regularity. So the best of '77 reaches peaks equal to the best of '74, but with a difference: The grooves are harder and deeper, owing to the addition of Mickey, but they tend to be *much* less exploratory, owing in part to same. It's been observed by Deadheads and said by band members alike that the band just couldn't turn the corners as quickly after Mickey's rejoining the band—in 1977 that energy is channeled into a harder-driving, more intent, and tighter sound.

The elements of the '77 sound are distinct. There is first and foremost a tightness in the band that borders on the telepathic, with Jerry and Phil playing in perfectly improvised counterpoint, with Keith stepping into Jerry's register the second he leaves it, and the whole thing held together with aggressive, martial drumming. A shining patina is added by the mix from Keith's organ and piano fills, Bob's *chukka-chukka* rhythm playing, and a shimmering overlay of cymbal-riding.

And the vocals, oh the vocals. This era represents a peak in Jerry's singing. It's true that his vocals from the eighties on took on a great gravitas and an irresistible feel of wizened wisdom, but here's his voice in full flower, matured past the sometimes reedy and nasal quality of earlier years, mellifluous and sweet, by turns youthful and innocent, sardonic and wry. He can make it break and he can give it enough throat for true soul on command. His range is fully in sync with his vocal imagination, which was both vast and eminently tasteful.

The curve of the quality of Bobby's voice is neither as easily traced nor as linear as Jerry's, but suffice it to say that this was also a good year for his singing. His vocal delivery seems very well considered and his interpretive powers are at the fore. He's not oversinging as he did at times in the early years, but he had that trait pretty much licked by 1972—think of all those beautiful Me and Bobby McGees and Black-Throated Winds. Add to this the (unfortunately rarer than one would hope) treat of Donna singing consistently on-key and, in the best of the '77 shows, beautifully and you have the Dead's best vocal mix to that point, unmatched until the introduction of Brent.

Of course regardless of the consistent quality of the vocals, '77's tightness can be seen as a double-edged sword. While the jams were often brilliantly innovative, the music tended to be less out-there than in the period before the retirement. The band did less full-bore opening up of tunes, choosing instead to do their improvisation, for the most part, within the song structure. Improvisation on 1977 tapes tends to mean the comping of solos within tunes rather than the spontaneous composition of new forms. This runs contrary to what a lot of people see as the essence of the Dead. On the other hand the Dead had a funkiness in '77—this is the era of "disco Dead," remember—that made the long Dancin' and Estimated jams, to name two songs that spring to mind, special in their own right.

Individual band members have said themselves at various times that the Dead's sets became more programmed—*ossified* was the word Phil used—after the introduction of the beautiful but less open-ended material from *American Beauty* and *Workingman's Dead*. The evidence in tapes and setlists bears this out to an extent: The Dead's sets become more varied from '69 onward, by the simple virtue of having more tunes to play. But if Dark Star → St. Stephen → The Eleven night after night doesn't seem all that varied on paper, well, just listen to the music play! And truth be told, the '67–'69 incarnation of the Grateful Dead found some fairly breathtaking ways to mix up a relatively small repertoire. They managed to do this in the period '69–'71 as well, with a much-expanded song list. The newer material with which they were mixing and matching, though, didn't allow for as much jamming room as the primal compositions, and the first signs of the first-set–second-set division are evident by early '70. Since the new song-based material wasn't so easy to "play through" (to borrow a golf term), one wasn't all that likely to see, say, a Dark Star → Cumberland → Other One. Such things happened, which is impressive, but not with overwhelming frequency. At least the old Pigpen numbers had been essentially blues and hence easily jammed upon. The acoustic sets of 1970 only seemed to speed and entrench the process of putting the "songs" in the first set and the "tunes/jams" in the second, which by 1972 was firmly in place.

The '72–'74 period is one in which the Dead tried to have their cake and eat it, too, regarding this demarcation of their material. Though the set-separation die is cast deeper in '72, there are, in first sets from that year, always a song or two for exploration, for example, Playin'. By 1973–74, famously the era of things being weird in the first set, getting weirder in the second, and flying out past the Oort Cloud in the third (when there was a third set to be had), the Dead were nonetheless picking and choosing where to open up. The large number of first-set tunes that one can fit onto ninety-minute tapes of this era's shows bears witness to this: There wasn't much "space" in these three- to six-minute versions of Loose Lucy, Deal, Promised Land, Beat It On Down, and so on, though the playing was generally loose, jazzy, and excellent. This was no doubt in part because the band knew that there would be plenty of exploration later in the program, and because, as with '72, there was generally a song in the first set that would allow some openness.

By '77 the Dead further codified the business of constructing a show, but with the result that each of the formerly brief first-set tunes increased in length and jamming. Unfortunately the areas for real spacey jamming, now pushed out of the first set nearly entirely, got smaller and smaller, eventually resulting in the compartmentalization of Drums and Space that began in the last stages of '77 but didn't really get fully under way until '78. The more predictable placement of Drums got under way in earnest, when the Dead returned to touring in the fall after canceling their summer tour.

Rock Scully's book, *Living with the Dead,* doesn't have all that much musical content (given the subject, that is), but it seems portentous that in discussing the 5/7/77 Boston show he digresses to give an exegesis of the drum duet and its popularity with the nondrumming segment of the band—a chance to chill, remediate, drink a cold one, eat a Ding Dong, whatever. In that show the drums fall at the later-to-become-nearly-carved-in-stone midway point in the second set. It's odd, though, that he should choose this show to extol the virtues of Drums as a time to chill—it's a real short one (because of the "mysterious elbow sequence" pictured in *Playing in the Band?*) and, at that early point in the year, still far from a regular occurrence.

What of the songs during this year? It was a big year for some of the tunes very clos-est to the hearts of Deadheads, both then and in retrospect—St. Stephen, Truckin', and Sugar Magnolias galore, the relatively recent Help $\rightarrow$ Slipknot $\rightarrow$ Franklin's suite, as yet unfragmented, the wondrous pairing of the new Estimated Prophet and the es-tablished masterwork Eyes of the World, and the instant classic Terrapin (alas, no Dark Stars, though—a fact more than slightly responsible for the lack of wide-open improvi-sational space, although this observation begs a "chicken or the egg"–type question). When I think of '77, I think of Lazy Lightning $\rightarrow$ Supplication, Samson and Delilah, The Music Never Stopped, Dancin'—all those shiny tunes, brassy and quicksilver slippery, with a hard beat. And though the setlists are a bit more standardized than in previous years, the oft-heard assertion that the '77 repertoire was in any way limited is more of a bum rap than Heads may realize: The Dead had a repertoire of about seventy tunes in 1974 (give or take some thematic jams); in 1976 they didn't even have sixty; by 1977 the number was back up to about eighty. On the other hand yet again, it is true that the band leaned very heavily on considerably fewer than eighty tunes.

It's interesting to me that, coming from the band, there's been very little—none that I could find—acknowledgment of 1977 as having been a special year for their playing. When speaking of Mickey's improved reintegration into the band after 1976, there's been, I suppose, the implication that 1977, coming after, was more musically successful on at least that score. More often '77 seems to get thrown together with accounts of the late-seventies Dead as burned out on touring and of the Keith/Donna problem and all that flowed into and from it. Scully's book certainly gives a hedonistic picture of that early-May run, replete with Kennedy kids and showgirls.

If the question of whether 1977 was the Dead's best year is a moot one, perhaps more compelling (and more provocative) is the question of whether it was the band's last con-sistently great year. It is of course an equally impossible question. But if by consistently great we mean the maintenance of a high batting average on all fronts—vocals, playing together, all graceful instruments making themselves known as such individually and together, what later year approaches '77? Donna and Keith's remaining years in the band sometimes achieve highs equal to the best of '77, but with much less frequency; '78 is *better* in some ways, as are '79 and '81—a couple of years with some very hot runs, but are generally regarded (and I think rightly so) as not having the consistency of '77 (and again one could argue until one is blue in the face as to the relative virtue of consistency, but I mean it in its most positive sense here); '82–'84, sick spring tours (and some great fall shows in '83 and '84 particularly) and sprawling Scarlet $\rightarrow$ Fires aside, are more hit-or-miss affairs than any of the years '77–'81; and though '85 was a killer year on a number of fronts (Garcia's solos come to mind, for one), the band also showed some definite fraying at the edges (Garcia's vocals come to mind, for one). The years '86, '87, and '88 can pretty much be discounted, I think—'86 for more or less obvious reasons, and '87 and '88 because of a rebuilding effort epitomized by the double thudding of a rhythm section often out of sync (with electronic drums, no less) and the odd, twangy sound of the guitars (especially Bobby). Nineteen eighty-seven epitomizes a version of the Dead that is playing it safe, a by-product of Jerry's recovery, many new audience members, and playing behind Dylan. Now . . . 1989–91—these are strong candidates: Outstanding song selections, a renewed commitment to musical weirdness, a very beautiful, round sound, the advent of MIDI among the ax wielders, Garcia's seeming reemergence as a full entity in the band—these all make a good case for either of these years. But the Dead were, it needs be conceded, at least a step slower. Does this matter? Perhaps not.

The changes, the changes. No perfect Dead. No best year. Better this, not so great that. Tomorrow's diamond in the rough may shine brighter than the whole of yesterday's "greatest" show. Such is life in real time. Many Heads go out of their way to slam '77 because of its being overtouted by others—opinions made against conventional wisdom are almost always couched in more incendiary rhetoric. "Overrated" becomes "ridiculously overrated." But if you happen to be among those convinced of the infallibility of '77 Dead, check out, for example, the horrendous Wheel from 10/30/77 Indiana University (although the Playin' → Other One → Drums that precedes it is totally sick).

3/18/77

W I N T E R L A N D

Here is some of the *Terrapin Station* material in its first blush, with a very young version of Estimated Prophet, the first and only Terrapin with the At a Siding, or L'Alhambra (an unusual title that has its roots in a Hart/Hunter collaboration that was eventually part of the Terrapin suite), appended, and the first Fire on the Mountain. Fire was originally intended for *Terrapin*—at least one studio recording was made—but did not see its official release until *Shakedown Street.* Actually Fire wasn't *originally* intended for a Dead album at all but for Mickey Hart's unreleased 1974 solo album. The Fire "rap" was recorded with Mickey on vocals, and a couple of versions have even surfaced with Steve Miller—of all people—handling vocal duties.

The first set features excellent versions of a number of tunes that would get a lot of stage time in '77: Half-Step, Sugaree, Peggy-O, Minglewood. Minglewood in particular is sick—full of fire. The big guns come out at the end of the set, though, prefaced by some tuning-related banter that calls to mind that of another night of debuts, 2/18/71—I guess careful tuning accompanied by nervous chatter is endemic to breakout shows. Phil announces the welcome news that "After about fifteen years in music each, we finally learned how to tune up last week. So we're gonna do it for you now, only this time—" Bobby interjects with "You'd be surprised at how much fun tuning up can be."

And then, deep breath, the first Scarlet → Fire is launched. Of course the audience doesn't know this yet—Scarlet Begonias has been in the repertoire for three years already. One of the first things of note in Scarlet is a good Jerryism, a slip of the tongue that makes "calling my eye" sound like "clawing my eye." It drags a bit in the beginning but starts to pick up a head of steam midway through. Donna sings her lilting, floating solo in the transition about as fully and powerfully as she ever has. The soloing, though, is still very rudimentary at this point. It's nevertheless a thrill to be able to witness this pivotal moment in Dead history. Fire itself, though immature, is well played, considering. Garcia establishes what will become a long-standing precedent by flubbing the second verse. The most intense moment comes with Garcia's quick slide down the neck of his guitar before playing the coda, to which the band *does* add some interesting elaborations, taking it beyond the bare bones, more so than they did for the transition jam.

The second set continues the new material with an early version of Estimated, which at this stage in its development is much less fluid than it would become—it's bouncier, choppier, with less of a groove. Bobby also sings some slightly different words here and there: Note ". . . ascend on wings of flame" and "My time come any *old* day."

The third-ever Terrapin gets off to a slow start but gathers momentum heading into "Inspiration . . ." Jerry's guitar wails above the ending theme. L'Alhambra—which begins with much the same sonic feel as '74 Mind Left Body Jams—is really hair-raising. Something about Jerry's guitar sound (is this insect fear?) in this eerie arabesque gets right into the pit of your stomach. It's a shame they didn't revisit this theme either as part of Terrapin or as a jam to be played out of Space, or wherever. Though rhythmically sloppy in places, it succeeds mightily in creating a mood distinct from that on the album.

Not Fade Away is given a booming intro out of Drums, and the song's middle sees the band breathe new life into this standard. They also add some new musical structure to the closing, with Jerry playing superheated Gibsonesque solo figures above the band, replete with harmonics and other esoteric effects. He slides his pick all the way down a string several times, surf-rock style (look out, Dick Dale!)—the first instance is very loud and you can hear Donna, genuinely surprised, yell, "Wow!" Versions such as this one serve as a reminder of the Dead's ability to discover new textures in even those songs they'd been playing for years. The closing vocal trio—Bobby, Jerry,

HELP ➠ SLIPKNOT! ➠ FRANKLIN'S OF NOTE

❋ 6/17/75 Winterland (Help ➠ Slipknot! without words)

❋ 8/13/75 Great American Music Hall (*One From the Vault*)

❋ 6/14/76 Beacon

❋ 6/19/76 Capitol Theater, Passaic, New Jersey

❋ 6/24/76 Tower Theater, Upper Darby, Pennsylvania

❋ 10/9/76 Oakland

❋ 2/26/77 San Bernardino

❋ 5/9/77 Buffalo

❋ 5/22/77 Pembroke Pines (*Dick's Picks Volume Three*)

❋ 6/9/77 Winterland

❋ 9/11/83 Sante Fe Downs

❋ 10/31/83 Marin

❋ 4/1/84 Marin

❋ 4/22/84 Philly

❋ 10/8/89 Hampton

❋ 10/19/89 Philly

❋ 3/24/90 Albany (*Without a Net* version, with Branford Marsalis)

❋ 3/30/90 Nassau

❋ 6/14/91 RFK

❋ 9/10/91 MSG (with Branford Marsalis)

❋ 6/28/92 Deer Creek

❋ 8/22/93 Eugene

❋ 9/22/93 MSG

❋ 5/26/95 Seattle

and Donna—is also a real treat. Is this the best Not Fade ever? Who knows. Does it come close? Yes, it does.

A slow St. Stephen follows—a pretty standard version of a great tune, succeeded by a great version of a standard tune, Around and Around. Keith and Jerry are in cahoots here, playing perfectly synchronous fills. Like St. Stephen, it starts out slow but it soon builds to a very hot groove, with Jerry taking solo turns in the intraverse spaces where he would generally play more chordally. Keith is just all over the place, especially in the double-time jam at the end, playing a rolling left-hand vamp while tickling the upper-register ivories with great aplomb. As Phil once said, that guy had it all. Here he shows some of the spark that was more evident in his early playing with the Dead. The Uncle John's encore is a really nice cap to an important show.

5/4/77
THE PALLADIUM

This is a big Phil show, with Jerry not as much of a presence as he would be in the days that followed. The second-set opening Estimated rocks as hard as any of the great editions in the '77 volume, though Garcia's soloing isn't quite as aggressive as in other (especially later) versions. Phil steps out in the Scarlet → Fire every bit as much as he does in the 5/8/77 version. Bobby does some really nice detail work here too—listen for the fragment of his China Cat intro lick in there. The transition is very different from that of just four days later. For a long while out of Scarlet Jerry is playing way down in the mix, with Bob, Keith, and the drums (lots of cymbal and high hat) playing circular staccato figures. Phil plays a rhythmic lead while Donna coos mellifluously. When Jerry does step out, he does so in a Kenny Burrell-esque jazz tone—more his Fender side than the Gibson alter ego more present at Cornell. The leads themselves are gentler as well. Fire is well jammed but lacks a certain amount of fluidity. The closing jam really picks up once Phil allows some air into the tightly packed notes he's been playing, loosening up with a melodic line that leaves Jerry some breathing room to really go to town. As a result Fire ends exceptionally well.

The Terrapin that follows is a good one, but gains more of its intensity from fine vocals and the exertions of the rhythm section than it does from Jerry's guitar. Jerry finally brings the Wolf out of hibernation for a masterfully rendered Playing in the Band, the show's highlight. Playin' is where the Dead discovered their most exploratory jams in 1977, and this one sees the band mining this rich vein with the zeal of prospectors. The closing jam is a long, dreamy unraveling that eventually drops the band right into a soulfully sung Comes a Time. Though the 5/9 version has the edge, this one is also extremely well sung and played. The Dead take particular care in constructing the bridge from Comes a Time back into Playin', producing a work of painstaking craftsmanship that is marvelous to behold. It's this Playing → Comes a Time sandwich that distinguishes this set from, and places it on a par with, the shows that follow.

5/5/77
NEW HAVEN

If the May 7th Boston show and May 9th at Buffalo tend to stand somewhat in the shadow of 5/8/77 Cornell (more the case for 5/7), then New Haven finds itself standing squarely *behind* the most famous of the Dead's May shows in 1977, for its song list makes it seem almost a sound check for that one. While not many of the shows from this May's edition of the Dead could be termed obscure (especially now that the 5/22 Pembroke Pines show has been released in the *Dick's Picks* series), this is probably the least-sought-after of the Bettyboards from this month. It's definitely cut from the same cloth as the others, and though many of its songs can be found in what may be deemed more successful versions in the May 7–9 space, it will still meet with hearty approval from any who enjoy those.

Bobby starts off the show by "asking that age-old question, 'Why doesn't it ever work?' " "It" proceeds to work just fine.

The opening Promised Land is made by the way Bobby enunciates the lyrics. Jibing nicely with the airplane-heavy lyrics of Promised Land is Bobby's apology after the tune: "We're sorry to be late, but you see a funny thing happened to us on the way to the show tonight: Our airplane went the wrong way."

Sugaree is huge, standing out even in a month with some of the best versions of this song ever played (both 5/19 and 5/22 leap to mind). Jerry's first solo break sees him alternating between cascading notes of molten lava and lightning strumming. After the second chorus a much longer jam gives the rest of the band a chance to stretch out, with Bobby and Keith playing nicely off each other. When Phil asserts himself, the theme is picked up, and it's then that Jerry cuts loose again, with a towering solo that spirals to its greatest height, appropriately, right before dropping the listener down again into the verse, an exercise in perfect timing that brings a wave of cheers audible even on this pristine soundboard.

One of Keith's best features as a musician was his ability to keep things going nicely in the quiet sections of songs, as he does to great effect in the next verse break. The band gets down so low it almost sounds as if the song is about to end, a gorgeous effect with the counterpoint of Phil's bass thudding ominously in the background. This passage evokes a wildflower-filled field beginning to be claimed by the shadows of thunderheads in a sunny springtime turning cold.

Tennessee Jed is bouncy and fun, with Jerry taking the care to give the lyrics the sardonic reading they really need for this song to be fully interesting. Jerry really struts his guitar stuff, too, in the last solo break, cramming all sorts of aside-type licks into the spaces provided by the solo on the main theme.

Nineteen seventy-seven was a year full of gorgeous Looks Like Rains, and the one played this night may be the finest of them all in every respect, probably the best version they had played since '72. Phil's measured bass lines provide the perfect counterpoint to Jerry's shimmering, soaring guitar and the lilt of Keith's piano. Bobby's vocal is subtle and expressive, and Donna's harmonies are on-key. I nominate her first two "Brave the storm to comes" at the end as one of her finest vocal moments ever with the band. And listen to the guitar rain that Jerry drizzles and dopples on everybody in the background. Shivers! Chills!

The way they bring this one all the way down to Bobby, Donna, and Jerry and then build it back up with Phil's thunder mark this as a definitive version. Perhaps it is not as precise as those of 1972, but it has more emotive impact.

Lazy Lightning → Supplication is a close cousin to the more famous 5/8/77 pairing—again, no faint praise. The two are so close in some respects in fact that I find myself bracing for the "whoosh" of the Bettyboard splice of May 8th in the "My lightnin' toos." In the end, however, it's still the Cornell version that's the hotter of the two, by dint of Jerry's more ferocious strumming and Bobby's more precisely attacked vocals in "Supplication." Peggy-O is given a beautiful treatment, and the Music Never Stopped that follows is huge, a thumping, rocking monster, with Jerry and Phil building to peak after bottom-drop-out peak, and Keith cascading down the other end of the summits with stop-on-a-dime piano rolls. Most people tend to give the edge to the 5/7/77 version, but my opinion is that this one rocks even harder.

The second set kicks off with a flawless Bertha, which is, on technical points, a hair better than the next one at Boston. The Dead were able to put such punch into perennial set workhorses such as Bertha during this era because they paid such close attention to the details of the musical arrangements. Note, for example, the percussive double-punch that comes after the "bended knees" line—especially the first time around.

Jerry takes some typically breathtaking envelope-filtered solos in Estimated, and then there's a Scarlet that positively blazes its way into Fire. This one is the last before the famous one at Cornell three days later, the best-known version from perhaps the most famed Dead show. I'm not going to commit any heresy here—the Cornell version is clearly the superior of the two—but this more than holds its own. And it does have a certain feel of being at least an unconscious dry run for the biggie. The rhythmic sureness, the funkiness, and the tempo are all in place. Jerry's guitar rips in Scarlet, too. In the New Haven transition, though, he is much less questing, as is he during the majority of Fire, only really stepping out near the end, and then a bit less fluently (remember that this is all relative!) than at Cornell. So think of this one as a basics track for one of the hottest tunes to come out of the Dead's favorite recording studio—the stage.

Fire slides effortlessly into Good Lovin', though with less drama than the thumping bass lines that signal the transition from Bertha in the 5/9 Buffalo show. This one, however, ultimately packs more of a punch. Jerry builds the lead through three different runs of the verses-chorus structure, trying new musical ideas each time, as if to say "Or I could do it like this. How do you want it, man?" (I'm convinced that if Jerry had been a basketball player—an improbable thought if ever there was one—he would have been a trash talker on a par with His Airness or Reggie "Cheryl" Miller.)

A long intertune break reveals tuning hints of St. Stephen, which is duly delivered, with a flawless opening from Jerry. It builds up a nice head of steam by the second verse, all in sync, save for a slight miscue where Donna comes in too soon (with the wrong line to boot) during Jerry's first solo break. But he isn't done yet, not by a long shot. If you've ever wondered what the Cornell St. Stephen would sound like if it had been left intact (that is, without the Not Fade sandwich), then you need do no more than listen to this one. It goes into some interesting spaces in the middle, with the percussion at one point seeming to suggest Truckin' (with corresponding audience reaction).

This very hot show ends with a large dose of Bobby, who shreds his vocal cords in an exuberant Sugar Magnolia but still manages to return for a raspy Johnny B. Goode encore.

5/7–9/77
BOSTON ● CORNELL ● BUFFALO

For many, these three nights in early May '77 represent the Dead at their very best. Others prefer the unpredictability of the preretirement years or the rich sonic mélange of the MIDI-fied post–Dark Star revival years, but if the Dead had only played from '76 to '78, it would be hard to dispute that these were among their finest concerts. Given their sound, repertoire, and performance parameters during this era, these dates achieved perfection.

They are reviewed together here because their setlists, despite some repitition of tunes, comprise a cycle of sorts of the songs the Dead were performing at the time. In three successive nights the band played forty-six of the roughly seventy-seven tunes in their repertoire in 1977. The performances complement each other very well and are certainly of a piece. Even excellent shows from later in the month—5/13, 5/19, 5/22—don't sound like these. Of those that come before, 5/5/77 comes closest in sound but does not match these three shows in tightness or the ineffable "X" factor. All three are also treated together here because perfection is tough to review—bouncing them off of one another takes them out of that vacuum.

Of the three I've always been partial to the first night—Boston. That's somewhat contrary to conventional Deadhead wisdom, in which the Cornell show is generally held up as the pinnacle and Buffalo is the show most often seized upon by "contrarians" (though regard for any one of these shows hardly makes one a contrarian). The Scarlet → Fire and the St. Stephen → Not Fade → St. Stephen and yes, the Dew from Cornell may make it more of a classic show, but there are moments from 5/7 that make me *fly*. And that's how those who prefer 5/9 feel as well, about the Comes a Time and the Help → Slip → Franklin's.

The first set from Boston just might rank as the best since the first-set—second-set division became entrenched; in other words, excluding wonders such as Doin' That Rag, Dark Star → St. Stephen → The Eleven → Lovelight. Going straight to the crux of the matter: Half-Step—just about the best ever played. In my book only 11/6/77 comes close, and 9/3/77 is more heat than light. It begins with Weir good-naturedly roasting Billy on the occasion of his "eighteenth" birthday, and then . . . whew, look out! The arrangement of this one, with the longest bout of soloing illustrating the just-sung "On my way" and spilling out into the cool easings of "Across . . . ," with another sick jam to close, shows an exquisite sense of timing. The vocals are gorgeous and powerful, Jerry singing clear as a bell and really climbing the ladder at the end of the "Rio Grand-eos." And the playing, particularly the Jerry-Phil interplay, is nothing short of phenomenal. Here is a quintessential example of Jerry's skill not only in playing but in constructing a solo. The way the interior jam slowly builds in tempo and complexity to dizzying heights is signature Jerry. The fanning at the end of this jam, punctuated by Keith's key roll, the little Phil solo in response to the line Jerry has just played during the slide into the bridge represents the Dead at their best. Add Bobby's grace notes and tight playing, some thudding tom runs from Mickey and Billy, Donna's excellent backups, and the cascading Phil runs in counterpoint to Jerry's ascending lines in the closing solo, and you've got one of the tastiest morsels of Dead there is. *And* it goes racing off fluently into an outstanding Big River.

The songs that come before and after are played with such enthusiasm and virtuosity as to make the Half-Step seem almost routine within the set's context. The opening Bertha, with Jerry and Donna's "Wooo!" echoing feedback and exuberant "anymores" tips the Dead's hand early—they're *psyched*. The band's energy courses through the little things like the "One, two, three, four!" count-off to Cassidy, Jerry's "little ears" improvisation in Deal, and the way he draws out "shoooz," the high-stepping excitement of the song's first solo—this is the stuff of which memorable shows are made. Make no mistake: This is one of those "Wait until that deal—*ga-wonggg*!" versions, Jerry seeming to revel in the sheer *metal*-ness of it all. Peggy-O builds irresistibly, polished by Bobby's grace notes, a patina of cymbals, and Keith's right-hand run at the end. Minglewood wins my vote as best ever, Jerry and Bobby giving it much raunch as the drums press their attack, Bobby's vocals ranging from the growl of "born in the desert" to the yelp of "wanted man . . ." and even doing a killer Elvis in "Yes and my number-one occupation . . ."

Everything they touch just turns to gold throughout the set as they close with all-time versions of Jed and Music, everyone (especially Garcia and Lesh) playing with a driving force and agility.

The quirky second set smokes as well. The jaunty Terrapin opener is perhaps a bit unripe but technically right on and interesting not only for its tempo but for its transition into a blazing Samson in which Phil goes off. A mid-tempo Friend Of and another '77 Estimated inferno round out the set's beginning. Eyes is led by Phil, with Jerry bubbling up and twisting around his bass notes like the tendrils of some rapid-growth aquatic vine. Drums is short and concise, leading into the patient construction of a paragon Wheel. Space is also short and to the point—Horsehead Nebula, warp nine; back to Earth again, warp nine. "Earth" in this case is Wharf Rat, another one for the books, closed up by a raging Around and U.S. Blues encore.

The next night at Cornell is one that is known to practically every Deadhead. Ever since the soundboard of this (and Boston and Buffalo as well) became available, it has been regarded as a classic that would inevitably be a part of those core first ten or so tapes in a Head's collection. The emergence of the Bettyboard of this show (so-named after Betty Cantor-Jackson, then sound engineer for the Dead; this and a wealth of other soundboard masters emerged into the tape-trading scene in 1987 after they were auctioned off as a lot because of unpaid storage fees; some, like the 6/77 Winterland run, began to circulate some years later) married pristine sonic clarity, rich in dynamic range, with an already well-known setlist and performance. (It should be noted that there is a very good audience recording of this show. It has practically ceased circulating due to the obvious superiority of the soundboard, but is worth having for the completist because it lacks the tough-to-stomach splice during the hot first-set Supplication jam.) The result was that it caused the show to be sought after, traded, collected, and lauded out of proportion even to its clear excellence. The show is so overwhelmingly popular—it regularly garners top honors in any number of categories in *DeadBase*'s reader polls—as to have inspired an almost virulent backlash among some Heads, which is again out of all proportion to its clear excellence (the same can be said about 1977 in general). Hey—it's a great show. And it's one of the best of the postretirement era.

Like the night before and after, its first set is fantastic, full of vigorous jamming. The Minglewood opener runs a very close second to the Boston version, and Loser, El Paso, and They Love Each Other each see some of their best performances here, though Keith's organ on Loser walks a thin line between strength and heavy-handedness. Jack Straw and Deal are powerhouses, easily equaling or surpassing their Boston predecessors. In retrospect it's interesting to see this pair, later a perennial opener and closer respectively, in the middle of the set—this gives a clue to the set's power. The highlight, though, has to be a Lazy Lightning → Supplication that merges real fire (Weir's superlative, growling vocals) with a smoothness that evokes the recording studio (Jerry and Bob's guitar, Keith's organ, the drums). The jamming is generous on this tune, Jerry scaling syncopated heights in an impressive collection of trademark runs. The set keeps on giving with landmark performances of the Jerry-Bobby yin-yang tunes Brown-Eyed Women and Mama Tried, and a phenomenal Dancin' as slick as the Studio 54 dance floor, as flammable as a 100 percent polyester white three-piece suit.

For the past ten years at least, the Cornell second set has been perhaps the most-listened-to eighty-odd minutes of live Dead, so I won't much belabor it here; if you haven't heard it, I suggest putting down this book and getting it from just about any tape collector, if only to hear what everyone is or has been talking about. It is, to be sure, a juggernaut, remarkable for the way in which it actually builds in intensity from the white-hot Scarlet → Fire opener (kicked off in fine fashion by a Take a Step Back that ranks with the great lead-ins of 8/13/75, 11/5/77, 6/15/85, and 9/14/90) through maybe the most kickin'-ly wah-wah-fied Estimated ever, to a St. Stephen → Not Fade → St. Stephen that approaches the superhuman in its improvisational smoothness and excitement—all into an awesome Dew that showcases some of Jerry's most affecting fanning. The Scarlet → Fire, like the other tunes of this set, wears an air of definitiveness (unfairly if not uncomfortably, many Heads would say) that tends to obscure its most sublime idiosyncrasy. When this one saw heavy play on my deck, it was not for Jerry's ubiquitous bubbling up in the transition (okay . . . that *helped*) but for the bouncing superball bass figures with which Phil announces Scarlet. The chiming Scarlet intro that Bobby usually plays is fantastic—quintessentially Dead—but I don't think there would have been too much complaining if Phil had superseded it with these licks more often. Speaking of complaining, I wonder how many picky Deadheads left Barton Hall muttering about the "short second set."

The third night of this troika has, as noted above, many devotees. If one can point to one mark of distinction between it and the preceding two shows, it might be the slightly raunchier cast to Jerry's guitar—his tone is generally rounder in Boston and Cornell. Like its predecessors, this is an out-and-out great performance.

The first set opens with one of the best Help → Slipknot → Franklin's of the year, probably second only to the 6/9 Winterland edition. Given how well the Dead performed this trio in '77, it's a real shame they didn't play it more—the one time they played it on the fall tour (10/11) was the last full suite until its '83 revival. Jerry plays with some hairy distortion in the Slipknot, and he engineers a sideways, almost playful entrance to Franklin's. It's great how Jerry blows a couple of lines in this Franklin's and then sings, "If you get confused . . . ," lending verity to the aphorism with about a minute's worth of intricate soloing (and how many times has *that* happened? 6/14/91, for one, comes to mind). Franklin's pulls into the station chugging full steam on the tracks of Weir and Garcia's locomotive strumming.

The set builds on its impressive start with outstanding versions of Brown-Eyed Women and Cassidy. Jed, though not quite as hard-rocking as the Boston edition, contains one of Garcia's best vocal performances in that song, especially in the way he elongates the Drink all day and correlative lines, and puts such emphasis on "the letters read. . . ." An excellent Big River and Peggy-O seem to be in response to requests from the crowd. Sunrise is not an apparent request filler, but it is powerful. Music is just as kicking here as it was in Boston, if not more so, Garcia fanning up a gale at the climax, marred only by a harsh reel splice.

The second set opens with one of the most fun, not to mention slow and laid-back, Bertha → Good Lovin' pairings, Phil ringing in Good Lovin' with those fat rolls of bass. Then it's Jerry's turn again, for which he delivers a Ship of Fools with a hugely favorable passion-to-technical-merit ratio. Estimated, which comes next, was played at all three of these shows; this is another glorious rendition. The Other One is great throughout, but what *makes* this one is Garcia's obsessive repetition of the fuzz-laden descending line he rides into a short Drums that functions primarily as a rhythmic setup for Not Fade Away. This one is firmly in the tradition of the best Not Fades, eschewing slavery to the beat in favor of sinuous, Allmanesque lines from the guitarists.

The highlight of the set and show, though, has to be Comes a Time. It is a masterpiece. The vocals are beautiful—flawless—but Jerry really does his expressive talking in a cursing and weeping guitar solo of such complexity and wrenching emotion as to be completely breathtaking. Soaring notes of hope are juxtaposed with deep, fuzzy mutterings and harmonic teardrops in a virtuoso instrumental interpretation of a

Leash Laws

I remember a rhetorical question about Cassidy asked by a friend of mine in college: "What the hell does that mean, 'I can tell by the mark he left, you were in his dream'? Did he, like, take a shit?" Higher education indeed.

raging inner conversation. And then the storm passes into tranquil, soothing lines, its fury spent.

As if in keeping with Comes a Time's ending, the show ends on a very upbeat note. Keith dapples an involving Sugar Magnolia with upper-register arpeggios to close the set in a summery mode, and a reggaefied Uncle John's—reclaiming the feel of the 1973–'74 versions—keeps the sunny vibe alive.

These shows are so popular and overhyped by some Deadheads that it's easy to approach them with cynicism in theory, but listening to them cannot help but leave one with the feeling that their exalted place in the Dead's canon is richly deserved.

5/19/77
FOX THEATER

Yet another excellent show from May '77, this one distinguishes itself not only through fine playing but through innovative set building in the second set as well, with a surprising Terrapin-initiated jam.

The first set kicks off with a strong Promised Land in which Keith acquits himself very well. Things really get rocking, though, with a Sugaree that serves as a one-way express to the zone, building hypnotically to a peak that grabs your frontal lobe by the ears and gives it a good tattooing. Jerry gives us a little of everything in the climax, first syncopating high on the neck and then fanning all listening into a frenzy. Bobby takes the opportunity to remind us that it's Ho Chi Minh's birthday after El Paso and then the Dead proceed to reel off a fine, dramatic Peggy-O, a Looks Like Rain with some very pretty Jerry "rain," and a good Row Jimmy.

Regardless of what follows, then, the quality of the set is already assuredly high. What follows, though, is probably the hottest stuff in the set. While Bill's fixing his drum because "something ain't right," you can plainly hear Donna yell, "Are you ready?" and then "Play real loud!" before ripping with Bobby into an outrageously hot Passenger. Donna's close harmonies with Bobby here are right on the money. Jerry of course rages and there's lots of Phil. A great Loser follows, Jerry delivering a cutting solo, and then Dancin' to close. This one is as hot as the best of its '77 brethren, which is saying a lot. Phil and Jerry play counterpoint as if they are two sides of the same musical brain.

The second set starts with Weir putting the crowd through some bizarre motions—having them "turn around real slow" with their hands in the air. Could this be what Jerry meant when he said that the potential power the Dead have over Deadheads was, if abused, "perilously close to fascism"? What benevolently trippy dictators!

A generic Samson starts things off, but Ramble On kicks out the stops with a high-steppin' ". . . hundred verses of ragtime" bridge. Estimated, though not bad, is undistinguished in a year with so many outstanding versions. The real second-set stuff gets under way with a taut Terrapin, Donna and the drums particularly on. Terrapin turns into a Playin' with a long main jam and then a bass-led section where Phil carves out some new territory. Jerry plays loping scale runs in a mode quite different from his speedy staccato jamming in this tune in the eighties. Here he sustains the top and bottom notes of the scales and is far more legato in his phrasing. So different and seemingly unrelated are Jerry and Phil's parts that it sounds as if the band is "going out"—dividing their rhythmic allegiance among Mickey and Billy and playing in different times of which the overarching time signature—10/4—is a multiple. When the band regroups on the plateau of the main thematic chords, they're really cooking. They tear into the Uncle John's intro, Jerry at the vanguard. The momentum of Uncle John's is carried into a real rolling-thunder Drums with very little letup on the way to a very well executed Wheel. The Dead achieve a sparkling clarity in the "won't you try . . ." section that sets this version apart.

Playing with great crispness and considerable momentum, the Dead decide to take a chance next by going from The Wheel into their first China Doll since '74. The result is one of quiet perfection that begs the question of why they didn't go on to play the tune more in '77. The transition back into Playin' is the most exciting part of the whole jam. The drummers establish a clocklike, metronomic pulse against which Jerry carries on a long, patient dialogue, a forerunner of some of his bouts of tasteful domination in '78. Bobby and the drums add momentum to Jerry's three A.M. meanderings; when they state the Playin' theme, first lightly and then in an ever-building wave of sound, it carries the force of an epiphany.

In a year where many shows sounded alike despite consistently excellent playing, this artfully constructed second-set jam hearkens back to the fabulous Playin' jams of '73.

ENGLISHTOWN

Now *this* is a show I'd call overrated, owing no doubt in part to the fact that it was so well attended (and so widely circulated due to a pretty good FM broadcast), a huge crowd turning out to see the first Dead show in three months and the only one of the summer. Despite some very hot moments, the teeming multitude must have been disappointed if they expected to hear the precision and intensity that marked the Dead's playing in May and early June. What they heard instead was the first incarnation of the more straight-ahead, arena-rock-ish incarnation of the band that would prevail over most of the fall tour and into '78.

The first set gets off to a fairly sluggish start, the band out of practice and taking a while to turn the engine over. Things get going with a vengeance, though, after a lively "Step Back" midway through the set. The Half-Step played next is one of the all-time best, though it does not match the intricacy and musical subtlety of 5/7 or 11/6/77. It is nonetheless fantastic on its own terms, the main jam long and generous and featuring some terribly exciting fanning up the neck from Jerry. He also plays some lovely, gossamer notes with accents from first Keith then the drums and Phil in the quiet space before the "Across . . ." bridge. It's not *the* best, but it's on the short list for sure.

The rest of the set is excellent, starting with a pretty Looks Like Rain in which Bobby and Donna interact very nicely. A sad, wistful Peggy-O moves along steadily with a fine build and a dynamic interverse jam. Minglewood is pretty hot, as '77 Minglewoods tend to be (Lord knows they played it enough that year), and Friend of the Devil is gorgeous, a stunner. It's fully jammed out, just as slow and shimmering as you please, with some great drum fills to boot—takes you to the zone and keeps you there for a long time. The set ends on a strong note with a laid-back and simmering Music Never Stopped that turns more agro at the end with some fearsome fanning.

The second frame starts auspiciously with Phil applauding the audience: "Okay, let's hear it for you 'cause this is the best crowd we've seen in a looong time." Bertha starts from there with Keith taking a long roll down the keys. The Bertha → Good Lovin' combo is one of the hotter versions of the year (especially the Good Lovin' half of the pair). The set really picks up, though, with a fiery Estimated into a beautiful and unique Eyes. Jerry's unadornedly percussive guitar here makes him sound almost like a piano as he makes those frolicking triplet runs. This one really sounds like no other Eyes, with two very pretty solos. It's followed up by a smoking Samson that shows the Wolf's range, moving from a basic Fender sound to a straight-up Gibson tone in the space of a tune. The Dead leave the stage briefly at the end of Samson—legend has it that this break was taken in order to review Truckin', but equipment problems offer a far more likely explanation.

The next song, He's Gone, is a mess unfortunately with flubbed entrances and lackluster playing. The band recovers strongly, though, with a long, jammy Not Fade Away. Then Mickey sounds the police whistle and . . . the triumphant return of Truckin'! This one's a trucker's Truckin', brawny and unshaven, heavy on guitars and drums, unabashedly *rocking* as hard as any passage in the Dead's history. A solid Terrapin encore rounds out the show in fine fashion.

11/5/77
ROCHESTER

The Dead's '77 fall tour evinced much of the same fire and almost offhanded excellence that characterized the legendary spring shows. The three-show upstate New York swing taken by the band in early November to end the tour represents what is perhaps its peak. This show, it should be noted, is not only generally hot but a total Phil Phest.

The first set opens with an all-time version of Minglewood that is given that extra spark by some excellent Jerry soloing in a country-blues mode, and peals of Phil thunder from the upper end of his register to the bottom. Half-Step drags a bit in the beginning—Keith's playing in particular is weak here, as it is through the whole of the first set—until Jerry and Bob breathe some life into it with some extrasharp playing, Bob laying down a number of his trademark arpeggiated licks. Phil manages to further pick up the slack in the solo break before the "Across . . ." bridge. Jerry lets rip here, playing soaring lines with wicked hooks as the rhythm section builds a thick wall that he just punches through with a stab of guitar light at the jam's pinnacle, a perfectly timed release that has all the force of a cannon shot. "Across . . ." is sung very sweetly, and it's instructive for younger Heads to note the cheers that greet Donna when she chimes in with some nice harmony here. Jerry's vocals are also great, especially when he starts to climb the ladder. They bring it down real low and then build it back up again as the launching pad for a white-hot closing jam. Though not as long as the 9/3/77 edition, nor perfect, as is 5/7/77, this one ranks among the very best for pure intensity.

Looks Like Rain starts out very spare, instrumentally, the better to hear Donna nailing her harmony part (and presumably the better for Donna to hear herself, which is no doubt a big part of *why* she nails it). Jerry's sound and phrasing are especially trumpetlike here, more so toward the end of the song. Phil once again asserts himself, playing some very loud lead lines. After Looks Like Rain we get an indication of the front-of-stage crowding at this show:

JERRY: "People up—uh, hello?—The people up front are getting smashed horribly again. If everyone on the floor could sorta try to move back it would be helpful."

PHIL/BOBBY: "Move back, move back, move back, move back, move back."

JERRY: "It's hard for us to get off seeing smashed human bodies up here. Give us a little mercy."

Jerry then launches into Dire Wolf, which seems to be his pet piece of musical commentary when confronted with hideous vids (also sung by him under death threats at Nassau '79 and Deer Creek '95). This version is played pretty fast, with enthusiastic vocals and Donna still right on. A very speedy Mama Tried, through which Jerry's solos simply ricochet, shares its last beat with the first beat of Big River, a masterful segue. Jerry's Candyman is so-so, but the set-closing Jack Straw → Deal is big and beefy.

Phil makes his presence known from the start of the second set, with a solo that the drums and Jerry join after a time, creating a sinuous backdrop for the only Take a Step Back that could be described as beautiful. It's kind of a shame, though, that what could have developed into a momentous set-opening improvisational jam was wasted on having to tell the audience not to crush one another. Sure, this jam saved lives, but too bad it was necessary. Eyes starts out strong, with Phil and Jerry going off right out of the gate, but it loses some of its drive when Bobby, apparently bored with holding down the rhythm part, starts playing noodly little figures in an increasingly tentative fashion, forcing Jerry to descend from the looping heights of his soloing to hold down the rhythm. Keith meanwhile does nothing *but* play the rhythm part, pounding out the same E-major-seventh chord over and over again. This period roughly marks the beginning of his decline within the Dead. Luckily Bobby regains his footing sufficient to assist Phil, Jerry, and the drums in making this the hot version it ends up being. Phil's big phat solo right in the middle doesn't hurt matters either. Momentum from the end of Eyes carries over into Samson, which just may be the hottest one ever—this and and the next night's stand out even among '77 versions. It seethes with Jerry's raunchy, crunching power chords and screaming southern rock leads. As for the drums, they sound as if they're trying to *flay* the head off the lion.

After such a scorching Samson, It Must Have Been the Roses comes as a splash of cool water, a chance for the band to take a breath and assess. All are clearly ennervated by what has come before, however, making this a very forward-leaning Roses. The heat returns with a ferocious Estimated, to which Keith's organ playing lends a real full-bodied flavor. The Dead cover a lot of territory in the closing jam. He's Gone experiences a nice slow build to the bridge and contains a long "Nothing's gonna bring him back" coda vamp before ceding to Drums. Phil, obviously feeling it, does some more soloing over Drums, which eventually insinuates itself slyly into The Other One, Jerry slithering in and out of a relentless rhythmic attack like some quicksilver Spanish snake. This long intro witnesses Jerry adopt a variety of sounds for his tireless soloing, until the song finally locks into the beginning with a *BAM!* as keyboards, guitars, and drums all come crashing down as one, throwing off the energy of a supernova. The Dead build to peak after peak in the stretch before the vocals, the sonic density relieved only by interludes of Jerry's flitting Spanish-flavored solo runs as the band executes awe-inspiring dynamic shifts, on a dime. It's surprising that one doesn't hear more about this version.

A suitably rocking Sugar Magnolia closes the set, and Saturday Night seems almost subdued in relation to what has come before as Weir and the band reflect bemusedly on a "crazy, crazy night." Then it's all over, with a "good night till next year."

11/6/77
BINGHAMTON

This is the show where the Dead ended their '77 perigrinations, wrapping up a fall tour in which they managed to rival the outstanding playing of the spring. As it turns out, they saved some of the best for last.

An all-time Half-Step makes a very good first set a must-have, and Weir gets the second frame under way in a biblical fashion. "It being Sunday, we're going to do a little tune of spiritual derivation" sayeth Bobby. Samson makes for a hot start, with all in the band interconnecting perfectly. Phil, especially, goes all out on this one. Jerry also seems pretty agro, a soupçon that is more than borne out by the end of the set.

One of the more successful versions of Sunrise is followed by a grooving Scarlet → Fire with impassioned vocals from Jerry and Donna. It's not quite Normal '78, but it's close. An excellent Good Lovin' sees Jerry cut loose over some tricky stop-start playing by the rhythm section. The separation of St.

Stephen and Not Fade Away by a brief Drums means that the transition between these two songs moves much more slowly and searchingly than, say, the storied 5/8/77 version. Out of Drums, Not Fade has an air of barely restrained power, unchained by Jerry with some nasty soloing at the end. Wharf Rat sees the band put the brakes on once more, making for a taut, muscular rendition; the same sense of tension pervades the end of St. Stephen played out of Wharf Rat.

Truckin' is where the dam bursts. The sting of Jerry's wrathful licks is first felt at the end of the first chorus. From then on he unleashes a torrent of blistering guitar attacks played way up on the neck at high volume. His assault reaches its acme after the last chorus as he climbs the ladder of the song's opening riff on the sturdy shoulders of Phil's bass playing. When that jam is brought down again, he steps up for some showboating the likes of which we've rarely heard from him before or since. The Dead, for this song at least, is clearly Garcia's backing band, setting up rhythmically each opening for Garcia's almost metalish lines. Wow! Look out, Jimmy Page! The only Truckin' that comes to mind as even touching this one is 5/19/74, but the comparison is of course a case of apples and oranges. This one is not jammed for long, but it burns with megawatt intensity as it streaks its way across the Dead firmament. It demands to be heard. Repeatedly.

12/29/77
WINTERLAND

There's a monster feel to this show (a likely future Vault release) that's evident even on tape at a remove of two decades. The booming triumphalism of the second set may mark the apex of the raucous arena-rock sound the Dead unveiled at Englishtown three months earlier.

The X factor makes an early appearance in a fiery and enthusiastic Bertha → Good Lovin' combo in which Jerry's soloing is not just hot but downright promiscuous. The Roses follow-up shows the band game for all modes of play, switching comfortably to mellower environs before Sunrise manages to contain fire and cool breezes alike in the same song. Donna is at her finest here, singing more sensually than ever.

Coincidence? I Think Not!

If one counts Drums and Space as songs, the Dead played exactly seventy-seven different tunes in 1977, seventy-eight in 1978. So *that's* why they broke out Dark Star on New Year's '78!

But the major attraction of the set is of course the Chinese Playin' triple-decker sandwich: Playin' → China Cat → Rider → China Doll → Playin' → Drums → Not Fade → Playin'! Playin' is whipped along from the beginning by an impatient rhythm section, Jerry and Keith complying happily. One of Donna's best, most controlled and musical Playin' wails heralds the Dead's emergence into an open jam. Jerry's guitar questing is relaxed yet determined in this shimmering world of cymbal and bottomless bass. The band mines a vein of pure gold as the jam peaks in a unique series of serene, twilighty passages that are at once exciting and reassuring—musical good news. Jerry disappears briefly from the jam at the end (according to those who were there, he also disappeared from the stage) as Phil guides the music through a bassy end and holding pattern. Then . . . bedlam. Jerry plays the opening figure to China Cat Sunflower, not heard since the Dead's "last" show in the same venue more than three years prior. The Dead do not skimp at all on the transition, which crests like a tidal wave but seems to leave Jerry a bit befuddled on the beach afterward, seemingly unable to find the handle to go into Rider. After circling for some time he and Donna finally sing the choral intro somewhat tentatively. Jerry really seems to get back into it, though, when Bobby takes the "sun gonna shine" line for the first time ever. Garcia lets loose a guitar barrage at this point and then delivers his "headlight" part with all the pining angst of the ages. After another, much surer run-through of the chorus, the unique, thrice-played coda is reduced to cinders in the inferno of Jerry's fanning.

This fiery Rider gives way to the ice of China Doll, though this one is not as brittle and bitterly cold as most. The legato feel of this version seems to lend more hope to the refrain that "it's only fractured. . . ." A brief foray back into Playin' serves as a bridge to a Drums that in turn becomes a rhythmic launching pad for a thumping Not Fade Away. The whole band sounds very fired up at this point, Jerry ad-libbing a little "Y'know that . . ." before "my love is bigger. . . ." What else is there to do from here but build up a Playin' reprise? The Dead bring it down to a drum and guitar whisper before marshaling a musical shout for the refrain. It's a fulfilling end to a fat jam in a hugely satisfying set and show.

Scarlet Begonias ➡ Fire on the Mountain

In its early years—from early '74 to early '77—Scarlet Begonias lived a happy life as a stand-alone tune, played mostly in the first set. Early in its childhood, however, its end jam began to get most triumphant, a place for exploration and musical questing. It was searching, it seemed, for a sibling, a sister tune to *go into.* Why should all that jamming be an end in itself? Why should it not serve as the spark for a . . . fire?

If you listen to a few of the pre-Fire Scarlets, you'll hear right away that the lion's share of what's become known as the Scarlet → Fire "transition jam" is actually the jamming out of Scarlet. And if one wants to get really nitpicky about it the pairing should really be referred to as Scarlet → Fire → Scarlet—the rhythmic figure with which almost all Fires end is actually the ending of Scarlet, which doesn't get played until that point when Fire is appended. Fire more than makes up for the relatively small portion it contributes to the intermediary jam, though, in fierce interverse jamming and its own exit jam, which in the best versions sees the band turn up the volume and the playing more than a few notches.

After the first Scarlet → Fire was introduced at the end of the first set at Winterland on 3/18/77, it soon became a foundation for second-set building, a position it enjoyed for the rest of its long, happy life in the Dead's repertoire. A notable exception to this "rule" was a brief period in late '89 and early '90, a period when the Dead were shaking things up in general (and more power to them, although Scarlet → Women can seem the very definition of "anticlimactic"), when Scarlet had a number of turns as a mid-second-set link in a jam chain, leading into tunes such as Women Are Smarter, Truckin', Estimated, and a few others. Sure enough, though, it eventually found its way back to its near-sure-thing relationship with Fire on the Mountain.

As is usual between quintessential Dead pairings, the relationship between the two songs has more to do with key relationships and rhythm than lyrical content. Fire's signature rhythm in fact is almost a mirror image—an inversion—of Scarlet's. Both tunes exist in that stop-start rhythmic world, defined to a large extent by Weir's guitar style, which is the unique domain of the Grateful Dead. There's not too much music by other bands—in rock and roll at least—that sounds like these songs (or Row Jimmy, or Jed, or Push, or . . .). There is one interesting coincidence of lyrics, however, though it's obscure: In the third verse of the tune (verses three and four, which can be found in Robert Hunter's book *Box of Rain,* were never sung by Jerry onstage) there appears the serendipitously appropriate line "Baby's in scarlet. . . ." Matches also make an appearance in both songs.

Both Scarlet and Fire fall into that category of Dead tunes that have been heard

BRIGHT SCARLET ➤ RED-HOT FIRES

❋ 3/18/77 Winterland
Get it for historical value, as it's the first, with a rudimentary transition for which Jerry compensates by playing some interesting variations on the Fire outro. He also offers some humorous vocal ad-libs in place of flubbed lines.

❋ 5/8/77 Cornell University
Widely regarded as the class of the field, a narrow view that nonetheless has some merit.

❋ 5/13/77 Auditorium Theater, Chicago
Phil leads the charge into Fire in such a way—one can hear Jerry shout "Yeah! Try it, Phil!"

❋ 2/5/78 Cedar Falls
A long, fiercely original approach to the pairing.

❋ 4/24/78 Normal
Jerry's vocal enthusiasm on this Fire contributed to the theory among Deadheads that it was his favorite tune to play.

❋ 4/3/82 Norfolk
A very long, transitory jam with the actual joining into Fire executed perfectly.

❋ 4/13/83 UVM
Epitomizes the huge Scarfires of the early eighties.

❋ 9/8/83 Red Rocks
Another raging '83 edition.

❋ 10/14/83 Hartford
Brent's "conga" sound makes a huge contribution to this very long version,

and sung along to so often that they've taken on a lyrical logic of their own. They are, as so many of Robert Hunter's lyrics are, imagistic in that sense. They evoke feelings and visions that seem in real time to be fairly self-explanatory; prolonged contemplation outside their musical settings, however, proves them to be somewhat more slippery, Fire more so than Scarlet.

Taken on face, Scarlet Begonias' narrative relates a chance meeting, an affair, probably what Jerry had in mind when he said in an '81 interview (with Blair Jackson and David Gans) that it, like Loose Lucy, was raunchy, "in a way." Is the woman in the song a prostitute? There are a number of possible hints at this in the lyric, such as the way she calls the narrator's eye, her flashy dress—rings, bells, flowers (although this could also describe the sartorial splendor of any number of Deadhead women—"She had an Indian-print blouse and that radiant glow / I knew without asking that her name was Rainbow...")—and the clues they give the narrator that she is "into the blues" (a mod? code?) and "not like other girls," her dodginess upon approach ("too pat to open..."), the defense that "there ain't nothing wrong with" her movements or that "love" (or "look," as Jerry sang it) in her eye, and finally, if one goes along with this reading, the repetition at the end of the song of the hoary (pun intended) cliché most often associated with hookers, the "heart of gold." In this in-now available on Dick's Picks Volume Six.

✹ 7/13/84 Greek
A justly famous Scarlet ➡ Touch ➡ Fire with white-hot, full-speed transitions.

✹ 6/16/85 Greek
The percussion paints in a gorgeous and unsettling tropical setting. Bobby shines.

✹ 7/1/85 Merriwether Post Pavilion
A biggie, the favorite of many from one of the best shows in a fecund year.

✹ 6/28/88 SPAC
Probably the year's best, with 3/28 or 7/15 a close second.

✹ 9/14/90 MSG
For Jerry's singing, the Scarlet exit jam, and a monster Fire.

✹ 3/21/91 Cap Center
Victim ➡ Scarlet ➡ Fire ➡ Stir It Up jam!

✹ 8/16/91 Shoreline
Scarlet ➡ Victim ➡ Fire. Astounding, seamless transitions.

✹ 6/19/94 Eugene
Quantity (thirty-five-plus minutes) meets quality.

✹ 10/14/94 MSG
One of the most electrifying episodes in the later days of the Dead, with some really big solos between the Fire verses.

terpretation, the "hooker with a heart of gold" shows him "the light"—certainly a strange place to get shown it. If one really wishes go out on a symbolic limb, there's the possibility that "Scarlet Begonias or a touch of the blues" is a sly reference to a case of venereal disease (through a prostitute strangers "shake hands"—"everybody's playing in . . ."). This would be in the same tradition as the nursery rhyme "Ring-Around-the-Rosy," which has its origins in the time of the Black Death—the bubonic plague; "ring-around-the-rosy" refers to the red "buboes" that marked plague victims, in the same way that "scarlet begonias" could allude to a rash. Remember, the narrator learned "the hard way to let her pass by."

Even if the preceding interpretation is way off the mark (do I hear a chorus of assent on that point?), the song does seem to be on one level about a one-night stand or brief relationship—the narrator has only "been there before" in a flash of déjà vu, and soon learns to "let her pass by." Of course all of this is tremendously at odds with the images that swirl through many Deadheads' heads while dancing away happily to the song in its musical setting. And even if the above analysis is true to the intent of the lyric on one level, Hunter imbues the song with enough ambiguity and depth that alternate and deeper meanings not only come to mind but demand extraction.

Most important, Scarlet has a tremendous sense of place. More precisely it's about the sense of place and

Before the Discovery of Fire: Three Great Stand-Alone Scarlets

✱ 6/28/74 Boston Garden

✱ 8/6/74 Roosevelt Stadium (the "meat" in a Playin' sandwich)

✱ 10/9/76 Oakland

Stand-Alone Fires of Note

✱ 9/16/78 Egypt

✱ 11/24/78 Capitol Theater

✱ 10/31/80 Radio City Music Hall

✱ 6/22/86 Greek

✱ 7/3/94 Shoreline (Eyes ➡ Fire!)

And More Than Worth a Listen . . .

✱ 11/2/77 Toronto

✱ 4/8/78 Jacksonville

✱ 12/31/78 Winterland

✱ 2/3/79 Indianapolis

✱ 8/6/82 St. Paul

✱ 10/14/83 Hartford

✱ 9/15/85 Chula Vista

✱ 8/23/87 Calaveras County Fairgrounds

✱ 3/16/88 Kaiser Center

✱ 7/15/88 Greek

✱ 8/6/89 Cal Expo

✱ 2/26/90 Oakland

✱ 3/22/90 Copps Coliseum, Hamilton, Canada

✱ 12/27/90 Oakland

✱ 4/27/91 Las Vegas

✱ 6/25/91 Sandstone

the intoxicating effects it can have on a person. It opens in Grosvener Square—in London—with the line "As I was walking," a nod to a convention of the English folk tradition, and then takes us to a room that is given concreteness with two simple brush strokes, the words *matches* and *door*. Then there's that marvelous flash of déjà vu, in which the teller realizes "he's been *there* before" (emphasis mine), followed by the revelation that one can see the light "in the strangest of *places*" (again my italics). *Strange* here can mean not only "odd" but its root definition, "foreign," which England obviously would be for Hunter, an American who lived there for a time (this is *not* to say that Hunter "is" the narrator).

There's a sense in the song of the feeling of intoxication and disorientation—the love in the air, the flashes of eerie remembrance, the inversion of the colors of the sky and sun—that can visit the traveler abroad. For one who's experienced it, especially when accompanied by love (an intoxicating and disorienting experience in and of itself), it's a wonderful intangible that Hunter manages to evoke here with subtle mastery.

Also worth noting are the mild contradictions Hunter builds into the text, which lends the song an additional sense of place-drunkenness: "Not a chill . . . but a nip," "too pat to open . . . too cool to bluff," "I ain't often right . . . I've never been wrong," "Scarlet . . . blues," and "sky was yellow . . .

* 5/21/92 Cal Expo
* 6/12/92 Albany
* 9/13/93 Philly
* 3/30/94 Atlanta
* 10/1/94 Boston Garden
* 5/23/95 Charlotte (with Bruce Hornsby)
* 5/25/95 Seattle

sun was blue." Finally Hunter manages to bring the song's threads together in the superbly crafted "wind in the willows" line, an apparent reference to "Blueberry Hill" (by Al Lewis, Larry Stock, and Vincent Rose, made famous by Fats Domino)—"The wind in the willows played love's sweet melody." He lets us know here that the narrator has "found his thrill," not on Blueberry Hill but rather in England, evoked by "Tea for Two." This song, like Hunter, is American, but the mention of "tea" here conjures England, and the narrator's act of hearing songs emanating from the landscape becomes another symptom of the romantic effect of a foreign locale.

Fire on the Mountain also lends itself to a variety of interpretations. Hunter notes in *Box of Rain* that he wrote it at Mickey Hart's ranch while watching a fire on the surrounding hills approach Mickey's recording studio, but that's only a clue as to the initial "spark" of inspiration that lent itself to the song's refrain.

Metaphorically what is a "fire on the mountain"? The phrase suggests a volcano, for one, an awesome outpouring of heat and energy. It is also a blaze atop a summit—a blaze of inspiration at a high point, an enhancement of a peak. Steve Silberman, coauthor of *Skeleton Key: A Dictionary for Deadheads,* once observed that the song seemed to be about the additional heights a creative person (in the song a musician) must continually seek to produce new art, and the need at times to try to force the creative process when the muse does not appear of its own volition. I must say that this perspective has stayed with me and seems an extremely valid one. The "long-distance runner" cannot rest, cannot "stand there." Complacency ("laughter") only results in "cold music." To invert a common saying, for the performing artist a creation must be lent not only the "light" of creation but the "heat" of performance. This can be exhausting—to have to not only invent but continually give interpretive meaning to the invention. Sometimes even a dragon needs matches.

Thus the song is addressed to a musician who can't seem to find the interpretive spark to deliver a "hot" version of the song or songs he's performing, for whom it's all he can do "just to stay on the beat." The lyric is a stern reminder that the act of creation alone is not enough if the musician-composer wants to stay true to his own aspirations: "You say it's a living...but you're here alone...." There are also elements of sympathy and empathy for the addressee's plight in the song's voice wishing "mercy" and "more than just ashes" for him—the hope that the realization of "dreams" and creative fruition

Beam Me Up, Jerry

Sublimely ridiculous are the MIDI effects first Jerry, then Bobby throw into the Seattle 5/25/95 Startrek → Fire, and reminiscent of the "bridge signal chime" is the noise right before the "shipping powders" line in the 11/7/85 Throwing Stones. A further example of the Deadhead-Trekkie connection first evidenced by Mickey's suggestion of the title "Warp Ten" for the Hart, Lagin, Lesh collaboration that became Seastones, and continued with his stint as Spock in the New Year's '87 closed-circuit broadcast. And anyone ever heard Leonard Nimoy's album of weird electronic music? Talk about Space—the final frontier indeed!

won't burn the artist out and will see the fires of inspiration still burning sufficient to stoke a performance—as well as in the rhetorical question "You gave all…why you wanta give more?" To paraphrase, "Hey, I know the life of the performing artist is a bitch—you don't have to do this, you know."

Another friend once suggested a darker interpretation of this song, in which it is addressed directly to Jerry, who by numerous accounts was addicted to the Persian, a pure opiate that he would smoke in an act referred to as "chasing the dragon." His noddings as a result, combined with his habit of smoking cigarettes, reportedly led to a number of hotel-room fires. This interpretation has Jerry as the "dragon with matches" on the loose. If Hunter wrote the song not long before the band recorded it for *Shakedown Street,* the time frame would jibe with most stories that put this as the time in which his addiction started to come into full swing. A number of Jerry's friends observed that his personality seemed to undergo a shift at this point as he became more withdrawn and less openly sincere, more likely to put a superficially sunny face on things to avoid direct confrontation, which may find echoes in "cold music" and "…laughter…dead to the core." It's also not hard to find the concerned voice of a friend trying to give a warning and pep talk to a guy at the pinnacle who the song's voice sees as endangering all he has (the fire imperiling the mountain), for a cheap high—it exists in lines such as "…there's no one to compete," "If mercy's in business…," and "you really can't fake." Perhaps most telling is a line from the unsung fourth verse: "lost to the world on that fifty-cent jive." If viewed in this light, the song takes on a very poignant cast, the sense of someone seeing a close friend slip away and doing his best to give him the message before it's too late. There's a sense of resignation in Days Between, Hunter and Garcia's last collaboration, that also reaches into this poignant space, this time looking back when it's too late.

This said, and in an effort to dissipate the gloom of such reflections: Jerry as a long-distance runner? C'mon! ("Gimme twenty laps, Garcia!")

Much More Than Egypt
1978

t's been said that the Dead's 1978 performances are cut from the same general cloth as those of 1977. This is certainly true to an extent—the band's membership was of course the same, and the Dead's music didn't "know" that the calendar had progressed. Nevertheless there are subtle yet tangible differences between the Dead's performances in the sanctified year of '77 and the period that followed.

It is not exclusively a question of quality, though that does enter into the equation, as 1977 was a benchmark of sorts for the period between Mickey's reenlistment and Keith and Donna's departure, and I don't think that there's much question that although 1977 is not without its clunker shows and weak moments even in generally rocking shows, 1978 is not up to the standards set by its calendar-year predecessor. Mostly, though, there are textural differences between the two years.

Nineteen seventy-seven earns its place in the Head's heart because of unbelievable ensemble work. In the best of that year's performances the whole band seemed not only to be on but to be directly wired into one another's musical minds. It was a year of many transitions that were not only flawless but superlatively intuitive—they were played in such a way as to make the marvelous seem offhand. The Jerry-Phil Bobby interplay was so tightly woven as to seem unconscious; Keith was often *right there* with a key fill when the musical space opened for it (even if he hadn't been doing anything except playing block chords in repetition before that space opened); Donna sang on-key more than ever before or since; Mickey and Billy had rediscovered their groove...well, see the essay on 1977. The Dead did not lose this synergy by 1978—Normal 4/24/78, to cite one example, is a show that could have come from the best of '77—but on the whole the Dead's performances in 1978 were less consistent in quality and more reliant on Jerry above the other band members. On the other hand the best of '78 possesses a musical adventurousness not always present in '77.

Discussing 1978 as a whole is problematic because it's a year in which the band's playing underwent some fairly dramatic changes. In the first part of the year, through Red Rocks, the band continued along a line of progression consistent with late '77—the more driving, rock-and-roll sound one hears in 11/6/77 and 12/29/77. Jerry's soloing in the 11/6/77 Truckin', for example, is wholly consistent with the way he stepped out in this part of '77, and on into '78. The sound of his guitar here also applies to this time frame.

In addition to the heated, fuzzy guitar sound employed by Jerry in this period, the more locked-in playing of the drums and Phil—especially evident in the excellent 4/24 Normal show—evinces a further departure from the jazziness of the preretirement years. Keith's more sedentary and chordal playing in 1978 is also a factor in this sound.

The band's playing and sound—particularly that of Jerry's guitar—underwent a rather marked shift around the time of the Egypt shows, with Jerry moving to a pinched, muted wah-wah sound—tight little pearly notes strung together. At the same time the Dead began playing more fluid, Jerry-led improvisations. Both these trends are exemplified to perfection in the 11/20/78 Playin' jam that starts the second set. This new sound and approach is also evident during the Winterland "From Egypt with Love" run, for example, and the band continued in this vein for the remainder of the year. It resurfaced in '81, albeit with Brent in the mix and Jerry on a new guitar.

There were some other, more readily apparent novelties in 1978 as well. This was the year the Dead made their first switch of onstage positions, with Jerry moving from the far left of the stage (from the audience's point of view) and carving out a space for himself between Donna and Phil. This lineup did not make it through the year, but while it lasted, it was the most immediate visual evidence that changes were afoot. Drums/Space, which had made sporadic appearances, both linked and separated, throughout the Dead's career had begun to lay sporadic claim on their later-customary mid-second-set spot in 1977. By 1978 they were together and entrenched, a feature of nearly every show, to be augmented the next year by the Beast.

Nineteen seventy-eight was also, infamously, the year in which Bobby took up slide guitar, a measure taken in no small part to provide the band with some sustain in the face of Keith's resistance to playing electric piano or organ on a regular basis. Now, much has been made of how Bobby learned how to play slide onstage, and his '78 slide playing was much maligned at the time. Interestingly, though, his slide work in that year surpassed his subsequent efforts for many years to come—it's plain beautiful in many songs—If I Had the World to Give, for example. Maybe it was beginner's luck. Maybe he caught wind of the criticism and, due to self-consciousness, regressed.

You will come across many references, both oral and written, to 1978 as a weak year. True, Keith was often a nonentity. True, Space began to eat up the jamming once spread more liberally throughout a Dead show. True, there is much uneven playing. But some of the Dead's (and Jerry's) hottest playing of the seventies is to be found here, and there are many surprises to be mined as well. Pass on '78 tapes at your own peril.

1/22/78
McARTHUR COURT

This early 1978 show in Oregon stands as one of the best of the year. The first set rocks, closing on an auspicious note with a powerful Music Never Stopped. After the joyous and very well done Bertha → Good Lovin' opener to the second set, the show takes on an indescribable quality of mounting energy and excitement. This is on the whole an incredibly intense performance, focused and *driving*. Jerry's guitar sound, somewhat changed from the main of his '77 performances, adds to the edgy feel of this show. The overheated Gibsonesque sound Jerry used before Egypt is exemplified well by his playing here. The rest of the band is somewhat subdued on this night, a fact that gives Jerry's slashing sound and licks the effect of someone shouting in a quiet, darkened room.

There is a release of sorts to be found in the perfectly executed "inspiration" in Terrapin, but Jerry proceeds to build the energy right back up again in a crunching, wailing, power-chord-driven Terrapin end jam. Terrapin flows into a brief, hard-hitting bout of Drums, which in turn SLAMS into The Other One with the strength of a force-five hurricane. There's so much to be psyched for here: the way Jerry's leads dart between Phil's crunching bass notes, the way Bobby and the drummers whip the music forward faster and faster, but perhaps the most subtle and sublime effect is the reverb from Keith's grand after each *WHAM* played in unison with Phil as the song's central thematic passage keeps comin', comin', comin' around. This is not the sound of a piano player grown apathetic.

There's a meltdown in the middle of The Other One, from which the band rises, phoenixlike, to return to the main theme with a vengeance—killer. The closing jam cooks with a tribal frenzy as Billy and Mickey really pour it on while Jerry loudly serves up menacing weirdness in a variety of guitar voices (some of which actually *do* sound like voices). This inspired jamming, after bringing the energy level to its apex, breaks forth orgasmically as the *Close Encounters* theme, which just seems to explode from Jerry's guitar.

That's not all, though, as Jerry quickly works himself up into a near-Tiger frenzy before again stating a variant on the *Close Encounters* theme that surges outward into a big St. Stephen intro. A long, questing Not Fade follows Stephen, reaching into a number of musical spaces, and the closing Around, despite getting off to a slow start, gets cooking itself. Even the U.S. Blues encore rips.

4/24/78
NORMAL

If you dig Scarlet → Fire (and I know that you do), this is one show you don't want to miss out on. The second set starts off with a huge one. What makes it so special? A big Scarlet starts off with rock-solid drumming and forward-leaning intensity, but that's not it. The transition builds from Garcia's wah-wah prowlings around Weir's slide lines to a raging Fire, but that's not quite it either. The drums get even more serious in Fire, making it throb with a tribal beat, but . . . okay, what makes this a Scarlet → Fire for the ages is all of these things but the pièce de résistance has to be what Jerry does late in the Fire. As the last chorus builds, he starts to get a notion, telling us he's "Talkin' 'bout fire," making sure that "you know there's a fire, yes" and then, the best improvisation of all, "Let it burn, let it burn." Stoic as Jerry could be, such vocal improvisations are truly noteworthy. Even when clearly into a tune, he was more likely to funnel his enthusiasm into his delivery of the lyrics as written or his guitar than engage in Bobbyesque improvisations. Hearing Jerry so obviously pumped up is a joy indeed.

This Scarlet → Fire would be no more than killer filler if the rest of the show wasn't so incredibly hot. The first set is exceptional. Cassidy is executed perfectly, if not as jammed out as later versions. In Brown-Eyed Women Jerry foreshadows his vocal expressiveness of later years by singing the "old man never was the same . . ." line as if he's fighting off tears. Passenger is a fiery, all-time version, as is Roses, which even has a bit of fire itself, with an unusually hot middle jam. And Jerry and Bobby's dueling in Music matches favorably with the best of the '77 versions.

A thumping Good Lovin' comes screaming like an engine out of Fire, followed by a crisp, faultless Terrapin. Mickey and Billy have clearly been driving the show, and they get their showcase in a tumultuous, lightning-

Better Try Wolfsbane...

A common configuration for the tape of this show has the encore on side A of the first set, which, when read aloud from set shorthand yields the phrase "Music Never Stopped Werewolves." Which of course became a cautionary motto among me and my friends.

handed Drums → Not Fade. The Black Peter → Around offers the usual end-of-show study in contrasts, with muscular versions of each.

And to top it all off, what else but Werewolves of London? This is one of the better played and most interesting versions, replete with Phil's Werewolves of Tamalpais. Obligatory pun for this show: a performance well, well above Normal.

9/16/78
EGYPT

This is the show in which the Dead most realized the promise of their surroundings at the Gizeh Sound and Light Theater amid the wonder of the Pyramids. It also marks the beginning of their ascendancy to the peak they would reach at the Winterland run that followed a month later.

An excellent first set is highlighted by a mellifluous Candyman with shimmering "falling rain" effects courtesy of Jerry and the Wolf and playful lines from Phil. A lovely Looks Like Rain features some interesting vocal phrasing from Bobby and Donna's strange contribution of a "meow" after the "... streetcats making love" line. Phil and Jerry make this a piece of Dead program music by each adding, respectively, thunder and rain. The Row Jimmy is simply unlike any version played before or since, with the band playing in a very stop-start staccato style over which Bobby lays long lines on the slide guitar. Like the rest of this show (and much of the remainder of '78), it's strange and beautiful.

The magic truly commences, though, with the second set's opening Ollin Arageed, featuring Hamza El Din and his Nubian Choir. A distance of thousands of years and miles melts away as the Dead, one by one, quietly join the drum chant. Phil is the first, laying down a bass line that simply follows Hamza's rhythm. Then Jerry sneaks in, weaving lovely, Eastern-flavored lines through the tars and chorus. The playing here brings to mind the intricate and significant knotwork on the reverse side of the finest Persian rugs. After Hamza and his choir leave the stage, the Dead continue in this vein with a few seconds of lovely bridgework between Ollin Arageed and a Fire that is most definitely influenced by what has preceded it, not to mention the environmental surroundings. Garcia's lead lines are transcendently influenced by the local muse. This is a loooong version that ventures into all sorts of mystical places with some very sensitive playing by all. Bobby, especially, plays some wonderfully textural passages here.

What starts out sounding like a graceful transition into Not Fade Away becomes instead an equally graceful move into Aiko which, with its strong rhythm and lyrics that convey as much through the sound of the words as through their actual meanings, seems an inspiredly universal choice. Donna bids adieu to Sunrise with a strong performance, and the Shakedown → Drums → Space → Truckin' → Stella Blue → Around that closes up the show features very strong versions of all these tunes, with some extraordinary jamming in the spaces between. Space itself is a masterwork of strange, Pyramid-induced beauty. The Shakedown and Stella Blue are particular standouts.

Despite a continuation of what must be regarded as uninspired song selection for these shows, the Dead proved on this night that it ain't what you play, it's how you play it. Mickey regarded this night as the end of their *first* trip to Egypt. It is a shame indeed that they never made it back.

10/17/78
WINTERLAND

This, the first show of the "From Egypt with Love" shows and indeed the first show at all since Egypt, amply shows that whatever the band was or was not able to bring with them *to* Egypt, they surely managed to bring something important back. For those who traveled with the band to Egypt and widely reported experiencing only one night of musical magic instead of the hoped-for three, this may have been scant consolation. But for Heads at large, for the Dead themselves, and for posterity as embodied in tapes, maybe this was the most important thing.

On this night a good first set closes with a dynamite Jack Straw. Though the second-set opening Scarlet is a disaster lyrically, the playing is exquisite. Bobby and Keith add some very tasteful (and tasty) fills. Donna's on, too, as are Phil and the drummers—okay, I think that's everyone: Let's face it, the whole band is on. Jerry does some nice soloing between verses in that alternately thin and crunching '78 guitar sound, so different from his '77 tone and already significantly evolved from the beginning of the year. Donna's end of Scarlet cooing is pretty (weird). There's some very lovely playing all around in the transition to Fire, with attention being paid to dynamics throughout, bringing it down real quiet before building back up on the wings of fluttering Garcia fancies. This one may win the prize for most seamless transition into Fire. Check out those tight little wah figures Jerry plays at the beginning of

Fire, which epitomize his almost-pinched guitar sound at this point. The playing within Fire is *so* clean, a glassy lake from which Garcia's guitar keeps bubbling up. It's well jammed to the end.

The band plays an interesting variation on the opening of Estimated—a three-note figure instead of the big single beat on the "one" to start. Bob adds some great, patently weird playing behind a hot intraverse Jerry solo, as Phil and the drums continue their fine playing as well. Once again it's the whole band lavishing attention on their parts, with Donna doing some nice work among the "Nah nah nah nah nooooh's." The interplay between Bobby and Jerry builds like mad before the junction to an Eyes that is an occasion for Mr. Garcia to do some stepping out again. Eyes features playing of the same quality as the rest of the show, which is to say jazzy, dynamically sensitive, and pretty.

Drums is notable for the rare pan work within, Space for a woman who perhaps was a wee bit into the pudding repeatedly asking Jerry for banjo lessons (it's clearly audible on the soundboard), to which Jerry politely demurs, intoning, "I don't teach anymore," while delivering blasts of sonic weirdness: "I don't [*diddy dee wah wah wah*] teach [*pliddely pliddely blaaat ba bwoowang wah*] anymore [*fiddle dee fiddle dee hum . . .*]." Someone eventually tells her either "give it a rest" or "you're under arrest" as she is presumably removed from the stage. Soon after this bizarre incident Jerry brings the Space down into If I Had the World to Give, which my romantic heart would like to think of as sort of sung to the addled girl who was looking for banjo lessons about thirteen years or so too late. The song itself is a smooth, thrilling ride—one can hear that, though Jerry is at least up for the challenge, it was the vocal range required for this tune that no doubt led to it being shelved.

Finally, it need be said that the Around and the U.S. Blues encore positively smoked.

10/21/78
WINTERLAND

This is yet another fine show in the superlative post–Egypt-Winterland run. The second set opens with a jaunty, tight Bertha → Good Lovin' pairing, followed by a lovely Roses. The Dead really start showing signs of life, though, during Estimated. Jerry's first solo in this tune shows some small twists on the standard reading, and his guitar voicing has less of a wah sound than those accustomed to the hot Estimateds of '77 (and post-'81 versions, as well) are used to. Jerry's greater willingness to furiously fan chords during his solos is another '78 innovation in his sound that is evident here, showing him to have started playing in more of a rock-guitarist mode than in his jazzier past.

Some frenzied Garcia noodling at the end of Estimated gives way to the slow rhythms of He's Gone, which is played as well as any and serves as the band's passage into Drums. Mickey and Billy's exciting work here is augmented by the plaintive wailing of blues harpist extraordinaire Lee Oskar. Jerry then emerges, sounding like a baritone being played at great speed before soaring off into the upper registers. The jam that emerges between Oskar and the Dead sounds for a time as if it is about to go into Dancin', but what we get instead is the surprise of what was to be the last Got My Mojo Workin', the first in about a year. It's an inspired choice, the ideal funky-blues fare for Oskar to do his thang, which the band step back and let him do to great effect. When Jerry joins him on slide guitar and they start trading licks, look out. When Bobby, also on slide, joins in the mix, well, look out too. This is the stuff.

The Dead go straight into The Other One with an air of "Okay, that's your music, Lee, check out *our* vid." It's interesting to hear how they adapt this version initially, presumably for Oskar's benefit, with Jerry playing a few variations on the lead line before slamming into it. If thoughtfulness to Oskar was the impetus for this methodical approach, it's soon forgotten, as Jerry builds the song to a fever pitch before the vocals kick in. Jerry bobs and weaves with unconscious mastery between perfect singing by Bobby and Donna, reaching some burning, piercing, unparalleled peaks. The power chords he lays down at the end are really most un-Jerry-like—in the most wonderful way. What is very Jerry-like is the way he brings it all down in an instant for Stella Blue, that *whoosh* of an energy drop he's spoken of. All the better to bring it back up again, as he and the band do several times in the course of an all-time version of this song, which is particularly notable for its strong vocals and—you guessed it—guitar work by Jerry.

A Sugar Magnolia and U.S. Blues wallop ensure this show's ending on a very high note.

11/20/78
CLEVELAND

This is a show that seems to exist according to its own logic, particularly in regard to a jewel box of a second set—small, unique, and almost mystically beautiful.

An introspective Jerry-led Playin' jam kicks off the second set. This is really one to love and listen to again and again, offering as it does some magical moments of lightning-fast runs played with a muted tone. It moves into Drums and emerges from the other side before dropping unexpectedly into the first Jack-A-Roe in more than a year. The choice seems more than a bit of a non sequitur (especially given the fact that Jack-A-Roe had never before appeared in the second set, and hasn't since), though it does share its predecessor's tempo. It's randomness simply adds to the intrigue of a set that is beginning to take a most peculiar shape.

The end of Jack-A-Roe brings the flow to a momentary stop, only to be resumed by a Playin' that could be subtitled "Tasteful, Exquisite Jamming, Part Two." This morsel flows seamlessly into a mellow and funky Shakedown. The body of the song and the closing jam are, as is the rest of the set, strangely subdued but nonetheless superb. Just as the jam has stuck around enough to start to rock in a more familiar manner, it descends in the most ethereal way into that rare gem If I Had the World to Give. Jerry's vocals at the beginning of this song start out unusually sure, and it promises to be the best of three versions extant until he misses a line. His vocals never completely recover—his frustration is evident in the chorus—but his and the band's playing remain excellent throughout, Bobby's plaintive slide guitar a sonic portrait of melancholy. A lovely transition jam brings them back into Playin' for the other end of this very tasty sandwich. As do so many hot shows from '78, this one closes with a good Around.

1979-1981
1979-1981
1979-1981
1979-1981
1979-1981
1979-1981
1979-1981
1979-1981
1979-1981
1979-1981
1979-1981
1979-1981
1979-1981
1979-1981
1979-1981
1979-1981
1979-1981
1979-1981
1979-1981
1979-1981

1979–1981

he first couple of years of Brent's tenure ⚘ constitute something of a "lost" period in the Dead's history. Obviously this is a metaphorical statement—in terms of tapes available, they're not lost at all, as *are* big chunks of the mid to late sixties'; then again, one certainly *hears* (and reads) a good deal more about the Dead's doings in this era than in the early eighties. The years 1979 to 1981 seem to be neglected in many—if not most—tapers' collections and esteem.

This is a state of affairs that begs to be remedied. And, to be sure, there are exceptions. There's the famed 10/16/81 Melk Weg show in Amsterdam, the Nassau Coliseum show from earlier that year, the acoustic-electric shows at the Warfield and Radio City Music Hall in 1980 (though the electric sets can be quite hard to find). Cape Cod '79 also gets some attention. But when three prime years are so underrepresented in the tape collections I see, discussions with friends real and virtual (i.e., Internet pals), and in more objective polls such as *DeadBase*'s "Feedback" section, well, here's a cause that needs to be championed.

First of all why *do* these years get ignored? Probably the most frequent objection to shows from the early end of Brent's tenure (and this is a complaint one hears about shows right up to and through 1985) is "that plinky keyboard sound." And it's true—his early-eighties sound was pretty plinky. I happen to like it; it added a real nice touch, especially when he would step up and play those fluid solo runs. Friend of the Devil from this period comes to mind. This modified Fender Rhodes sound was easy to hear in the band's mix and gave the music a real fast, quicksilver tone in the upper registers and had that nifty *CHock* sound, with the quick decay in the lower oc-

> ⚘ Q: WHAT WAS BRENT'S FIRST SHOW WITH THE DEAD?
>
> A: 4/22/79, SPARTAN STADIUM, SAN JOSE, CALIFORNIA. THE SHOW WAS NO GREAT SHAKES, WITH THE DEAD PLAYING IT PRETTY SAFE, DOUBTLESS IN DEFERENCE TO THE NEW GUY IN THE HOT SEAT, BUT THE SCARLET ➤ FIRE AND WHARF RAT IN THE SECOND SET MAKE THIS TAPE MORE THAN SOLELY AN HISTORICAL CURIO.

taves. That said, the criticism is well understood when put in the context of the greater development of Brent's sound—at its apex it was that lush, multifaceted cryptical envelope for the band one finds especially on boots from '85 and '89. It *is* puzzling, given how many times the core members of the Dead have said that their biggest musical beef with Keith (aside from his apathy near the end of his stint) was that he didn't provide the band with any real sustain (or did so rarely, a pity in light of some of his organ work, particularly that of 1975), that when Brent arrived he would work this percussive electric-piano sound so hard. The band was also real hungry for color, though, and that's something that Brent provided from the beginning, as tapes from his early years attest to.

These were also the years where the Dead began having arid stretches without too many trips to the songwriting well. After the *Go to Heaven* material was introduced in 1979, 1980 and 1981 marked the first two years in which no new originals were brought into the Dead's repertoire. In addition perhaps (*perhaps*) the two most beloved Dead tunes—Dark Star and St. Stephen—were also largely absent in these years. Further, these were the years in which the Dead set (given the years involved, you'll pardon the unintended pun) completed its last stages of solidification/ossification. The introduction of the Beast and accompanying percussion fest that grew out of the *Apocalypse Now* sessions—"Drumz," "Rhythm Devils"—whatever name you know it by, becoming firmly planted in the second set to stay, and either-or tunes such as China → Rider and Playin' in their last days of being frequently heard in the first set.

The flip side of the coin is, hey, there was some fine new material from *Go to Heaven:* Stranger became a jamming opener, as did Alabama Getaway; Althea, along with Alabama, featured some of Hunter's finest songwriting (the Alabama → Greatest pairing got many a show off to a roaring, biblical start) and Lost Sailor → Saint was a powerhouse Bobfest for years. Even Easy to Love You has its charms, though it is decidedly a pop song with a capital *P*. Plus, and this is a big plus, there is all that great

> Q: DARK STAR WAS IN FACT PLAYED ONLY THREE TIMES DURING THE YEARS 1979–81, AND ST. STEPHEN ONLY ONCE. CAN YOU CITE THE SHOWS?
>
> A: DARK STAR RAISED ITS LOVELY HEAD TWICE IN THE BEGINNING OF 1979—1/10/79 NASSAU COLISEUM AND 1/20/79 BUFFALO—AND, JUST IN TIME TO BE COUNTED, ON 12/31/81 OAKLAND. THE ONLY ST. STEPHEN FROM THIS ERA WAS PLAYED AT THE SAME SHOW AS THE FIRST '79 DARK STAR—1/10/79. FOR EXTRA CREDIT, WHICH OF THESE SHOWS FEATURED A PERSONNEL ANOMALY AMONG THE BAND (I DON'T MEAN A GUEST ARTIST, SO IT'S NOT NEW YEAR'S '81), AND WHAT WAS IT? ALSO, WHEN WAS THE NEXT ST. STEPHEN PLAYED AFTER 1/10/79? EXTRA-CREDIT ANSWER: 1/20/79 WAS ONE OF THE EARLY '79 SHOWS ON WHICH DONNA TOOK A PASS. ST. STEPHEN, AS WE ALL KNOW, DIDN'T REAPPEAR AGAIN UNTIL 1983, WHEN IT WAS PLAYED THREE TIMES IN THE MONTH OF OCTOBER, STARTING ON OCTOBER 11TH. AFTER THE LAST TIME—HALLOWEEN '83—IT WAS GONE FOR GOOD. NOTHING'S GONNA BRING IT BACK.

acoustic material that was brought back in 1980, not to mention what occasioned its return—some wonderful acoustic shows.

As for the sclerotic quality of the show structure, why not look at the glass as half full? Sure the sets are more structured than in earlier years, but they're positively chaotic compared with any subsequent year until 1989. In these years one can find some of the most unpredictably mapped shows of the Brent years.

What it all boils down to, though, is the playing, and the band featured on tapes from the era '79–'81 is one that is clearly energized from having shed the Keith/Donna millstone and by adding, in the person of Brent, a component with as fine a tonal ear as any, a great voice, and a hell of a lot of punch.

1/15/79
S P R I N G F I E L D

Five great reasons to check out this show:

1. Phil is abducted by aliens in the set break, which clearly affects his playing.
2. The insane Miracle → Shakedown.
3. Some of Donna's most soulful singing ever, in From the Heart of Me.
4. The Terrapin → Playin' → Drums → Playin' → Casey Jones that comprises the remainder of the second set.
5. The insane Miracle → Shakedown.

The set opens with Bobby reporting the news that "our bass player was last seen consorting with a couple of aliens." From this evidence we can only assume that an actual extraterrestrial abduction took place. Phil's being beamed back to the stage is marked by a bass note or two, then a big fat bomb, accompanied by Jerry's opening Miracle lick.

Miracle is blazing in and of itself, with Jerry pouring on some licks in the postlyric jam very reminiscent of those in the 11/6/77 Truckin'. What really marks this version, though, is the sudden climb Garcia makes up and up and up the scale until he finds the note he wants and sustains it, at which point Keith rolls from that note down to the one from which he had started. He is met there by a cacophonous crash of bass, drums, and guitar, his piano reverberating for a good second or two afterward on the Shakedown D-minor "fate" chord. This surprising transition is one of those moments that begs to be played again and again, at successively higher volumes. As Mickey would say, "If it's worth playing, it's worth playing loud!"

Donna's Heart of Me is great, with very sympatico playing from Jerry. Terrapin is a very fine, thoroughly jammed-out version, and the Playin' into which it moves is home to all that makes this tune exceptional—long, questing, hypnotic jams. Playin's energy is carried through Drums → Space and finally poured into the worthy vessel of Casey Jones, a hell of a closer.

Now—listen to that Miracle → Shakedown transition again. Turn it to 11. As for Phil's abduction,

THE DANGERS OF DATING ANOTHER DEADHEAD—ONE MAN'S STORY

"*A*nd what about your girlfriend's tapes? Every Head I know had a girlfriend whose tapes were always such an atrocious mess. Songs cut off, tapes labeled merely 'Dead,' horrible quality, no boxes, all jumbled together. My brother and I now have a running joke referring to an old flame; whenever a song cuts off before the end, we look at each other and say, 'Heather!' "

—S. K.

the repercussions of this event upon the Dead were felt even into the early eighties, when Jerry and Phil switched places in response to Brent's complaints that he was "sick and tired of playing next to that fuckin' alien." Mr. Lesh is believed to have since reclaimed his terrestrial bioform.

7/1/79
SEATTLE

The first set of this show is remarkable for two reasons: its exceptionally high "western" content (out of ten tunes total there's Half-Step, Mama Tried, Mexicali, Minglewood, Stagger Lee, El Paso, and Brown-Eyed Women) and the fact that the band makes it all the way through without flubbing a single line (though Bobby comes close in Minglewood, singing "wanted man in Trexas").

The Half-Step → Franklin's opener really shines, with Garcia's soaring licks in Half-Step boding well for the rest of the show. Newcomer Brent adds some lightning runs in the upper register before the first chorus of Franklin's, which Jerry sings with surety throughout. An energetic Mama Tried → Mexicali and a sparkling, up-tempo Peggy-O with strong Phil show the band to be in fine form. Brent takes a nice solo turn in Minglewood, which is also graced by an exciting Bobby slide solo. Bobby's slide work is also impressive in Stagger Lee, as is Jerry's. A solid El Paso is followed by an excellent Brown-

Eyed Women that sees a restless Jerry give an extra go-round or two to all his solos, always a good omen in the first set. He brings some vocal innovation to this edition, too, clearly paying attention to his delivery. Once again, Bobby's slide playing is pretty damn good.

The set ends on the strongest note possible with a *blazing* Passenger, packed with lightning Garcia runs and all the guitar raunch for which the song was designed.

After Bobby announces some technical difficulties to which the "crack equipment crew" is attending (during which someone onstage asks, "Isn't it Weir's birthday?"), we're Ease'd in to the second set (Don't Ease wouldn't become a first-set closer for some years yet) with a rocking, percussion-fueled version. Bobby stays on the slide for this and the Samson that follows, still playing strongly. Jerry more than compensates for some lyrical flubs (the first of the show!) in the beginning of Sugaree with some *fast* guitar work and impassioned singing of the choruses. This is an outstanding version. (Bobby slide-guitar watch: still on it, still playing very well.) The Terrapin that follows is pretty lackluster in the main body, but starts to pick up steam with the postlyric jam. Unfortunately this is right about the point where there is a tape splice on the soundboard.

Next up is Playin', which takes best-of-show honors on the strength of a superlative jam. Jerry mesmerizes with blindingly fast circular figures before spinning off into a jam that, like that in the 6/30/84 version, contains subtle Spanish Jam hints. Here's where Brent kicks into high gear, climbing the scale in unison with Jerry until they just can't get any higher or hotter. Brent's contribution here cannot be stressed too strongly (the person from whom I sourced this tape had this portion of the set labeled "Playin' → Jam → Brent on Keys → Drums," which is apt)—his swirling key fills send this one into another dimension.

The Drums continue for a good while at Playin' tempo, Mickey and Billy building to one heart-attack rush after another before Mickey brings things back down with some sensitive tar playing. Just as Jerry begins playing in Space, Mickey adds to the mix what sounds like sandpaper being rubbed against a microphone. Brent's Prophet V holds sway over a Space that truly earns its name. Electronic weirdness suggestive of interplanetary travel moves from slightly whimsical to vaguely sinister with the addition of ghostlike shouts and synthesized babies crying right before easing ever so gently into Stella Blue. The best Stellas can guide you through a humid, lapis-hued dream space, propelled by the majestic, pipe-organ strains of Jerry's guitar. This one, slow and poignant, accomplishes that before making a seamless and surprising transition into a Truckin' → Around combo to close the set. Though both are hot, the trauma of being yanked from the womb of Stella Blue can seem at times equal to that of birth. Luckily there is a Shakedown encore (and a '79 Shakedown, to boot) to show us that life outside the womb ain't so bad after all.

The Deadhead Pantheon

✿ JOHN BELUSHI, ACTOR/COMEDIAN

Maybe it's not fair to put someone in the category of Deadhead who once shared the stage with the Dead (the *Blues Brothers* opened at the Closing of Winterland, New Year's '78/'79), but I had to work the old samurai in somewhere. A good friend to the band, he played host to some hedonistic, star-filled jam sessions at his private after-hours bar in New York, of which various members of the Dead were a part. He was one of the prime planters of a Deadhead seed among the cast and crew of *Saturday Night Live,* as evidenced by the band's appearances (over the initial misgivings of creator Lorne Michaels that they were not "hip" enough—well, who was hipper in 1990, Lorne?) on the show and the cropping up of Dead references like the "Day on the Green" Skull and Roses T-shirt worn by the Conehead daughter. Belushi, who died in 1982, is loosely memorialized in West L.A. Fadeaway (Belushi met his final reward at the Chateau Marmont).

✿ THE CLINTON-GORE ADMINISTRATION

Although Bill and Al's Excellent Adventure has no doubt turned sour for many Heads since its rightward lurch after 1994 (and then again, Deadheads not being a monolithic group, it's probably sweetened for others), the question to be asked is, Did LBJ, Nixon, Ford, Carter, Reagan, or Bush ever invite the Dead or any of its members to the White House? No, but this administration did. Sure, Bill didn't happen to *be* there at the time (plausible deniability), but Tipper and Al showed Bobby, Mickey, and Jerry around and had them back to their house for dinner. Sure Tipper has her enemies in the rock-music world from her PMRC days, but she's an avowed Deadhead (she's even been backstage), as is her husband. And Clinton did have the good grace to say a few kind words upon Jerry's death.

✿ FRANCIS FORD COPPOLA, DIRECTOR, PRODUCER; FOUNDER, ZOETROPE STUDIOS

This one's not that hard to figure out—Hart, Kreutzmann and Lesh, among others, were tapped to create the *Apocalypse Now* sound track. But Coppola has also stood as yet another gratifying example of someone at the top of a creative field who's clearly held the opinion that the Dead are something special. He got the idea to use Mickey and Bill (Phil ended up joining the fray as well) after seeing a Dead show with his family in 1979. The main reason he earns a place in the pantheon, though? The *Apocalypse Now* sessions (*Rhythm Devils Play River Music*) spawned the Beast.

✻ MATT GROENING, CARTOONIST (*LIFE IN HELL, THE SIMPSONS*)

How could I resist the opportunity to do honor to the creator of *The Simpsons*, a man who also happens to be a Deadhead? Whether at Groening's initiative or not, *The Simpsons* teems with references that are, if not direct allusions to the Dead, sure to catch the notice of Deadhead *Simpsons* fans (and there are many): Marge's "Keep On Truckin'" patch on the family quilt (yes, this could be more of a nod to R. Crumb), Barney ranting about "the dank," the "Simpsons Sing" album (in the episode where the Simpsons are rich and famous), for which we see the recording of "Man Smart, Woman Smarter," the bong teenage Homer sneaks into the prom, and, yes, the Steal Your Face—wearing, microbus-driving Deadhead who gives Homer's mom a lift in the episode where Homer discovers she's still alive. Groening's *Life in Hell* strip the week Jerry died contained a very touching eulogy to Garcia, depicting how the Dead had helped young Groening escape a straight world that mocked and humiliated him.

✻ PHIL JACKSON, HEAD COACH, CHICAGO BULLS

Continues the odd Dead-basketball connection. Zen hoopster Jackson, who recently guided the Bulls to the winningest season in pro-basketball history, has been known to use the Dead as a metaphor for teamwork. Presumably he's the influence behind pop-culture icon Dennis Rodman's self-assessing quote that he saw himself as "a Grateful Dead–type person." Another merciful Head in a straight world that's getting more bent by the minute.

✻ U.S. SENATOR PAT LEAHY (D-VT.)

He won forever a place in the hearts of fellow Heads by eulogizing Jerry from the Senate floor, a touching tribute that also represented a long-overdue official recognition of the Dead for being an American icon (a mere week after Senator Duncan of Tennessee decried the "horrible" Deadhead culture, introducing a *Washington Post* article titled "UnGrateful Deadheads: My Long, Strange Trip Through a Tie-Dyed Hell" into the Congressional Record, on Jerry's *birthday,* no less). He got on the bus after attending a show with his son.

✻ GEORGE LUCAS, DIRECTOR, PRODUCER; FOUNDER, LUCASFILM

One of the persistent rumors that's made its way through Deaddom of late is that Lucasfilm bought Grateful Dead Merchandising (in some versions of the rumor he bought the whole Grateful Dead kit and kaboodle) a few years back and is behind the explosion of Dead knickknacks for sale through the *Grateful Dead Almanac,* the Dead's newsletter and music/merchandise catalog—the "Steal Your Face Golf Club Covers" syndrome. Even the *Dick's Picks* series has been seen as a symptom of this alleged change at the till: While Heads applaud the effort being taken to open wider the doors of the Vault, they also note acidly that there was a time when the band, or whoever (usually Dan Healy), would simply put boards of good or hard-to-find shows in circulation. I for one am glad for (the *very* reasonably priced) *Dick's Picks,* and tapes still get circulated gratis out of the Dead hoard, though admittedly not as frequently, and only after first being put through an analog-cassette generation to stump bootleggers. Oh yeah, George Lucas. Well, it's not hard to see what the Dead and Lucas would have in common. They both have a gift and an appetite for providing startling visuals and pushing the envelope of media experience. And there's clearly *something* up—"Lucasfilm—George Lucas" is given thanks in the *Built to Last* liner notes (they recorded parts of the album at the state-of-the-art studios at Lucas's Skywalker Ranch), and in some '89 and '90 shows you can clearly hear Jerry sing "*Death* Star crashes. . . ." (Note for the overly literal-minded: George Lucas did *not* buy GDM.)

✻ HUNTER S. THOMPSON, WRITER

There's no real evidence he's actually a Deadhead, but just as sure as he wouldn't cotton to the label is the probability that he's taken in some shows. None of that really matters, though. He makes the pantheon hands down on the strength of this simple fact: Hunter's the one who introduced Ken Kesey to the Hell's Angels.

✻ BILL WALTON, FORMER CENTER, PORTLAND TRAILBLAZERS AND BOSTON CELTICS, CURRENTLY SPORTS ANNOUNCER FOR NBC

Never hard to spot at Centrum shows, Walton was the redheaded tree dancing off to the side of the stage. He used to get psyched up for games by listening to shows on headphones. For years he's been one of the foremost Head "spies" in the straight world—advancing the feeling that we are in fact everywhere. There's always been a thrill attendant on the knowledge that the guy doing color for Marv Albert is the same one who freaked freely in Egypt and elsewhere with the Dead, particularly when he sneaks Dead song references into his commentary. When Walton joined the Celtics, the organist at the Boston Garden would play Touch of Gray and Uncle John's between quarters. Conversely the Dead's '87 Ventura shows started late because the band and crew were engrossed in the Celtics-Lakers finals, which they broadcast over the PA.

10/27/79
CAPE COD

Funky keys and a vibrant tenor—Brent's arrival and the changes it wrought are amply highlighted in one of the best second sets of the year. The Dancin' opener finds Bobby forgetting that they're no longer opening the song vocally with the "Dancin', dancin' dancin' in the streets" duet that he and Donna used to sing. Donna's absence is not felt for long, though, as Brent sings right in her register with apparent ease. This arrangement works so well with Brent in fact that one must assume that their subsequent rearrangement of the song that brought it closer to the Dead's original preretirement arrangement (which is in turn much closer to the Martha and the Vandellas version) was a matter of musical preference rather than necessity. It's Brent and Jerry going at it instrumentally here, with Mydland alternating between the straight-ahead Fender sound and a *funky*-ass wah-

wah key effect that weaves in and out of and at times envelops Jerry's more rounded wah tone. If this is the sound of disco Dead, well, then call me a Dancin' fool. Unfortunately Brent experiences some technical difficulties with the bug-squashing funky keys and has to retreat to sole use of the "plinky" keys, a distraction that briefly robs the jam of some of its drive. Not to worry, though, they promptly get it back on track. Everyone makes their presence felt—the drums and Phil lay down a fat, fat beat (Mickey throwing a rim shot into a quiet space with a solar plexus—hitting "crack!"), and Bobby's rhythm fills are right on as well.

Franklin's Tower sucks up the ends of Dancin' like the *Götterhooverung* (vacuum cleaner of the gods), subsuming its rhythm in a way that's quite a marvel to behold. As stand-alone Franklin's go, this one is one of the best jammed out. The sound of Brent's keys over percussion that heralds the next song almost seems to hint at a Brent tune; instead its an outstanding He's Gone. This one goes down real smooth. Just as it seems it's about to twinkle gracefully off into Drums, Garcia and Lesh grow restive. Jerry's noodlings grow into the beginning runs of the Caution jam, and Bobby soon joins in with alacrity. There's an interesting bit of improvisational teamwork to be witnessed here as Phil uses his bass to prise open a space in the mix for Garcia's attack of the theme. It's a short-lived one unfortunately, though Brent does manage to fit in some frenzied dueling with Jerry late in the jam. Just as the playing is beginning to meander, Phil refocuses the minds of all by carpet bombing the coliseum with one of the most ferocious—almost angry-sounding—Other One intros he's ever laid down. Not surprisingly he dominates the entire tune, to marvelous effect.

Sightings

As seen on TV:
Roseanne to Dan, on the CBS series *Roseanne:* "You have no self-control. You're like Jerry Garcia without the music!" Roseanne is actually quite the Deadhead.

A fairly ordinary Drums lends its tribal beat to Not Fade Away. Phil slips into the drum rhythm, fattening it considerably, while Jerry initiates a slow, menacing guitar growl above. Brent's entrance in the upper register adds the final element to a deliciously restrained build to an excellent version. Alas, next come Black Peter and Around, both solid versions but nothing compared with the sinfully rich groove they follow. Taken as a whole, this tape's a must.

The Best of the Rest: Extraordinary Versions of the Very Ordinary

AROUND AND AROUND
3/18/77
5/7/77
10/17/78
9/11/83

U.S. BLUES
5/19/74
6/28/74
1/22/78
10/17/78
10/21/78

MINGLEWOOD BLUES
3/18/77
5/7/77
5/8/77
1/13/80

EL PASO
2/15/73
5/26/73

ME & MY UNCLE
3/18/67 (well, maybe the weirdest...)
4/29/71
12/1/71
12/5/71
2/9/73
12/12/73
11/6/77 (quite the transition from Mexicali)

ONE MORE SATURDAY NIGHT
9/6/80
7/4/81 (one more Fourth of July)
3/24/90

MEXICALI BLUES
5/9/77
11/6/77

12/1/79
STANLEY THEATER

An awesome, fantastically well jammed China → Rider opens one of the most fulfilling second sets of 1979. The Looks Like Rain that follows is of similar quality, though definitely the less for no longer receiving the benefit of Donna's backing vocals—this was one song in which her embellishments were almost always welcome, sort of the inverse of Playin' in this respect. Bobby goes some way toward compensating for her absence by trying out some interesting and quite effective vocal improvisations in the ending. He leans on "Oh Lord" (as in, "Oh Lord, here come the rain") in this version more than in any other of which I'm aware. Usually this word just gets sung as "Oh-whooaa-oh."

If Looks Like Rain calls to mind Donna's absence, He's Gone plays up the benefits of now having Brent around. His raspy tenor adds just the right element to the bittersweet refrain. This is a laid-back and restrained version even for this tune. It's all the more surprising, then, when a sudden surge of energy pulls the band into a positively smoking Gloria jam. Like the Not Fade later in the set, there are broad hints of a Caution jam here as well. The transition into the first C. C. Rider is exciting and, obviously, unexpected—even by most of the band. It's humorous to note the frantic back-and-forth among band members as the song emerges, kind of "Just what the hell *are* we playing?" Strangely, and a bit disappointingly, the Dead don't take a blues jam into Drums, switching instead to a fast, rather generic jam of the Playin' mold. As jams of this sort go, though, it's a good one, with even a slight hint of the Spanish Jam to be found.

The Not Fade Away out of Space achieves a deep, purposeful groove. It seems as if Not Fade always used to get its energy and find its rhythm in the intro jam, which must be part of why all those Throwin' → Not Fades, which threw the band right into Not Fade, seemed so empty and alike after a while. Jerry fans away here like mad, ensuring this Not Fade's distinction. The Black Peter that follows is hardly a downer either. Jerry's emotional vocals and improvisational repetition of the "run and see" line spur the band to some fierce playing on the way out of the tune. This is easily one of the best electric versions, at least, of this oft and unjustly maligned tune. The energy level by the end is such that the switch to Sugar Magnolia does not sound at all forced—the obligatory end-of-second-set shift from Jerry ballad to Bobby rocker seems a natural fit in this case. The Dead would achieve this effect with greater regularity in the nineties as Jerry really beefed up the codas to his ballads—Standing on the Moon is a prime example.

If you haven't much experience with '79 shows, December of this year is definitely a good place to start, a month throughout the whole of which the Dead played at their peak. And what better show to start December with than the first?

1/13/80
OAKLAND

This one-set-only benefit for Cambodian refugees can be considered a one-tape Dead sampler of sorts, with a balance of first- and second-set tunes, pretty and aggressive playing, and a few guest artists, to boot, in the persons of John Cipollina, Carlos Santana, and Greg Errico.

The show opens with a big Jack Straw into which Phil drops a couple of atomic bombs. There's also some impressive drum work in between the lines of the "gotta settle one old score" verse, and fat jamming throughout. Franklin's, too, is mighty kind, striking the perfect balance between sensitive and rocking playing. Phil, it should be noted, continues his bombing run here. A *great* Minglewood and very good Jed both have a larger-than-first-set feel to them appropriate to the format. Playin' is marked by a deep, questing jam that receives each band member's full participation on its way into Drums.

Mickey and Billy get the audience to clap along to a sixteen-beat pattern in the excellent Drums, which is not followed by any real Space but rather a long, tension-filled Not Fade intro that is in its own right more than a little bit spacey. Brent and Bobby are the notable participants here, each laying down some *funky* lines. Additionally the guitar interaction between Cipollina, Weir, Santana, and Garcia conspires to make this one for the ages. Talk about your psychedelic all-stars! This is one "all-star jam" that doesn't amount to less than the sum of its parts. The big band steers Not Fade into a closing Sugar Magnolia that brims with energy and serious fun. A hot U.S. Blues with Greg Errico ties up this very satisfying single-set performance nicely.

6/20/80
ANCHORAGE

The middle show of the Dead's first and only Alaska run serves as a fine indicator of how the band sounded on a good night in 1980. The very standard composition of both first and second sets provides a useful "control."

The first set begins with the then-common pairing of Jack Straw and Franklin's Tower, both solidly played here. There's a quintessential Bobby moment in the Mexicali that follows as he shouts with glee that "Eveerybody loves a polka!" Perhaps he was trying to convince the drummers. An excellent Friend of the Devil features some of the sparkling Brent and Jerry solo turns

PLAYIN' VERY WELL INDEED IN THE BAND

* 4/4/71 Manhattan Center
* 7/18/72 Roosevelt Stadium
* 8/27/72 Veneta
* 11/19/72 Hofheinz Pavilion
* 2/9/73 Stanford
* 6/22/73 Vancouver
* 11/10/73 Winterland
* 11/17/73 Pauley Pavilion
* 12/2/73 Boston Music Hall
* 5/21/74 Seattle
* 5/19/77 Fox Theater
* 7/1/79 Seattle
* 8/4/79 Oakland
* 12/28/79 Oakland
* 7/4/81 Manor Downs, Texas
* 4/17/83 Byrne
* 6/30/84 Indianapolis
* 10/12/84 Augusta (Playin' reprise only)
* 3/31/85 Portland, Maine (inverted Playin')
* 11/21/85 Kaiser
* 7/2/88 Oxford Plains
* 7/29/88 Laguna Seca
* 10/9/89 Hampton
* 3/19/90 Hartford
* 5/26/93 Cal Expo

that mark versions from this era. Althea provides ample evidence that this set is getting hot, fire courtesy of Jerry's piercing licks. A "Shave and a Haircut" tuning precedes a very good Lost Sailor → Saint, both of which have their share of cutting Garcia solos. The same goes for the big Deal that closes the set.

Alabama → Greatest, another set-opening pair from this era, begin the second frame. I've always thought that this combo was not only musically excellent but inspired in terms of the songs' shared religious references. This and the Ship of Fools that follow are well played if not standout versions. Estimated Prophet, however, represents a shifting of gears. The body of the song is brawny and firm, and the closing of the song bristles with a fast, staccato jam that Phil, with some well-chosen peals of thunder, magically transforms into a *very* fast Other One. The playing is very tight here under Jerry's vicious lead lines; unfortunately it ends abruptly after the last chorus. Even Billy and Mickey seem surprised—a moment or two passes before Drums begins.

And a loopy Drums it is, full of virtuoso rhythm workouts leavened by Billy's downright goofiness. At one point, alternating between the toms and the snare for some jazzy fills, he gives vocal

✸ 9/26/93 Boston

✸ 7/5/95 St. Louis (the last one)

echo to what he's just played: "Boogedy, boogedy, boogedy, shoop!" drawing laughter and a cryptic percussion response from Mickey. At another, Billy takes up a duck call, which he riffs on while giggling uncontrollably. Mickey and he get into dueling bird calls here, with Mickey answering Billy's lines in a higher pitched version of the sound he's employing.

The full band eschews the customary spacey noodling upon taking the stage again for Space, diving instead into a funky, bizarre jam. Weir and Mydland acquit themselves particularly well here, the two of them getting real down and wah-wah raunchy. Garcia contents himself (and the listener) with fueling a feedback groove in the background. The jam takes full shape as a very fresh Not Fade Away. Black Peter, the highlight of the show, continues the excellent playing and sees it reach its peak. The first, slow solo is a perfect example of Jerry's unsurpassed skill in melodic phrasing. Part and parcel of this is his uncanny rhythmic sensibility—the way he lets certain notes almost die out completely before hitting the next at the *exact* nanosecond to produce maximum emotional impact. His singing is also superb here, especially in the "... as poor as me" line. Note the little harmonic jewels he plays behind his vocals. And Bobby's tasteful slide work. And the boisterous solo Jerry plays after "run and see." And . . .

The rest of the set is pretty straightforward, three rockers in a row: Around, Johnny B. Goode, and a Don't Ease encore, of which Johnny B. Goode is the rockingest.

9/6/80

LEWISTON, MAINE

The second set of this show has a great deal to recommend it—almost an embarrassment of riches. That the huge Playin' sandwich in the middle of the set isn't the only highlight speaks volumes.

Shakedown is a tune that just kept getting hotter from '79 on, with Brent clearly the impetus, and the one that opens the second frame here is no exception. This one gets real down and funky in the end jam especially, as Brent and Jerry kick each other around the stage in the midst of a monster groove—whew! The Lost Sailor → Saint that follows is good, though not quite up to the epic scale of the rest of the show, but it's followed by a finely rendered, always-a-pleasure Althea.

Then comes the monster jam that defines and dominates this show: Playin' → Uncle John's → Drums → Space → NFA → Wheel → Uncle John's → Playin' → Sugar Magnolia! The menu for this sandwich—nay, hero (sub, hoagie, or whatever you call it locally)—is mouthwatering in and of itself, but the playing itself is the real delicacy here. A Playin' appetizer bursts at the seams with fast, fantastic jamming on its way to an Uncle John's transition in which the band simply fights its way through the encroaching Drums. Uncle John's itself is played exceptionally well and with a great deal of energy, with which the exit jam in particular fairly crackles.

Coming out of Drums, Not Fade manages to incorporate its predecessor's rhythm but not wholly accede to it. They play this one with a great deal of thoughtful musicianship, the way it used to be done, Brent, Bobby, and Jerry weaving an electric tapestry of psychedelic jamming. A fine Wheel brings the band back around to a Playin' reprise into which they storm as if eager to be back home. They carry the celebration over into a rollicking Sugar Magnolia to complete the jam. Although Weir's voice is shown to be the worse for wear in

"One of the many things I'll miss most about Dead shows, and which I think a lot of Heads were sorry to see slipping away in the last few years or so, was that amazing feeling of trust you could get from most of the people even in a crowd of tens of thousands. You hear the word *family* a lot in talking about the Dead and Deadheads and it's one of those words that one hears so often and in so many different places that it's lost some of its impact. People no longer really think about what it means. Well, even at a huge and (justly) bad-rapped place like the Meadowlands, it meant that you could get a drink of water or slice of orange if you were bumming and you would gladly offer same. That's the thing, stuff like that was *offered* all the time— miracle tickets (or at least tickets at cost or below), a pull on a bowl, a desperately needed cool quaff, even a back rub. The Dead scene, at its best, was Eden.

"A small example, the likes of which every Deadhead has seen countless times: I met this guy Zeus on the train into the city the first night of the spring Byrne shows in '88. I was missing that show because of a wedding in New York but was hopping back on the bus the next night. Zeus was obviously going to the show that night. I, already in my wedding attire, obviously was *not*. I struck up a conversation about the tour, though, how hot the Hampton shows had been and all that. I wished him a good show, and that was that. The next night, in the parking lot, I was bumming because I couldn't find my friends who had my ticket. I *did* run into Zeus, though, who selflessly helped me look for about an hour (granted he didn't know what my friends *looked* like, but I was happy for the company) and tried to line up a fallback ticket for me from among his friends. As showtime neared (and oh, to have *that* feeling again...) and I resigned myself to hanging in the lot (the fallback, alas, hadn't materialized), he asked if I would hang on to his skateboard for him. I said sure, took the board, and a minute later ran into Dave, who had my ticket. After the show, I waited for Zeus in the general area I'd said I'd be in. As it got closer and closer to time to split, I left the board with instructions with my friends, who were just hanging in the postshow glow, rapping, playing Frisbee, and set out to the area where his friends were parked. I couldn't find him or his friends, and I arrived back at my camp to find Zeus hanging with my friends, skateboard safely in hand. He'd run into them a few minutes after I left to find them skating on his board. He was psyched to have found it, and the thought that they were doing anything but having fun while safeguarding it never crossed his mind—no suspicions of theft or sketchiness there. This openness and willingness to help people typified Deadheads at their best.

the Saturday Night encore, it must be said that it *rocks.* The follow-up of Brokedown to seal the tour makes it all the sweeter.

5/4/81
PHILLY SPECTRUM

Caught between two better known shows in a big spring tour, this night tends to get overlooked. But while the second set of this show can't touch 5/6 at Nassau, it's superior in almost every respect to that of the 5/1 Hampton performance.

A jaunty China Cat kicks off the second frame, aurally defined by "that plinky Brent keyboard sound." It works well here, sounding almost like vibes as Brent plays the melodic lead over Bob's excellent rhythm playing, similar here to his work in the 6/30/85 Shakedown, in the well-developed transition. The Rider that follows is solid, if not spectacular, highlighted by Jerry's quick rhythmic scrubbing between lines of the "headlight" verse. Samson is sung with conviction by both Bobby and Jerry, whose backing vocals are once again impeccable. The middle jam, in which Brent positively goes off on the Hammond B, is played with stop-on-a-dime precision. A respectable To Lay Me Down never really takes

"Of course the scene was not always at its best, and those elements in it that were malignant seemed, in contrast to those who would make the scene a paradise, to be emissaries from that other place. The vibes that the best Deadheads send out, though, can, like the ocean, cleanse much that is foul. Every Head has seen the phenomenon of frat-type guys mellowing out at shows, even if its only for that one night in the year. And though there was some smugness in the scene about seeing some people don their "Deadhead" persona for a show like a Sears tie-dye, I always thought it was a beautiful thing. This must be the transformative quality that fired the imaginations of the social revolutionaries in the early Haight—hey, all we have to do is turn on the world!

"Without getting too crypto-theological about the whole thing, I think this could be (aside from all that amazing music!) the Dead's most enduring legacy. As the scene inevitably splinters, we should embrace chaos and spread all that love and trust we once kept insular to those who haven't yet turned on to the fact that trust begets trust, that it shouldn't just be shown to one's biological family or even acquired families of friends, tour buddies, and the like.

"Then again, never trust a Prankster (who wears his head too tight). **99**

—Matthew Rus

off, though apparently not for want of effort.

The energy level picks back up with a crisp Playin' that gets a quirky lead-in from an excellent Camptown Racers tuning that goes awry à la Merry-Go-Round Broke Down at the end. Brent's keys are again a big factor here. The long Playin' jam into Drums is played with plenty of fire, Jerry going to the wah effect with great results. Drums is short but intriguing, best described as serpentine, an accent seized upon by Jerry and Bobby in their intro for the breakout Nobody's Fault that follows. This version is appropriately soulful, if perfunctory, unique in the way it is driven by the clip-cloppy rhythm of the preceding Drums. It leads into a somewhat spacey Lost Sailor, in which Bobby gives us his James Brown impersonation ("I need some help now") and informs us that the rainbow does indeed end "right here in Philly" (who'da thunk it?). Ragging aside, it's well done and sires a very exciting Saint.

The Jerry-sad, Bobby-happy end-of-show trip is particularly well done here. Black Peter is even more emotional than usual, and Jerry makes the end jam count by wringing some authoritative blues licks out of the Tiger. On the flip side, Sugar Magnolia is especially exuberant, highlighted by the verve of Bobby's very forward-leaning rhythm riffs. It's capped off by a sick Sunshine Daydream, Bobby rapping "c'mon over here" and other entreaties to his summer lover. The warmly sung Brokedown encore approaches the feel of We Bid You Goodnight—a big good-bye hug from the band.

The Dead That We Said: The Other Lyrics

THEY'RE OFTEN tasteless, or burnt, or seemingly cruel to the band, but when 90 percent of what's running through your head at any given moment are Dead lyrics, you're going to come up with some, um, interesting variations. Surround yourself at a show with twenty thousand other people whose thoughts are also running in this manner and . . . well, you know what they say about the roomful of chimps on typewriters. So here, for what it's worth (not a whole hell of a lot, I'll grant you) and in no particular order, are some intentionally altered lyrics from over the years and tours:

Brown-Eyed Women
"The bottle was dusty but the liquor was clean"
"The blotter was dusty but the liquid was clean"

Jack Straw
"We can share the women, we can share the wine"
"We can share the women, we can share the kind"
"We can share the lemon, we can share the lime"

"We used to play for silver, now we play for life"
"We used to play for acid, now we play for lines"
(actually sung once by Bobby!)

Dark Star
". . . pouring its life into ashes"
". . . pouring its life into acid"

Bertha
"I had a hard run, running from your window"
"I had a hard-on, running from your window"

"I ducked back into a bar door"
"I ducked back into Novato"

"Test me, test me—why don't you arrest me?"
"Testes, testes—why don't you caress these?"

Pride of Cucamonga

"Whoa-ho, Pride of Cucamonga"
"Whoa-ho, Pride of Jimmy's* momma"

Uncle John's Band

"Goddamn, well, I declare, have you seen the like?"
"Goddamn, a wide éclair, it's creamy and so light!"

"How does the song go?"
"Where does this bong go?"

Ship of Fools

"I cannot share your laughter, Ship of Fools"
"I cannot dig your menthol, pack of Kools"

Estimated Prophet

"And might and glory gonna be my name"
"And Mike and Gloria gonna be my name"

Sugar Magnolia

"She don't come and I don't follow"
"She don't come and I don't swallow"

Victim Or the Crime

"Whatever happened to his precious self-control?"
"Whatever happened to my TV remote control?"

So Many Roads

"So many roads to ease my soul"
"So many shows to ease my soul"

Hey Pocky Way

"He-ey, Heeeey, Hey Pocky Way"
"He-ey, Heeeey, No Fuckin' Way"

* Obviously the name is to be substituted with that of the victim of your low-grade sophomoric humor.

A Touch of Gray

"I see you've got your list out, say your peace and get out"
"I see you've got your dick out, take a piss and get out"
(Some Heads claim Jerry actually sings this in the 10/27/91 Touch. I'd say it's [a] unlikely in general and [b] especially unlikely given the somber nature of this run—the Bill Graham memorial shows.)

Man Smart, Woman Smarter

"That's right, the women are smarter"
"That's right, the women of Sparta"
"That's right, we're swimming in water"

Cassidy

"A catch colt draws a coffin cart"
"I catch cold at a coffee cart"

Wharf Rat

"I love my Pearly Baker best"
"I love my curly baco-bits"
"I love my girlie paperbacks"

Wave That Flag

"Wave that flag, pop the bag"
"Wave that flag, cop a bag"

Hell in a Bucket

"I may be going to hell in a bucket, but at least I'm enjoying the ride"
"I may be going to hell in a bucket, but at least it's a joyful imbibe"

It Must Have Been the Roses

"... maybe it was the roses"
"... maybe it was cirrhosis"
"... maybe it was the doses"

Feel Like a Stranger

"You know it's gonna get stranger, so let's
get on with the show!"
"You know it's gonna get stoneder, so let's
get on with that bowl!"

Throwing Stones

"A peaceful place, or so it looks from space"
"A pizza place, or so it looks from space"

"We are all alone . . . all alone!"
"We are on the phone . . . on the phone!"

Eyes of the World

"Wake up to find out that you are the eyes of the world"
"Wake up to find out that you are the size of the world"
(Actually sung by Jerry at Greek 8/17/89, a horrible show)

Scarlet Begonias

"She wore scarlet begonias . . ."
"She wore a scarlet Patagonia . . ."

In the Attics of My Life

"In the attics of my life . . ."
"In the antics of my life . . ."

> " *A* funny story from the
> Cornell show, I think in
> May '81, with a
> longtime touring buddy: An
> extremely weird-looking long-haired
> guy dressed in yellow sweats dotted
> with dozens of red Cosmic Wimp-out
> stickers sold us each five little pieces of
> paper. He said, 'It's from San
> Francisco, very fresh.' I took his words
> to heart, but my buddy scoffed and
> promptly ate all five. My favorite quote
> from him came after the show when he
> asked me in all seriousness, 'Did they
> ever come and take me up on stage and
> shine all the lights on me?' "
> —CAPTAIN K.

5/6/81
NASSAU

It's interesting that Nassau Coliseum, a venue upon which the Dead have heaped scorn because of the way its community's police have used the band as "bait" for drug arrests of Deadheads, has played host to so many hot shows over the years. Perhaps the Dead put in an extra effort to compensate Heads for any hassles they might encounter there. This just may be the best of the bunch (with all due respect to Branford and devotees of 3/29/90), due to a second set that's just one long, flowing river of a jam.

It starts with a trickle after a stand-alone Minglewood opener—an average High Time. The gathering waters pick up speed, though, with a fast Lost Sailor that overcomes Bobby's hoarseness to feature one of the most exciting passages into Saint on tape, whitewater sluicing suddenly over the falls, bearing with it a shouting Bobby in a barrel. After this torrent the river enters a serene glade of slow esses and muddy banks with He's Gone for Bobby Sands (the IRA hunger-striker who had just died), played appropriately slowly, quietly, and mournfully. The harmonies are particularly good; also very soothing is Jerry's fluid and relaxed lead line. Jerry's singing sounds genuinely sad and restrained—note how he downplays the "steal your face" line the second time through and how his voice cracks on the last couple of "nothing's gonna bring him backs" before the coda. The song fades to near total quiet, the stillness of standing pools rippling only to Brent's synthesizer breeze moving across the face of the waters.

Out of nowhere, though, *whitewater.* Jerry suddenly plays *lightning* runs on the He's Gone scale—as fast as he's ever played. The rapid runs emerge into a full-fledged, hysterically hot Caution jam, a bolt from the blue if ever there was one. Garcia plays on like a man possessed while Phil lays down a thick undercurrent of bass and Brent begins to match Jerry, alternating with great speed between the Hammond and the Fender.

We briefly find ourselves in a nether territory, with Jerry running up and down scales and Phil and Brent, especially, coming up big behind him—Brent adds some insane psychedelic color here. Where to go but . . . Iberia! The Spanish Jam in all its glory. Is this '81 or '72? The jam is played in a virtuoso staccato variation, with heavy atmospherics provided by Bobby and the drums. Jerry dances around the theme for quite some time before stating it with an indescribably satisfying flourish. Rank this spate of jamming among the very, very best in the Dead's history—it's that good.

A run through the land of Drums continues the frenetic pace of the Spanish Jam. Most noteworthy here is the mad beating of bass drum and toms that occurs near the end, followed by accents of higher-pitched percussion. Mickey changes to a rhythm with strong Middle Eastern accents just before Jerry reappears and takes up the theme with enthusiasm. Bobby and Phil rejoin the mix as the drums lock into a more intense, direct variation of the beat (compare the playing here to what some Heads have dubbed the "Baghdad" Space out of Close Encounters on 7/15/89); the effect is galvanizing, electric. The ravishing Moorish jamming continues for a time until Jerry points all in the direction hinted at earlier by Billy and Mickey—The Other One. And, boy, do Phil and Brent *nail* the intro to this one! It flames over the surface of the jam's river, burning quickly but with acetylene intensity until it is cooled by a breezy Goin' Down the Road, which strikes a perfect elemental balance. Before long Jerry conspires to turn up the heat on this one, too, playing it loud with a big-time feel. It's interesting to note that he foregoes the We Bid You Goodnight coda and launches directly into Wharf Rat instead—it takes some quick thinking to beat Bobby to the tune call! Jerry justifies his precipitousness by delivering a muscular version fully worthy of its esteemed company in the set.

As a final measure of the degree to which the group mind was at work in this show, listen to the end of Wharf Rat: Jerry's beginning to noodle in search of the next tune when Bobby plays a *tiny* snatch of the Good Lovin' intro behind him, which Jerry picks up instantly, stepping in without missing a beat. The drums crash in at the next available downbeat. Good Lovin' cooks all the way through, as does Don't Ease. This one's a jaw-dropping stunner all the way through; it makes for mighty exhilarating rafting.

10/6/81
RAINBOW THEATER, LONDON

This show, which is relatively obscure, would probably get a lot more attention if it weren't for the novelty of the Melk Weg performance on Bob Weir's birthday. While the Amsterdam show certainly has more going for it than novelty alone, this one's a more accurate portrait of the Dead's sound in late 1981. As for the playing itself, well, London is not without its own surprises.

Bobby gives the second set a randy start with a great Man Smart, Woman Smarter, which he embellishes with a number of "Ha!"s thrown in for good measure. Jerry quells the rowdiness with a strange, floaty, feathery delivery of High Time that's pretty disconcerting. A less charitable reviewer might simply write that he was straining vocally, but that alone does not explain the odd, seemingly intentional "delay" in his voice. The weirdness continues with what must rank as the most bizarre Estimated ever. Brent's innovative keyboard figures in the intro get things off to an odd start and exert a disproportionate influence on the whole of the song, owing to Jerry's subdued presence. When Jerry does take his solo, it bears little resemblance to the one he generally delivers. Bobby's delivery is breathless, with his vocal improvisations more manic than usual. The wonderfully twisted closing jam sounds as if it's being played underwater. The jam maintains its strange character in the climax, after which it sounds as if the band is veering off into Eyes. Instead they find a sunny, shimmering musical place between songs, in which they idle briefly before Jerry leads the way into He's Gone. This is a strong version that dissolves into another unusual jam. Mysterious and compelling from the start, it becomes even more so as it heads into Drums, with Brent steering the jam and adding some accents in concert with the drummers' beat. This last section sounds like a deconstruction of the Other One jam—played backward.

Drums comes on like a force of nature. Billy can be heard at one point urging "Harry" (Popick?) to "c'mon, man, jam with us—c'mon, don't be bashful." While Billy tattoos the set, Mickey begins to *work* the tar. Billy swings with him, cracking rimshots and providing counterpoint on his floor toms. The duet turns terrifying at one point when both drummers are at their sets and begin alternating suddenly and unpredictably between staccato ticks on the drum rims and all-out *war* on the bass drums: *BAMMA BAMMA BAM BAM tick tick tick tick tick BAM BAM BAM BAMMA BAM tick tick tick BAM BAM....*

The full band's return brings a rare treat, the first Blues for Allah jam, crickets and all. There are some moments in this jam where time seems to stand completely still—this is some of the most transportational music the Dead have ever played, trippy in the extreme. Especially affecting are Brent's legato keyboard effects. From this masterful space the band begins a Wheel intro that is just so . . . right. It occupies the moment to the exclusion of all other sensory input, exerting a powerful emotional hold upon the listener. Part of this effect is due to the remarkable unity of sound and dynamics the band achieves here. The spell does not dissipate throughout the song, and Jerry begins to weave it again in the outro before Bobby interjects with what seems like the singularly uninspired choice of Sugar Magnolia. Weir's vocal mugging, particularly in the "walk around" part of the song, is enough to make one wonder just what the hell he thinks he's doing. Before we know it, though, we're at the closing jam, Jerry going off happily on guitar (I guess if Jerry was okay with it . . .), and there's Bobby, laying down some mean-ass, completely crazy riffs that could only be his. From goat to hero in a matter of minutes.

There's something about the stillness of the Stella Blue that follows that's utterly transfixing. Jerry's vocal delivery is outstanding. The jam that builds out of it is mesmerizing as well before Bobby decides to cut it short in order to deliver the oh-so-momentous tune Good Lovin'. Jerry ends the line he was playing with a "crunch" that seems born of frustration and joins in resignedly. Bobby's continued vocal cuteness is particularly aggravating after this trespass.

The Dead end this oner of a show by playing an encore that consists of the Sunshine Daydream they had left off of Sugar Mags into a nice Brokedown, which unfortunately gets cut, even on a one-hundred-minute tape. A compelling reminder not to neglect that part of the tour that did not take place in a hash bar.

FALL

1

2

3 *9/3/77 Englishtown*
   9/3/85 Starlight

4 *Gary Duncan, b. 1946*

5

6 *9/6/80 Lewiston, Maine*

7 *9/7/85 Red Rocks* ❋ *First Hey Jude finale out of*
   Fantasy

8 *Pigpen (né Ron McKernan), b. 1945*

9

10 *9/10/91 MSG* ❋ *With Branford Marsalis*

11 *Mickey Hart, b. 1943* ❋ *Peter Tosh, d. 1987* ❋
    9/11/83 Santa Fe Downs ❋ *Help* ➤ *Slip*
    ➤ *Frank's, Dew!*

12

13 *Bill Monroe, b. 1911* ❋ *9/13/93 Philly* ❋
    Tubular bells

14 *9/14/90 MSG*

15

16 *9/16/78 Egypt* ❋ *With Hamza El Din* ❋
    Full lunar eclipse

17 *Hank Williams, b. 1923* ❋ *Ken Kesey, b. 1935*
    ❋ *Keith Moon, d. 1978*

18 *9/18/87 MSG* ❋ *Dew!*

19 *9/19/70 Fillmore East* ❋ *"Fuck" Lovelight*
    9/19/90 MSG

20 *9/20/70 Fillmore East*
    9/20/91 Boston Garden ❋ *Help* ➤ *Slip*
    ➤ *Fire!*

21 *First day of autumn* ❋ *9/21/72 Philly*

22

23

Fall. Summer has flown and August has died, and the world is growing dark. Close the windows, put on a sweater, and try to increase summer's lease with some great fall tours preserved on tape. Try on '77 or '78 for warmth. Or '85. Nineteen eighty-seven's a fun one—dancing to Good Lovin' → La Bamba → Good Lovin' should heat you up a bit. And while you're at it, might as well sample those tasty runs from '90 and '91.

Time was when fall was the time for collegiate Deadheads to fall hopelessly behind in their classes, putting off studying for midterms to catch the Boys in as many towns as one could make, *fall fall fall fall fall fall fall fall fall fall fall fall fall fall fall fall fall fall*

24

25 *9/25/80 Warfield* ✲ *Acoustic breakout fest*

26 *Johnny "Appleseed" Chapman, b. 1774* ✲ *9/26/91 Boston*

27 *Samuel Adams, b. 1722*

28 *Miles Davis, d. 1991* ✲ *9/28/72 Jersey City*

29 *9/29/67 Straight Theater* ✲ *Mickey's first show*

30 *9/30/71 Santa Venetia, California* ✲ *Rehearsal with Keith*

hoping to run into some friends from Vermont (or Humbolt) to reap the fruits of that year's harvest. If you were from northern climes, it was a chance to catch the Dead at the "cosmic taco shell" that was Hampton, the mellowest East Coast venue, and hopefully catch some warmer weather in the bargain. On both coasts, having the Dead on or near a college campus during freshman orientation meant a Head start for meeting those who shared your interests. "Oh, dude—you blew off that ice-cream social too?" This fact was not lost on the administration of U.C. Berkeley; the Dead played the Greek right before orientation there in 1989 and never returned. And if the Brown University (Providence, Rhode Island) administration is still wondering why the

1

2 *10/2/77 Portland, Oregon*

3 *Woody Guthrie, d. 1967* ✻ *German reunification, 1990*

4 *Janis Joplin, d. 1970*

5

6 *10/6/81 London*

7

8 *10/8/89 Hampton* ✻ *Help* ➥ *Slip* ➥ *Frank's breakout*

9 *Peter Tosh, b. 1944* ✻ *10/9/76 Oakland* ✻ *Day on the Green* ✻ *10/9/89 Hampton* ✻ *Dark Star!!!*

10 *Vice-president Spiro Agnew resigns, 1973*

11 *10/11/83 MSG* ✻ *St. Stephen breakout*

12 *10/12/84 Augusta*

13 *10/13/81 Russelsheim, Germany*

14 *10/14/83 Hartford*

15

16 *Bob Weir, b. 1947* ✻ *10/16/81 Amsterdam* ✻ *10/16/89 Byrne*

17 *10/17/83 Lake Placid* ✻ *Sugaree!*

18

19 *10/19/89 Philly*

20 *Tom Petty, b. 1952* ✻ *10/20/74 Winterland* ✻ *"The Last One"*

21 *10/21/78 Winterland* ✻ *"From Egypt with Love"*
10/21/83 Worcester

22

23

24

freshmen in 1987 were such a "problem" so early in the school year, well, now you know.

To be sung to the tune of Easy to Slip:

"It's so easy to trip
It's so to do fall tour
And let your courseload
drift and do nothing at
all
All the shows that you
missed,
And the setlists that you
can't recall…
Did they really exist at
all?"

Autumn shades seem to bring out the simple farmer in all of us as we don flannels and even we most citified or suburban types might harvest a pumpkin and a few gourds *fall fall fall fall fall fall fall fall fall fall fall fall fall fall fall fall fall fall fall fall*

25 *China invades Tibet, 1950* ✹ *Bill Graham, d. 1991* ✹ *10/25/73 Madison*

26 *10/26/89 Miami*

27 *James Marshall Hendrix (né Johnny Allen), b. 1942* ✹ *10/27/79 Cape Cod*

28

29 *Peter Green (né Peter Greenbaum), b. 1946* ✹ *Duane Allman, d. 1971* ✹ *10/29/77 DeKalb, Illinois*

30 *Grace Slick (née Grace Barnett Wing), b. 1939* ✹ *10/30/68 Matrix* ✹ *With Elvin Bishop and Jack Casady*

31 *All Hallows' Eve, or Samhain* ✹ *10/31/91 Oakland* ✹ *Bill Graham memorial rap by Ken Kesey* ✹ *10/31/80 Radio City*

from the patch or take up rake and clear the front yard. Going to see the Dead in the fall meant reaping the benefits of fellowship and the glow of good music. Summer-tour friendships, breezy and uncomplicated, seemed, like the season, as if they would last forever. A hello-again hug in the fall, though, now that was something to hold close.

For the Dead, fall came in 1985, with a blaze of autumnal color. Frost was on the pumpkin, but that touch of gray didn't seem so gray at all with Jerry off the hard stuff (for the time being, at least) and the shows starting to smoke once again. Like all falls, it had its moments of chills, as when Jerry fought death in '86, but it also had its Indian summer—the unseasonable warmth of '89–'91 and the memories of brighter days in the

1 *All Saints' Day* ☀ *U.S. Post Office introduces money orders, thus making mail order possible, 1864* ☀ *11/1/85 Richmond*

2 *All Souls' Day* ☀ *11/2/77 Toronto* ☀ *11/2/84 BCT*

3 *11/3/84 BCT*

4 *11/4/85 Worcester*

5 *11/5/77 Rochester*
11/5/85 Worcester

6

7 *Pacific first sighted by Lewis and Clark, 1805* ☀ *Joni Mitchell, b. 1943* ☀ *11/7/71 Harding Theater*

8 *Louvre opened to public, 1793* ☀ *11/8/69 Fillmore*

9 *Berlin Wall comes down, 1989*

10

11 *11/11/67 Shrine*
11/11/73 Winterland
11/11/78 Saturday Night Live ☀ *First appearance*

12

13

14 *Claude Monet, b. 1840* ☀ *Aaron Copland, b. 1900* ☀ *11/14/73 San Diego*

15

16

17 *11/17/73 Pauley Pavilion*

18

19 *11/19/66 Fillmore*

20 *Gettysburg Address, 1863* ☀ *Dr. John ("Mac" Rebennack), b. 1942* ☀ *Duane Allman, b. 1946* ☀ *11/20/78 Cleveland*

revival of so many great songs. And just when the days were getting colder and clouds covering more, Here Comes Sunshine through the gray of November and even an Unbroken Chain riding out to us on the cold railroad.

21 *11/21/85 Kaiser Center*

22 *JFK assassinated in Dallas, 1963*

23

24 *11/24/78 Capitol Theater, Passaic*

25 *Bruce Hornsby, b. 1955* ✸ *Neil Young, b. 1945*

26

27

28

29 *Discovery of King Tutankhamen's tomb, 1922*

30 *11/30/80 Fox Theater* ✸ *The Fox*
   11/30/81 Dayton ✸ *Only Mack the Knife*

f logical explanations can be arrived at—rightly or wrongly—for the Dead's exceptional playing in the favored years 1974 and 1977, the special quality of 1985 came, by contrast, as something of a bolt from the blue. I used to think that I held this year in special regard because it was when I had seen my first show. And I've heard the arguments that 1985 is held in such esteem primarily because of the easy availability of many excellent soundboards (a similar argument to one heard against the primacy of '77). I will grant that my first live run-in with the Dead on March 27th of that year has predisposed me to the rest of the year's opus. I will also allow that, sure, there are '85 shows that are overrated because of tape quality, as there are in many years, and that the year as a whole may be a bit inflated for this reason. But it has got to be more than the mere availability of crisp tapes that causes so very many Heads to spin the '85 opus with such relish. The crispness that is most evident to me on tapes like 6/15/85 has more to do with the playing than the quality of the recording. Still, it's not really a year that *should* have been so good.

Okay, you might think or hope that the Dead would try to rise to the occasion of their twentieth-anniversary year. But anyone who knows the Dead knows that they never put much stock in that sort of thing. Even if they had, a sense of occasion has never been in and of itself a guarantor of that patented excitement—witness Woodstock, Monterey, and Egypt. As it was, the Dead *did* rise to the occasion of the twentieth-anniversary celebration, in a big way. But a good, historically significant run is hardly enough to sustain a year. And 1985 was a year that began, infamously, with Jerry's January 18th run-in with Officer Gamble in Golden Gate Park and the resulting charge for suspected possession of heroin and cocaine. (Just prior to this incident the band had done an intervention with Jerry.) The very next year he lapsed into his life-threatening coma. Little retrospective danger signs for the year's performances, you'd think.

Actually both Jerry and other sources have stated that he stopped taking drugs after the bust (others have said he merely abated) and was still off them when he fell into a diabetic coma on July 10, 1986. In later interviews he expressed surprise that his body would have broken down at a point after he had not been using drugs for some time. Jerry's newly cleaned-up act is probably the greatest clue to the quality of 1985 as compared with the three very uneven years that predated it.

By all rights the Dead *should* have been pretty damn good by the mid eighties. Brent had been with the band long enough to have fully assimilated their live approach, and all the other band members had that many more years of experience under their belts— hell, you would think that each year from Brent's introduction on would be stronger than the last. The years 1979, 1980, and 1981 were all very hot, but the next few years, as I say, fell short. Although Jerry's excessively documented problems with the Persian during this time were no doubt a major factor in this three-year setback, the band has also given the impression in interviews that this was a period of general disillusionment for them. Nevertheless there were flashes in that "lost" period—great spring tours in '82 and '83 (and some standout fall shows such as 10/17/83 Lake Placid), and a very strong summer-fall span (7/13/84 Greek; 10/12/84 Augusta, Maine) in '84—and in the best of '83 and '84 (the Greek '84 Scarlet → Touch → Fire, for example) the Dead achieved the fluidity and fullness of sound and lack of rhythmic slack that became the hallmarks of their '85 shows.

John McIntire, the Dead's on-again, off-again manager, who had been off-again for some time, went to see the band for the first time in years in 1984, attending their Kansas City show on July 3rd. The scene he described in a 1988 interview with Blair Jackson for *Golden Road* was a pretty depressing one. What it amounted to in his eyes was a concert by a band that had lost its inventive spark. Touch, Bucket, and the bulk of the tunes that would eventually find their way onto *In the Dark* were by that time almost two years old. Time was that two years was a long span for the Dead not to have a batch of new (original) tunes! By the time 1985 rolled around, the aforementioned tunes were beginning to fall into relative disuse, a decline made precipitous by the truncated nature of 1986, when Touch, for example, was only played nine times. (There are of course maybe one or two Deadheads who feel the band may have made up for this in 1987.) McIntire also noted that the band's playing seemed uninspired. Now, maybe John caught the Boys on an off night—we've all learned not to judge a tour by one show—but the band wasn't exactly arguing with him, it seems, after hearing his assessment. At any rate he found his first taste of the Dead since the seventies less than satisfying.

As fate would have it, Bob Weir took McIntire out to dinner after the show and asked him to come back and manage the band, as Danny Rifkin was about to take a paternity leave. Though his immediate answer was no, Weir bade him think it over. Some months later McIntire called Robert Hunter (who had even warned him against attending the show) for the lowdown. Hunter reported that things had begun to change since the July show, that the Dead were starting to "take some responsibility for their careers."

The beginnings of the '85 upswing? McIntire took the gig. Methinks he helped the process along.

At any rate, where to stand on 1985? Wildly overrated? When Heads have more '85 tapes than '68–'74 tapes in their collection, yes. When the years '79–'81 are, by comparison, ignored, sure, you betcha. When held up as some kind of apex in the band's career? Well, it's the best they played in the mid-eighties . . . but taken as a high point of relative consistency in the '82–'88 continuum (with all due understanding given to the bands' performances in '86 and '87), no, it's not overrated. There's some awfully fine playing in this here year, some interesting setlists, and let's not forget the return of Cryptical, Comes a Time, and bustouts of other, "smaller" tunes, such as Big Boy Pete, Walking the Dog, and even Frozen Logger. Even if Cryptical was ultimately deemed less than totally successful by the band and most discerning ears, the revival of the full That's It for the Other One suite (for the first time since 1971, save one performance in 1972!) should, I think, be taken as ample evidence that the band was truly feeling it that year.

6/14/85
GREEK

The Dead's twentieth-anniversary run had its Scarlet → Fire show, its China → Rider show, and its wild-card show. This first show in 1985's finest run was the wild card.

The snippet of "Sgt. Pepper's Lonely Heart's Club Band" ("It was twenty years ago today . . .") that precedes the band's entrance sets the scene dramatically, if a bit self-consciously, for an historic concert. In a humorous stylistic touch the band initially tunes with what sound like "orchestra" tuning noises, probably provided by a Brent sample—this was a stand where he let fly a number of these electronic gewgaws that would become staples of the year's summer tour.

The first set this night is easily the best of the run; I should say *sets* actually, given the miniset occasioned by the band having to quit the stage for a time five tunes into the first due to equipment hassles. The opening fanfare of Dancin' in the Streets harkens an inspired lead-off choice, a song steeped in Dead history. The execu-

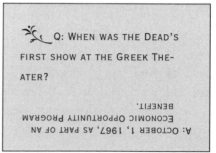

Q: WHEN WAS THE DEAD'S FIRST SHOW AT THE GREEK THEATER?

A: OCTOBER 1, 1967, AS PART OF AN ECONOMIC OPPORTUNITY PROGRAM BENEFIT.

tion here is excellent and full of vitality, an invitation to terpsichorean ecstasy right off the bat. The West L.A. follow-up, a bit of Garcia darkness clouding Dancin's summer day, is of similarly high quality, with Jerry playing some menacing leads. Brent gives us another sample of sample weirdness after West L.A. Fade with his woman's voice or falsetto voicings of "Bobby, Bobby," accompanied by kissing sounds.

It's Bobby we get, on an especially hot C. C. Rider. Brent's torrid Hammond runs prove a welcome respite here from Bobby's slide solos. An up-tempo, jiglike Peggy-O and Bucket (with Bobby singing of the "infamous" Catherine the Great) rounds out the first set, take one. At the end of Bucket, the buzzing from the PA that had been noticeable during the last two tunes gets really bad, prompting a premature end to the set due to "technical difficulties."

The festivities resume with Bobby asking, perhaps of the gods, "What am I doing here? Ah, there we go." Phil starts to clown around with a mike set with a delay effect: "Hello, hello." (Bob: "Dan, can you hear me?") "Echo, echo, help, help," which all piles up into a heap of hysterical panic that must have sent at least one dosed freak in the audience back on his heels.

Three gigantic Phil notes then announce "Here's one o' mine." It turns out to be Derek and the Dominoes' Keep On Growing, featuring Phil and Brent trading off verses to evident mutual delight. It is joy in which any listener can share; an FOB I have of this set clearly indicates that the crowd did, to the utmost degree. The Lesh-Mydland synergy is at its height in this tune, which makes all the more vexing the fact that they didn't play it much more often (though the truly awful 2/14/86 edition goes a way toward clearing that up).

The band doesn't let a drop of energy dissipate, as the barrel from the tasty end jam of Keep On Growing right into words not heard from Jerry's lips since 1982: "Nineteen forty, X-mas Eve . . ." An already high level of excitement continues to grow, right into Let It Grow, making this a very horticultural little set indeed. It's a near-flawless version, with great jamming; the Dead show that they're feeling it, too, by going into Deal for a scorching double closer.

The second set opens with Brent unleashing a full sample barrage on the gathered multitudes—burps (Phil?—they're very bassy . . .); Mickey calling out, "Harry, turn up the bass drum!"; kissing noises; "Bobby, Bobby"; maniacal laughter (again sounds like Phil)—all brought to a close with what sounds (again) like Mr. Lesh summing up, "You know what I means."

Soon enough we *do* find out what Phil means: BOMB—a Dew opener! It's a very powerful version, a rough way for the band to start the second set because it's so hard to top. They manage to do so immediately, however, with

DANCIN': A GOOD SHREEP

* 3/18/67 Winterland
* 2/14/70 Fillmore East
* 5/2/70 Harpur College
* 5/6/70 MIT
* 6/12/76 Boston Music Hall
* 6/24/76 Tower Theater
* 5/8/77 Cornell
* 5/19/77 Fox Theater
* 5/22/77 Pembroke Pines (*Dick's Picks Volume Three*)
* 5/9/78 Syracuse
* 10/27/79 Cape Cod
* 6/14/85 Greek
* 7/1/85 Merriwether

one of the best Playin's of the eighties—adventurous and trippy but melodic through and through. The China Doll into which Playin' flows is monumental, a dreamlike, stately version that trickles into a jaunty little rhythmic jam to which Jerry adds some pretty melodic elaborations before it winds down. Brent remains onstage to play a rousing, triumphant keyboard accompaniment to the beginning of Drums—more than five minutes' worth.

Drums and Space are, by '85 standards and relative to what comes before, unremarkable; the Truckin' out of Drums is also a bit ragged. A resounding Smokestack Lightning gets things back on track nicely, just in time for Jerry to pull another goodie out of his hat with a much more momentous breakout than the Stagger Lee of the first set—the first Comes a Time in five years. While this revival edition doesn't reach some of the peaks of some of the subsequent '85 versions—Jerry's vocals are less sure and the band doesn't cohere as well—it provides its share of thrills, obviously establishing a firm enough foundation to encourage Jerry to explore it further that year. Sugar Magnolia provides a good traditional cap to the show, but it and the Day Job encore can hardly help but seem anticlimactic after such an epic set.

6/16/85
GREEK

The closing show of the superb twentieth-anniversary run does not sport nearly as impressive a first set(s) as the opening night, though a gravel-voiced Jed, Esau, and Big Railroad Blues all stand out, as does a heartfelt Looks Like

Rain, with an innovative rap and stirring climax, and a rocking Promised Land closer. But the second set more than holds its own with the other two from the run.

Before the first note of Scarlet Begonias we are given an idea of some of the rich tonal color in store as Phil, Bobby, and Brent's warm-up playing shimmers in anticipatory waves. It's out of these heat ripples that Scarlet opens, Bobby and the drums creating a humid, tropical feel that's part Caribbean, part jungle. It isn't only the vaguely calypso rhythm that Bobby lays down, it's the wet suffocation of Phil's bass, Jerry's dripping guitar lines, and the way Brent's keyboard sparkles like light dappling through a lush canopy of vegetation. Jerry's playing is crisply excellent here, as it is throughout the show, but it is the rest of the band who really dress up this Scarlet, and Bobby is first among them.

Weir plays with a similarly exalted palette in the transition; indeed it seems to be he who is leading the band. Fire, while not jammed to monstrous proportions, is exquisite throughout. Bobby next reminds us it's Sunday with a live-wire Samson, after which there's a long pause. On the soundboard you can hear a member of the audience close to the stage yell, "Aiko Aiko!" and it sounds as if Garcia mutters in response, "Yeah, that New Orleans shit." Then again, maybe that isn't what he says. At any rate Aiko is not destined to be the next tune, as the band can be heard discussing how they're going to go from "Cryptical into The Other One" (a nice piece of supporting evidence, by the way, for that being the proper appellation for the suite's components). This first Cryptical since 1972 is consistent with its successors in '85, which is to say that it's not a success vocally (what was it about this song that made it so hard for Garcia to sing?), but it is played well and is just plain exciting to hear performed by a mid-eighties incarnation of the Dead. This one also seems to give an extra charge to the Other One that follows it—it comes bolting out of the gate with its tail on fire. Despite the breakneck pace of this one and its relative brevity compared with early seventies editions, the Dead manage to break some new ground here—listen to the way Garcia alternates between rhythm and the lead toward the end of both of the internal jams.

The Other One goes ripping into a Drums/Space that is among the finest of the year. Mickey lends Drums a vibrant, world-music flavor, and Brent's keyboard samples coupled with Jerry's guitar birdcalls create a Space that presages Jerry's later *Blues for the Rainforest* work with Merl Saunders. Brent's running-water sample is put to particularly evocative use here. Even the high-pitched whisper of "Bobby," potentially goofy in other situations, sounds here like a faraway voice calling you from a dream. Not long after that, Jerry begins to head back to the "waking" world of Goin' Down the Road, furthering the illusion of reverie interrupted. Even the silly sample of Phil (?) intoning "You know what I means" seems to carry some key to a larger significance in this set ripe with the sound of mystery and other lands. The dopey cadence of the words also fits nicely with this Goin' Down's appealing looseness. I Need a Miracle is ushered in by a fitting sample as well, maniacal laughter that also sounds as if its source is Phil. Miracle is fittingly manic, a taut, growling performance. Lovelight reclaims the bounciness of Goin' Down, and then the show ends with the obligatory Brokedown encore, which provides nice symmetry by reprising the ringing clarity of the set-opening Scarlet, epitomized by Bobby's harmonics-rich guitar sound.

An appropriately historic and virtuoso ending to one of the Dead's great stands, this show stands synesthetically as the third primary color—red—to the opener's blue and the middle show's yellow. Between the three of them one can find all the tonal hues of the spectrum.

6/24/85
RIVER BEND

Yet another excellent June '85 performance, the second set of this show rewards the listener with many delicious moments.

The opening Aiko, in which Weir takes a "Say, Dixie boy on the battle front, Brother John is gone" verse, gets extended play—all the better for additional dancing and carrying on. On the board of this show you can hear Jerry yell "Hey Weir!" before Aiko, presumably to remind him of the verse change, this being the only time I'm aware of that Bobby has taken *any* verse in Aiko. Aiko itself carries on into a *ripping* Samson and Delilah. This one doesn't have the drum intro, but Billy and Mickey are definitely a force throughout. Jerry's backing vocals here epitomize much of what makes '85 a special year—the little things matter in a beast as potentially unwieldy as the Grateful Dead.

He's Gone could be tighter, but this version has a certain punchiness on its side. That, and a sardonic flavor that carries the song's original intent— there's more I-told-you-so than elegy here. Note Jerry's crisp enunciation the "cat on a tin roof" line and the way he bellows "Nothin left to do . . ."— so, so tasty, as are his feedback effects in the main solo break. A long bout of vocal riffing on the coda, which puts it in such company as the 5/26/73 He's

Gone on this score, engenders a Smokestack Lightning that's randy as hell. One of the finest, yes indeedy. That Smokestack should melt into Cryptical Envelopment is, to say the least, a surprise. This and the He's Gone → Cryptical incursion a week later in Maryland point to the gameness of '85. Cryptical may not have ultimately worked out, but the Boys were at least not playing it safe.

Cryptical burns into a Drums that is, not surprisingly, heavily seasoned with Other One accents. Space also plays with the Other One theme almost from the start. Toward the end it gets *very* quiet and then resumes with a little bit of Other One–based noodling that of course drops right into the unmistakable opening notes of . . . Comes a Time?! Add this one to the long list of superb '85 versions.

A kind of no-man's-land immediately follows Comes a Time, where the Dead is playing The Other One but with evident lack of forethought as to how its beginning would take shape. Not to worry, though, they find the "one" (it's where they thought it was) with a Phil-Jerry *whump-boom!* and race headlong into what may be the hottest Other One of the year. Brent's work throughout is very strong, particularly in the beginning. It's all tied up nicely at the end with a brief Cryptical close-parenthesis to complete the suite. From there the Dead move without hesitation into a supremely powerful Wharf Rat, the strength of which is made clear from Jerry's delivery of the first line. The band seem privy to the fact that this one's special, and respond in kind—check out, for example, the cymbal sting after Jerry sings, "Half of my life . . . ," and Brent and Bobby's gorgeous backing vocals in the bridge. Jerry's solo after the "Got up and wandered" verse is a scorcher too. This one's truly an all-timer.

It's amusing to note how eager Jerry seems to be to put Bobby through the paces—witness how quickly he begins Around out of Wharf Rat before any other tune can rear its head, and how he imposes Good Lovin' right on its heels. To his credit he fulfills his obligations as the one who called the tunes by singing his backing part with added gusto. Good Lovin' has a great Bobby rap, too, Weir adding "you gotta *fight!*" to his "push back the night" bit.

When U.S. Blues rocks as hard as it does here, chances are it's been a great show. This is no exception.

A Rose by Any Other Name...

THE GRATEFUL Dead, in various incarnations and give or take a few members, performed under a variety of names over the course of their thirty-year run. Perhaps best known is the sobriquet Mickey and the Hartbeats, which the Dead, minus Bobby and Pigpen, adopted for some legendary shows in 1968 and '69. A bunch more follow. Can you supply the circumstance (not a performance in every case) for each name below?

1. The Just Exactly Perfect Brothers Band
2. Interferon and the Desmodrones
3. Formerly the Warlocks
4. The Jones Gang
5. Phil Lesh and Friends
6. The Emergency Crew
7. Bobby Ace and His Cards from the Bottom of the Deck
8. The Sun-Stroked Serenaders
9. The Acoustic Grateful Dead (misapplied)
10. David and the Dorks
11. The Rainbow Makers

ANSWERS

1. A name given the band by Weir at the beginning of the 12/29/77 Winterland show: "We're gonna try to get everything just exactly perfect, on account of our new name is going to be the Just Exactly Perfect Brothers Band." In an epic show where they revived China → Rider in style, the Dead came very close to living up to the appellation.

2. This is the name Phil gave to a fantastically geeky picture of himself and fellow rhythm-section mates Billy and Mickey. It can be seen on page 75 of David Gans's *Playing in the Band.*

3. This is a billing that the Dead have worn twice, both times at significant turning points in their career. The second time was of course at the legendary Hampton run—10/8–9/89—where they revived Dark Star, the full Help → Slipknot! → Franklin's, and Attics. The first time was on 1/14/66, at their third Fillmore gig, where they were actually billed as the "Grateful Dead, Formerly the Warlocks."

4. Phil's tag for the band while introducing it during equipment problems in the beginning of the second set at Colgate on 11/4/77. The full intro:

BOB: "In case you're wondering, something doesn't work. We're gonna try and *make* it work."

PHIL: "Well, at this time I think it would be propitious to introduce the band. We're the Jones Gang, folks. Over here on stage le-, uh stage right, we have Mr. Keith Jones on the keyboards. To his immediate left on, uh, the eee-lectric guitar we have Jerry Jones. And of course, on drums, the one and only Julius P. Jones. In center stage, ladies and gentlemen, a star whose name has gone beyond him, even unto the farthest galaxies—heh—Bob Jones. On drums back here we have also . . . actually, I'm Phil Jones and that's Mick Jones. And now I'd like to introduce all the other Joneses. Would all the other Joneses please step right out here and, we have Harry Jones over here, we have Alex Jones over there, we have—"

BOB: "—Momma, she was a good old girl."

PHIL: "—Steve Jones back there, we have John Jones back there, we have Larry Jones, we have, we have Jones."

JERRY: "Freshly deported from Canada, ladies and gentlemen." ✑

PHIL: "We have Donna Jones."

5. A billing presumably intended not to offend the drummers (and/or minimize ticket madness), who were not in attendance for the acoustic benefit show played by Phil, Jerry, Bobby, and Vince on 9/24/94 at the Berkeley Community Theater. The benefit was for music in Berkeley schools, very much Phil's baby, as he was a product of this extraordinary but endangered program.

✑ THIS IS AN ALLUSION TO THE DEAD'S MOST RECENT GIG, AT SENECA COLLEGE IN TORONTO ON 11/2/77. THEY HAD BEEN PUT THROUGH THE WRINGER GOING THROUGH CUSTOMS FROM BOTH SIDES OF THE BORDER BECAUSE OF THE BEE POLLEN WEIR HAD BEEN CARRYING. THE CUSTOMS OFFICERS HADN'T THE FAINTEST IDEA WHAT IT WAS, BUT ASSUMED IT MUST BE SOME SORT OF ILLEGAL DRUG.

6. The name the Warlocks took for the Autumn Records demo they cut at Golden State Studios in San Francisco on 11/3/65, shortly before they changed their name to the Grateful Dead.

7. The name Bobby gave to his short-lived and sporadic country-western spin-off band, which was sort of the flip side to Mickey and the Hartbeats. The lineup, in addition to Weir: Tom Constanten—piano; John Dawson—guitar; Jerry Garcia—guitar; Peter

Grant—pedal steel guitar; Hart—drums; Lesh—bass; David Nelson—guitar, autoharp, and vocals.

8. Early in the second set on a hellishly hot August day in Oregon in 1972 (8/27/72, to be exact), Bobby announced that "We're changing our names to the Sunstroked Serenaders."

9. This could of course apply to any number of acoustic shows/sets, but notice I specified "misapplied." "Acoustic Grateful Dead" was the billing given the quartet composed of David Crosby, Garcia, Hart, and Lesh when they played Pepperland in San Rafael on 12/21/70. Which brings us to . . .

10. A humorous name assumed by the above Crosby-Garcia-Hart-Lesh quartet. Tapes of the 12/15/70 show by this group at the Matrix, the only surviving/circulating record of this inspired collaboration, frequently bear this title, which reeks of Garcia's sense of humor.

11. The appellation given the Dead by Wavy Gravy or his friend Asa at the end of a pre-second-set appeal for funds to help rebuild a teaching hospital in North Vietnam that had been leveled by American bombers.

6/30/85
MERRIWETHER POST PAVILION

This show and the next night at Merriwether deserve their reputation as two of the best shows of '85, by dint of spectacular playing that yields some epic versions of favorite tunes.

In this, the first night, the festivities truly get under way with the powerful, suspense-filled opening chord of an outstanding Shakedown. Bobby lends this one some inspired slide-guitar weirdness, with Jerry and Phil keeping time. Jerry eventually resumes his soloing duties over a cooking synth-and-drums background, building to a dizzying peak before dropping us back down into the final chorus, after which he's back at it again. The Sunday Samson that follows is, though somewhat obligatory, played with alacrity.

The soundboard of this show reveals a debate among the band as to whether they should play Gimme Some Lovin' next. Happily they do, turning in a superheated version driven as much by the guitar players as by Brent.

The musical one-upmanship that results between Brent, Jerry, and Bobby pushes the song to aural heights that even this crowd pleaser rarely attained. He's Gone proves a fine forum for the Dead's excellent Brent-era vocal mix, with Bobby holding down the low-to-midrange, Brent soaring above, and Jerry twanging playfully between the two. What's most memorable about this He's Gone, though, is the breathtaking, utterly surprising transition into Cryptical Envelopment. Instead of The Other One, this Cryptical takes a roundabout path through Drums.

The Drums and Space that follow are, true to '85 form, tuneful, shimmering, and highly hallucinatory. To be found within this one are Bobby's guitar wailing in inspired mayhem, sparkling notes in the upper register from Brent, and what seem to be more of Brent's samples from this period: radio-tuning-type noises and what sounds like Phil breathily speaking nonsense syllables. The overall effect is not unlike that of the Beatles' "Revolution 9."

Once Jerry's guitar runs begin to quote The Other One, though, we know we're on the way back out. He circles and circles for a landing while Phil readies himself, then resumes playing scales and arpeggios in The Other One key, utilizing a number of different voicings. The suspense builds, only to be heightened by the drums kicking in. Almost before you realize it, you're speeding down a hill, brakeless, with Cowboy Neal at the wheel. The interior jam turns into an all-out war, Phil carpet-bombing the Pavilion, Jerry's guitar the shriek of incoming shells, and the drummers' tom fills the concussion when they hit. Bobby's guitar thrashings are the red confusion of combat. This one's a biggie.

DO DEW THAT VOODOO . . .

* 5/2/70 Harpur College
* 5/26/72 London
* 11/10/73 Winterland
* 2/24/74 Winterland
* 6/18/74 Louisville
* 10/18/74 Winterland
* 5/8/77 Cornell
* 7/22/84 Ventura
* 10/12/84 Augusta
* 6/14/85 Greek
* 6/28/85 Hershey
* 3/24/86 Philly
* 9/18/87 MSG
* 3/31/89 Greensboro
* 3/26/90 Albany
* 9/16/90 MSG
* 8/17/91 Shoreline
* 5/24/92 Shoreline
* 6/24/94 Las Vegas
* 6/21/95 Albany

Dead to the Core

The Stella Blue that flows from this martial Other One provides a contrast, to say the least. More than that, though, it's lent a sense of heightened drama by strong effects and color work by the whole band. They manage to produce live what sound like the fruits of a fully equipped recording studio. After such quiet and understated excellence, Around and Around is frankly an unwelcome mood breaker, but then again that's really nothing new. The Sugar Mags that follows reveals Bobby's voice to be totally thrashed, rendering inevitable a Jerry encore. The U.S. Blues we get is okay, but doesn't really do justice to the best parts of this intense show.

7/1/85
MERRIWETHER POST PAVILION

If anything, the second night of this '85 run surpasses the first—no mean feat, that. The first set of this show doesn't quite match the previous night's string of rockers, but I think you'd have to rate any set that includes Dupree's, Stagger Lee, and Jack-A-Roe, three great Jerry takes on traditionals, not to mention Esau and the curious pairing of Let It Grow → Day Job, as at least interesting. Actually the Let It Grow is huge, and I know many at this show were relieved to have Day Job dispensed with in the first set, thus clearing up the encore spot for more appetizing fare.

The clear showstopper here, though, is the gigantic Scarlet → Fire that opens the second set, truly one of the best of the eighties, a decade with a great number of standout versions. A current of crispness and enthusiasm runs through much of the Dead's '85 shows, particularly evident in the mid June-to-early-July stretch of which this show is a part. You can hear that winning combination in this Scar → Fire in the soaring energy of Jerry's guitars, the exclamatory crack of the toms after his lead passages, and the multiple turns taken on the interverse jams. Even the pre-Scarlet tuning glissando signals the magic about to unfold. The band really leans into the transition, with Jerry driving the band to the edge of the cliff that is the jumping-off point for Fire. Jerry pauses for a moment, then jumps into the abyss with a plantive first Fire *wah*, probably the paragon of this always-special moment that signifies that the transition is complete. Moments later his initial riffing on the Fire theme sounds almost defiant. When the vocals come around, Jerry of course flubs them completely. It's a fair trade-off in a life filled with compromises.

There's a sing-song, almost contemplative flavor to Fire's interior jam, as if Jerry's trying to decide something on his guitar—a decision is made, he builds

AIKO-AIKO

❋ 9/2/80
Rrrrroooocccckkkkssss!!!

❋ 8/10/82 U. Iowa
A meaty Aiko, no bouncy dance toss-off, this one fully justifies its position out of Space, back when that transition was fairly standard practice.

❋ 3/31/85 Portland
Like the rest of the show, crazy and uninhibited.

❋ 6/24/85 Cincinnati
Bobby's verse somehow manages to up the energy ante.

❋ 2/11/86 Kaiser
If ever a tune was meant for the Dead with the Neville Brothers, Aiko (or "Iko Iko," as the Nevilles call it) is it—here's a strong example of just such a collaboration.

❋ 12/30/86 Kaiser
Another great Aiko with the Nevilles. In addition to some very trippy drumming, this one holds the answer to that eternal question of just what is the difference between Aiko and Women, anyway? The transition into Aiko's close sibling here reveals the difference to be in key (up two steps for Women).

❋ 3/18/90 Hartford
The Dead as swing orchestra, courtesy of Jerry's MIDI saxophone. I defy you not to drop whatever you're doing and dance.

❋ 9/10/91
Swingin' with the B-man.

the associated phrases to a peak, then, Jerry-like, deflates his "statement" with wah-rounded mutterings of doubt. When the verse comes around this time, it seems to echo these guitar-voiced statements perfectly. Just when Fire seems to be winding down, the Dead go into a kickin' little almost-double-time jam that sends the pairing into history with style. The fest continues with a Playin' that features sharp playing by all. The drum fills here are especially exciting. The band carries the momentum into an Uncle John's in which the "Goddamn, well I declare" line is hit even bigger than usual and given fierce punctuation by Messrs. Hart and Kreutzmann.

Yet another excellent '85 Space has Jerry and Brent collaborating on what sounds like a B-grade horror-suspense-movie sound track; Brent breaks the tension briefly with a video-game sample. The effect loses its innocuousness, however, as he works it into a mélange that also includes sounds akin to heavily distorted screaming voices (the overall feel of this part of Space is, as is the previous night's edition, strongly reminiscent of "Revolution 9." It also carries shades of the end of "On the Run" right before it goes into "Breathe" on Pink Floyd's *Dark Side of the Moon*). Or perhaps it's the sound of the interstellar pinball machine from the *Grateful*

✼ 3/18/95

March 18th was a good day for Aiko, a tune they played well to the end, especially after a much-needed revamping during Mardi Gras '95—some tempo adjustments and the addition of the "See that girl all dressed in red" verse.

✼ 3/27/95

Another great late Aiko, one of the best in the new arrangement.

Dead Movie, tilted to the max and barreling into a haunted house. After this passage Mydland and Garcia go back to work on the "horror-sound-track theme," which has taken on an even more sinister air after the strange effects that punctuated its midsection.

The dark clouds lift when Jerry pulls out of a minor-key run with a tentative statement of the Dear Mr. Fantasy intro line, which he states again more fully once he has the attention of the band. Though Brent's singing here is technically fine (as always), there's a curious emotional flatness to his delivery. Luckily Jerry more than compensates with superb backing vocals—particularly noteworthy is his "Oh, Mr. Fantasy" at the end of the last verse. Bobby's choice of Good Lovin' is a nice one to end the set. He does his "push back the night" rap here and also manages to bring geopolitical relevance to the song with an allusion to the hostages in Beiruit at the time. Do *I* think that those people who took the hostages away woulda done it if they had good lovin' anyway? Hard to say, Bob, but keep asking the tough questions. (Ain't no easy answers, that's what he's got to say.)

Finally, a sixties greatest-hits pairing of Satisfaction → Baby Blue for the encore is a real yummie, a nice mix of raucousness and more thoughtful cover fare.

9/3/85
STARLIGHT THEATER

Every stab Jerry took at Cryptical in '85 should be appreciated. Unfortunately it just didn't really happen for him. This is the night it happened least of all. And in one respect at least this is the night it happened most of all. On technical points this is the most poorly executed of the bunch, with Jerry simply bailing out for a good portion of the song and mumbling the rest. Phil and the drums try to jump-start the Dead engine with a pounding Other One intro. Jerry follows their lead with some very good soloing over this strong rhythmic foundation. Nothing earth-shattering here, just good, solid playing. The song really starts to pick up, though, when Brent begins to punctuate the vocals with some dazzling lead lines in his Fender Rhodes sound. He and Jerry interact well throughout, pushing each other on the solo. It's a short Other One, though, and all too soon we're back into Cryptical, with Jerry still mumbling. So what "happens" to make this version so memorable? Jerry takes his leave of this song forever, ceasing his mumblings with a tremendous bellow of "YOU KNOW HE HAD TO DIE!!!" It's an electric moment that draws an immediate response from both audience and band, pulling the song out of the fire. One can imagine that the shout reflected Garcia's feelings regarding a song he just couldn't seem to sing despite several game attempts. That *was* it for the other part of The Other One.

Once he's put all that behind him, Jerry loses no time swinging into an Eyes in which he does some interesting soloing amid more shining turns on the keys by Brent. Unfortunately this Eyes suffers from a rhythmic astigmatism. Billy and Mickey manage to rectify the situation with a dramatic double-take flourish right before Jerry goes into the "Sometimes we live . . ." line. The realignment is short-lived, however, and the song begins to fall apart soon after the last verse.

The band, cutting their losses, begins to surrender the stage to Drums, or so it seems, until Brent brings everyone back on stage for Don't Need Love. Everyone, it seems, except for Jerry, who bails out during this tune as was his wont for many a pre-Drums Brent tune. ꗞ The Drums that follows is short but sweet, punctuated at the end with a long sliiiiide down the Beam that creates a nice segue into Space. Jerry restlessly shifts from mood to mood here, starting the proceedings with some majestic chords before playing some blues figures in which he drops a hint or two of Stella Blue before settling on, of all things, Nobody's Fault. It's a

"...And I Don't Need You"

ꗞ Don't Need Love was the Brent tune everyone was sure Jerry hated, given his near universal leave-taking upon its opening lines. Was this really the case? Stories abound of Brent singing particularly vehement versions that many took as aimed at Jerry ("...and I sure the fuck don't need you!"). Though with Brent and vehemence, who can tell? Was Jerry (a) Dying for a butt and/or tired? (He left for a number of pre-Drums tunes—not just Brent's—in '85 and leading up to his coma in '86.); (b) Leaving the soloing space for Brent and of the opinion that two guitars on rhythm just clogged up the mix?; or (c) Just wanting to appreciate Brent's fine tunes from a spectator's point of view?

Actually Jerry's exits might be viewed as right on time (according to *his* schedule, at least), with all who remained onstage simply prolonging the pre-Drums portion of the set. Billy once reported in a *Golden Road* interview that, in response to Brent's frustration over the Dead not wanting to do his tunes, he had told him to simply remain onstage into Drums and that he and Mickey would back him up.

mournful rendition that is augmented nicely by some competent slide playing by Weir. Jerry's vocals, though soulful, are less than perfect, which is understandable given this song's more than four-year hiatus prior to this performance. The Brent, Jerry, and Bobby jam at the end is unfortunately not given a full chance to develop before Jerry pushes the band into Truckin', which carries more than a hint of Nobody's Fault in the intro. This is where the set finally seems to really hit its stride.

Truckin' is hot through and through, and it's great to see Weir drag Garcia into another Smokestack Lightning by stepping up with a roaring "Whoaoh, SMOKESTACK LIGHTNING" as Jer's winding down Truckin', preempting whatever he may have had in mind. Smokestack also simmers. Jerry finally finds his footing in the Comes a Time that follows, which is gorgeous, a knockout. Jerry's clear, supremely emotive singing and plaintive, molten lead lines link this one strongly to the standout 11/1/85 version. The closing Lovelight gets up a nice head of steam and is leavened by a humorous Weir nonrap: "Sometimes you get up here and you can't think of a thing to say, y'know?" and "You get up here from time to time and you try to make things come out in rhyme," and let's not forget "Not much of a message here tonight," to which, on the audience tape I have, someone in the crowd gives the apt answer, "Oh no!" Fortunately the percussion section really keeps things kicking during the rap.

Jerry's Baby Blue encore, one of his best tunes even from the earliest days, sees him continue the momentum he had worked up during Comes a Time. His innovative phrasing—especially in the first and the "leave your steppingstones behind" verses—as well as his attention to dynamics make this version extra fine.

It's a show with its ups and downs, to be sure, but it's good on balance, and consistently interesting.

9/7/85
RED ROCKS

The second set of this show is notable less for any flights of musical craziness than for the exquisite playing throughout and a well-crafted setlist. The one musical oddity contained herein—the first-ever Hey Jude finale out of Dear Mr. Fantasy—is probably the weakest link in the show musically.

The set opens with a Shakedown plump with bass and wah-wah. Jerry's vocal, though imperfect, imparts a nuanced sense of skepticism, as if he's not really sure he *can* hear the town's heart beat out loud and only asks the song's addressee not to tell him otherwise out of fear of confirming his worst suspicions. The Jerry-Brent vocal interchange at the end of the song is particularly exciting, with Jerry repeating the "you just gotta poke around" line as if it were a mantra on curiosity and Brent echoing his sentiments with elaborations. The song's well jammed out, with heavy doses of Bobby's strange mid-to-late-eighties cosmic twang, that *twing-a-ling, chi-chook, twaaaang, chi-chook, twaaaang* sound.

Crazy Fingers is sad and beautiful, with Jerry and Brent lending subtle emotional color to the "gone are the days" passages. Samson offers a hot response to the introspection of Crazy Fingers, and the Uncle John's that follows it is perhaps the highlight of the set. Jerry's opening solo has an authoritative air to it in this version and the Jerry-Brent vocal mix on the chorus is again exemplary. Uncle John's flows into its yang, a Playing in the Band notable for its spacey exit jam into Drums. Space is another mind-blowing '85 version, with trippy phase effects and a very haunting Jerry-led jam into Dear Mr. Fantasy. The Hey Jude finale played here seems wholly extemporaneous this first time out, with Brent discovering the melodic line on his organ and Jerry picking it up immediately. The incorporation of Hey Jude is distinct as well, with Brent going back into Fantasy to close off the sandwich. A solid Truckin' ends with the opening

THESE ARE IT FOR THE OTHER ONE

✳ 11/11/67 Shrine

✳ 10/30/68 Matrix (Mickey and the Hartbeats)

✳ 2/22/69 Vallejo

✳ 3/1/69 Fillmore West

✳ 4/4/69 Avalon

✳ 2/13/70 Fillmore East

✳ 5/2/70 Harpur College

✳ 4/28/71 Fillmore East

✳ 12/1/71 Boston Music Hall

✳ 9/28/72 Stanley Theater

✳ 6/18/74 Louisville

✳ 11/5/77 Rochester

✳ 1/22/78 McArthur Court

✳ 2/5/78 Cedar Falls

✳ 10/21/78 Winterland

✳ 10/27/79 Cape Cod

✳ 5/6/81 Nassau

✳ 6/16/85 Greek

✳ 6/30/85 Merriwether

✳ 8/19/89 Greek

✳ 2/20/91 Oakland

✳ 6/19/94 Eugene

triad of Comes a Time, thrice played by Jerry in a sort of tease before he counters with the resolving three notes of the phrase. This is one of the best, marked by soulful, oh-so soulful singing and plaintive soloing by Jerry that perfectly matches arcing high notes with low feedback growl—a solo that speaks of anguished sorrow. The set ends on a strong note with a laid-back, easy-swinging Lovelight in which Bobby's delivery of the rap is given drama by an excellent sense of timing.

A double encore brings the show to a close with a bit of everything. First there's the raucousness of Johnny B. Goode, played with gusto and enhanced by Jerry's backing vocals; next there's the more tempered Baby Blue, which shows Jerry to still be in exceptionally good voice at show's end. Jerry said that he was able to inhabit Dylan's lyrics even better at times than he was Hunter's; this seems to be one of those times. Garcia truly makes the song his own, singing with authority and distinction. He and the band also pay close attention to dynamics here, which brings the full weight of the song's emotional impact to bear—listen, for example, to the way the "leave your stepping-stones behind" line explodes from the quiet space that precedes it. Another gorgeous subtlety is to be found here in Bobby's cascading guitar beneath Jerry's vocals as he sings the "vagabond who's rapping . . ." line.

It's moments of quiet professionalism such as this last that make this show.

Dylan and the Dead

t's perhaps unsurprising that Bob Dylan and the longest-running show in rock and roll should have so much shared history, but I'll bet that when the Dead played "It's All Over Now, Baby Blue" and "She Belongs to Me" for the first time on January 7, 1966, they never guessed they would serve as backing band for Dylan some twenty-odd years later. Actually this is cheating for rhetorical purposes; it's only the first time documented—numerous sources place at least "Baby Blue" in their repertoire from their earliest days as the Warlocks in '65. The point is that the Dead started out with Dylan as an idol and ended up sharing the stage with him.

Or maybe, seeing as how a mere six months later the Dead had their first onstage guests in the persons of Joan Baez and Mimi Fariña—two performers inextricably tied to the legend of you-know-who—they wondered just why it took so long. The Fariñas were also frequent guests at that crucible of beat transformation into freakdom, the Chateau.

It's well established that the Dead admired Dylan since their inception, and it would seem that Dylan had a little Deadhead in him as well. Bob took in his first show at the final Fillmore East run on 4/27/71 and it was a good one, though hardly a representative slice: one-offs of "Riot in Cell Block Number Nine," "Help Me Rhonda," "Okie from Muskogee" performed with the Beach Boys and their final performance of the Leiber and Stoller tune "Searchin'." Rock Scully gives a droll account of the lengths to which Bill Graham went to accommodate Dylan, installing him quite literally upon a throne in a luxury balcony from which to view the entertainments.

Dylan's next known appearance on tour was the Dead's second show after Pigpen's last, 7/18/72 at Roosevelt Stadium in Jersey City, a three-set wonder with a Birdsong breakout in the first set (just in time to get it good and practiced up for 8/27/72). Dylan first saw the Dead at a time when they were more than a little bit country, as was he at that juncture—no doubt that's where much of the resonance lay for him.

It was a staple of the seventies rock-and-roll rumor mill that there was a finished Dylan-

Dead studio album in the can, either gathering dust due to the artists' caprice or about to be announced or released, depending on which branch of the grapevine you heard it off of. Either that was just wishful mongering or the album in question is the most secret and least-bootlegged unreleased album ever—not bloody likely when you consider Deadheads and their Dylan counterparts, as virulent a bunch of tape traders and (especially in the case of Dylan fans) bootleg vinyl/CD buyers as has ever been assembled.

Garcia did, however, add some pretty licks to Dylan's 11/16/80 ("To Ramona" shines in Jerry's hands) show at the Warfield, part of a twelve-concert run presented by Bill Graham, who facilitated the musical meeting, it is said, by letting on that Bob had personally requested Jerry's backing. He hadn't, but Jerry allowed nonetheless that playing with Dylan, who was then at a low ebb commercially and critically amid the poor reception of his "born again" material, had been the fulfillment of a personal dream.

Maybe a collaboration was something they had always meant to do but hadn't gotten around to sooner, like those maddening moments in *Golden Road* interviews with Jerry or Bobby where they'd say, "Yeah, we've been meaning to break out [insert the song you've been waiting your entire tour life to hear]—maybe someday we'll get together and rehearse it."

Unfortunately when the collaboration finally did take place in the form of a summer stadium minitour of both coasts in 1987, it was a disappointment to many who had eagerly awaited the sights and sounds of their favorite band giving an injection of Good Ole Grateful Dead to the poet laureate of the counterculture's tunes and trademark singing. For those who believe in Dead-tour omens, it could not have been a good one that Dylan had last come onstage with the band on 7/7/86 at RFK, the last show before Jerry's coma. Dylan was touring with the Dead and Tom Petty and the Heartbreakers, who also served as his backing band. (And let's not forget that Dylan opened for the Dead on their disastrous '95 summer tour. What's with this guy? Could it be Dylan who turned Garcia on to red T-shirts?)

For starters 1987 was not exactly a banner year for either act (despite a number of hot Scarlet → Fires to the contrary). Both had their share of hot shows, but judged against the continuum of their performing careers, the late eighties for both the Dead and Dylan (especially Dylan) aren't quite the years one looks for first when considering that next bootleg trade or purchase. Indeed both took a dramatic upswing as the decade turned, though the Dead's came sooner—in '89, with flashes in '88—than Dylan's, whose shows became consistently mouthwatering events again in the early nineties.

I have no doubt, however, that this famously accomplished group of artists could have had a storied collaboration had they taken to the studio for focused, intense rehearsals in preparation for a tour of intimate venues. Of course that is exactly what did not happen, with the Bob putting the Boys through, as Weir recounted, his usual pretour routine, rehearsing "maybe a hundred songs two or three times" over several sessions at Club Front in mid May 1987. The sessions have, of course, found their way into the hands of tape traders: *DeadBase* lists the songs that are in most common circulation, forty-four tunes (some performed more than once) that span a couple of tapes in various configurations, which often carry—inexplicably* and incorrectly—either the date 3/14 or 3/4/87. There's also a lesser-known tape with eleven more tunes, six of which are unique to this recording.

The rehearsal tapes tell a frankly mixed story. On the one hand, yes, most songs are only given a desultory run-through, with beginnings and endings generally left very ragged. Garcia would later comment that fashioning beginnings and endings for the songs was a problem that carried over into the performances as well, with Dylan giving the matter no attention. It's unclear why the Dead didn't then take matters into their own hands in crafting the arrangements, but, well, it was DYLAN after all, who is generally allowed to call the shots in the studio, often to his detriment. Doubtless the band for whom "avoidance of confrontation is like a religious point" just decided to leave well enough alone rather than fiddle with the arrangements of some of the bedrock of the rock-and-roll canon. Or at least they would wait until after their tour with Dylan to truly give some of the Dylan tunes that found their way into their repertoire the full Dead treatment.

It's also dismaying that Dylan apparently didn't sing from a songbook at the rehearsals, as the lyrics and the placement of the verses are, for the most part, either forgotten or scrambled or both. This, and Dylan's very casual delivery, tend to undermine the seriousness of the practice sessions.

If the playing is not all that smooth, there are, however, times that the band gets a groove going such as they rarely achieved in the concert performances of these songs. Ironically the Dead seem to be much more themselves in the studio in this case— backing one of their musical heroes—than they did in performance before a stadium's worth of people. It's been said by more than one Dead-savvy reviewer, and I'll second it, that the shows and particularly the cuts chosen for the *Dylan and the Dead* album show the Grateful Dead playing with perhaps too much caution. There's less of that in the rehearsal tapes, no doubt owing to the informality of the setting. There's also an interesting moment early in one of the rehearsal tapes where the band really starts to get cooking on Dylan's "Man of Peace"; Jerry's comping a hot solo, and just as things start to reach a peak, the whole thing comes to a sudden stop. One wonders if the band wasn't reacting to a nonverbal cue from Dylan that he wanted to get on to the next song. This inability to connect musically seems to plague the entire '87 collaboration. Interestingly the rehearsal tapes reveal Dylan and the Dead to be most together when they are playing someone else's tunes, such as "Boy in the Bubble" and "Oh Boy."

---

* Actually one possible explanation is that Deadhead detective work deduced that the rehearsal occurred at that date because it falls between the end of an early-March run at the Kaiser and the start of the '87 spring tour of the East Coast, at Hampton Coliseum on March 22nd.

It's well known that the Dead repertoire absorbed quite a few more Dylan tunes after the Dylan-Dead shows ("When I Paint My Masterpiece" and "All Along the Watchtower" actually debuted after the May '87 rehearsals but before the shows). In fact rare was the 1988 Dead show where Bob Weir did not sing at least one song by the other Bob. In the nineties Jerry brought back "It Takes a Lot to Laugh, It Takes a Train to Cry" (which he had played once before, on 6/10/73), and Phil, spending more time in front of the microphone in general, delivered quite a few more "Just Like Tom Thumb's Blues." A fact about which Deadheads may be less aware is the effect the Dead, particularly Jerry it seems, had on Dylan in the wake of this collaboration and a brief joint tour in the summer of '95.

Dylan recorded two Robert Hunter lyrics, "Silvio" and "The Ugliest Girl in the World" in 1988 for his album Down in the Groove, and in the nineties "Friend of the Devil" started making appearances in Dylan's concerts. His second of two recent albums of traditionals and blues standards, World Gone Wrong, released in 1993, features a version of "Two Soldiers" nearly identical to the Garcia-Grisman arrangement; indeed he credits Jerry Garcia in his (mind-blowing) liner notes for teaching him this "battle song extraordinaire." Interestingly the song appears on the CD sandwiched between "Stackalee" and "Jack-A-Roe." Of these two, only "Jack-A-Roe" bears much resemblance to the Dead's version. Dylan credits Tom Paley, a member of the New Lost City Ramblers, with the arrangement. It's not surprising that Dylan should perform the song in a manner similar to the Dead, since the Dead's rendition is in essence a speeded-up version of Joan Baez's early sixties treatment of the song. World Gone Wrong's liner notes also refer to Dylan's 1993 tour as the Dont [sic] Let Your Deal Go Down Tour.

Garcia's death seemed to hit his friend Dylan especially hard. In elegy he praised Jerry's playing in the highest possible terms, also saying that no amount of praise could do it justice. There was a phrase in the middle of his statement that captured better than anyone else ever has Jerry's musical nature in all its acoustic and electric glory: "He is the very spirit personified of whatever is muddy-river country at its core and screams up into the spheres. He really had no equal." At Jerry's funeral he is reported to have said to Deborah Koons Garcia, "He was there for me when nobody was." Perhaps he was alluding to the 11/16/80 Warfield Dylan show Jerry played; Dylan's popularity was at a low ebb at this time. Dylan has played "Alabama Getaway" as an encore throughout his 1995 and 1996 legs of the Never Ending Tour, an unusual tribute. "Friend of the Devil" has also made frequent set appearances throughout that tour, as has "Silvio." ❧ "West L.A. Fade Away" and "Black Muddy River" are two recent additions. Most remarkable,

"This One's for Jerry Garcia"

❧ This is how Patti Smith introduced her thumping, rapped-over versions of Not Fade Away when she opened for Dylan on several dates of his fall '95 tour.

though, is the degree to which Dylan's playing and that of his backing band seem to be taking on Dead-like overtones. Lately there is much more jamming out of tunes, with some passages, particularly in "Silvio," that are very evocative of the Dead. And so it has come full circle.

THE DYLAN-DEAD REHEARSALS

One of the things that strikes Heads immediately about Dylan and the Dead's stage collaboration is how careful the band sounds behind Bob—too careful, as if they're afraid to really cut loose. Indeed the Dead could be said to play it safe in more than just the Dylan performances that year, partially in deference to Jerry's musical readjustment after his coma and in part due to an awareness that they were playing to many new Heads in the wake of *In the Dark*. The Dylan-Dead rehearsal tapes indicate that the caution might have been at least partly owing to an unfamiliarity with the material, as what's in circulation jibes with Weir's report that many tunes were sampled and just about all were given only a cursory run-through. The other story told by these rehearsal tapes, however, is one of a type of playing that was at times more spirited and relaxed than what made it to the stage, if one can get past the decidedly "rehearsal" nature of the song versions here. This is no Watkins Glen or Omni sound check; songs begin and end very raggedly and are more often than not fragmentary (Garcia's primary criticism of Dylan's approach in general). When you get such storied performers as the Dead and Dylan together in the same studio and roll the tape, you're bound to come up with something interesting.

The most commonly circulating tape begins with "The Times They Are A-Changin'," which exemplifies the haphazard nature of the run-throughs here, starting as it does on the "Line it is drawn . . ." verse and falling apart rather quickly. A similarly desultory treatment of "Masterpiece," however, yields more interesting results. The band has a real loose *Basement Tapes*-ish feel on this song.

"Man of Peace" really starts to smoke, Dylan playing vocally off of Mickey and Billy's snazzy syncopated drumming and Jerry leaning into the solo in a way he didn't during the tour. Just as he really gets going, though, the band just stops, inexplicably. One wonders if Dylan wasn't perhaps looking bored or impatient. Whatever the reason, it's a pity. "I'll Be Your Baby Tonight" offers the treat, also witnessed on stage, of Jerry playing pedal steel. Some excellent backing vocals (it almost sounds as if there's a woman singing here) get the song kicking from the first chorus on for a great version

The List for the Lesser-Known
Dylan-Dead Rehearsal Tape
Club Front, San Rafael, California

Mid-May 1987

"Under Your Spell"
"I'm So Lonesome I Could Cry"
"Blues, Stay Away from Me"
"If Not for You"
"Ballad of Frankie Lee and Judas Priest"
"Señor"
"I'll Be Your Baby Tonight"
"I'm Free"
"They Killed Him"
"Pledging My Time"
"Oh Boy"

SONGS REHEARSED BY DYLAN AND THE DEAD AT CLUB FRONT IN MID MAY 1987 (IN CIRCULATION)

1. "The Times They Are A-Changin'" (Bob Dylan, *The Times They Are A-Changin'*)
2. "When I Paint My Masterpiece" (Bob Dylan, *Greatest Hits, Vol. II*)
3. "Man of Peace" (Bob Dylan, *Infidels*)
4. "I'll Be Your Baby Tonight" (Bob Dylan, *John Wesley Harding*)
5. "Ballad of Ira Hayes" (Peter La Farge)
6. "I Want You" (Bob Dylan, *Blonde on Blonde*)
7. "Ballad of a Thin Man" (Bob Dylan, *Highway 61 Revisited*)
8. "Stuck Inside of Mobile with the Memphis Blues Again" (Bob Dylan, *Blonde on Blonde*)
9. "Dead Man, Dead Man" (Bob Dylan, *Shot of Love*)
10. "Queen Jane Approximately" (Bob Dylan, *Highway 61 Revisited*)
11. "The Boy in the Bubble" (Paul Simon)
12. "French Girl (Ian and Sylvia)
13. "In the Summertime" (Bob Dylan, *Shot of Love*)
14. "Union Sundown" (Bob Dylan, *Infidels*)
15. "It's All Over Now, Baby Blue" (Bob Dylan, *Bringing It All Back Home*)
16. "Joey" (Bob Dylan and Jacques Levy, *Desire*)
17. "If Not for You" (Bob Dylan, *New Morning*)
18. "Slow Train Coming" (Bob Dylan, *Slow Train Coming*)
19. "Tomorrow Is a Long Time" (Bob Dylan, unreleased—available on bootlegs of Dylan's Witmark Studio demos)
20. "Walkin' Down the Line" (Bob Dylan, *The Bootleg Series*)
21. "Gotta Serve Somebody" (Bob Dylan, *Slow Train Coming*)
22. "Gonna Change My Way of Thinking" (*Slow Train Coming*)
23. "Maggie's Farm" (Bob Dylan, *Bringing It All Back Home*)
24. "Chimes of Freedom" (Bob Dylan, *Another Side of Bob Dylan*)
25. "All I Really Want to Do" (Bob Dylan, *Another Side of Bob Dylan*)
26. "John Brown" (Bob Dylan, available in official release only in the rare *Broadside Ballads, Vol. 1* and on bootlegs of the Witmark demo sessions from early 1963)
27. "Heart of Mine" (Bob Dylan, *Shot of Love*)
28. "Rolling in My Sweet Baby's Arms" (traditional)
29. "John Wesley Harding" (Bob Dylan, *John Wesley Harding*)
30. "Pledging My Time" (Bob Dylan, *Blonde on Blonde*)
31. "Ballad of Frankie Lee and Judas Priest" (Bob Dylan, *John Wesley Harding*)

32. "Don't Keep Me Waiting Too Long" (traditional)
33. "Stealin'" (traditional—first Dead version: 1966 single [b/w Don't Ease Me In])
34. "I Want You" (Bob Dylan, *Blonde on Blonde*)
35. "Oh Boy" (Buddy Holly)
36. "Tangled Up in Blue" (Bob Dylan, *Blood on the Tracks*)
37. "Simple Twist of Fate" (Bob Dylan, *Blood on the Tracks*)
38. "Señor" (Bob Dylan, *Street Legal*)
39. "Wicked Messenger" (Bob Dylan, *John Wesley Harding*)
40. "Watching the River Flow" (Bob Dylan, *More Greatest Hits*)
41. "Under Your Spell" (Bob Dylan, *Knocked Out Loaded*)
42. "I'm So Lonesome I Could Cry" (Hank Williams)
43. "Blues Stay Away from Me" (Alton Delmore, Henry Glover, Wayne Raney)
44. "I'm Free" (The Rolling Stones)
45. "They Killed Him" (written by Kris Kristofferson, performed by Dylan on *Knocked Out Loaded*)

SONGS REHEARSED BY DYLAN AND THE DEAD AT CLUB FRONT IN MID MAY 1987 (IN CIRCULATION)

1. "Tangled Up in Blue"
2. "I'll Be Your Baby Tonight"
3. "Man of Peace"
4. "Ballad of Frankie Lee and Judas Priest"
5. "John Brown"
6. "Simple Twist of Fate"
7. "Ballad of a Thin Man"
8. "Stuck Inside of Mobile with the Memphis Blues Again"
9. "Chimes of Freedom"
10. "Queen Jane Approximately"
11. "Gotta Serve Somebody"
12. "Joey"
13. "All Along the Watchtower"*
14. "Touch of Gray"**
15. "Slow Train Coming"
16. "Tomorrow Is a Long Time"
17. "Highway 61"
18. "It's All Over Now, Baby Blue"
19. "Wicked Messenger"
20. "The Times They Are A-Changin'"
21. "Maggie's Farm"
22. "Dead Man, Dead Man"
23. "Watching the River Flow"
24. "Heart of Mine"
25. "Rainy Day Women #12 and #35"
26. "I Want You"
27. "Shelter from the Storm"
28. "Knockin' on Heaven's Door"*
29. "Mr. Tambourine Man"*

* Not on known rehearsal tapes.
** Jerry sings lead vocal.

So, if we discount "Touch of Gray," that's at least forty-five tunes rehearsed (and Weir spoke of double that number) to yield twenty-nine.

despite the unsteady tempo. "The Ballad of Ira Hayes" comes next, notable for Dylan's audible-yet-cryptic words of instruction as he stops the band a few bars in: "Like church, church on this. . . ." To which Jerry understandably replies, "Church?" to receive only "Yeah" in response. It's humorous indeed to hear Jerry, giving it the old college try, yell, "Organ!" as they start the tune back up again. Like the tape as a whole, "I Want You" shows some tantalizing moments of potential greatness despite its general sloppiness. Jerry starts with great confidence and Bob breaks out his harmonica—it's great to hear these two masters together in this way. But then Dylan misses a few chances to enter and proceeds to flub the whole verse, coming in strong only on the chorus. It also sounds as if Jerry's dying to cut loose on the main riff.

Jerry comes in like the wrath of God on "Thin Man," though a verse and a chorus is all they play of the song. "Memphis Blues Again" has Jerry finally getting to play a full-fledged solo, which seems to energize Dylan, as this time he's ready when the verse comes around again. This one definitely shows signs of becoming, as it did, one of the more successful fruits of the collaboration as well as a tune that would work well for the Dead. "Dead Man" and "Queen Jane," up next, feature good, full workouts.

The next tune, a clearly "for our ears only" version of Paul Simon's "Boy in the Bubble" is one of the more fascinating tracks here, truly affording a fly-on-the-wall sensation. It's definitely a vid. Bobby (Weir) obviously knows the song well and sings it capably despite spacing a couple of lines—but hey, he did that all the time with Dead songs. The whole band seems very comfortable with the song, the drums especially giving it a real workout. Jerry comes up real sharp on the second verse. It's definitely funny to hear Dylan sing backup on this tune. Mickey and Billy start to head off into Other One territory at the end of this tune before stopping.

A second run-through of "Man of Peace" gives a window into the evolution of these tunes as the Dead and Dylan performed them, with the later version stronger in general but featuring a far more restrained Jerry on guitar. It's followed by a reggaefied "Union Sundown" definitely not the song's original setting, a glimpse at Dylan's legendary penchant for changing the arrangements of tunes almost wholesale in the studio and onstage.

Given the Dead's long history with "Baby Blue," it's no surprise that it's one of the songs that's done best here. What *is* surprising, however, is the way they play it, giving it a cool, slow build as the Dead fall into place behind Dylan one by one. The momentum seems to carry over into the next tune, "Joey" (if these songs, with splices in between them, are indeed in order). Although Dylan coughs his way through the first verse, he sings the whole song with conviction. An interesting change for Dylanophiles: In this version Joey is thrown into the hole for trying to *cause* a strike.

After Jerry's comments regarding Dylan and the beginnings and endings of tunes (he said that he had no concept of them, but that what lay between was "pure gold"), it's funny to hear Bob say, ". . . and, uh, I forget how it ends," when laying out the structure of "If Not for You." The tape ends on a strong note nonetheless, with Jerry playing heavily distorted and appropriately indignant licks over the groove of "Slow Train" and then, in stark contrast, back on pedal steel again for a lovely "Tomorrow Is a Long Time."

The lesser-known list of rehearsal tunes almost strikes one as being from another, later session, given the appreciable improvement in the performances. It starts with an interesting (if somewhat tuneless) version of the obscure *Knocked Out Loaded* tune "Under Your Spell" and then moves on to a couple of excellent covers—Hank Williams's "I'm So Lonesome I Could Cry" and the obscure "Blues Stay Away from Me." Both reflect the easygoing nature of these rehearsals, which were by several accounts a refreshing change of pace for Dylan. Dylan plays acoustic on "I'm So Lonesome," and what a treat it is to hear Jerry and he take a stab at this classic. Dylan, Weir, and Garcia come up with a very appealing vocal mix on "Stay Away," Dylan breaking up laughing at a couple of points due to lyrical miscues.

Another treatment of "If Not for You" amply displays the best and worst of this collaboration. It drags terribly, in part because the Dead are learning it, sure, but also because that's what a band with two drummers tends to do even on Dylan's midtempo songs. On the other hand the vocal mix is great, and Jerry lends the song some beautifully ornamentative guitar playing.

"The Ballad of Frankie Lee and Judas Priest" is perhaps the real highlight of these tapes for Dylan fans, just as him playing this live was the Dylan highlight of the tour. It's far from perfect here but nonetheless a joy to behold, made all the more so by the way Jerry's guitar lines skip through the song. Jerry takes the lead vocal himself on "Señor," pulling a "Deadhead" on Dylan, that is, showing himself to know the song better than its original performing artist, which is pretty funny as Dylan flubs and Jerry plows on straight ahead. What's even funnier, though, is what Garcia says to Dylan after the song: "You phrase it differently." A version of "I'll Be Your Baby Tonight" is probably the most stage-ready performance out of all the known rehearsed tunes. This strong session ends with an almost vintage '66 reading of "Pledging My Time," and the unbridled fun of all cutting loose with "Oh Boy," Jerry taking the lead vocal and Dylan singing backup with evident relish.

t's difficult to convey the sense of gratification with which those on the bus at the time greeted the developments of late 1989. Wading through the late eighties, it seemed every tour was an occasion for group support ("Jerry looks great, I think he's lost weight." "He's definitely lost weight." "I think they're playing hotter than last tour—what about Oxford?") that was beginning to seem perilously close to self-delusion and denial. There were plenty of hot shows to be taken in, sure, but one found oneself all too often staring wistfully at setlists of yore. It wasn't only the setlists, though. Even some of the best shows of '88—the spring-tour Hampton run, the summer Oxford shows—didn't make all that good a translation to tape. Oxford, especially, seemed to suffer from the lack of context (granted one shouldn't expect a *tape* to cause the *Aoxomoxoa* skull and crossbones to come floating out of an overcast sky during Row Jimmy). Were the band's best days behind them (and us)? Were we just telling ourselves the Dead seemed to be getting better in order to avoid unbearable conclusions? Or was confirmation of our hopes and banishment of our fears just around the corner?

Hopefully this serves to put the later events of 1989 into perspective. The deluge that followed Hampton—10/9/89—was as manna from heaven, the confirmation that "just around the corner" wasn't illusory, that our perspective of steady improvement since Jerry's return from the coma was not clouded by so much wishful thinking, that opening the first set of the summer tour with Playin' was indeed a good omen.

In retrospect it seemed the Deer Creek Close Encounters (7/15/89) was the catalyst, the mother ship beaming the instructions for Dark Star, Death Don't Have No Mercy, Attics, We Bid You Good Night—those glistening, almost illusory pieces of primal Dead—back into Jerry, Phil, Bobby, et al.'s frontal lobes. The results were felt immediately: The very next show, at Alpine, the Boys closed with We Bid You Good Night (and, as we can now say with certainty, pushed When Push Comes to Shove out for good). It was humorous indeed (or least became humorous once hopes were fulfilled) to see how various of us took the news of the pre-Hampton bustouts. There's a strain of superstition in many a Deadhead that rivals that of baseball players. So there was always that, Death Don't at Shoreline? No shit!" (contemplation of full possible implications, checking of impulse to venture a guess as to whether they'll break out Dark... no, no, no, don't jinx it... just smile that Deadhead Cheshire Cat smile and say...) "Cool." (He's thinking it, too, I can tell...).

It was into this hotbed of speculation and wonder that the Dead threw the "Formerly the Warlocks" shows. Why would they bill themselves as the Warlocks, we asked ourselves and each other. That it might be an effort to thin unmanageable crowds was a thought far too prosaic to be contemplated. The reason seemed clear: This was to be a gathering of the faithful for a very special occasion.

Well, both turned out to be true, and with the full Help → Slipknot! → Franklin's, Dark Star, and Attics back in the rotation along with the previously decanted goodies, the prospect of missing this or that show suddenly took on a greater gravity, as did attempts to divine the show in a run where they would play "It."

What gave the jubilation over the revamped repertoire an added dimension was the way the band was playing. In a word, on. What were we hearing? We were hearing what 1986 *should* have sounded like; that is to say, what 1986 could have been without Jerry's deteriorating health—an evolutionary building on the success and renewed commitment evinced in the best of 1985. Somewhere along the line the Dead had found that ensemble strength, that hearty appetite for lengthy musical exploration, that ineffable groove, and they were playing a good head above 1985.

When the magic of MIDI was factored in, our cup ranneth over. For a time it was only an enrichment to Space, but once Jerry and Bobby and then Phil got it "on board" their guitars, MIDI became a passport to musical realms of unimagined orchestral permutations. More important than the beauty, trippiness, and sheer entertainment value of MIDI instrumentation for Deadheads, however, was that it seemed to be giving the band the same. Here was novelty in playing instruments they had played for more than a quarter century! Suddenly there were compelling reasons to follow the rabbit of a germ of a musical idea running across the stage down the rabbit hole and through the looking glass, where Deadheads would have been all too happy to follow the band. It seems as if the advent of MIDI definitely acted as a spark to the powder keg of chops that had steadily improved since Garcia's comeback, through '87 and '88.

The '90 spring tour saw the Dead on a self-assured roll. If one can make allowances of the "that was then, this is now" sort necessary to compare the apples and oranges of the Dead's various historical incarnations, then one must surely concede that March '90, culminating in the Knickerbocker Arena and Nassau Coliseum shows, was one the Dead's finest performance months ever. The band was on an incredible roll; that jazz saxophonist Branford Marsalis caught them at this peak on March 29th at Nassau

🌿 Not everyone agreed, though. Here's what *Rolling Stone* writer Eric Flaum, who compiled an annotated, selected Garcia discography for *RS's Garcia* book, had to say about *Without a Net*: "The pity...is that the Dead chose this lackluster tour.... Branford Marsalis sits in on 'Eyes of the World' with minimal impact."

represents one of the more fortuitous convergences in the latter history of the Dead. The result was—*is*—legendary. 🌿

All the more's the tragedy, then, when Brent Mydland died after a strong summer tour. Just as the Dead seemed to be realizing the full promise of what they could be in the "Brent" era, a lush flowering of skillful, muscular playing and kaleidoscopic sonic color, the band lost an inventive instrumental component of the ensemble and an integral part of their vocal mix. It's beyond sad to contemplate what effect continued inspired playing by the band might have had on his happiness. That the Dead were never quite the same again is undeniable; many also feel that despite the momentum they carried into the latter half of '90 and then '91, they were never again quite as good either.

7/15/89
DEER CREEK

The aliens returned in the second set this night....

It begins with a ragged Foolish Heart, which manages to improve somewhat by the uplifting end jam. Bobby follows up with a respectable Victim.

The Hot Seat, Part IV

There were two bits of tour-observed lore concerning Brent's death that were downright eerie: that his last show fell ten years *to the day* after his predecessor Keith Godchaux's death, and that his last words (or last *lead* vocal anyway) onstage with the band were the end of his verse in The Weight: "I've got to go, but my friends can stick around...." Weird. The absolute weariness with which Brent sings his last verse of The Weight on the tape of 7/23/90 World Music Theater is positively chilling.

Crazy Fingers is well played but a mess lyrically, a situation helped not at all by Weir sticking to his guns on a backing vocal that contradicts the one Garcia's singing. This bit of cheekiness obviously flusters Jerry, who goes on to blow the next few lines completely.

An epic Truckin' contains some licks reminiscent of the ones Jerry played in the epic 11/6/77 "Jerry-as-Jimmy-Page Truckin'." The transition to Smokestack Lightning is also executed with considerable panache. Bobby's vocals are a bit thin and forced here, but there's some great blues jamming at the end. The band starts to head into Drums, but Jerry keeps the music playing with a little impromptu jam the likes of which was seen quite a bit in '89. Space reflects the joy the band members were taking in their new MIDI rigs—it's a musique concrète fest from which the *Close Encounters* theme seems to come out of nowhere. It's not the orgasmic release of 1/22/78, but it's definitely a trip to hear. Jerry doesn't really explore it farther, though, initiating instead a jam with a Far Eastern flavor. Via much MIDI weirdness it emerges into what some of us have come to label the "Baghdad Jam," an evocative piece of music that calls to mind a hot evening spent smoking from a hookah in a café on the Tigris. This *may* be a slightly idealized picture of Iraq's capital; the jam is touched by and engenders this same idealism. This Middle Eastern music floats into a stately China Doll intro, Jerry's flügelhorn MIDI solo is exquisite; the change in tone also serves as catalyst for some stunning alterations of the solo arrangement. And there's just the merest hint of a closing jam like that of 6/14/85 before Jerry fuzzes out for Watchtower. The jamming's good in this version, if truncated by Stella Blue.

No matter, though, this Stella (in which Jerry sings "I've *slept* in every blue light . . .") is, as are the best, dripping with silvery-blue guitar lines. The near-inevitable Sugar Magnolia is fortunately an especially lively and elating one, with some great key runs from Brent to help end the show in smiling style.

10/9/89
HAMPTON

Dark Star. This is it, the *long*-anticipated breakout. The thing is, this show is so hot that it would rank high up in the year's shows even without the momentous occasion in the second set. But just as the situational play of baseball does not allow one to presume that a solo homer hit after a running error by the team at bat would have been a two-run homer, one cannot perhaps assume that the Dead would have been so deep in the zone *without* Dark Star in the show. In baseball the counter to the "fallacy of the assumed run" states that the pitcher may well have pitched differently with a runner on base. Perhaps the Dead wouldn't have played with such intensity had they not been anticipating the moment when they would break out Dark Star. Or maybe they wouldn't have played Dark Star at all that night if they hadn't been playing so well. Thankfully the question is moot. The show rocks, Dark Star was played.

The first set, kicked off by a crackling Stranger (featured on *Without a Net*) shows the band to be locked in from the get-go. A long, crazy night indeed. The Dead maintain the energy through a well-rounded (in terms of dynamics) set of material that, with the exception of Ramble On Rose, is wholly postretirement in vintage. It's capped by a great, long Music Never Stopped.

The second set is, famously, a whole 'nother ball of wax. The fest of primality begins, appropriately enough, with Playin'. Brent plays some interesting variations during the intro, the sort of on-the-spot mutations that would make him so sorely missed less than a year later. They jam this one out very well, Jerry taking some imaginative MIDI solos. The second one, in a flute voice, is a masterpiece unique to this Playin'. He begins to deconstruct the jam until he is playing only single notes in syncopated fashion and then builds the solo back up spectacularly; Brent's synth-flute echos are a wonderful touch here. The Uncle John's intro, while hardly seamless, is nevertheless beautiful. Jerry's first solo break possesses an almost tear-jerking emotional acuity, at once playful and contemplative. The vocals are also very fine. Garcia sings his part lower than usual in some places, a gambit that serves to accentuate Brent's high-flying tenor. The transition back into Playin' is deftly accomplished, and once back in the tune Jerry hits the little country licks at the end of each line with a crispness sometimes lacking in other shows.

Next is . . . well, I think we all know what happens next. Jerry, Phil, and Brent twice play the four most famous notes in Deaddom to a reaction that, even on the soundboard, is clearly one of absolute bedlam. Audience tapes of this show render more clearly the nuances of what actually transpired: the notes were followed by a pregnant pause during which everyone exchanged glances with their neighbors for a reality check. Then, assured that it was, indeed, *true,* everyone *freaked* in unison. The band takes the direct route to the first verse of Dark Star, Jerry nailing the vocal with a full-throated wail at the edge of his range. He makes a slight break from past vocal arrangements (including the 7/13/84 revival, the last time it was played) by singing "through" from the "transitive nightfall" line at the point where he formerly sang the "the" that follows; instead of giving "the" two syllables, he lends one of its syllables to "through."

It's not long after the first verse that the Dead also show themselves more willing to step out than in '84. Brent, with a "vibe" solo, heralds a passage from close variations on the theme to a spacier place. Once Bobby shakes loose from the main theme, an even greater looseness is achieved, with only the tempo and Jerry's occasional thematic statements to mark the song. In the elegant passageways through which the band journeys next, Jerry plays a "bassoon" solo with touches of both The Other One and the Spanish Jam. Still spacier playing follows, in which Brent and Jerry are the prime instigators. As Space goes, though, it's still fairly melodic, and soon heads back into the second verse.

The end of the second verse, however, yields an anxious musical reality informed by the minor key of Dark Star. The spaciness ends with some keening Garcia guitar and a short feedback fest, the firsthand intensity of which—what with the band silhouetted onstage while bizarre sounds whooshed around the quadrophenic system—no tape can hope to fully capture. Drums is pretty standard in light of what it follows, but Space is beautiful and highly evocative, reminiscent of some of the best of the '85 Spaces—6/16 and 7/1/85 come to mind. Out of Space, the primal run continues with the recently revived Death Don't Have No Mercy. Jerry manages a virtuoso gospel vocal run on the "land" at the end of his verse. Bobby also nails his verse. Jerry takes a huge solo between Bobby's and Brent's verses, redolent of peaks achieved in monster Dews. Brent then provides the vocal equivalent, his Hammond solo afterward keeping the song roaring heavenward. All this passion finds a ready vessel in Jerry's rendition of the final verse, where he pushes his range into the red zone and more than pulls it off. He sings with as much emotion here as I've ever heard him muster.

Poor Dear Mr. Fantasy, having to come after all that. It is nonetheless a muscular version and the Hey Jude finale → Throwing Stones → Good Lovin' that follows could make one think that here was a show in which the Dead could do no wrong. Jerry's solos in Fantasy; Brent's vocals in same; Bob's riffs in Throwing; the way Jerry joins Bobby on the ". . . his cover's blown" line; the fact that the band, led by Brent, laughingly eschews Not Fade for Good Lovin'—all point to this conclusion. The verse Brent takes in Good Lovin' and his "Be my girl" improvisations seem to throw Bobby a bit, but this fact is more than mitigated by the *joie de vivre* they evince.

The "Formerly the Warlocks" billing for this run and rumors of portentous sound checks led many to at least fervently hope for Dark Star, though none dared *expect* it. I think it's fair to say, though, that this night's encore came as a surprise to all: the first Attics of My Life since 1972. Jerry had spoken of bringing it back as far back as 1988 in an interview with Blair Jackson, but . . . well, who knew he was serious? This revival, vocally complicated as it is, is stronger than even could have been hoped, owing in no small part to Brent nailing down the high end. A fitting ending to a truly epic show: the revival everyone had desired for years plus one they didn't even know they wanted, an amazing playlist all around, and fantastic playing. There was a long-standing ovation after the show that night in Hampton. Instead of the usual

Cosmic Taco Saga

Once upon a time, not so long ago, there lived six very powerful magicians. These wizards, or warlocks, had many splendrous abilities: They could create multifaceted crystals out of almost thin air, and they had the peculiar ability to draw on the sacred cosmic yippee, to draw inspiration and enlightenment from the sky. And they made terrific taco fillings. But how could they share their gift, they wondered?

Soon they had a plan. They would hold communion at the cosmic taco shell. So word was sent out, and a week later the gift was shared. Sacred songs invoked the spirits of the very earth, the sky, and the great unknown, the cosmic unity Itself! The end?

—ROB HODIL,
TACO-FILLING ENTHUSIAST
(WHO PREFERS CRISPY SHELLS)

Written on the inside cover of his copy of 10/9/89 (a very short story due to spatial considerations).

race to the lot, all stood and savored a beautiful moment in recognition of the Boys having given such a rare gift.

3/24/90
ALBANY

Maybe it was the fact that live sixteen-track recordings of these shows were being made for what would become *Without a Net*, maybe the band was rejuvenated for another East Coast swing after the incredible song revivals of the previous fall, and maybe—probably—there was just a good dose of that ol' spring-tour magic in the air . . . but whatever lay behind the effect, the band was *on*, simultaneously attacking downbeats with a vengeance and intellectually nimble enough for surprising musical explorations with just the right effect, nuance, or phrase at the right time.

Let the Good Times Roll is a fun show starter as always, but it gives no hint of what is to come—only the second first-set Help → Slipknot → Franklin's since its resurrection the previous year at Hampton. What a way to get things going! And this is no cursory version either. A solid Help really gets a kick from Brent and the rhythm section during the Slipknot, which leads into a joyous Franklin's. Walking Blues and Loser are top-notch versions, the Dead opening them both up farther than usual for some really hot jamming (one has to wonder about Brent's scat-singing in Walkin', though—a man on the edge?) and Loser literally exploding at the "Last fair deal in the country" peak after the jam. Saturday Night is, in all deference to the many superlative '77 versions (and many, many, more throughout the years—lots—maybe one or two more than some of us would have liked) quite simply one of the hottest ever. I've never been a big fan of this song (or its close cousin, Around and Around), but the tightness and heat of the jamming, especially the Garcia-

Lesh interplay, as well as its unusual placement, set this one apart. The band apparently thought so, too, as they put this version on *Without a Net*.

Although the second-set song list doesn't match the first set's for peculiarity, the performances more than fulfill the promise of the first frame. Playin' is tight yet exploratory, packed with virtuoso bass Phils, and seriously weird in the midst of a spacey end jam that features some inspired Brent-Jerry interplay. This is one of those shows where you keep thinking you can put your finger on who is especially on ("It's Bobby—listen to that rhythm line!" "No, check out those synth-drum fills!" "What about those bell sounds Brent's playing?") as if that would somehow reveal what is driving such transportative music. The answer, though, is everything at once. The transition to Uncle John's is so musically clever as to inspire awe, with Jerry and Bobby agreeing on a modulation in the key to slip from the D scale into the G almost simultaneously and then keeping the change close to their vests as the rest of the band, one thread at a time, weaves a loose cloth of musical concurrence until it's all there: rhythm, melody, tempo, Jerry's opening solo—Uncle John's Band and you can't figure out when it all started.

Uncle John's is good all the way through, followed by an equally polished Terrapin, the end jam of which melts into the most special part of the second set, a long, building Mind Left Body Jam (or, as we have been informed, the Mud Love Buddy Jam) the first since the early eighties. It doesn't start out as much, but once Jerry gets the guitar sound just right, Bobby gets the hang of the changes, and Brent starts in again with the aforementioned bell sounds, it becomes a version that could even stand up to (no, not surpass, but contend with) the benchmark Boston '74 version. It definitely shares the '74 edition's gooseflesh-raising, solar-plexus-tugging quality. It's catchy-weird, haunting, acid-drenched pop.

Drums is as shreepy as the promise of its predecessor, with sound effects reminiscent of those on *Blues for the Rainforest* and the Greek 6/16/85 Space, replete with exotic birdcalls. Jerry launches into a bizarre deconstruction (with a MIDI effect that sounds like a twisted hybrid of harpsichord and bagpipe from hell) of The Wheel's opening notes, and spends the rest of the Space taking it farther and farther from its source, then of course brings it right back to go into The Wheel out of Space. This is one Wheel that is self-contained and not merely an intersong bridge.

Even if The Wheel were to be merely a bridge to the Watchtower that follows, boy, would it have been worth the journey! It never ceases to amaze me how many licks and filigrees Jerry could pack into this song, all at a lightning speed between verses. This rendition shows his playing at a particularly inspired pitch. The inspiration carries over into a heartfelt Stella Blue and a Not

Fade Away like they write about—a thoughtfully jammed-out version that recalls the '71 and '77 incarnations of a song that the Dead played too often as if on "autopilot."

One more treat lies in store, though, and it's a double. We Bid You Goodnight is always a performance to be cherished, a link to storied primal days; this one is sublime, the best since they brought it back in '89. The harmonies are right on, as is the timing of the "round"-type construction. When Jerry sings the "Walkin' in Jerusalem" part, it will make your hair stand on end, not for the first time in listening to this tape.

A goose-bumps show—one of the pick of the 1990 litter.

Now We Play for Gold

Atlanta '96—The Dead Olympics

Watching NBC's television broadcast of the 1996 Summer Games was a very strange experience indeed. This may not have been the best-run Olympics, and sure, the ugly specters of terrorism and rampant capitalism reared their ugly heads in a big way, but the Centennial Games definitely ranked first in Dead content, surpassing even the Barcelona Games' Lithuanian basketball-team hoopla.

It started with the very first notes of the Opening Ceremony, cocomposed by Mickey Hart and Philip Glass and accompanied by some pretty trippy visuals before settling into good old American-cheerleader flash and country-music glitter. It continued with the revelation that Gary Hall on the U.S. swimming team was a big Deadhead—the narrator also talked about how he would drive his coach crazy because he had so much native talent but only practiced when the mood struck him (sound familiar to anyone out there?), and the fleeting playing of Stella Blue as the sound track for an "up close and personal" story on gymnast Vitaly Sherbod. It kicked into high gear of course with a basketball game be-

3/28/90
NASSAU

Oh, cruel fate to befall a show, to live perpetually in the shadow of one of the favorites of Deaddom! So will it forever be for perfectly excellent performances the likes of 5/7/77 and 2/14/70. While this one surely does not rank with the above, it is safe to say that one would hear more about this one had Branford Marsalis not joined the Boys onstage the next night.

The second set gets off to a promising start with a very well done Foolish Heart that's positively brimming with vitality. Jerry has his troubles with the lyrics, to be sure, but perhaps that's to be expected with any tune he's been singing for less than a decade. A series of rhythmic stop-starts are particularly well-executed—one can hear the audience getting off on them, and their thrill translates nicely to tape. Some of the jamming in this tune, too,

tween the Dream Team and Team Lithuania. Lithuania was in the light uniforms for this game, so the only tie-dye present was in the uniforms' piping.

But the camera panned over the bench to show one of the Lithuanian coaches in a dye, and the play-by-play announcer started talking about the Dead's support of the team and how they were wearing a black band on their uniform in memory of Jerry. That was all Bill Walton, who was providing color commentary, needed. He started saying how the Dead were among those who recognized the connection between sports and music, the constant improvisation and creation in the moment, and went on to laud the Dead for their charitable work and for always being there for the underdog. Casey Jones was also played at the end of NBC's coverage of the game, and a Coke commercial that aired right after Walton's comments featured the Lithuanian b-ball team against a tie-dyed backdrop and some Madison Avenue psychedelic music—this was part of the "Always Coca-Cola" campaign, so the end of the ad featured a Coke bottle top with the slogan "Always Truckin', Always Coca-Cola."

The Dead Olympics wound down with Tennessee Jed as the sound track for a piece on the kayaking competition, which took place on the Ocoee River in Tennessee.

Truly a watershed in the strange emergence of the Dead into the mainstream after their disbanding.

is extraordinarily transportative, a sign of this tune's evolution in a span of less than two years. The Looks Like Rain that follows, which made its way onto *Without a Net,* really moves.

Cumberland fairly bounces off the walls, featuring some affecting vocals from Garcia and Weir as well as a combustive Jerry-Bob duet in the middle jam. Magic is brought to the stage next with the debut of The Weight, an outstanding cover choice. With the success of this tune and Jerry's Garcia Band treatment of The Night They Drove Ol' Dixie Down, it's too bad they didn't try their hand at more Band songs. In one of those maddening *Golden Road* interview moments, Phil once professed a desire to work up a version of King Harvest (Has Surely Come), and Hunter is a big fan of the Band, with an avowed atmospheric debt to their songwriting. Imagine Jerry singing This Wheel's on Fire, for one. Ah, well. The Weight at any rate certainly whets the appetite. The Dead's rough-hewn, masculine voices capture the spirit of the song perfectly, Jerry and Brent standing out in particular here. A nervous Phil blows only the end of his verse, what with the crowds going nuts over his taking a verse at all. The vocal mix on the choral parts is superb.

An interesting if not spectacular Space evolves into an introspective, Phil-dominated Other One. A good rendition of Wharf Rat is countered

by Bobby's Good Lovin', to which Brent adds some bravura backing vocals. Note his "Would you be my girl" interjection. The encore is the Dead's last rendition of Revolution, though the Dead's version might be more accurately termed "Revolution I"—it's got that same shuffling, skiffle sound. A treatment closer to the original Beatles' "Revolution" may have worked better and been less Dead-generic. Those paired triplets Jerry plays between vocal lines call to mind the way the Dead play Let the Good Times Roll, When Push Comes to Shove, and numerous other tunes.

It's not a show that will turn you into a quivering mass of jelly, but it has its moments, in abundance. It also functions as a good "control" for gauging the full effect Marsalis had on their performance the next night.

ttending the sorrow and shock Dead-
heads felt at news of Brent's death
was an almost shamefully mitigating
sense of relief. Especially for those
who at first only heard—as I did—
that "someone in the Grateful Dead
died" (from a non-Deadhead girlfriend), there was the feeling that, well, since it isn't
Jerry, Bobby, or Phil, or the equally core drummers, the Dead would probably carry on.
It's not a proud reflection, and it was not one that dulled the sense of Brent's loss, but
it did offer the solace that the music would likely continue.

After the mourning the speculation began. Bruce Hornsby, who had toured
with the Dead along with his band, the Range, and sat in from time to time on accordion, seemed a good prospect—and one to be devoutly wished for. A fanciful hope of
many (including my friends and I) was Mac Rebennac—Dr. John. He had, after all,
turned in a cut (Deal) on the *Deadicated* compilation. He did not, however, have the
tenor that the Dead also sought to hold up the top end of their harmonies (indeed it
should be noted that he was never a contender and was probably not considered at
all).

The eventual choice—Vince Welnick, late of the Tubes—was fielded from a
number of auditionees, including two who had done keys work for Starship, Tim
Gordon (also a veteran of Jefferson Airplane and Who tours) and Pete Sears. For
those Heads unfamiliar with the theatrical rock work of the Tubes (many, if not most),
the choice didn't so much engender surprise as curiosity: Who was this guy? How
would he fit in? (Not to mention dread of the possible "White Punks on Dope"
bustout.)

Fears were assuaged and hopes fueled when the Dead returned for their fall tour,
missing only the first three dates at Shoreline. Vince brought a new approach to many
of the core tunes in the repertoire, seemed to play well with the group, and added interesting color. When Bruce Hornsby added his fingers to the mix at the second show of a
reassuringly hot Madison Square Garden run, the two struck an ideal balance. Bruce
played assertive, percussive lead lines on a grand piano, à la Keith, going occasionally to

a synthesizer atop the grand. Vince became more of a colorist, adding to the MIDI'd mix with a variety of sounds including horns (trumpet, baritone saxophone) and exciting effects such as the "breaking glass" sound Brent had pioneered within the band in Victim or the Crime.

Hornsby also energized the Dead. Here was a musician who seemed to know the material well (he had, after all, been in a band in college that did Dead covers) and could not only stay with the Dead through freewheeling inspiration but could lead them new places as well. His impressive soloing was an obvious inspirational kick for Garcia, leading to outstanding musical duels onstage. Hornsby's extra-Dead career, however, frequently called him elsewhere, and by the beginning of '92 he had ceased to be a regular.

When both Bruce and Vince were together, the Dead magic flowed more freely, as it did throughout one of the band's best European tours and equally impressive summer and fall tours in '91. When Vince was left to his own devices, however, the results were decidedly more mixed. Some of the effects and novel approaches he brought to the band's repertoire saw very little variation as time wore on, and this same repetitive streak was borne out within songs as well, Vince riding the same riff throughout an entire tune in a manner unpleasantly reminiscent of Keith's last couple of tours with the Dead.

So Vince wasn't as consistently inventive as Brent—but they were two different musicians and such a thing can be forgiven. What made the Vince-era Dead, even at their hottest, hard to take at times was not only Vince's predilection for repetition but his prominence in the mix. He had a heavy-handed way of playing some of his most banal riffs that would drown the other players out in a reedy synth wash. The sonic density was sometimes such that avenues of jamming would be gridlocked—perhaps a symptom of not listening well enough to the rest of the band or maybe just evidence of Vince's monitor mix not telling him all that he needed to know.

The fact that Vince is an accomplished, creative player capable of excellent jazzy improvisation was evidenced in many shows; his problems with dynamics, sensitivity, and the demands of constant improvisation, however, made Brent's absence all the more palpable.

9/14/90
MSG

Some shows, without anything earth-shattering or completely weird happening, seem just right—quintessential Dead shows. The opening night of the '90 Madison Square Garden run is one of these.

The first set is distinguished by impeccable song selection and playing to match. The second set starts on a dime with Scarlet → Fire, the trippy phasing of the "Grateful Dead" intro still echoing. Jerry makes the vocals as special as the jams here with an inspired, alert delivery. One of Jerry's greatest strengths as a singer was the attention he gave diction. He enunciated his consonants (when he was aware of which words he was singing, that is), sometimes to trippy effect, as with the delayed *duh* at the end of "Heart of Gold Band" in this Scarlet. Jerry, Bob, and Phil have one of their more spirited conversations in the Scarlet exit jam. It's not one of the longest or hottest, but it is far above average in terms of complexity. Fire is just a gift that keeps on giving, with the whole band very into it. It stands at that precise point where exceptional playing meets an unmatched ability to convey raw emotion through musical notes and rhythm.

The set keeps giving with a Truckin' that features some inspired rhythmic variations under Jerry's soloing. Terrapin is likewise a winner, a fourth tune in the set that carries over onto the other side of a ninety-minute tape. It's hard to find any faults with this version, but there is great virtue in the long, involved MIDI jam on the Terrapin theme into Drums. A suitably bizarre Other One–dominated Space sires an Other One with trippy effects on most of Weir's vocals. When the effects are off, his singing on this version is revealed to be some of the best he's turned in for this song. Even the predictability of Wharf Rat and Sugar Magnolia is mitigated by the muscular versions played here. The slightly different vocal take Bobby gave Sugar Mags in later years— the way he'd go up and lean on the *-ia* at the end of *magnolia*—is showcased well here, and the jam at the end in which Jerry and he duel it out is just insane.

A fine way to start a great run, this show was at the time a resoundingly positive answer to the question "Will the Dead be able to sustain their momentum with this new guy Vince?"

9/20/90
M S G

Despite the jubilation that greeted the return of El Paso to the first set, the real highlights of this show were—believe it or not—to be found elsewhere. Specifically in one of the best post–'77 Brown-Eyed Women and a killer second set.

Truckin' to kick off the second set seems as good an indicator as any that the band's cooking with gas, and this version bears that out. An excellent China → Rider is notable for Jerry's big, full-throated roar on the "head-

TERRIFIC TERRAPINS

✵ 2/26/77 Swing Auditorium
The first one is a good one, very much worth having for more than historical reasons.

✵ 3/18/77 Winterland
Rendered magical by L'Alhambra.

✵ 5/7/77 Boston Garden
Bouncy, fast, and airy; unformed still, but it works.

✵ 5/19/77 Fox Theater
A tight version that serves as portal to a fantastic song cycle.

✵ 5/22/77 Pembroke Pines
The dying strains of Wharf Rat eschew the "Lady with a Fan" section to meld seamlessly into the beginning of the Terrapin Station, which serves as the perfect bridge and intensity builder en route to Dew, a transition that is also astounding. Available on Dick's Picks Volume Three.

✵ 1/22/78 Eugene
The tension builds, is released in a beautifully sung "inspiration," then builds more and more with crunching power chords from Garcia and Weir.

✵ 11/6/79 Philly Spectrum
In an unusual set-opening position, a very well jammed-out Terrapin leads into a sick Playin'.

✵ 12/31/85 Oakland
A seminal version in a very good New Year's show.

✵ 12/31/87 Oakland
Another excellent New Year's Terrapin.

light" line in Rider and Bruce's sparkling solo runs in same. Here's as fine an example as any of how Bruce served as an artistic prod for Jerry at times—check out the blistering run with which Garcia answers Hornsby's first solo. A spirited Women Are Smarter leads the rhythmic charge into Drums.

A very long, quiet, and complex Space leads to a late-second-setlist to roll away those predictable post-Drums blues. The opening notes of the Dark Star everyone had been waiting for on this run emerge out of Space to a huge roar (okay, that much *is* predictable) and from then on it's anyone's guess as to where things will go. And go they do in one of the year's most far-out Dark Stars. Phil in particular serves as a one-man clearinghouse for MIDI madness in this version, playing in voices emulating bowed bass and cello. The initial jam leads into a reprise of the previous night's Playin', then quickly back into atonal meltdown after atonal meltdown until finally giving away to a fantastic Throwin' Stones that mercifully eschews Not Fade for a rousing Touch.

The closing night of one of the band's strongest stands at the Garden, this show skimps not on jamming, improvisation, or surprises.

Dead to the Core

❊ 7/2/88 Oxford
Arising unexpectedly out of Uncle John's, this one truly climbs the heights of inspiration.

❊ 3/31/89 Greensboro
A great closing jam, replete with Andean clay flute sounds.

❊ 3/15/90 Cap Centre
Phil's birthday—a "Dear Prudence"-ish jam afterward sets the stage for Albany.

❊ 3/24/90 Albany
That "Dear Prudence"-ish jam they'd been playing at the end finds full flower in the first Mind Left Body Jam in years.

❊ 6/16/90 Shoreline
A raging exit jam gives birth to a distinct, equally excellent piece of improvisation.

❊ 7/18/90 Deer Creek
An especially eerie version.

❊ 6/23/93 Deer Creek
Terrapin pours its life into an insanely hot jam.

12/27/90
OAKLAND

The list for the second set of this show follows one of the Dead's classic templates: a Scarlet → Fire opener, an Estimated pairing into Drums / Space, and Miracle, Wheel, Throwing Stones post-Drums. Looks mighty familiar, right? For a while this was like, every fourth show. So how did the Dead manage to play sets such as this one for years and still keep things interesting? By making subtle variations, such as they do here, that completely change the "standard" character of the set.

I've been intentionally vague with the partial setlist I've given above. The Estimated pairing is not Estimated → Eyes, but Estimated → Comes a Time. Throwing Stones is not the first part of a hackneyed Throwing → Not Fade combo but of a considerably fresher if not rare Throwing → Lovelight. These are small changes on face, but they engender a fairly significant change in the set's rhythm. Replacing Eyes with a Jerry ballad frees (and obligates) Mickey and Billy to find their own tempo in Drums and, in this particular case, sets up a contrast with an up-tempo beginning to the drum duet. Similarly the removal of the Jerry ballad from the post-Drums string establishes a nearly unbroken flow of momentum from Miracle to Lovelight. One of the best things about the way the Dead arranged their sets according to a fairly established paradigm was the sense of adventure they created each time they broke these "rules."

The opening Scarlet is rock solid, Bobby's rhythm playing in fine form. The transition to Fire is outstanding, reminiscent of the great 7/1/85 version. Bobby again stands out here with some extremely funky guitar playing augmented by an idiosyncratic electronic sound. The bubbling notes that gurgle out of Jerry's guitar show his playing in this era to be undiminished.

The first thumping downbeat of Estimated Prophet is full of portent; it's fulfilled in an outstanding version, one for the ages. To start, Bobby sings with fire, even providing his own echo effect: "'Cause I know, I know, I know. . . ." The X factor makes an unmistakable appearance in the jamming of this tune, with band and crowd egging one another on to heights of wild abandon by the time Bobby sings the thoughts of all: "Might and glory gonna be my name!" The interior Jerry solo is the locus for the peak of this song's insanity (and how true that is of so many tunes!): Phil and the drummers prod him on mercilessly and Bobby chases him the rest of the way to the mountaintop, nipping at his heels with rabid, buzzing riffs. Avalanches of toms cascade all around. Oh, delirious chaos, I call thee Dead!!! Ahem. It should also be noted that Vince's tripped-out alto sax-synth bursts during Bobby's "don't worry about me's" at the end of the song were still a novelty at the time of this show. If you can listen without the prejudice of the many times you've heard the same effect in the same place since, the resulting effect is nicely bizarro.

Estimated dwindles in time to only Vince and Bruce. And Jerry, who takes this opportunity to deal one from the bottom of the deck, dropping hints of Comes a Time but playing it close to the vest. A long cascade of unresolved notes brings the anticipation to a fever pitch—serious roar building from the crowd now—until Jerry repeats the opening six notes, at first quiet and tentatively, then with loud certainty, bringing the house down. The clamor doubles when he sings the opening line. It's a gorgeous performance all the way through, Jerry delivering and more with heartfelt vocals and cut-crystal guitar lines.

The Drums come marching in with speed and regimental flair. There's a quick detour as Billy and Mickey adopt a Not Fade Away cadence, but they soon reclaim their martial air, complete with call-and-response courtesy of Billy. A jazzy duet is conjured out of thin air, which they ride into the inner workings of a clock where ticking noises and the whir of gears reverberate with unnerving proximity. Hamza El Din and his Nubian Choir provide a soothing respite afterward. All in all, a fantastic, transportative Drums.

Space begins with a MIDI effect from Jerry that sounds like the creaking of a door, which he then elaborates into a creepy Bela Lugosi sound track. It's almost as if this loud, abrupt change of pace from Hamza El Din is his way of saying "Remember those loud American *freaks*? We're baa-aacckk. . . ." Phil, Bobby, and Bruce pick up the feel of Jerry's explorations to produce a very far out Space. Somehow, though, it slides into Miracle, which opens amid hints of The Other One and Truckin'. The great band-audience synergy at this show

THE BEST OF TIMES: SOME COMES A TIMES FOR THE AGES

* 10/19/71 Minneapolis
* 10/30/71 Cincinnati
* 7/18/72 Roosevelt Stadium
* 7/26/72 Portland, Oregon
* 5/4/77 Palladium
* 5/9/77 Buffalo
* 6/24/85 Cincinnati
* 9/7/85 Red Rocks
* 11/1/85 Richmond
* 12/27/90 Oakland
* 6/25/91 Sandstone

makes Bobby's Miracle sing-along a smashing success, and Jerry and Vince dominate a smoking exit jam. The drummers take charge of Wheel after the first bar, speeding it up radically—this one cooks along at quite a pace. The drumming here, as throughout the show, is top-notch.

The Throwing Stones → Lovelight pairing brings a rocking post-Drums to a festive close. Throwing is distinguished by Phil and Jerry's playing in the closing solo, Lovelight by some interesting time changes at the end and by Vince's Clarence Clemons turns. The outstanding Baby Blue encore contains a vintage Jerry-ism: "Strike another match, they will not follow you"—found art!

A final note: I don't know if soundboards of this show circulate, but take my word for it, you want one of the several exceptional audience tapes in circulation. This is a show where the band-audience interplay was definitely at a high.

A Rose by Any Other Name, Part Two

SOME OF THE FOLLOWING takes on song names are conversational in nature, others can be found on J-cards (the inserts in tape cases—some of the J-card humor is pretty dry, for example, "Do Not Ease" for Don't Ease. Oh, you mean dry *doesn't* mean "not funny"?). They're all a little slice of Deadhead humor. It should be noted that some of the original titles listed here—"Miracle," for example, are already slangy abbreviations.

❋ Big River
Big Liver

❋ Black Muddy River
Swamp

❋ Black-Throated Wind
Black-Throated Lung

❋ Corrinna
Borrinna
Velveeta

❋ Don't Ease
Don't Sleaze
Dough Knees
Jolene

❋ Easy Answers
Cheesy Answers
Queasy Hamsters

❋ El Paso
El Bob

❋ Half-Step
4/8 Step (or some equivalent fraction)

❋ I Will Take You Home
I Will Take You Down

❋ Just a Little Light
Just a Miller Lite

❋ Let Me Sing Your Blues Away
Shittyball

❋ Me and My Uncle
Me and My Monocle

❋ Mexicali Blues
Montezuma's Revenge

❋ Might as Well
Mighty Swell
Minus Twelve

❋ Miracle
Miracle Whip

❋ Picasso Moon
Ricotta Moon

❋ Playing in the Band → Uncle John's Band
Playin' in the John

❋ Queen Jane
Queen Hein ("When you're sick and tired of all this repetition")

❋ Stella Blue
Stella Burnt
Stella D'Oro

❋ Throwing Stones → Not Fade Away
Throwaway
Throwing in the Towel (my favorite, because that's what this closer began to signify for me after about the millionth time)

* Tons of Steel
  Tons of Brent
  Tons of Shit
  900,000 Tons of Veal

* Truckin'
  Juggin' (an appellation given this new tune by a Rolling Stone *review of*

the show in which it debuted, Fillmore West 8/18/70)

* U.S. Blues
  Useless Blues
  U.S. Snooze

* You Ain't Woman Enough
  You Ain't Donna Enough

2/20/91

OAKLAND

The Dead rang in the Chinese New Year and their new year as well with a fine run that showed them not to have lost any momentum from their strong playing in the last half of 1990. The previous night's electrifying New Speedway breakout and the guest drumming of Airto Moreira for several tunes the following night tend to overshadow this show, but this middle night of the stand should not be overlooked, as it possesses playing that's at least on a par with all three and a long, delectable pre-Drums.

The second set kicks off with a Scarlet that proceeds at a fairly mellow pace until Jerry gooses it with a guitar run that mercifully drowns out Vince's riff for a moment (who, I wonder, decided that he should be the loudest in the mix?). Jerry continues to assert himself in a long Fire jam, competing once again for primacy in the mix, this time with both Bobby and Vince. Vince's accumulated synth delay produces what I think of as a Vince Tiger, which gives the effect of a cloud rolling forth and billowing toward you, only to be parted suddenly by Jerry's guitar screaming out of the haze. Phil also unleashes a torrent of *extremely* loud bass notes midway through. Unfortunately Jerry's smoking leads in the closing jam are partly buried again under Bobby's loud rhythm playing; Weir plays well here, but c'mon!

The mix problems ebb somewhat in an excellent Estimated, allowing one fully to appreciate the epic duel in which Jerry and Bob engage before the "Don't worry about me's." Jerry plays a very relaxed (yet musically tight) end jam, making superb use of first a Pan-flute MIDI voicing and then a standard flute, which yields slightly better technical results.

He's Gone finds Jerry still discovering new ways to deliver the vocals in a song that is almost two decades old at this point. He gives the coda a long vocal workout as well before the band embarks upon a generous jam that, while Other One–flavored, is distinctly its own animal. Drums is short but intoxicating, enhanced greatly by Baba Olatunji and Sikiru Adepoju, whom the full band join onstage for a hot jam that starts out fully formed and moves swiftly through a nocturnal terrain as if borne by an Arab charger. It features some wild Jerry runs and slinky bass accompaniments by Phil to Olatunji's drum riff. After some early postjam Other One hints, a full-fledged Space develops, centered around Jerry's haunting and sonorous "Gregorian chant" and string MIDI voices, Bobby and Phil throwing some electric wrenches into the proceedings at opportune moments.

A searing Other One comes racing out of Space. Weir finds a novel vocal delivery for this tune as well, and plays some great MIDI "trumpet," while Jerry's guitar screams to the spheres. From there it's a very strong Wharf Rat and an Around that reveals Bobby's voice to be as hoarse as it's ever been. It's not a perfect show by any means, but one that is well stocked with exemplary moments of combustion.

> "There was the time at Giants Stadium when my buddy and I were up on the upper level before the show. We peered over the edge at the crowds below us, and my buddy's Ray-Bans fell off his head and straight down about four levels and landed in an aisle below us. Whereupon we saw some Deadhead scamper out of his seat and pick up the glasses. Through massive effort we were able to scam our way down all those levels. We even had to use the famous two-man section-buster move, where one guy with a ticket for a different section hassles the guard, and the second man slips in behind in the confusion. When he finally got to the spot where the glasses landed, he just looked back up at the crowd and said loudly, 'Well, who's got my sunglasses?' They were promptly returned. "
>
> —C. B.

3/21/91
CAP CENTER

The pre-Drums portion of this show's second set is one of the most consistently interesting stretches of the Vince period, showcasing as it does some of his better licks of electronic weirdness. The set opens with a Victim that is, despite some early vocal lapses, one of the finest exemplars of the fierce feedback beast this sublimely "hideous" song (Garcia's quote) had become. Vince's crazed, claustrophobic synth is never more appropriate than it is here, especially in an all-out barrage at the end out of which Scarlet emerges in a way that recalls transitions out of '72 and '73 Dark Star meltdowns. Even when the wondrous cacophony subsides, Vince lays down a number of irregularly spaced surges that evoke the residual power spurts of a severed high-voltage cable.

It is from these ashes that Scarlet rises, picking up energy on its way to a hot Fire. Weir really asserts himself midway through, giving the tune a bit of raunch that contrasts nicely with Hornsby's steel-drum-tinged keys. It's Jerry who takes over before the last verse, though, building the jam to an inferno. He apparently gets pretty pumped up from all this himself, stepping out on a par with Normal '78 on the chorus, roaring that he's "Talkin' 'bout a fire, fire. . . ." This is the stuff.

The Phoenix-like origins of Scarlet from Victim, Jerry's fire in Fire—all this already qualifies this version for an esteemed place in the Scarlet → Fire pantheon, but Jerry takes it farther still by taking Fire right into the first Stir It Up Jam, building it with slow majesty. As is so often the case with the Dead's thematic jams, these passages make you want to turn your face skyward and weep for the joy of music's gift. Jerry's not alone in making this special—high marks also go to Bruce, Bobby, and Vince, who add all the right touches to round out the jam. When Jerry starts to play the lead melodic line over their foundation, it sets off another round of chills.

Space is highlighted by a thrilling jam led by Jerry on MIDI trumpet; it speaks of a dawn run through a foggy, cobblestoned European capital, a thousand thoughts and doubts coursing through one's head. It eventually gives way to an excellent Goin' Down the Road, in which Bruce does some fine soloing, into an all-too-familiar but well-played Throwin' → Not Fade. The audience-singing-the-refrain "bop-bops" were hackneyed at this point, but this one does work very well. When the band takes the stage again for a pretty Box of Rain encore, Jerry and Bobby have a little laughing fun with the still-chanting masses, going up and up the necks of their guitars with the rhythm part before commencing Box.

In the scheme of things this show is vastly underrated, an inevitable side effect of so many shows in this period having the primal trappings of Dark Star and other pieces of vintage Dead. But I'd take one of these shows over any sloppily played setlist fest like 9/26/91.

4/1/91
GREENSBORO

The song list for this show's second set could have floated in from 1972; the playing therein suggests that perhaps it did. It's one of the finest shows of the year, if not *the* best, and it wears the stamp of "primal Dead" with easy grace.

Phil has the helm for the opening China Cat, which means that it's one fat, bouncy Cat. The transition to Rider is perhaps a tad premature, but is nonetheless very exciting. Jerry comes alive during Rider, delivering a number of piercing solos. Bruce also takes a hot solo turn at the end (he's all over this China → Rider) over Vince's sensitively applied synth wash. Weir follows with a fantastic Looks Like Rain in which vocal delay is used to fine emotional effect. But Bobby is already in fine voice, not to mention the excellence of his rhythm playing here. Jerry and Bruce also add some poignant touches.

The centerpiece of the set is Dark Star, but of course. The band gives it an extravagantly long opening, Bruce's sparkling piano proving the perfect complement to Jerry's climbing ice-blade lead lines. Vince, Bobby, and Phil provide a lustrous, full sound underneath Garcia and Hornsby's upper-register explorations. Just as the jam seems bound for the first verse, Jerry takes a leisurely turn with his flute MIDI voice, prolonging the instrumental bliss. His singing is very hoarse on the verse that follows, but so what? Such considerations are mere trifles in the face of what is shaping up to be one of the most fully realized Dark Stars since the '89 revival. Jerry and the band behind him assume a more angular, argumentative tone after the verse, becoming increasingly dissonant as the jam peaks. Jerry slips into an ever more brassy MIDI voice as the music becomes a crazily collapsing piece of modernist sculpture. He and Vince pile up synthetic delay for a real meltdown, nineties style. Jerry, now screaming above the fray in trumpet and flute voicings, soon dives into the sharp-edged jam fragments with abandon. Just as it seems that the band is going to cede the stage to Drums, Jerry takes charge again with his "saxophone," leading the band headlong through a short, odd jam into another mystic cloud. Bobby and Phil remain onstage for quite some time after the others have left to work out a menacing outer-funk jam with Mickey and Billy.

A deeply introspective Space magically coheres by incremental degrees back into Dark Star. The process is so gradual as to be almost subliminal. As soon as it's to-

> "*I* was sad because there would be no more shows, until I met a man who had never seen even one."
> —STEPHEN KOLOZSVARY

gether, the band wastes no time getting to the second verse, a completion of the song that's most satisfying. They take the time to build a nice Playin' intro out of the verse, though the body of Playin' is run through fairly quickly. The performance is strong, though.

Even though not much could arise comfortably in the wake of such exquisite jamming, the Dead do sustain the sixties'/seventies' atmosphere with strong versions of Black Peter and Lovelight. The Baby Blue encore is marred only by too much Vince in the mix—Jerry's singing has apparently recovered from his Dark Star troubles, enabling him to sing this one with the strength and emotive impact that made this (along with Brokedown) one of the Dead's best regular encore for years.

9/10/91
MSG

Although this is probably not the most spectacular of Branford Marsalis's onstage collaborations with the Dead, it does mark the first time he sat in with the Boys for the entire show (and the only time he played with them on *every* tune). Rest assured, both sets contain more than their share of great moments.

The promise of a full show is felt from the very beginning, with some lovely interaction between he and Bruce in the tuneup before Shakedown. Shakedown itself, a perfect tune for the Garden, is somewhat flat from the start, or at least played a bit cautiously. It picks up, though, with a nice jam at the end.

It's rare that I have very much nice to say about C. C. Rider, but it's a *little* better with Branford soloing instead of Bobby on slide. This version grows even better as it becomes the basis for a seamless transition into It Takes a Lot to Laugh, It Takes a Train to Cry. This was the third time the band played this pairing, and its success caused it to become the norm for the remainder of C. C. Rider's run. Jerry sang this Dylan blues tune with authority and innovative phrasing that made it his own.

Black-Throated Wind, to which Branford contributes some great licks at the beginning, and High Time create a mellow space. Branford, as one might expect, adds some exceptional color to both songs. The set ends on an up note with Cassidy and Deal.

One of the best things about Branford's guest spots was the salutory effect he had not only on the Dead's playing but on their setlists. The Dead, in an effort not to bore him, trotted out some of their best material at the Branford shows; hence a Shakedown opener and Black-Throated Wind, High Time, Cassidy, Deal to end the first set. That was nothing, though, compared with the charms to be found in set two, which opened with Help → Slip → Franklin's and just got better from there.

Help on the Way is highlighted by Phil's string-slapping jazz technique, appropriate indeed given the company at hand, and Slipknot! benefits mightily from Branford's presence, opening up into a loose, jazzy space. The ensemble takes some time to work through some flatness in Franklin's and their perseverence pays off. Though it's not any kind of all-time performance, there are definitely some moments in the jamming out of this tune that possess a good deal of complexity.

The Estimated that follows has a certain dark flavor—there's something about Branford's prowling around during Weir's vocals that lends a back-alley edge to this one. Jerry lets Branford take the main solo here, which is understandably less nuanced than Jerry's usual turn (he hasn't been playing the tune for fifteen years, after all). Vince's employment of his oft-used baritone-sax sound seems at first an inspired stroke here, and Branford initially plays off it nicely. But as was unfortunately all too often the case with Mr. Welnick, it soon becomes too much of a good thing. And since he's both louder than and unable to stay with Marsalis, the esteemed jazz man retreats for a bit until Vince abates. The mellow dissolution of Estimated is full of portent, and it is Bobby who first hints at what is to come—Dark Star. Seconds later Jerry and Branford join in for a shining opening jam that soon leads into the first verse. The playing that follows is very loose and fluid, with first one player, then another asserting themselves in the mix, engendering a kaleidoscopic effect with varied tonal color and melodic hues.

Dark Star's second verse emerges from the Drums/Space into which it had initially poured. More spaciness follows, consisting mainly of scalar runs by Jerry, Branford, Phil, and Bruce, with Bobby playing insistent licks and tinkering with feedback underneath. Later he turns up with a brash and brassy MIDI trumpet sound. A wonderful point of maximum density is reached when Vince pours on the "Victim" synth effect (that sustained broken-glass sound) and all three axmen pile on with MIDI weirdness. The tightly packed sonic quality of these few moments renders the ear all the more receptive to the looser, quiter playing that follows as the group casts about for a new direction. All are listening and responding to each other admirably at this juncture as they seek a resolution. They find one in the key of Miracle, which they begin building toward in exceptional fashion. The tune blazes all the way through.

SOME TANTALIZING TEASES, REAL AND IMAGINED

I have a friend who thought he heard St. Stephen in every Space. In this he was not alone—St. Stephen tease "hearings" are among the most widely reported and most controversial form of the Dead "tease." Here are some other noted examples through the years:

❋ 4/29/71 Fillmore East
St. Stephen tease in Not Fade ➧ *Goin' Down transition.*

❋ 5/11/72 Rotterdam
Major Bird Song teases in Dark Star.

❋ 9/28/72 Stanley Theater
St. Stephen tease in Greatest Story.

❋ 3/13/82 Reno
"Dear Prudence" tease between The Other One and Black Peter.

❋ 6/17/91 Giants Stadium
The "Dark Star Tease" show—when the refrain of New Speedway Boogie came around in the second set, it seemed especially appropriate: After four different teases this darkness got to give, indeed!

❋ 6/28/91 Denver
Dark Star tease in the middle jam of Wharf Rat.

❋ 12/8/93 L.A.
Jerry plays St. Stephen melody out of Space into Last Time.

❋ 2/27/94 Oakland
Major Cosmic Charlie tease between The Other One and Wharf Rat.

While it's true that the combination of Bruce and Branford adds a bit of an MOR sound to a ballad like Standing on the Moon, it's an assessment that fails to take into account the skill and inventiveness of their playing. The result of fine playing all around here (Phil especially deserves mention) and Jerry's impassioned vocals is a standout version of this affecting song.

Lovelight is Bobby's happy choice to close, though one wishes he wouldn't have cut off some great riffing by Branford with his vocals. Fortunately there's ample jamming in the crazed closing of the tune, with a joyful mélange of Jerry, Branford, and Bobby's "trumpet" fills. And to top off a fine show, Baby Blue.

The Branford shows always provide plenty of fodder for close listening and aggressive yet sensitive jamming, and this one's no exception, with an exceptional setlist to boot.

9/26/91
BOSTON

A star-studded night sky is described by Hornsby's piano at the opening of the second set, colored with bass and guitar floating through in slow motion. Dark Star emerges from a nebula just visible on the horizon. This is a very open, jazzy version, the band giving it ample time to develop before going into the verse. Jerry leads a bout of nervous jamming out of the verse, which dissolves after a time in a glistening array of keyboard sounds. The Dead stop, realign, and take off in a new direction with Saint of Circumstance, certainly a surprise.

Eyes is a bit shopworn in places but manages to find some interesting spaces at the end of its various meanderings, leading finally into an inventive and pleasingly melodic Drums. Mickey and Billy cover a lot of different ground here. Space shimmers with Dark Star overtones but moves into an almost contemplative Other One. It finally begins to catch fire just before going back into Dark Star for the second verse, which in turn pours its life into Attics of My Life. The band starts Attics pretty weakly—particularly on the vocals—but achieves enough confidence to deliver a creditable rendition of a song that was a treat to hear in any form in the nineties.

Good Lovin' shines from the beginning, with credit especially due Hornsby. Weir delivers his "push back the night" rap to rousing effect, ending the show on a high note.

The Brokedown encore is just gorgeous, as Garcia's attention to vocal phrasing is especially palpable here. His immediate turn into a fully *a capella* We Bid You Goodnight puts an extra-special cap on the show and on a fine fall tour.

This show is more than a bit overrated, owing no doubt to its fine setlist. I've given it the benefit of the doubt at times here, but some of the playing feels frankly tired. Nevertheless the good moments shine all the more brightly when they occur in songs such as these.

10/31/91
OAKLAND

In a year of many fine shows, the one the Dead played on Halloween in the wake of Bill Graham's death may be the finest. The playing throughout is inspired, encompassing deep emotion and unconscious jamming. The song list, too, is very strong.

The first set gets off to a running start with Help → Slipknot! → Franklin's, which the Dead had been using to enliven first sets ever since the previous year's spring tour. Having these tunes in the first set does wonders for a show, bringing an excellent forum for jamming to the opening frame and rendering all that follows, including the second set, all so much icing on

Beat the It Down On-line, or, "With a Net"

One of the unexpected results of Jerry's death was its precipitation of the first real Internet "event." In the same way that the Kennedy-Nixon debate, the moon walk, and Vietnam combat footage defined the emerging medium of television—TV images became inextricably linked with the way the nation experienced these events—the worldwide sharing of grief and remembrance on August 9, 1995, and the days that followed will, for many Heads, be remembered as at least partly a cyber-experience. The Dead newsgroup, rec.music.gdead, became a gathering place for those looking to vent and seeking sympathetic voices, as did the WELL. Thousands of Dead home pages went into a state of mourning exemplified by poignant writing and artwork.

This would not have been the case had not Deadheads already staked out considerable territory on the Internet. Newsgroups and chat rooms devoted to discussion of the Dead, sharing of tour information, and tape trading were among the first such entities and have thrived in the years since they were pioneered; the WELL (Whole Earth 'Lectronic Link) has long been a virtual home for many Heads, in newsgroups, chat rooms, and subscribers' home pages; and countless on-line Deadheads have their own web pages devoted to the band. Many of these sites are small, homespun affairs—some Steal Your Face "wallpaper," the proprietor's tape list, some links, maybe a few scanned tour pictures—but others are tremendously ambi-

the cake. The Help here is very strong, and Slipknot! carries the muscle of some elephantine Phil lines. Jerry's vocal delivery in Franklin's (save one blown entrance) is electrifying—clear, crisp, and well considered. Of particular note here is his repetition of "home again," a sure sign that he was very conscious of how he was singing this one. The band really rolls this one out, too, playing very well as a unit and clearly listening to one another. Its only flaw is in the brevity of the closing jam.

Although Bobby's slide-guitar solos, even at this late date, are still more exercises in volume and venturing up the neck than displays of real artistry, Rooster does manage to generate some genuine heat. The Loser that follows tops it, though, with Garcia continuing to lay a very strong hand vocally. This is about the best they've played this tune. The set keeps getting better as Phil steps up for an outstanding Tom Thumb's Blues, in which he yet again manages some very interesting twists in the delivery of Dylan's lyrics and his own permutations thereof. Amazingly the band manage to turn it up yet another notch from here, closing with perhaps the best-played Let It Grow of the nineties.

The second set picks up where the first left off, with a solid Scarlet → Fire that features some downright vicious Weir licks in Fire. Bobby, as is his wont, spaces some lyrics in Truckin' to humorous effect before sliding into a blues mode for a pretty hot Spoonful.

tious affairs, featuring exegesis of songs, discographies, archives of reviews, and more, all of which represent many, many hours of work on the part of their creators.

Another by-product of such a prodigious linking of Deadheads is the hope that by casting a net both far and wide it will bring to the surface obscure audience tapes from the Dead's early history, or overseas treasures such as a high-quality recording of the Dead's Radio Luxembourg show. The Internet has already facilitated countless tape trades, some through one-on-one contact initiated by a posting to a newsgroup inviting tape trades, others by way of "grovels" ("ISO [In Search Of] First Show—4/1/88 Byrne"), and large volumes via "taper trees," in which "branches" propagate "shoots" for a geometric expansion of the "gene pool" of a given show (I get a tape and spin it for five people, who in turn spin it for five people . . .).

Gary Duncan, sitting in, adds some searing blues licks to this last.

Dark Star begins as a very good version, but when Ken Kesey steps up and delivers his rap on Bill Graham's death, replete with e. e. cummings poem, it is transformed into a classic. It isn't just the fact of Kesey's presence that accomplishes this—it's in the way the Dead spur on his rap. Many a band might bring it way down in back of such a "reading," or cheese out with punctuations such as rim shots, tinkling piano, and the like. Not the Dead. They just play more and more frenzied behind their old compadre, building in volume until he has to shout to be heard. They devour him and the rap in chaos that speaks volumes about the formlessness and darkness of the universe and serves as a reminder that the insanity of the Acid Tests still lives within these souls. These few moments in Dark Star stand as among the most memorable in the band's entire history.

A very dark Drums → Space is transformed by a Duncan-initiated blues jam, but Jerry eventually brings the musical conversation back around to Dark Star. The post-Drums portion of the song seems to offer some redemption from the ominous nature of the first section. The music here speaks of a parting of the clouds, a soft clearing and respite from an angry storm. The "Shall we go . . ." of the second verse becomes an invitation up into a now-cloudless night sky, a final benediction for Bill Graham sent on shining wings of piano and guitar.

The transition into Last Time comes as a surprise, but a good one. The Dead deliver this song with considerable gusto, although Bobby's screaming at the end is just awful, not in the least bit musical or even emotional. As ever, Jerry is ready with an immediate contrast. Though he clearly struggles with the opening verse or two of Standing on the Moon, he manages to turn the technical failings of his voice to emotional advantage. His delivery gains confidence as the song builds—from the "somewhere in San Francisco" line (which draws the requisite roar from the local crowd) on, the song provides one chill after another. The repeated lament of the song's coda feels like another, very personal, elegy for Graham.

The rest of the set, alas, holds no real surprises, though the Not Fade end of a Throwin' → NFA is better than usual. The Werewolves encore is fun too.

Some Key Stops for the Deadhead Cruising the Information Superhighway

✳ **The Official Grateful Dead Home Page (www.dead.net/)**

The name tells it: This is the beautfully designed site maintained by the Dead organization, the place to go for the latest official word on tour info (sadly, now only Further, Ratdog, Mystery Box, etc.), rumors, news from the band, Vault releases, and so on. There's also a catalog of Grateful Dead label recordings, merchandise, and Hulogosi Books. Take the time to check out Robert Hunter's on-line journal, a surprisingly frank work-in-progress. Hunter has also paid for a software upgrade out of his own pocket, setting up a usenet-like site dubbed DeadNet Central, linked to the Dead home page.

✳ **rec.music.gdead**

The Grateful Dead newsgroup, a hugely popular site on usenet where Deadheads meet for tape exchanges, swapping of rumors and opinions of hottest versions, and sometimes banal, sometimes fascinating Dead-related insights.

✳ **ftp://gdead.berkeley.edu**

An FTP (file transfer protocol) archive at Berkeley, fat with files of a mostly statistical nature—setlists, and so on. The highlight, though, is Ihor Slabicky's discography, which is by far the most comprehensive yet assembled on the recordings of the Dead as a group and as individual musicians.

✳ **David Dodd's Annotated Grateful Dead Lyrics (www.uccs.edu/ddodd/ gdhome.html)**

A work-in-progress by David Dodd, Assistant Professor, Library, at the University of Colorado at Colorado Springs. The Dead's lyrics are rich in allusion and meaning, and this highly enlightening and entertaining site provides a reference to the songs' references, as well as a concordance between

Dead lyrics and significant words and phrases, freewheeling interpretive essays (and one of Robert Hunter's replies to same), discographies, and plenty of other treats to keep you up late in front of the computer. If you've always wondered what a "Buck Dancer's Choice" is or who Billy Bojangles was, this is the site for you.

❋ Roots of the Grateful Dead (www.taco.com/roots/)

Makes a nice companion to David Dodd's annotated lyrics site. Here are the origins of the folk, country, blues, bluegrass, and other roots tunes played by the Dead. Another very impressive piece of on-line Deadhead research.

❋ *DeadBase* (www.deadbase.com)

Includes information on the gestalt of the *DeadBase* project, a directory of tapers, *DeadBase* ordering information and progress updates, and of course setlists.

❋ Jeff Tiedrich's Resources for Tape Traders (www.tiedrich.com)

A fascinating site that goes a long way toward answering the question that occurs to so many perusing *DeadBase*—which and how many of these tapes are in circulation, and in what form? Tiedrich is a taper's taper, a self-avowed completist, and his painstaking research and that of others featured here is an invaluable resource for the serious tape collector.

❋ WELL Conferences About the Grateful Dead and Deadheads (www.well.com/conf/gd.html)

The WELL (Whole Earth 'Lectronic Link) is to Deadheads what AOL is to the average American on-

Not Fade Away: The On-line World Remembers Jerry Garcia, *Edited by David Gans, with a Foreword by Steve Silberman*

At first glance, this might appear to be another quickie celebrity death payday but Gans and Silberman's involvement in the project is all the assurance that Heads should need that this is nothing of the sort. Their reflections on Jerry are as always right on, and the material that David Gans has collected rings with insight, fond reminiscence, and loss. A fine document of one of the most articulate on-line communities in what was both its darkest and its finest hour.

line. As such it features a variety of forums for Dead-related news and chat, as well as many other forums and member web pages of tangential interest to Heads. Many of its features, including the Dead ones, are available to registered guests as well as WELL customers.

☼ **The Dead Sled (www.voicenet.com/~ yakko/gdead.html)**

"The Deadhead VW Tour Bus to the Information Superhighway." Sort of an Internet starter kit for Deadheads, this is a nuts-and-bolts guide to outfitting yourself as an on-line Deadhead, with many useful links to other sites. Everything from Grateful Dead screensavers to J-cards (tape-box insert cards) to info on cassette players, and more.

☼ **Ed Bick's Grateful Guitar Page (www.connix.com/~ebick/tabindex.htm)**

The site for the Deadhead guitar player. Here you'll find tablature and chords as worked out by Ed and other Heads, basic guitar theory, links to other Dead and guitar-related sites, and more.

☼ **Grateful Dead Tapelists (http://www.demonsys.com/jim/tapelists.html)**

The fruits of Deadhead James Denaro's mission to build a close community of active tapers. The tapers in the network have collections that range from vast to tiny. A good site for getting serious about on-line trading.

☼ **Sunflower Studios (www.Sunflower_Studios.com)**

A collection of beautiful J-cards, some of which are truly astounding, that can be downloaded free of charge. Also check out the Taper's Domain, where dozens of traders have registered, and the Shakedown Street catalog, which, as the name implies, is a virtual lot vending scene.

☼ **Mark Leone's Grateful Dead Site**

RIP. Alas, this classic collection of links and info, the portal through which so many Netheads first passed, is no longer. It is gone, but not forgotten.

WINTER

DECEMBER

1 *Rosa Parks arrested for refusing to cede her seat to a
white man, 1955* ✱ *12/1/79 Stanley Theater*

2 *12/2/73 Boston Music Hall*

3 *12/3/92 Denver* ✱ *Terrapin!*

4 *12/4/65 Big Nig's House* ✱ *First appearance as
the Grateful Dead* ✱ *San Jose Acid Test*

5 *Eighteenth Amendment (Prohibition) repealed,
1933* ✱ *12/5/71 Felt Forum*

6 *Altamont, 1969* ✱ *Ira Gershwin, b. 1896*

7

8 *Gregg Allman, b. 1947* ✱ *John Lennon, d. 1980*

9

10 *12/10/93 L.A.* ✱ *Scarlet*  *Fire with
Branford*

11 *12/11/94 Oakland* ✱ *Days Between!*

12 *12/12/73 Omni* ✱ *Don't forget the sound
check*

13

14

15 *Bill of Rights ratified, 1791* ✱ *12/15/71 Ann
Arbor* ✱ *12/15/86 Oakland* ✱ *Jerry's
comeback show*

16 *12/16/88 Oakland* ✱ *Estimated*
Eyes!

17 *12/17/93 Oakland*

18

19 *12/19/73 Tampa* ✱ *Dick's Picks Volume One*

20

21

22

23 *Jorma Kaukonen, b. 1940*

24 *Christmas Eve*

25 *Christmas*

Winter has traditionally
been the season for West
Coast Deadheads to reap
the rewards of living in the
Dead's backyard, a place
where it never snows ten
feet 'neath the ground.
December was generally a
month when, the year's
touring over, the Boys
played in the Bay Area:
Winterland, Oakland, the
Kaiser Center—all the
home-turf haunts that
made West Coast shows
feel like family gatherings.

December was also the
month for Deadicated
Heads all across the land to
make travel arrangements
to escape the cold rain and
snow for the best New
Year's Eve party around.
Though Jerry disparaged
the New Year's shows as
mediocre at best, more

parties than concerts, they were the height of the Deadhead "social season." A far cry from the manufactured, boozy joy of most New Year's gatherings, they seemed the very epicenter of thrills. On tape they comprise some of the bedrock shows in a Head's collection, musical smorgasboards happily housed over several tapes: 12/31/72, with its Truckin' ➡ Other One ➡ Drums ➡ Other One ➡ Dew; 12/31/78, the epic "Farewell to Winterland," a marathon show that featured revivals of Dark Star, the Sunshine Daydream coda to Sugar Magnolia, and We Bid You Goodnight to top it all off; the four-set acoustic-electric wonder that was 12/31/81, with another Dark Star revival and the last time around for several acoustic tunes, with Joan

1 *New Year's Day* ❈ *Hank Williams, d. 1953* ❈
   Breakfast at Winterland, 1979

2

3 *Stephen Stills, b. 1945*

4

5 *George Washington Carver, d. 1943*

6 *Carl Sandburg, b. 1878*

7 *1/7/78 San Diego* ❈ *Garcia laryngitis show*

8 *Bill Graham (né Wolfgang Grajonza), b. 1931*

9 *Joan Baez, b. 1941*

10 *Buffalo Bill, d. 1917* ❈ *1/10/70 San Diego*

11

12

13 *1/13/80 Oakland* ❈ *With John Cipollina,*
   Carlos Santana, and Greg Errico

14 *1/14/67 Golden Gate Park* ❈ *The Great*
   Human Be-In

15 *1/15/79 Springfield* ❈ *Miracle* ➽
   Shakedown!

16

17

18

19 *Janis Joplin, b. 1943*

20

21

22 *1/22/66 Trips Festival*
   1/22/78 McArthur Court

23 *1/23/66 Trips Festival*

24

25

26

27 *Wolfgang Amadeus Mozart, b. 1756*

28 *Space shuttle* Challenger *exploded, 1986*

Baez no less; the three-way *soul*ar blast of the Dead with Etta James and the Tower of Power horns on 12/31/82; and the last Bill Graham New Year's, 12/31/90, where Branford Marsalis's saxophone breathed gorgeous life into a superbly played show highlighted by Bird Song and a second set that was one fat Not Fade Away sandwich stuffed with Eyes, Dark Star, and The Other One. Now that the Dead are no longer with us, much of the color has seeped from our mind's-eye view of the passage from 1999 to 2000.

Winter, too, was the season for the new year's shows—that is, the first shows of the new year, usually in February. These

29 *Jesse Fuller, d. 1976* ✻ *Willie Dixon, d. 1992*
30 *Release of first commercial jazz recording, 1917*
✻ *Marty Balin (né Martyn Jerel Buchwald), b.*
1943
31 *Philip Glass, b. 1937*

could be counted on to be special as well, either a continuation of the celebration with Chinese New Year's or Mardi Gras as the occasion, or a time for the band to break out new tunes. In 1986 the Dead pulled off a hat trick, starting out with Chinese New Year's and Mardi Gras in succession in California, then playing their first tour dates (and last gigs of the winter) a month later in Hampton, breaking out Visions of Johanna and Box of Rain. Three paragons of the February breakout show are of course 2/18/71, 2/9/73, and 2/26/77. The February '85 Kaiser run and '91 Oakland stand also stand out among Chinese New Year's celebrations, with some fresh tunes for good measure.

It's that feeling of anticipation, wondering what "this year's model"

1

2 *Groundhog Day*

3 *Neal Cassady, d. 1968*

4

5 *2/5/78 Cedar Falls*

6 *Bob Marley, b. 1945*

7

8 *Neal Cassady, b. 1926*

9 *2/9/73 Stanford* ❀ *Eyes, China Doll, They Love Each Other, Here Comes Sunshine debut*

10

11 *Thomas Edison, b. 1847* ❀ *2/11/70 Fillmore East* ❀ *With Duane and Gregg Allman and Peter Green*

12 *Abraham Lincoln, b. 1809*

13 *2/13/70 Fillmore East*

14 *St. Valentine's Day* ❀ *2/14/68 Carousel* ❀ *Foundation for Anthem of the Sun.*

15 *2/15/73 Madison*

16

17 *Thelonious Monk, d. 1982* ❀ *2/17/73 St. Paul* ❀ *Here Comes Sunshine* ➥ *China* ➥ *Rider*

18 *2/18/71 Port Chester* ❀ *Bertha, Loser, Johnny B. Goode, Wharf Rat, Playin' debut*

19 *2/19/71 Port Chester* ❀ *Bird Song, Deal debut*

20

21 *2/21/71 Port Chester* ❀ *Ripple!*

22 *Vince Welnick, b. 1952* ❀ *George Washington, b. 1732* ❀ *2/22/69 Dream Bowl*

23 *2/23/93 Oakland* ❀ *With Ornette Coleman*

24 *2/24/74 Winterland*

of the Boys will sound like, that will be missed more than New Year's, even, which had already gone missing for three years. Now that August has died and the roof's caved in, that feeling is gone. Fortunate are we, then, to have so many memories and so many shows. So throw another log on the fire and warm up to a nice Sugaree. And happy holidays.

25 *Auguste Renoir, b. 1841* ✻ *George Harrison, b. 1943*

26 *2/26/90 Oakland*

27 *2/27/69 Fillmore West* ✻ Live/Dead *show*

28 *2/28/69 Fillmore West*

(29) *Leap-year day* ✻ *The Dead have never played on leap-year day*

"*It* was New Year's '89–'90 and we were on the floor, maybe thirty-five rows back, and I can't remember what they were playing, but it was pretty sick. It was the New Year's set—Bill Graham had just spurted across the crowd on a giant mushroom, I remember little kids throwing roses into the crowd. We weren't in costume, but people all around us were dressed as jesters, so it was a pretty trippy situation. When New Year's hit, they dropped thousands and thousands of colored balloons, some sparkly, but mostly just all different colors—everywhere—that seemed to drop from the ceiling for five minutes as the house lights were thrown on. When it was through, you couldn't even see the stage anymore, just these swirling spheres of color. And then the Dead started to play Aiko, which came bouncing to us in through all the balloon bubbles. It was just an unbelievable experience. "

—BRAD KHAN

Appendix A
Additional Show Reviews

✤ 8/4/67 O'Keefe Centre, Toronto

Three songs survive—Alligator, New Potato Caboose, and Viola Lee Blues, although Alligator may actually be from the following night. All three are amazing, swirling seas of musical color—chugging organ, grinding guitar, car-wreck bass—all seemingly stirred by Jerry's furious guitar dervishing. There's a self-assurance to these performances that seems to indicate that the band had an idea that they were creating something very special. Listen to the playful, almost experimental backing vocals for Alligator, the surf-bass line that rolls in Viola Blues—these guys meant business.

✤ 2/14/68 Carousel

A classic in every sense of the word: This is, famously, Phil's favorite show, a large part of the foundation for *Anthem of the Sun,* and the night where Jerry pushed Phil down the stairs because he thought Lesh had given up musically at some point in the show. As you might guess from the above, the performance is a biggie. A complete That's It for the Other One bolts out of the gates, New Potato Caboose is a fantastic edition in that song's development, and Born Cross-Eyed also represents a high point for that tune. Phil is omnipresent and takes the lead in a Spanish Jam that starts out strong. Listen closely and decide for yourself whether the detour into Space was intentional or the result of Weir losing the rhythm—Jerry, always able to speak through his guitar, sounds frustrated. The Alligator → Caution jam that served as the basis for that sequence on *Anthem* is legendary and rightfully so, especially topped off as it is here with a crazed bout of Feedback. An epic. The second set is commonly available in pretty good quality due to an FM broadcast.

✤ 2/28/69 Fillmore West

Dick Latvala has tapped this one, which is "screaming" at him from the Vault, as a likely future release. Let's see—a show highly recommended by the Dead's archivist, from the February-March '69 Fillmore West run, with, say, a jam of Cryptical → Other One → Cryptical → Dark Star → St. Stephen → The Eleven → Death Don't . . . *you* do the math.

❄ 2/28/69 Hollywood Pop Festival

Here's a show that illustrates just how much the Dead changed between the beginning of 1969 and its end. Among the rich array of largely new (soon-to-be *Workingman's*) material here, particular standouts are of course the China → Rider → High Time and the closing four—terrific versions of Cold Rain, Hard to Handle, Mason's Children, and Lovelight. There's also some great stage chatter concerning the precariousness of the light towers at this festival after too many adventurous souls had decided to try to climb them. Both Jerry and Pigpen's personalities come through loud and strong, particularly Jerry's compassion for the archetypal scared, timid guy in the crowd.

❄ 4/5/69 Avalon

The Dead's 1969 shows are rich in the sweetest of song linkings, strings of pearls plucked from the maw of the primal Dead oyster. This show has one of the most lustrous editions of the basic *Live/Dead* jam configuration: Dark Star → St. Stephen → The Eleven → Feedback, Lovelight. The Dead's playing here is smooth and thrilling, particularly on the superb, oh-so-smooth Stephen.

❄ 2/13/70 Fillmore East

A classic show that features one of the best and most revered Dark Stars ever played, an intent and relatively unmannered foray straight to the heart of the Zone. It's also the touchstone for an absolutely superb jam that passes through the full That's It for the Other One suite and exits to the jubilance of Lovelight. This greatly celebrated run has been mined by the Dead for official live releases since Owsley chose from among its bounty for *Bear's Choice* in 1973. Now that it's Dick who's doing the picking, this night and the following have been combined to form the sensational *Dick's Picks Volume Four*.

❄ 2/14/70 Fillmore East

Although the night before is undeniably more popular, this Valentine's Day acoustic set probably has the edge over 2/13. Like 2/13, the whole show is great, but the real meat in the electric portion is to be found in the Not Fade → Mason's → Caution. The entrance into this last-ever Mason's Children is a bit awkward—the song worked better from a standing start—but the rest of this three-tune jam is pure gold.

❄ 4/18/71 SUNY Cortland

In an era where it's often hard to find fault with the Dead's playing, this is probably as close as the Dead come to an off night. But this is still a great show to have for the intangible element that makes it entertaining despite its technical flaws. There's some hysterical stage banter aimed at the lightman (Pigpen: "If you don't turn those lights down now, Mr. Lightman, we're gonna hog-tie ya and throw your ass outta here!") and a general feeling of fun prevails. The China → Rider is the highlight, a clean, simple exemplar of the pairing at that point in the Dead's history.

✽ 11/7/71 Harding Theater

The Dead were on a roll in the fall of '71, as the many blisteringly hot shows from this period attest. Here's another one to add to the list. The playing is outstanding throughout, Keith adding a great deal and the band obviously deriving energy from their new member's presence. The centerpiece is a jam from Dark Star through Drums into an Other One sandwiching Me & My Uncle. At the beginning of Dark Star Jerry lets loose with a note that he sustains for a good ten seconds or so, under which Phil advances the lead. It's a galvanizing moment that sets this Dark Star, which wastes no time at all getting into outer space, on edge. I know of no other version of Dark Star that explores so many distinct musical landscapes in so brief a time; it's a stunning, evocative work. The Other One presages the huge '72 versions, especially in the way it wraps itself around a simpler tune. The return to The Other One out of Uncle is wonderfully meandering, containing hints of the Spanish Jam and even New Potato Caboose.

✽ 12/5/71 Felt Forum

The Dead ended 1971 on the highest of notes, having quickly found a world-class groove with Keith, the new guy in the hot seat with the phat mad skills. There's a clarity and acuity to the performances in this show that is epitomized by Jerry's clean, direct, and seemingly unconscious playing. The effortless excellence the band brings to Truckin', Sugaree, Sugar Magnolia—indeed just about every song in this show—evinces a comfort level with their playing and material that doubtless led to the more rambling, exploratory second-set work of 1972. Plan for a band with a new guy on keys: Get confident on the material, *blaze,* then set out for new territory. One can see the outlines of that *terra incognito* in the wildly inventive Dark Star, sans lyrics, that envelops Uncle in wavy, percussion-laced weirdness before rocking off into Sittin' on Top of the World.

✽ 7/26/72 Portland

The lovely soundboard of this show that entered into circulation in 1991 has a very comforting, almost homey feel to it. With the shenanigans of the first set and a lovely, lyrical Dark Star into a beautiful Comes a Time, it's a performance that's lovable, warts and all. Black-Throated Wind sees one of its best performances here (Bobby is so obnoxious in getting his monitor mix right before the tune, and so eloquently sincere in his delivery of the song—a brief lesson in duality), and Playin' has that crisp '72 first-set feel that makes that year's versions stand out in the continuum. The stage banter throughout the show is hilarious, highlighted by Weir's death threats on Bear, and classic quotes by Phil ("Minor technical difficulties turning into major technical difficulties—that's the story of my life.") and Bobby, dedicating Sugar Magnolia: "This next one's dedicated to Portland's skid row. For no reason at all. Just to prove my point that life is like a symphony."

❋ 9/20/74 Palais des Sports, Paris

This well-known show was the penultimate of the Dead's "last" European tour. Although shows from fall '74 definitely show some fraying at the edges, as does this one, there's more than enough inspired and energetic playing here to gain this tape time on the deck. China → Rider is very well done and dominated by big Phil lines, over which Jerry lays down some staccato gun-slinger picking. He takes an admirably novel approach on the vocals to Brown-Eyed Women, which is followed by a fast and furious Greatest and a pretty Brokedown. The Truckin'-initiated jam that comes next is the highlight of the show, and Phil's fingerprints are all over this one. He alternates between playing along with the vocal and creeping through the mix to put his weight behind this section or that. In the end jam he and Jerry duel furiously, Lesh cutting loose with mad fusillades while Garcia charges up the neck of his guitar. Not content to rest on his laurels, Phil then proceeds to initiate a most un-Truckin'-like jam that culminates in some Tiger-like growls from Jerry before taking a turn into Eyes. This one starts out a bit dull but eventually finds a very nice groove indeed. The '73–'74 rhythmic jam at the end proves an excellent bridge to a Not Fade Away in which Jerry's playing is at its most conversational.

❋ 6/17/75 Winterland

The combination of Keith's *Blues for Allah*–era keyboard sound and the cavernous acoustics of ice-rink *cum* concert-hall Winterland conspire to imbue the audience tape of this show with a very spooky, distinct feel. There's palpable excitement and awe among the Winterland faithful as the Dead begin the show by unveiling Crazy Fingers—a lovely performance, fairly true to the album cut—end the first set with an awesome debut of Help → Slipknot! → Franklin's (Help on the Way without lyrics), and then kick off the second set with a long jam composed of the first Blues for Allah sandwiching Stronger Than Dirt and Drums. *This* must have blown some minds. The older material played at this show also shines, none greater than a Peggy-O for the ages. The frantic battery-checking of the group of tapers responsible for the heavily circulated aud of this show is humorous, if distracting.

❋ 8/13/75 Great American Music Hall

Due to an eventual FM broadcast and classic bootleg (*Make Believe Ballroom*), this invitation-only release party for *Blues for Allah* probably holds the distinction of being the most widely circulated Dead show, which is ironic because it was performed in front of one of the smallest audiences to witness a midseventies Dead show. It's a gem through and through, the first set opening with an excitement-building Bill Graham intro to an epic Help → Slip → Franklin's (the first Help with lyrics) and closing with a jam of Eyes → Drums → Stronger Than Dirt. The second set is home to a towering Sugaree, the debut of Sage and Spirit, and the desert's breath of Blues for Allah to close. Sage and Spirit contains some of the most gorgeous interplay between Jerry and Bob ever recorded—it is breathtaking. More than in any other show where an acute spotlight has been on the band, the Dead manage to play here with a care that never becomes cautious, a virtuosic exactitude that nonetheless allows bouts of unrestrained jamming.

❋ 9/28/75 Golden Gate Park

There's a live-wire energy attendant on this show, what with a baby being born in the crowd and much humorous stage chatter, that speaks most clearly in the music through Jerry's Travis Bean guitar. He was right—that silly-looking thing *did* sound great. The clear highlight here is the Truckin' (note: no "g")-initiated jam that leaps from an insane version of that tune to the unbridled thrill and surprise of the Eleven (jammed only), continuing on in a rhythmic mode through Drums, Stronger Than Dirt, and Not Fade Away. Too many people get Winterland and Great American Music Hall and then call it a day as far as 1975 is concerned; this is a huge mistake. Do not be one of those people.

❋ 6/10/76 Boston Music Hall

A Bettyboarded classic with a crystalline early Help → Slipknot! → Franklin's, a tour-de-force Playin', and a Friend of the Devil that's still finding its footing in the slower tempo but features gorgeous playing by Keith nonetheless. This is definitely one of the year's must-haves.

❋ 6/12/76 Boston Music Hall

This closing night of the superb East Coast comeback stand in Boston simply features excellent, shimmering versions of Let It Grow, Cassidy, Music, and Wheel as well as a stunning Mission in the Rain. Listen for Jerry cracking up in the U.S. Blues encore as he sings the "Charlie Chan" line—funny stuff.

✹ 6/14/76 Beacon

This first night at the Beacon is the better of the two, adorned as it is by what is perhaps the best performance of Crazy Fingers the Dead have ever put in, after superb versions of the Wheel, High Time, and the Music Never Stopped. The Help → Slip → Franklin's gets very spacey in the Slipknot!, as the 6/19 version does in Help on the Way.

✹ 6/15/76 Beacon

Though the performance here isn't as sharp as that of the previous night, a dreamy second-set songlist makes familiarity with both imperative. Stephen → Not Fade and Sugar Magnolia → Scarlet → Sunshine Daydream are the big fish here—Let 'em fry! While they're sizzling in the brain pan, listen for the Other One hint that Phil drops during Not Fade. Farther in the show there's a moment of serendipity when Jerry's hurried entrance in Wheel (you can hear Bobby shouting to him "Wheel! Wheel!" as he presumably draws a blank on the intro to this newish tune) causes his guitar to lurch forward into the opening solo in a sound that is wonderfully evocative of a wheel finding traction on slippery ground.

✹ 6/19/76 Capitol Theater (Passaic, New Jersey)

An outstanding first set from early in the Dead's comeback. The show begins with a spacey Help on the Way to kick off a very fine Help → Slip → Frank's. Every song is performed just about to perfection, with an exquisite Looks Like Rain and an extremely adventurous Playin' the standouts. Playin' is about as close as you'll get to '74 after the retirement, and it's so successful that one must wonder about all that talk of not being able to turn corners as quickly with Mickey back in the band.

✹ 6/24/76 Tower Theater

Here's a show that really deserves more attention. A sparkling audience tape circulates very lightly. The second set displays some of the smoothest playing of 1976, from one of the very best early Help → Slip → Franklin's through a long, scorching Dancin', to a complete That's It for the Other One with some breakneck passages, beautiful playing throughout. It's well worth the hunt.

✹ 10/9/76 Oakland

This is the first of two "Day on the Green" shows with the Who. Weir has said that this show was too cautious, but they really cut loose to play a much better show on the tenth—just goes to show, nobody knows the Dead less than the Dead themselves! Sharing the bill with the Who seems to have brought out the Dead's stadium rock brawn, as evidenced in an especially muscular St.

Stephen → Not Fade. Jerry becomes a blues-licks clearinghouse in this one, which sports a nice Bobby-Donna call-and-response on the coda before crashing back into Stephen. The splitting of Slipknot! (Help → Slip → Drums → Space → Samson → Slip → Franklin's) is a master stroke: The sound of Jerry's questing lines searching for and then locking on to the Slipknot! groove after Samson comprises one of those magic moments that stands out in the Dead's performance history. The first set is not to be missed either, with what may be the finest pre-Fire Scarlet played (just *begging* to have Fire appended) and a Lazy Lightning that builds to a fever pitch with Bobby and Donna's crescendo of traded "My lightning toos."

✻ 2/26/77 San Bernardino

The Dead's first show of 1977 began the year in style, with debuts of the soon-to-become core tunes Estimated and Terrapin. Both fare extremely well for the first time out, though Estimated was yet to undergo some slight lyrical revision. The first set ends in the strongest possible fashion with a crispy Playin' → Wheel → Playin' sequence, and the Help → Slip → Franklin's and knockout Eyes → Dancin' make the second set even better. A very important addition to the tape collection.

✻ 4/27/77 Capitol Theater

Another show that delivers the '77 yummies in a big way. The clear highlight of the first set is a long, roller coaster of a Sugaree that more than holds its own against the standout 5/19 and 5/22 versions from later in the tour. Row Jimmy is also very fine, as is a Half-Step that, while not on a par with 5/7/77, is definitely cut from the same cloth. Looks Like Rain is lovely. In a tour where songs often sounded very similar (albeit excellent) from show to show, the Estimated Prophet in the second set sounds like no other, Keith doing some *very* freaky organ stuff during the closing jam. What else? Well, there's an excellent Terrapin, a typically blazing '77 Samson, and a sick set-closing Dew.

✻ 2/5/78 Cedar Falls

Bobby's Sahara Forest kneeslapper introduces an outstanding second set that plays host to a titanic Scarlet → Fire and more. The *long* Scarlet → Fire transition jam features blissful cascades of Keith and Jerry, with no seeming end in sight. When the Dead finally do enter Fire, they truly make it count, capitalizing on its full jamming potential. This Fire is truly unique, made so by Jerry's floating, flutelike wah-wah solos in the lazy interior jams. Garcia's a creative force here, experimenting beautifully with the musical sensations of soaring, diving, and bubbling back up. Mickey's police whistle announces the other wild ride of the set, a rocking Truckin' that passes through a short Drums into an Other One with the driving force of a locomotive. Jerry is again the driving force, his restless, questing guitar building the jam to a screaming, jagged peak of fanning before it all slams down, reverberations from Keith's grand and all. Listen for the lovely, soft shower of notes into Wharf Rat, where Jerry's soloing resumes the floating feel of Fire.

✸ 6/4/78 U.C.S.B.

Bobby begins the second set of this very exciting show by saying that "you may think it's easy being a rock-and-roll star, but it requires intense concentration and, and, and, uh, fine-tuning, and painstaking planning. And we've been making a plan." Okay. . . . The thing is, the plan—whatever it was— seems to have worked. We see it in action in a long, questing Estimated paired with a very fast and lively Eyes. Jerry's enthusiasm shines through in the "yes it does" he ad-libs after the ". . . of its own" line in the chorus. A revving Harley in Space ushers in the Not Fade rhythm, Bob and Jerry duelling like mad in the intro with chainsaw-distorted guitars. Unfortunately (or rather, amusingly) this Not Fade is also notable for being home to one of the most unbearable and prolonged Donna solo assaults on tape—it's truly unbelievable! There's more fun to be had in this Not Fade, though, as it takes a screaming detour into a Nobody's Fault jam before coming back into Not Fade. It's an epic version, Hogs, guitar attack, Donna scream, Nobody's jam, and all. It is followed by a similarly insane Goin' Down the Road, with Jerry simply on fire. The "hot '78 show rule" is upheld with the choice of Around for the closer. There's another great Donna moment here as she chides "Spit it out, Bob!" when Weir stutters, "When the p-police knocked." The U.S. Blues encore is very hot, marked by Jerry going nuts vocally at the end. This was the show where the Dead gave Bill Graham his accursed "Uncle Bobo" nickname, Weir getting the crowd to say "Thank you Uncle Bobo" before the band launches into a Sugar Magnolia second encore for the newly coined Uncle.

✸ 12/28/79 Oakland

The show opens with an all-time Sugaree and picks up from there. The second set is sick from start to end, starting with a very clearly sung and played Alabama → Greatest and a Terrapin → Playin' that's nothing short of phenomenal. Jerry's singing in the Terrapin is very sensitive, and the band jams it out fully before going into a Playin' of historic proportions, highlighted by Brent's lush, otherworldly synth runs. The post-Drums cascade is a series of momentum-building, flawless transitions between exciting versions of Uncle John's, Miracle, Bertha, and Good Lovin'. The Casey Jones encore, like the rest of the show, has that little bit more that kicks it into another realm. This one's hot, a must-have.

❊ 10/6/80 Warfield

The acoustic set from this show is one of the better ones from this generally excellent run, distinguished by Jack-A-Roe and Heaven Help the Fool, and most of all by the Bird Song → Ripple pairing at the end of the set. These acoustic versions of the freshly broken-out Bird Song are as spacey and beautiful as any electric versions. Bird Song and warm, clap-along performances of Ripple to close the sets generally stand out as highlights in the shows that included them, hence the great appeal of this pairing.

❊ 5/1/81 Hampton

This solid but not great show nevertheless contains some hints of hotter nights to follow on the tour. The second-set-opening Stranger, for one, crackles and screams with feedback-laden energy, Bobby experimenting with unusual strum patterns and quirky chord formations to engrossing effect. He's Gone is also a big one, in a year that saw many excellent versions of this tune. As for Lost Sailor, see if you, too, hear Bobby sing, "Now that Phil Lesh beckons. . . ."

❊ 7/4/81 Manor Downs, Texas

It's Texas on the Fourth of July, so Jack Straw must be the opener. It's as if Bobby can't believe his luck, so he swallows *the line,* singing what sounds like "T for Texas, fourth day of July." No matter, it's a hot Jack Straw and an excellent show all the way through. The Stranger → Bird Song → Playin' to open the second set is a mother lode of inspired jamming, amply showing why '81 deserves more recognition. The "One More Fourth of July" encore drives home the point.

❊ 10/16/81 Amsterdam

The Dead, with time on their hands due to a pair of canceled shows in the South of France, repaired to Amsterdam to give two concerts at the Melk Weg (Milky Way), a hash bar (Jerry and Bobby had played there acoustically on the 11th). The results, while not representing any sort of technical heights, were fun, interesting, and definitely historic, as a number of tunes were revived and debuted. This night, Bobby's birthday, is the better-known of the two shows with good reason, despite the first-ever Spoonful and Phil solo into an outstanding Other One the night before. The show opens with the crowd singing "Happy Birthday" to Weir, and gets loose early with Bob humorously correcting a blown line in On the Road Again, to laughter from band and crowd alike. The centerpiece of this fine acoustic set is a Bird Song that is every bit as spacey and scintillating as its electric brethren. A fun Monkey and the Engineer, humorously introduced as "a song about disaster narrowly averted," and a supremely melancholy It Ain't No Lie also stand out. The electric set is just a big ol' party, full of garage-band raunch classics as the Dead trot out Hully Gully and Gloria. Gloria famously gives way to, as Phil put it, the "orgasm" of the first post-Pigpen Lovelight, Weir handling it pretty well after some initial tentativeness. The Playin's pretty good, too, and the whole set's simply a blast. The Dead, who except for Phil were playing on borrowed instruments, actually do an admirable job of re-creating their trademark sound—the only very noticeable difference is in the timbre of Brent's keys (he was playing what he later described as a very funky Fender).

✻ 3/14/82 U.C. Davis

A good, fairly popular show in which the Dead are pretty laid back despite a rare Saturday Night opener. The show's centerpiece is a Playin' → Scarlet → Fire. Playin' is good, and the Scarlet → Fire transition is an unusual one, open and resonant as opposed to driving (a microcosmic description of this show). Listen for the ascending "do-do-de-doo" vamp Brent plays at the opening of Scarlet—this was a figure Brent would play a number of times in Scarlet over the years; Vince, however, played it *a lot,* practically to the exclusion of innovation. Brent also steps up nicely in the solo spots in Fire, more so, almost, than Jerry. There's a long pause before Sunshine Daydream kicks in at the end of the show, as the band stalls in anticipation of midnight and it becoming Phil's birthday. It should also be noted that this was the last show before "The Switch" wherein Jerry and Phil changed places onstage.

✻ 4/17/82 Hartford

A Brent-led Spanish Jam (Brent leads because Jerry was not onstage) with heavy Lost Sailor overtones—residue from the Lost Sailor → Saint that precedes it—highlights the pre-Drums in a great second set. Space resolves itself into a knockout Uncle John's replete with duck call after "How does the song go."

✻ 4/18/82 Hartford

This is the tape with the famed Phil Earthquake Space, in which Phil revisits the infamous 1906 San Francisco earthquake on its seventy-sixth anniversary and creates some high–Richter-scale tremors of his own in the far-from-the-Fault confines of Hartford. Trey Anastasio of Phish has told of having a musical epiphany during this run—he was not alone.

✸ 4/19/82 Baltimore

What was *with* Phil during these two shows? (Perhaps his plea of "No more nitrous!" during Space provides a clue.) He follows his Earthquake Space with the Raven Space in the city that houses Edgar Allan Poe's bones: "Quoth the raven, 'nevermore' . . . or was it *evermore*?" The pre-Drums is especially fine, with the opening Stranger and the Terrapin into Drums the real standouts.

✸ 5/28/82 Moscone Center

This unusual show was for a Vietnam veterans benefit. It might be most accurately termed a single-set show with four encores and it is often labeled that way. The first set, or main body of the show, cooks, with a hot Alabama → Greatest opening pair, an especially good Althea, and one of the better Jeds played. Airto Moreira, who plays with the Dead throughout the show, adds an extra kick to Drums. The second, or encore, set is certainly interesting, with John Cipollina sitting in and Boz Scaggs handling most of the vocals. Note how similar Bobby's subsequent Walking Blues vocal phrasings are to Boz Scagg's delivery here.

✸ 7/18/82 Ventura

A pretty ho-hum affair on the whole, though the post-Drums → Space is stronger than what comes before, especially a laid-back Not Fade out of Space, a not-at-all laid-back Other One, and the closing Sugar Magnolia. More a hole filler than anything else, though.

✸ 7/25/82 Compton Terrace

Fairly ordinary, though worth having and hearing for the unusual Scarlet → Fire transition and a couple of very good jams, one of which leads into a hot Not Fade.

✸ 8/10/82 U. Iowa

This show has a sizable cult following, owing to a second set in which the band gooses the tunes with that extra little bit that can make a routine setlist special. The pre-Drums China → Rider, Lost Sailor → Saint → Eyes are all superb, energetic versions. The transitions in the China → Rider and Lost Sailor → Saint are made at the optimum point in the jamming for maximum excitement, and the Eyes is especially bouncy. The Aiko out of Space is one of the best, and it's both humorous and gratifying to hear Weir nix Jerry's Around out of a fine Stella Blue in favor of Sugar Magnolia. Bobby more than justifies the choice by delivering a fantastic rendition.

❄ 4/13/83 UVM

In one of the best shows of the fine-all-around '83 spring tour, Brent and Jerry construct a humongous, sprawling Scarlet → Fire. The rest of the show is above par as well, especially the Dew (despite the harsh splice).

❄ 4/17/83 Byrne

The second consecutive night that Stephen Stills sat in with the Boys is marked by a rousing Love the One You're With, a real Dead cover tune in waiting if ever there was one, even if this performance lacks the singular drive and intensity of the previous night's Black Queen. If Stills hadn't guested that night, though, this show would be known first and foremost for the long, exploratory Playin', rendered positively gothic by sonorous chimes.

❄ 4/19/83 U. Maine

The second-set-opening Sugaree → Samson is truly memorable, and a Space → Spanish Jam → Truckin' is nothing to be trifled with, but the first set, a real Brent showcase, just may have the edge in this show. Brent's keys, Fender bright and sustained alike, grace truly outstanding versions of Jack Straw, Friend Of, Dire Wolf, and Dupree's, complemented perfectly by Jerry's ricocheting, earthy guitar sound, which contains more than a hint of banjo.

❄ 4/20/83 Providence

A very high-energy show. The second-set pre-Drums features an excellent early Esau, for those who like this sadly deserted tune, and an awesome Estimated → Eyes. Jerry's solo breaks in Estimated are the stuff of which hot shows are made, and Eyes is if anything even better. The Space Jam is very exciting, Jerry and Bobby cooking up a brew with traces of Slipknot! and Dark Star before going into the opening figure of Throwin' Stones (Bobby lyric watch: This is the era of "stars and celestial balls"). Dew is fast enough to mark it as a curiosity, the closing Sugar Magnolia hot enough to make it more than a formality.

❄ 8/29/83 Hult

An unoriginal song list belies a fiercely energetic second set that begins with a full-bodied China → Rider, continues through a very fast Estimated → Eyes, and roars into The Other One out of Space. The set ends with one of the most exciting Johnny B. Goode's there is.

✲ 9/11/83 Santa Fe Downs

Easily one of the best and most interesting shows (or at least second sets) of the year. The first set is well played though truly unspectacular in song selection (Alabama → Greatest is a fine combo, sure, but boy was it overplayed in the early eighties!), save Althea. The second set, though, begins with a huge Help → Slip → Franklin's. This one, though plenty psychedelic, has kind of a raunchy edge to it. A rare second-set Let It Grow keeps the energy swirling, and He's Gone gives birth to a nice long pre-Drums jam. The post-Space occasions more exclamation points on the J-card, with a jammy Wang Dang Doodle (not rare in the second set then—it had only recently debuted, and been played once in each set—but "rare" for Act II in retrospect, if one thinks anachronistically), an all-time Dew (!) and an Around that for once makes Sugar Magnolia a second choice (high praise indeed given the quality of this Sugar Mag).

✲ 10/17/83 Lake Placid

A good show all around, but the opening Sugaree renders all that follows inevitably anticlimactic—it's hugely intense, building to several insane peaks. If not the best ever, it's certainly in the top three, Jerry's guitar and vocal delivery alike burning with creativity. Though the second set's good, with an excellent breakout version of To Lay Me Down, the focus of the show is clearly the first frame. After the Sugaree we get great Jerry vocals and Brent Fender runs in a jewel of a Friend of the Devil, an exciting early-vintage Esau, a Bird Song that could go much farther than it does but is still satisfying, and a sensational Deal played with Garcia Band–like verve. In the comic-relief department, check out Bobby's vocal turn on Bucket—amid repeated ". . . enjoying the rides" he lets loose with the improvisation, "Like a friend of mine used to say, 'Ride, Sally Ride!' " He continues in this vein for several bars.

✲ 10/21/83 Worcester

The opening Music Never Stopped is on a par with 6/28/85—these are probably the two best Brent versions—and the whole first set is smoking, especially Loser. The Scarlet → Fire in the second set is longer than the *Dick's Picks Volume Six* version, clocking in at thirty-five minutes plus. The "conga" sound Brent uses in the 10/14 Scarlet → Fire also makes an appearance here, to similarly delicious effect. The Uncle John's → Playin' combo is predictably well done, and the Sage and Spirit theme makes an appearance during Space. Space, of course, leads to Touch (!), and the show continues in this magnificent vein. Check out the very cool Wharf Rat → Miracle transition. A *great* show from a superlative spring tour.

❋ 4/1/84 Marin

This very popular show, the closing night of the first Rex Foundation benefit run, features one of the most celebrated Help → Slipknot → Franklin's. It's a good one, to be sure, as are the sweetly sung Terrapin and Dew. Good Lovin' also stands out, with an excellent Bobby rap in which he does his bit where he pays homage to Pigpen—"It's like an old friend of mine used to say, that love is the healing way. . . ." The Touch encore is a complete mess but worth it for the priceless Jerryism, "Dog can read at seventeen."

❋ 4/21/84 Philly

Another monstrous spring '84 Help → Slip → Franklin's (I'd actually give this one the edge—by a fair margin—over 4/1) kicks off a very big second set—Playin', China Doll, and Throwin' Stones → NFA are all standouts, with Phil rattling floorboards throughout. A very high-energy show—check out Jerry in his first Not Fade solo break!

❋ 6/24/84 SPAC

The most exciting part of this show is the Dancin' breakout opener. After that there's a good song list—particularly for the second set—but not all that much fire. The most interesting aspect of the second set is the delay on Jerry's voice during Wharf Rat, which lends it a very haunting quality.

❋ 6/30/84 Indianapolis

This show positively begs for more attention. The first set is home to a Jack Straw that bolts out of the gate with some very hot ensemble jamming, a Minglewood in which Bobby plays a truly earsplitting slide solo that is nonetheless strangely effective, and a Dupree's to which Brent's swirling organ lends some of the song's halcyon feel. It's in Dupree's that Jerry's soloing really starts to heat up, setting the stage for a huge second set. A sizzling Shakedown opener gets things moving in the right direction, right into Playin', which is given a long, twilighty intro—very nice—then, *bam,* it's on, and what a smoker it is. Jerry states the Spanish Jam theme briefly but firmly early on in this one and makes broad allusions to it throughout. The jam features one of the best examples I've heard of Jerry's early-to-mid-eighties manic fretboarding in this tune, fingerknotting thirty-second-note scale runs punctuated by machine-gun drumming from Billy and Mickey. Terrapin is exquisite, Jerry not copping out of a single note. The long lead line before "Inspiration . . ." is played as well here as anywhere else. Drums → Space is marked by some especially intriguing musical conversations before going back into a deft Playin' reprise. As Playin' dwindles, Mickey sounds the police whistle, and Jerry, obviously feeling it this night, bobs and weaves through the whistle on his guitar with witty variations on the opening triplets. His bravura backing vocals speak eloquently of just how much he's getting off on this Truckin', which is truly one for the ages. It ends with a seamless *ritard* into Spoonful—check out how Jerry finishes Bobby's first line for him. And OH MY GOD, IS THAT REALLY BOBBY ON SLIDE GUITAR? He and Jerry play some double leads here worthy of the best Southern rock bands. The golden yummies continue with Stella Blue, which starts out just perfectly until Jerry flubs a verse badly. What to do if you're Jerry? Why, vent your frustration in a blistering solo out of the bridge of course, which is just what he does here, getting Stella back on track nicely. Jerry jumps out of Stella's closing *fermata* a bit prematurely, no doubt to preempt the inevitable Sugar Magnolia or Around ("Hell, if Bobby gets a twofer, why shouldn't I?"), and launches into a joyous Goin' Down the Road. When Jerry's this randy, it's always a joy to listen to.

❀ 10/12/84 Augusta

A great Cold Rain opens the second set, and you *know* that's a good sign. The Lost Sailor → Saint that follows bears out this augury, with a tape-deck-melting transition into Saint, Jerry wailing away on the Tiger while Bobby simply *thrashes* on his guitar. Jerry's lightning scale runs in Uncle John's Band bring the mood way back up again after Brent's buzz-crushing Don't Need Love. Jerry gives a guitar-phrasing clinic here, placing this version high on the all-time list. It ends up in a pre-Drums jam that hints very strongly at Playin', amid pounding tribal drums and chest-vibrating feedback from Bobby. Jerry makes an early appearance among the drummers, initiating a very moving Space full of sinuous Spanish lines and including an Other One hint. Just as Jerry's playing is at its most Iberian, he leans heavily into the Playin' theme, then falls back again to Spanish fluttering, alternating back and forth and letting the tension build tremendously. When the drums finally kick in to announce the first-ever Playin' reprise, it's a moment of ecstatic release. The closing Dew is also phenomenal, with some liquid moments of quiet before Brent's great Hammond roar takes it on its ride to the summit.

❀ 11/2/84 BCT

An outstanding show. The second set is relentless, from the HUGE Help → Slip → Frank's opener through a raucous Lost Sailor → Saint, to the first-ever Gimme Some Lovin', the crowd positively eating it up. Lesh commented on this performance in Gans's *Playing in the Band:* "I heard that famous roar comin' back at us when we started that . . . the first time I ever heard it while I was singing lead." The Casey Jones encore was the last time anyone heard that tune for a long while.

✴ 11/3/84 BCT

An unusual pre-Drums includes a jamming Stranger and Cumberland making set appearances with style. Things get weirder when Gloria is the next tune, followed by a Why Don't We Do It in the Road in which the vocals are handled by the committee of Jerry, Brent, and Bobby (was Phil miffed because the rest of the band didn't take up his Lovelight hints out of Gloria?). An excellent Drums/Space gives way to a Fantasy in which Jerry sings the lead and Brent the backup. The Throwin' → Lovelight closer is very hot, with Bobby singing the old "The lights go on and off and the nightbird calls" line in Throwin'.

✴ 3/27/85 Nassau

The first set of this show is a blast, commencing with Half-Step, which is revived with style, played better here than just about any other subsequent '85 version. The other historical episode in the set, Phil's debut of Just Like Tom Thumb's Blues, is most certainly a vid. It's highly entertaining, but I can't believe he passes up the sure applause line "I'm going back to New York . . ." in favor of the quirky, more personal "I'm going back to San Anselmo." That Phil, always shunning the adoration of the crowd.

✴ 3/28/85 Nassau

This was the first show to open with Truckin' in a *long* time, the last previous occasion being 9/28/72—impressive lineage indeed. While this second night of a hot spring Lawn Guyland stand doesn't quite meet that exalted standard, it's sure no slouch, impressively played throughout. It also sports the delicious rarity of a China → Rider and a Scarlet → Fire in the same show. The Scarlet → Fire has the edge over China → Rider here, and is easily the highlight of the second set. The first frame belongs to the Truckin' opener and an emotional High Time. The only shame about Truckin' is that it doesn't go on longer, segueing quickly instead into Smokestack Lightning, where Matt Kelly's guest harp-playing serves as ample compensation for Truckin's truncation. High Time is distinguished by the way Garcia sings strongly through his raspiness, a serendipitous vocal effect of his later years that creates a compelling duality of frailty and strength, almost analogous to Miles Davis's playing.

✴ 3/31/85 Portland

Legend has it that this was a night of mucho acid all around, which would help to explain the very loose yet totally joyful flavor of the playing—and the abysmal performance the next night, which is generally considered to be the worst show of 1985. This night, though, possessed ideal conditions for Aiko, which thrives, as do the rave-ups Miracle, Day Tripper, and Don't Ease. And check out that inverted (reprise first) Playin'—wild and wacky stuff, I tells ya. . . .

❀ 6/15/85 Greek

The second set of this middle show from the twentieth-anniversary Greek run is, well, just perfect. The Brent vamp that opens China Cat augurs big things to come, and they are duly delivered in one of the best China → Riders ever. The playing is flawless, subtle, and energetic, and the transition is timed perfectly. Bobby counters with the most triumphant and satisfying Lost Sailor → Saint he and the band have ever pulled off. A beautiful Terrapin sends the show into a typically fine '85 Drums → Space. The Wheel out of Space is superb, and the show continues in this vein, topped off by no less than a double Jerry encore, including She Belongs to Me. This one's a must.

❀ 6/27/85 SPAC

This one's not as good as some of the June shows (the next night, for instance) but it has an energy of its own. The highlights of the first set are a bold, full-bodied Stagger Lee and a finely wrought Crazy Fingers into—who'd a thunk it?—a quicksilver Supplication jam → High Time. Yum. The second set burns out of the gates with Stranger into a *very* fast Eyes to kick off an exciting second set. The Man Smart, Woman Smarter here gets my vote for best ever.

❀ 6/28/85 Hershey Park

Mmmm . . . chocolate. This is a huge Phil show—he's loud in the mix and a major presence throughout, especially on a hot Tom Thumb's (despite early mike troubles) and a knockout Dew with bombs galore. The second-set-opening Music, which begins with some "Singing in the Rain" weirdness, takes best-of-the-eighties honors (along with 10/21/83). The pre-Drums nears perfection with a fantastic Estimated → Terrapin pairing, and the first set, with its great Cold Rain opener and Jerry hat trick (Bird Song → Comes a Time → Deal) flirts with greatness as well.

❀ 11/1/85 Richmond

This fall classic finds its snug little corner in the Deadhead heart on the strength of its abundance of Jerry excellence. The first set is a forum for some of his best up-tempo tunes—an outstanding Cold Rain, and great versions also of Stagger Lee and Brown-Eyed Women join impressive Bobby turns in Dancin' and Jack Straw. The second set is a Jerry ballad fest, with High Time, He's Gone, Comes a Time, and She Belongs to Me. In every one of them—Comes a Time especially—his singing is achingly expressive and his heated, edgy guitar lines even more so. Just one of these performed at the level they are here would have made the set. To get them all is a dream. But wait, there's more! Bobby's Spoonful serves as the ideal, bluesy bridge between He's Gone and Comes a Time, with much help from Brent's sensational Hammond work. Weir also plays a Lost Sailor → Saint split by Drums → Space to very interesting effect, and follows up the sensitive She Belongs to Me with the inspired counterpoint of Gloria. This is truly a great one.

✸ 11/4/85 Worcester

Though it doesn't really hold a candle to the next night's show, this one's definitely not a weakling. The first set's better than the first, with Jerry really connecting on his tunes. Alabama and Big Railroad are very good, West L.A. Fade is one for the books, and Might As Well is truly fat. The second set, though possessing a good setlist, is a bit perfunctory. The opening China → Rider is the best thing here, though Truckin' and Sugar Magnolia also have their moments.

✸ 11/5/85 Worcester

They say you can't judge a show by the song list, but a Supplication jam → Playin' jam smack dab in the second set is a pretty good indication that there's something special brewing. And indeed there is, from the Happy Birthday for Bill Walton to start the second set, through a hot Shakedown, all-time Women Are Smarter, heartfelt Ship, and the fluidity and quick grace of the paired jams. The transition between Supplication and Playin' is the very definition of seamless. The first set rocks, too, all the way through. Kansas City is performed so well that one really has to wonder why they didn't pull that one out more, and the Bird Song → Looks Like Rain is outstanding. The second set cools down a little post-Drums (there are much better versions of Tom Thumb's), but the Brokedown is one of the most wrenching they've ever done.

✸ 11/7/85 Rochester

This popular show may be a bit overrated, but that doesn't mean it's not damn good. The overriding highlight? High Time, hands down. This is a clear, piercing performance that raises chills. The second set is also notable for a few weird moments, such as Mickey admonishing the audience to clap louder during Drums ("Louder! Right on! One more time!"), quipping "Best drum class I ever had!" when it's done. Brent also gets strange in the Gimme Some Lovin' intro out of Space, unloading a barrage of his '85 samples, playing ray guns and "Bobby" in a high-voice rhythmically in the opening. There's also a moment in Throwing Stones, right before the "shipping powders" line, where Brent bends a single note in a manner highly evocative of a signal chime on the bridge of the U.S.S. *Enterprise.*

✻ 11/11/85 Byrne

It's hard to understand why one hears so little about this excellent '85 show. Perhaps its cookie-cutter setlist (the oft-repeated Scarlet → Fire, Estimated → Eyes kicks off a second set that ends with Throwin' → Lovelight; no surprises in between) has discouraged many a taper from giving it a spin. The playing, though, is gold. Althea and the closing trio of Bird Song → Looks Like Rain → Don't Ease stand out from a very good first set, and the second set is superbly played from start to finish: Scarlet → Fire, Estimated → Eyes is the best kind of predictable, and all components are played here with originality.

✻ 2/11/86 Kaiser

A good show with a split personality. The first set has the Dead playing very well without stepping out all that much—highlights are a tasty Stagger Lee, a Bird Song in which the band does stretch out a bit, and a stomping Music. The second set is largely a loose jam session with various of the Neville Brothers to which the audience has been invited. It's sloppy but achieves some real heat owing to the easy familiarity between the Dead and the Nevilles—a real Mardi Gras party. The long, rambling Aiko is a case in point, a rollicking, seat-of-the-pants jam. The Not Fade → Hey Bo Diddley → Goin' Down encore is also an expression of sheer exuberance. Somewhat overlooked in this show is a highly original Truckin' out of Space. Jerry's intro is downright bizarre, and his lead lines throughout stray quite a bit from the ordinary.

✻ 3/20/86 Hampton

This is a fine show overall, but it is rendered priceless for the audience reaction—giving new meaning to the phrase "bringing the house down"—to the Box of Rain revival at the end of the first set.

✻ 3/27/86 Portland

This jam-stuffed show gets my vote as best of 1986. It kicks off with a Jack Straw that rages out of the gate, followed by a Peggy-O that gets that song's slow build just right. Things get unusual with the intriguing one-off Revolutionary Hamstrung Blues, and more still with a Wang Dang Doodle bustout. The weirdness gets downright wonderful when the band breaks into an exhilirating Supplication jam. Jerry builds the second-set-opening China → Rider to a screaming peak in the transition, rendering this relatively unheralded version practically an all-timer. Estimated → Eyes is also hot, with a nice long jam after Eyes. Finally, the Spanish Jam revival is exceptionally well played, Jerry's guitar searing through the mix into a very hot Truckin'.

✹ 4/4/86 Hartford

The Greek, Winterland, Frost, the Fillmores, MSG—all rightly earn their place in the Head's heart as venues that have hosted more than their share of excellent shows. I'd like to cast a vote for the oft-overlooked "Harshford," which has definitely seen some goodies over the years. There's nothing extraordinary here, just a very finely played show from the better end of '86, more than worth a listen and the commitment of a couple of tapes. Particularly good are the second-set-opening Touch and the He's Gone → Smokestack Lightning. The very good Box encore deserves mention as being an early postrevival version.

✹ 6/21/86 Greek

A great second set, very well played for late '86 (the next night was excellent too). The set opens with Phil responding to the "We Want Phil" chant with "Yes, you want, you want, but *what* do you want? You want music, right? Well, here you go. . . ." To which Jerry rejoins, "We'll give you Phil *after* the show." Phil: "Speak for yourself, Garcia." The opening Saint is pretty ragged, but the crowd gets Phil soon enough with a robust Gimme Some Lovin'. He's Gone, which Phil dedicates to Len Bias, really picks up steam after a rough beginning. Bobby's Smokestack vocals are positively spiteful, resulting in a very fiery performance. Check out the passage in Drums that evokes Pink Floyd's "Meddle"—very tense and exciting. Tense and exciting also describes the lusciously long intro to The Other One, the tension relieved in a maelstrom of bass and guitar.

✹ 12/15/86 Oakland

Now, here's a show that is impossible to separate from its context. This was, famously and triumphantly, Jerry's comeback show after his coma and recovery. The cliché one hears about this show is true—there *wasn't* a dry eye in the house when he hit those magic words in Touch. Candyman, too, brought a moment of triumph, Jerry raising his fist in the air on the "Candyman's in town" line. Ironically (or perhaps understandably, given the circumstances) this is a show that highlights Bobby's skills more than Jerry's—all his tunes are very well played and delivered, especially a great first-set-closing Let It Grow. Jerry debuts both When Push Comes to Shove and Black Muddy River strongly and handles the polar moods of Aiko and Wharf Rat with aplomb. This is a show for which you definitely want an audience tape.

❋ 3/26/87 Hartford

A strong show throughout, highlighted by Midnight Hour and a very good Bird Song in the first set, and a hot China → Rider to open the second

❋ 4/2/87 Worcester

One of the year's stronger shows, with a fine first set—Cold Rain opener, Dupree's, Beat It On Down, and a Bird Song—Music double whammy—and an excellent second-set pre-Drums: Scarlet → Fire, Looks Like Rain → Eyes—well chosen and well played. Black Peter is particularly emotional, as those after Jerry's comeback tended to be—chalk one up for good audience tapes

❋ 4/6/87 Byrne

While not a show to run out and get, it is worth a listen for a fine Jack Straw → Deal end to the first set and the Terrapin → Other One → Stella Blue run out of Space in the second.

❋ 5/9/87 Laguna Seca

This show is played safe for the most part, but very well throughout. An excellent first set is given a fine start with Sugar Magnolia → Sugaree and is capped by an outrageous Let It Grow. The second set, though not as entertaining as the first, plays host to a very good He's Gone and Wharf Rat, and an ecstatic, paranthesis-closing Sunshine Daydream.

❋ 5/10/87 Laguna Seca

Though it receives less attention than the previous day's show at the speedway, this one deserves props for an outstanding first set, including landmark versions of Box and Desolation Row, topped off by an ecstatic Don't Ease. The Bucket → Scarlet → Fire in the second frame is nothing to sneeze at either.

❋ 7/10/87 JFK

This rates as one of the strongest Dylan-Dead shows. There's a strong Tangled to open the Dylan set, followed immediately by the gift of Jerry on pedal steel for I'll Be Your Baby Tonight. Dylan keeps things lively by playing a number of his rare tunes, all rendered impressively. Man of Peace is played with as much punch as anything the Dead and Dylan played together, and the Ballad of Frankie Lee and Judas Priest, a real shot out of left field, is a tour-de-force, as is an affecting Chimes of Freedom. Even Joey has more than a little *bop* to it this night.

❋ 7/12/87 Giants Stadium

While not up to the standard of 7/10, this one does have its moments, the highest one of which is Jerry's pedal steel turn on the gorgeous Tomorrow Is a Long Time, another inspired choice by Dylan and the Boys. Other stand-outs from the Dylan set are Baby Blue, Wicked Messenger, Queen Jane Approximately, and—once again—Chimes of Freedom.

❋ 7/19/87 Eugene

On the Dead-Dylan continuum of show quality, this one falls a bit behind the curve. Excellent tune selection helps this one out a good deal, with strong versions of Dead Man, Watching the River Flow, Heart of Mine, and another good Queen Jane. The Touch → Watchtower encore is terrific.

❋ 8/20/87 Park West

A great second set begins with Phil playing the bass line to "Whole Lotta Love" while the band is fiddling up (to use Paul Krassner's term) for China Cat—a welcome portent of friskiness. The Truckin' → Smokestack combo rip, and a phenomenal post-Space is highlighted by a pumping, driving Gimme Some Lovin' and a Watchtower from an era when Jerry was still clearly enthralled with teasing out this tune's intricacies.

❋ 3/27/88 Hampton

An excellent show all the way through, perhaps the best of the year. The first set is highlighted by an all-time To Lay Me Down and rounded out by the first Ballad of a Thin Man and strong versions of Rooster, Stagger Lee, and Cumberland. The second set starts off with some playful riffing on Miles Davis's "So What," but it's no more than a tuning jam, really. This, however, did not stop *Rolling Stone* from announcing that the Dead had added the song to their repertoire on the spring '88 tour. Not that anyone would have minded. . . . The pre-Drums is huge, with an awesome Scarlet → Fire, Estimated → Eyes sequence.

❋ 4/1/88 Byrne

Though unsurprising (perhaps this was the Dead's perverse April Fool's stunt for the year; then again they *did* start with a "Little Bunny Foo-Foo" tuning . . .), this has a lot of what one might ask for in a very good show: An excellent first set kicks off with Half-Step → Jack Straw → To Lay Me Down, touches down for the last Thin Man (to the relief of many a doser), and ends with a Cumberland, Deal one-two, Phil going off in the Deal. The second set is very standard but well played throughout, the China → Rider particularly good, and Brokedown always a nice ending.

❈ 4/9/88 Worcester

The Dead play it good but safe on this closing night of the spring Worcester run. The second set starts off with a very hot Bucket, Garcia's distortion runs fast and well enunciated. The momentum does not dissipate in a great Aiko. Terrapin, which rounds out the short pre-Drums, is also a good rendition, though not as much of a standout as the first two tunes. The rest of the show is pretty standard, if well played, with the exception of Throwin' Stones, which is a particularly strong version. It's also nice to hear Jerry having so much fun during Fantasy → Jude, audibly fighting off laughter at points in both.

❈ 6/25/88 Buckeye Lake

The show whence came the classic Garcia quote regarding Hornsby: "We don't let just anyone sit in on the accordion," before letting him do just that for an idiosyncratic, highly entertaining Sugaree. Of course Sugaree follows an outstanding Box. Memphis Blues with Bruce on accordian crosses the polka-dotted line a bit, but the rest of the first set is very solid—West L.A. Fade, Cassidy, and Deal are all strong. The second set is a bit of a wash, though interesting. The Victim—Blow Away—Foolish Heart trio undergo evident growing pains (Oxford has the edge on all three), and the post-Space setlist, at least, is as automatic as they come. A really nice Terrapin makes it worthwhile, though.

❈ 6/28/88 SPAC

One of the better shows of the summer tour, widely available from an FM broadcast. The first set kills, with an outstanding Bucket, Jerry hitting every note, some sick Phil runs in Bertha (to compensate for Jerry's flat guitar), and a wonderfully expressive reading of Candyman. Weir handles Masterpiece with lusty authority. The second-set Scarlet → Fire is very big indeed, as is the Estimated → Crazy Fingers that follows.

❈ 7/2/88 Oxford

An amazing show with a positively *ripe* setlist, the first night at Oxford nevertheless suffers a bit from the "you had to be there" syndrome. That said, Jack Straw and Row Jimmy in the first set are right up there with the best of the eighties, at least, and the Blow Away, Victim, Foolish Heart troika of new tunes to close the frame are caught at a time when all three were beginning to show some serious signs. As for the second set, despite some raggedness, there's very little not to like in a Crazy Fingers → Playin' → Uncle John's → Terrapin pre-Drums, and a Watchtower → Dew → Sugar Magnolia to close.

❋ 7/3/88 Oxford

. . . And there are those who prefer the second night at Oxford. It's a tough call (and one that need not be made), but those of this opinion cite arguably better playing, a long, dreamy Bird Song to close the first set, and a pre-Drums that smokes with an all-time Hey Pocky Way, an epic Looks Like Rain, and a very good Estimated → Eyes.

❋ 7/15/88 Greek

The second set, like the first (Shakedown opener), starts out very strong with a meaty Scarlet → Fire and an extra-good Women Are Smarter. The big start sets the tone for the rest of the set, which is highlighted by an excellent Ship, a better-than-average Estimated, and a brilliant Dew. The post-Drums is highly energetic—from Estimated on, it's a trail of fire to the Dew.

❋ 3/31/89 Greensboro

The second set kicks off with the jolt of Hey Pocky Way and never relents. There's no slack here—Truckin' is played with fire, Terrapin is well done, with a gorgeous jam afterward, Drums and Space are arresting, the transition between a very nice Take You Home and Watchtower is exciting. But the biggie here is a Dew that shows signs early on and builds to a towering peak, Bobby and Jerry fanning each other up the mountain. The closing Good Lovin' is given some added juice by Brent's participation. Brokedown is just as pretty as you could like, with a thrilling little solo break where Bobby rings along to Jerry's molten lead.

❋ 4/15/89 Milwaukee

A strong second set kicks off with a very good China → Rider followed by an even better Playin' and Terrapin into Drums. Jerry pulls off some very slippery guitar lines in the transition between I Will Take You Home and Watchtower, making the contrast even more dramatic than on 3/31 or 4/12 of that tour. In a period of monster Dews, this is another one to cherish.

❋ 7/2/89 Foxboro

Though this venue was much maligned, the Dead kicked off their '89 summer tour there with considerable élan, debuting Jan Sawka's gorgeous, shape-shifting backdrop. It's a topsy-turvy show that's full of surprises, with a rare Playin' show opener into an even rarer first-set Crazy Fingers, and Friend of the Devil to open the second set. Mickey only gave the first set a "C+" in local newspaper coverage, but a listen to the hot Jed, the Cassidy → Don't Ease closer, and the always welcome To Lay Me Down may cause one to beg to differ. He's Gone → Eyes and a very strong Fantasy anchor the second frame, in addition to the excellent Friend Of.

✸ 7/9/89 Giants Stadium

By no means a great or even very good show, but solidly played if very pre-dictable throughout. The first set is more interesting than the second, with a good Shakedown opener and fine versions of West L.A. Fade, Brown-Eyed Women, and Bird Song. The pre-Drums placement of the Jerry ballad (Built to Last) makes for a second set that is at least highly energetic.

✸ 10/8/89 Hampton

There were many for whom the revival of the full Help → Slipknot! → Franklin's was as much of an epic occasion as the Dark Star breakout the next night. The playing was just as fine in Hampton round one, the song choices nearly as extraordinary. That the following show could top this one was one of the most mind-blowing aspects of that very special time in Virginia. The quality of the performance translates well to tape.

✸ 10/19/89 Philly

An excellent second set is highlighted by a Help → Slip → Frank's in which Franklin's Tower positively shines, an Estimated to which Brent adds that something special, and an Eyes with a very tasty and tasteful Jerry MIDI trumpet coda. The post-Drums/Space is also very fine, Wheel, Death Don't, and Baby Blue standing out particularly.

✸ 3/18/90 Hartford

Given the extraordinary quality of this spring tour, it's not surprising that shows like this one are somewhat overlooked. This one shouldn't be, though, with a fine first set (particularly the Stagger Lee, Ramble On, and Music) and a superbly well-paced second act that kicks off with maybe the best MIDIfied Aiko.

✸ 3/29/90 Nassau

The fates smiled on all as Branford Marsalis made his first appearance on stage with the Dead during one of their best tours in recent memory. Marsalis's saxophone leads and embellishments added a whole new dimen-sion to the band's playing in a collaboration that raised spirits and eyebrows. This mind-blowing show was the result—it absolutely, positively, must not be missed.

✸ 6/24/90 Eugene

A scrumptious first set, opening with a muscular, nuanced Help → Slip → Frank's and continuing from there to what may be the best Masterpiece the Boys have done, delivered with lots of punch. Loose Lucy and Candyman are also fantastic, Jerry's vocals rich and sure, the playing strong. The set ends with a long Let It Grow featuring an outstanding Jerry MIDI trumpet solo. Jerry doesn't keep his "trumpet" in its case very long, busting out another show-stopping solo in Man Smart, Woman Smarter. The other big highlight of set two is a great Other One out of Space. A very good show over all, with the edge going to the first set.

❋ 11/1/90 London

The second set is full of musical treats big and small, from the brief Drums opener into a great Victim, through a sensitively jammed Playin', to a transcendent Drums with hints of whalesong and a Space where Bruce and Jerry pair for some beautiful melodic runs. The post-Space second verse of Dark Star is exemplary, with one atonal freakout after another, each more interesting than the next. The buildup to the Playin' reprise is one of the most satisfying of the nineties, Jerry even pulling the drums back at one point so as to give it more time to develop. A Standing on the Moon tease drifts across the stage before Wharf Rat, and even the obligatory Throwin' → Not Fade is more fully jammed out than usual.

❋ 4/27/91 Las Vegas

Here's one show of which it is impossible to tire. Jerry's at his best, and Phil is in bomb mode throughout. The first set is merely good, but the second set is phenomenal, staggering. Tunes you've heard a thousand times are given new emphasis, energy, and interpretation—and the intensity is sustained throughout the set. Sugar → Scarlet → Fire opens, and each song is ripe with astounding jams, the Scarlet → Fire one of the best ever, long and inspired. Jerry gets into the Fire on a par with 3/21/91 and Normal '78. Playin' → Uncle John's are played with similar verve, the Drums and Space are fascinating, Miracle rocks . . . and Black Peter may just be the best ever, Jerry emoting with his guitar on a par with the best Comes a Times (and singing beautifully). The Weight encore is gorgeous, Bruce doing it real piano justice. A real must, a must, a must!!!

❋ 6/24/91 Bonner Springs

The second set opens with a good China → Rider, both Vince and Bruce doing fine work. The post-Space Other One → Dew is somewhat underwhelming for its brevity and, given the tunes in question, execution. But that's okay because the real centerpiece of the set is the breathtaking transition from the Supplication jam (itself well conceived and played out of Estimated) into Uncle John's, which is huge.

Dead to the Core

✹ 6/14/92 Giants Stadium

In an off year for the Dead, this and the next night at the home of the hated yellowjackets may well represent a nadir. Though the Candyman and Jack-A-Roe are comparative bright spots, and the Smokestack/Spoonful weirdness in the second set is interesting, this and 6/15 are really for completists only—and haven't you completists got better shows to go after? If you must, be consoled that the Samson and Ship, at least, come across better on tape.

✹ 12/16/92 Oakland

This is by far the best show of the year, featuring great performances of Shakedown and Playin' and a Casey Jones encore, not to mention Dark Star's second verse out of Space.

✹ 3/17/93 Cap Center

A jewel of a show. Playin' → Dark Star pre-Drums is topped by one of the Dead's most entrancing Drums → Space segments. Many worlds are visited even before the sublime Handsome Cabin Boy jam. The Other One out of Space is top-notch, and Days Between, while not the best-sung version, is one of the most tear-jerking. And all this is topped off with the first ever Lucy in the Sky with Diamonds. Sensational.

✹ 5/16/93 Las Vegas

This show is surely not without its clams, but they come among some very hot moments. The second set is the better of the two, due to a smoking Help → Slip → Frank's and a deep Wharf Rat that stirs the soul despite a blown harmony entrance by Vince.

✹ 5/26/93 Cal Expo

Definitely one of the best shows of '93. The Broken Arrow in the first set may be the finest version of this welcome late-Dead Phil cover, and the second set is centered around a fantastically well-jammed Crazy Fingers → Playin'. Playin' gives birth to a jam that is practically its own entity, making for a monster version that is long and inspired. The Liberty encore is one of the best.

✹ 8/21/93 Eugene

This is the kickoff to an excellent late-August run. Many prefer the next night to this one, but who can pass up the chance to hear Huey Lewis sit in on harp with the Dead? Who, I ask. Mr. Lewis acquits himself quite well, precipitating a Schoolgirl breakout. The set-opening China → Rider is also more than worth noting, it being perhaps the best of the year. Standing on the Moon is given the full-bore Jerry vocal treatment. Here Comes Sunshine and

Bird Song in the first set are okay, but the real concentration of goodies here is in set number two.

✲ 10/17/94 MSG

A long, long Eyes starts the second set, rendering what follows almost superfluous. Though it admittedly plods in some places, this is an Eyes one can curl up and get lost in—happily. The Estimated later in the set is suitably fierce. The Rainy Day Women encore marks the last time the Dead and Dylan appeared onstage together, though Dylan did open for the Dead on a few dates in summer '95.

✲ 3/27/95 Omni

One of the better shows of the Dead's last spring tour is highlighted in the first set by a Sugaree that manages to impress despite a false ending, a So Many Roads rendered positively eerie by Jerry's high-pitched whisper, and a big Let It Grow. An outstanding, newly revamped Aiko begins a sixty-minutes-plus pre-Drums, which also includes a very inventive jam out of Uncle John's.

✲ 5/26/95 Seattle

This is probably the best show of '95, opening with a standout post-Brent Help → Slip → Franklin's and a second set that features a very trippy, Star Trek-ified Scarlet → Fire and a vocally outrageous Stella Blue.

Appendix B
All Good Things
Some Essential Jerry Solo Shows

by Rob Hodil

From his early, jazzy forays with Howard Wales to the Motown and early rock 'n' roll–inspired romps with Merl Saunders—which evolved into the Legion of Mary and his lifelong side band, the Jerry Garcia Band—to the bluegrass Old and In the Way and other acoustic projects—the Great American String Band, Jerry Garcia Acoustic Band, work with John Kahn and David Grisman—to the disco-influenced(!) Reconstruction, Garcia's excursions from "The Boys" covered vast musical territory.

Condensing these various musical outfits (the JGB alone went through at least fourteen different combinations of musicians with attendant stylistic recombination) into a short list of recommended tapes is akin to making a molehill out of a mountain—none of Garcia's solo outfits can be given the breadth and scope of treatment they deserve. The archetypal shows I have assembled here are easily available in good quality and cut a fairly broad swath across Garcia's musical palette. There are, needless to say, many objections or alternates that could be raised to the choices below, but they represent what is probably as good an "essential shows" starting point as any. If hunting out and listening to these selections inspire you, I strongly urge delving deeper into the relatively obscure world of Jerry tapes, where many like treasures await.

A quick note about this list: The excellent official recordings of Old and In the Way and Jerry Garcia Acoustic Band provide such a good sampling of those bands' abilities and repertoires that no particular tape can offer them serious competition as introductions to their respective groups. Other shows are, of course, worth collecting, especially since some excellent songs have not yet made it onto official releases; with such seminal recordings readily available, however, it makes sense to start there. I have also left the Great American String Band off of so short a list because of its relative obscurity and Garcia's role in this ensemble, which was more that of sideman; tapes of this group are also well worth checking out, though.

1. **Garcia, Kahn, Kreutzmann, and Saunders—Pacific High Studios, 2/6/72**

An early FM broadcast, widely available in beautiful sound. Kreutzmann stakes an early claim here to indisputable Best Drummer Jerry Ever Had status. The Rockin' K is simply dazzling on this tape. Highlights include a geared-up "It Takes a Lot to Laugh . . . ," an extended workout on "Expressway (To Your Heart)," which barrels along like a semi without brakes, and the funky "Save Mother Earth." The zenith of the tape, though, is a lovely, haunting instrumental of John Lennon's "Imagine." Other standouts include a typically spunky "That's Alright, Mama"; another luminous instrumental, "I Was Made to Love Her"; and—no joke—an absolutely ripping "Masterpiece."

2. **Legion of Mary—Scranton, Pennsylvania, 4/12/75 (late show)**

One of the best of many available Legion soundboards includes top-notch versions of "Tough Mama," "I'll Take a Melody," and "Boogie On, Reggae Woman." Martin Fierro's flute adds poignancy to "Wonderin' Why" and Dylan's chilling "Going, Going, Gone." Fierro also provides the show's centerpiece, a flute-led pastoral (dubbed "Lala" by *DeadBase*) that is guaranteed to soothe the most beleaguered soul. One can imagine a Disney-esque tableau of small, furry woodland creatures emerging cautiously from behind the amps and effects racks to slowly surround the band during this tune.

3. **JGB—Winterland, 12/20/75**

This is the band in its Nicky Hopkins incarnation. An enjoyable show all around, this one's worth getting especially for the seamless "Let's Spend the Night Together → Edward" medley at the end of the set. "Let's Spend the Night" has a huge, chunky shuffle feel and quickly departs for a transitory jam, a rare thing in the largely stand-alone world of the JGB repertoire. It's a driving transition at that, with the pace of a "China → Rider" in full swing. Edward is an exuberant, keyboard-led jam with a slightly similar feel to "Expressway." The previous night's show, of which soundboards are also abundant, is itself a fine addition to any collection.

4. **JGB—Moore's Egyptian Theater, 3/6/76**

A great show from an era when the JGB sported a terrific lineup: Keith and Donna Godchaux, perennial member John Kahn on bass, and John Tutt from Elvis's band of the fifties on drums. Excellent audience recordings of the second set are available, which is highlighted by a gorgeous treatment of the Rolling Stones' "Moonlight Mile," Jerry, Donna, and Keith achieving a vocal blend about which Garcia would rhapsodize for years to come. Although this version is much slower than the Stones', it possesses an eerie, ethereal quality their versions have never approached, owing to the drawn-out, pitch-bent notes sung by Garcia. A couple of sloppy moments do not take much away from this performance, the only easily available JGB "Moonlight Mile." The second big tune on this tape is the Beatles' "I Want to Tell You," a trailing, jammed-out arrangement of the Harrison Tune that simply puts later Dead versions to shame. The set-opening "Harder They Come" is also strong, Jerry comping like mad at the end, and "Friend of the Devil" and "After Midnight" are both present here in strong versions.

5. JGB—Keystone, Berkeley, 7/8/76

This fairly common soundboard contains a great version of the slow and slightly menacing gospel tune "Who Was John." As with the Seattle show, the Jerry-Donna-Keith vocal blend is present here at its finest. An early version of "Don't Let Go" is surprisingly quiet and gentle, with Jerry using a slide to explore the high end of his fretboard to unique effect. Also of note are Donna's beautiful lead vocals on "Stir It Up," and strong versions of "Mission in the Rain" and "The Way You Do the Things You Do."

6. JGB—Warner Theater, 3/18/78 (late show)

This classic, the easiest tape to choose for this list, seems to be the most common tape with which a JGB collection begins. The reasons are many, including the fact that, as an FM broadcast, it is available in very good quality. The Keith, Donna, and Maria Muldaur version of the band is shown to fine effect here, playing seminal versions of much of the *Cats Under Stars* material, including the title track, "Gomorrah," and the only known live version of "Palm Sunday," as the show fell on that occasion. The real jamming highlight is the rarely played Flatt and Scruggs tune, "Lonesome and a Long Way from Home" (also covered by Eric Clapton on his first solo album). This propulsive rendition unexpectedly veers off into space madness with a free jazz twist before returning back to Earth—a feel-good song with a detour deep into the Zone. Donna and Maria's beautiful gospel duet, "I'll Be with Thee," is another treat from this show, along with very good versions of "Midnight Moonlight" and "The Harder They Come."

7. Reconstruction—Keystone, Palo Alto, 6/22/79

The centerpiece here is the funkified instrumental version of the Doobie Brothers' "Long Train Running": You *will* dance. Other highlights include an instrumental jam with an "Expressway"-like groove, "Tellin' My

Friends," "Strugglin' Man," and "Dear Prudence" in a tremendous horn arrangement.

8. JGB—The Stone, 2/2/80

A terrific version of the rare "After Midnight → Eleanor Rigby → After Midnight" medley is the reason to add this one to your collection. "After Midnight" starts out strong and, after the lyrics, breaks into a jazzy intertune space, Jerry using his envelope filter wah to great effect. The transition into "Eleanor Rigby" is long and sophisticated, the chords and notes aligning themselves little by little. "Eleanor Rigby" itself, an instrumental as with all its JGB performances, is well played through several interesting elaborations, including a double-time jam at the end before giving way again to "After Midnight." A soundboard of this show is available, though finding it may require some persistence.

9. JGB—Keane College, 2/28/80

And here's a completely different version of "After Midnight → Eleanor Rigby → After Midnight," no less essential than that from the Stone. Jerry rides out to the ragged edge of distortion, making jaw-dropping use of layers of sustained feedback on the way out of "After Midnight." Exercise caution: This jam, unlike anything I've ever heard, may melt your tape deck. "Eleanor Rigby" is sloppier than those from the Stone or Rodeo, but it doesn't lose the momentum it gains from the preceding jam. Jerry absolutely *kills* at the end of the "After Midnight" reprise. An excellent audience tape exists of this one, forty-five minutes with a top-notch "How Sweet It Is" for good measure. The search may be difficult, but the rewards are oh-so-sweet, so YOU MUST.

10. JGB—Hempstead (yes, Hemp-stead), New York, 2/29/80

Without meaning to overemphasize a particular period of the JGB, this show cannot be overlooked, because Robert Hunter makes a guest appearance, one of the few occasions where Garcia and Hunter shared a stage after the Wildwood Boys. Jerry plays slithery, countryish lines throughout "Tiger Rose," as if he'd been playing it every night for years. "Promontory Rider" shines even brighter, a tune that was made for the Garcia treatment—it's almost hard to believe that he didn't come up with the melody and chord changes himself. First-class versions of "How Sweet It Is," "Masterpiece," "Midnight Moonlight," and especially "Dear Prudence" render Hunter's cameo icing on the cake.

11. **Jerry Garcia—Capitol Theater, Passaic, 4/10/82 (early show)**

This is it, the famed solo acoustic show, with great versions of "Gomorrah," "Valerie," "Dire Wolf," "Reuben and Cherise," "I've Been All Around this World," and a sweetly sung Elizabeth Cotton medley of "Freight Train → Oh Babe, It Ain't No Lie." After the late show this night Jerry placed a call to John Kahn, who joined him for the rest of the "solo" bookings; he never again performed all alone, a real shame given the evidence of this night. Soundboards of this unique performance abound.

12. **JGB—Music Mountain, 6/16/82**

This show reaches its pinnacle with an all-time version of "Don't Let Go" that is by turns gregariously rocking and sublimely subtle. This most exploratory tune in the standard JGB repertoire doesn't get much better than this. Audience tapes of the show are fairly common.

13. **JGB—Cleveland, 11/25/83**

This show may well be one of the primary reasons why the Rock 'n' Roll Hall of Fame is located in the improbable city of Cleveland. The entire show is solid, but the second set is where the sparks truly fly as Jerry unleashes a titanic "Sugaree." Next is the soothing reggae of "Love in the Afternoon." If this show's "Sugaree" is a monster, the "Rhapsody in Red" that follows is the Bride of Frankenstein—Melvin propels it into orbit as Jerry shreds like Oliver North on a double-espresso-and-Nicaraguan-coke binge. All-star versions of "The Night They Drove Old Dixie Down" and "Dear Prudence" round out a classic show.

14. **Garcia and Kahn—Santa Cruz, 10/16/85**

An excellent and easily obtained Garcia-Kahn acoustic soundboard. Garcia's vocals are pretty ragged, but his guitar is crisp and clear on standout versions of "Deep Elem Blues," "Little Sadie," "Reuben and Cherise," "Gomorrah," "She Belongs to Me," and more.

15. **JGB—Eel River, 6/10/89**

I'll admit that I'm partial to this show because I was there, but even without the sight of the evergreens and mountains rising up behind the small stage of this natural amphitheater, or the waters of the nearby Eel River to cool off in during the set break, the magic shines through. Melvin toys with the *Close Encounters* theme before the beautiful and luxurious "I'll Take a Melody" opener, a sure sign of good things to come. After that are great versions of much of the standard repertoire from this era (though both sets are longer than usual for this time). "They Love Each Other," "Get Out of My Life," "Mission," and "Don't Let Go" are all standouts. Another very nice inclusion is the uplifting rarity "I Hope It Won't Be This Way," which feels like a long-lost sibling of "My Sisters and Brothers."

16. **Garcia and Grisman—The Warfield 2/2/91**

The first large Garcia-Grisman gig, this is a widely available soundboard. Highlights include an extended romp through Miles Davis's "So What," "The Thrill Is Gone," "Arabia," and "Grateful Dawg," as well as a host of lesser-known songs, such as "The Handsome Cabin Boy," "I Truly Understand," and "Little Glass of Wine." Garcia's vocals are excellent throughout, the two maestros performing marvelously.

17. **JGB—Oakland Coliseum, 10/31/92**

Jerry's return to performing after a two-month absence (including a canceled East Coast tour) was greeted by considerable relief by one of the largest crowds ever gathered on the West Coast for a Jerry Garcia Band show. The first set includes great versions of "Lay Down, Sally" and "The Maker." The second set opens with a typically heartfelt "Shining Star," filled with ethereal noodling. The lengthy groove of "Ain't No Bread in the Breadbox" and a smoking "Tangled Up in Blue" are also notable, as is a fine performance of Louis Armstrong's "What a Wonderful World," which is bound to elicit bittersweet pangs. A spry Halloween encore of "Werewolves of London" brings things to a suitably upbeat and macabre finish.

18. **JGB—Buffalo War Memorial, 11/5/93**

This is probably the best show from an East Coast tour where the performances consistently ranged from very good to excellent. "Cats Under the Stars" gives the show an energetic kickoff, and showcase versions of "Mission," "That's What Love Will Make You Do," "Breadbox," "Like a Road," and the perennial JGB tour-de-force "Deal" complete the set. The second frame includes a blissfully melting "Shining Star," "The Maker," "Reuben and Cherise," and "Gomorrah." Jerry also broke from formula this night and ended the show on a joyous note with "How Sweet It Is."

Acknowledgments

In my days as an editor I used to wonder at long acknowledgments; now I more than understand and wonder only if I can amply thank all whom I should in the space I have.

Thanks go first of all to Hank Schlessinger for the idea to put all this Dead in my head down in a book. I am deeply indebted to my very good friend Jacob Hoye of Dell/Delacorte, editor extraordinaire, for his unfailingly perceptive suggestions and undying patience. My gratitude also extends to Dell Editor in Chief Leslie Schnur, whose support of my new career path has been both touching and a great help. I would not have gotten very far at all on this project without the love shown me by Jennifer Tomkins, and my parents, Betty and George Wybenga—I send it back to them with thanks from the bottom of my heart. George Wybenga also designed the characters that grace the chapter openings. One other who absolutely must be mentioned at the start is my old college housemate, Rob Hodil.

Rob Hodil contributed a wealth of knowledge (and cases of tapes!) to the book and also provided an invaluable "Deadit" of the manuscript. His intelligence, wit, and insight breathe through most of what is best herein. He also wrote the essay on and reviews of essential Garcia Band shows at the end of this book. I cannot thank him enough.

Kathy Allen, Ted McCutcheon, and Andrew McNaught also made generous loans of their Dead collections, providing countless nuggets for me to mine happily. Andrew is also to be thanked for many shared insights and for putting me up for weeks in San Francisco, along with his housemate Shelby Gaines, who was perhaps a Deadhead in another life. David Onek, who provided me with some of my very first tapes years ago, was also most hospitable in San Francisco. Nick Reeder is another San Francisco Head and friend who lent a hand and has been a source of the crispy, ultradoublekind boards from years back. Jade Hoye's research assistance was invaluable and a real time saver and Tom Wybenga provided some last-minute Dutch proofing— thanks to both of them.

A big thank-you also goes out to Brad Khan, Alan Klein, Steve Kolozsvary, Jon Leibner, Jeffrey MacDonald, Steve Milewski, Aaron Richardson, and all the others who weighed in with insights and reminiscences. Susan Schwartz, Mike Shohl, and Johanna Tani, of Dell, all made my job easier by letting me make theirs harder—thanks a lot, folks, I truly appreciate it. Thanks to Susan Maksuta, MarySara Quinn, and Bonni Leon-Berman for a great-looking book design. Stanley Mouse blew me away by accepting the cover commission and producing a work of art that exceeded my imaginings. Thank you Ed Bick, James Denaro, David Dodd, Ralph Hubble, Jr., Randy Jackson, Aaron Richardson, and Jeff Tiedrich for permission to print information on your web pages. Finally, thank you to Jim Fitzgerald and Geoff Kloske for just being good guys; to Steve Silberman, who provided encouragement on the final lap; and to the folks who research, write, and publish *DeadBase*. Writing this book would have been immeasurably more difficult without this valuable and fascinating setlist reference—if you don't own a copy, you should.